国际服装丛书·营销

服装专业双语教材

Fashion Marketing

时装营销

[英] 迈克·伊西　编著

梁亚林　安妮　译

中国纺织出版社

内 容 提 要

本书阐述了时装营销的性质和范畴，分析了应该如何了解和调研消费者，以及由此展开的目标市场营销和服装营销组合。全书综合论述了如何选择可获利市场并加以定位，并为满足顾客的需求采取行动即营销组合；专业营销团队怎样设计营销方案以及确保时装的准确定价，并适时、适地地投入市场以及达成良好的流通。

时装营销具有挑战性，要有整个时装营销过程的规划和协调，并建立起一个为消费者提供优质的时装设计并产生利润的系统。

原文书名： Fashion Marketing,3rd Edition

原作者名： Mike Easey

著作权合同登记号：图字：01-2009-7362

图书在版编目（CIP）数据

时装营销 /（英）伊西编著；梁亚林等译．—北京：中国纺织出版社，2014.9

（国际服装丛书．营销）

书名原文：fashion marketing，third edition

ISBN 978-7-5180-1029-5

Ⅰ．①时…　Ⅱ．①伊…②梁…　Ⅲ．①时装－营销　Ⅳ．① F768.3

中国版本图书馆 CIP 数据核字（2014）第 227004 号

策划编辑：金　昊　　责任编辑：陈静杰　　责任校对：楼旭红

责任设计：何　建　　责任印制：储志伟

中国纺织出版社出版发行

地址：北京市朝阳区百子湾东里A407号楼　邮政编码：100124

销售电话：010—67004422　传真：010—87155801

http://www.c-textilep.com

E-mail:faxing@c-textilep.com

中国纺织出版社天猫旗舰店

官方微博 http://weibo.com/2119887771

北京睿特印刷厂印刷　各地新华书店经销

2014年9月第1版第1次印刷

开本：787×1092　1/16　印张：18.75

字数：524千字　定价：48.00元

凡购本书，如有缺页、倒页、脱页，由本社图书营销中心调换

译者序

《时装营销》这本书的翻译历时2年多，一遍又一遍审阅、修改，终于交付了译稿。

在校园里，看到学生鞋带开了，我会忍不住告诉那人："哎，鞋带开了！"一次两次之后，曾经有同事笑说我有强迫症，对此我一笑而过、不以为然。但后来我做过一次测试，结果是我有比较严重的强迫症，我这才觉得我真的可能是有强迫症，要不别人翻译的初稿我审一遍又一遍，改一遍又一遍，直到觉得意思对了、读起来顺了、感觉舒服了，才会满意地放下。2年来就是这样，可以说是经历了一个相对漫长的审译过程。

本书第一章由北京服装学院陈佳翻译；第二章前半部分由厦门理工学院外国语学院何雅媚翻译，后半部分由厦门理工学院设计艺术与服装工程学院孙可可翻译；第三章、第七章由山东泰安市泰山区教育局乔婷翻译；第四、五、六章由西南大学纺织服装学院安妮翻译；第八章由厦门理工学院设计艺术与服装工程学院范晓轩翻译；第九章、第十章由厦门理工学院外国语学院何雅媚翻译；其余部分由厦门理工学院设计艺术与服装工程学院梁亚林翻译。全书审稿、统稿由梁亚林负责完成。

感谢所有翻译者对本书的贡献，在你们翻译的基础上，我结合自己近30年在服装市场营销方面教学经验的积累，完成了本书的全部审阅、修改和最终定稿。感谢本书的出版单位中国纺织出版社服装图书分社，在速度就是效益、以效益制胜的当今社会，你们一直没有放弃对我们翻译组的信任和支持，才有了这本书与读者见面的机会。还要提前感谢购买、阅读本书的所有读者，希望你们阅读后留下好的意见和建议并及时反馈给我们，也希望我们这本书对你们了解英国服装产业、了解英国服装市场营销状况和营销策略等有所帮助。

2014年7月

梁亚林

译者简介

梁亚林，教授，硕士生导师。工商管理硕士毕业，1988 年 7 月 ~2006 年 7 月在西安工程大学（原西北纺织工学院）服装与艺术设计学院任教，2006 年 7 月至今，在厦门理工学院设计艺术与服装工程学院任教。

从事服装市场营销理论与实务、服装产业经济等方面的教学与科研工作，讲授服装市场营销、服装贸易实务、服装商品企划等课程。工作至今发表教学和科研论文近 70 篇，参编国家级“十五”规划教材《数字化服装设计与管理》（中国纺织出版社）、《服装生产技术与管理》（东华大学出版社），主编厦门理工学院教材《服装市场营销》等。主持或参与国家级、省部级、市级及横向合作科研项目 18 项，获得国家级奖励一项，省、部级奖励一项，校级奖励等多项。

安妮，西南大学纺织服装学院讲师，伦敦艺术大学访问学者， 苏州大学服装设计与工程专业在读博士。从事服装市场企划与品牌运营的教学和科研工作，近年发表《3D打印技术在女性束身衣生产中的应用》《线上店铺虚拟试衣技术的实现方式对比分析》《新型试衣技术在实体店的应用》《纺织企业创建和发展服装品牌的模式探讨》《真人模特橱窗发展趋势》等多篇论文。主持、主研省级、市级和校级课题多项。独立主编完成教材《服装品牌企划与运营》（北京大学出版社出版）。

何雅媚，厦门理工学院外国语学院副书记、副院长、副教授，英语语言文学硕士。

从事英汉语比较与翻译、社会心理语言学研究与科研工作。近年发表《“定语+人称代词”结构的翻译审美》《言语交际中亲疏关系信息的传递》《将中华优秀文化纳入英语教学的思考》等多篇论文。主持完成省、市、校级课题多项。主编教材《大学比较英语教程 2》（学生用书）《大学比较英语教程 2》（学习手册）。

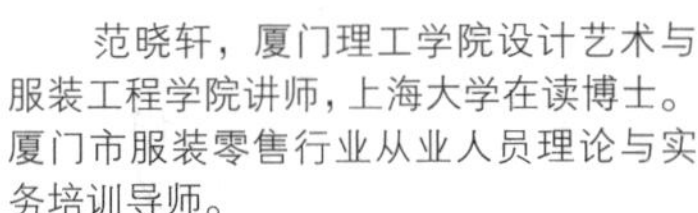

范晓轩，厦门理工学院设计艺术与服装工程学院讲师，上海大学在读博士。厦门市服装零售行业从业人员理论与实务培训导师。

主要从事服饰设计、色彩与文化的教学与科研工作，指导学生多次入围各类服装设计比赛并获得奖项。参与翻译马丁坎普的著作《艺术的科学》，近年发表《龟兹壁画人物配饰研究》《服装整体美展示与局部处理》《诠释万变 把握流行——女装流行趋势分析 》等多篇论文，参与厦门华懋企业横向课题等。

乔婷，工学硕士。2007 年 10 月 ~2013 年 5 月山东服装职业学院服装工程系讲师，2013 年 5 月至今，在山东泰安市泰山区教育局工作。

在山东服装职业学院从事服装专业教学期间，参编化学工业出版社《华裳天下丛书：历朝历代服饰》《服装结构设计》《服装贸易实务》等出版项目。参与并完成山东省艺术科学重点课题《齐鲁文化对山东服装企业文化的影响》等项目。发表《宋代服饰特点的研究与探析》《纺织服装出口微利的博弈分析》《山东省童装市场初探》等多篇论文。

孙可可，厦门理工学院设计艺术与服装工程学院讲师，工学硕士。曾就职深圳歌力思服饰股份有限公司，现为厦门容嘉服饰有限公司执行董事。

主讲服装结构设计、服装商品企划、服装专业英语、服装 CAD 等专业课程。近年发表《对服装双语教学的思考》《基于品牌市场的服装结构设计创新实践分析》《Research of Non-contact Body Measurement Technology in Natural Wearing State》（EI Conference）等数篇学术论文。翻译《简约包装设计》一书。主持并完成“基于品牌市场的服装结构设计创新教育模式研究与实践”等教研课题，指导学生参加“COCOON 杯”中国国际女装设计大奖赛、“中华杯”国际服装设计大赛、中国国际面料设计大赛、“大连杯”青年服装设计师大赛、NAFA 杯国际青年裘皮服装设计大赛、中国（大朗）毛织服装设计大赛、黛安芬创意设计大赛等若干专业比赛参赛并获奖。

Preface
前 言

If you are interested or involved in fashion you will already be aware that it is an exciting area of constant change, creativity and global commercial activity. However, skills in fashion are not enough to guarantee success, as even when those skills are exceptional there is still the constant risk of failure and bankruptcy. A knowledge of marketing is essential to help ensure success and lessen the possibility of failure. To paraphrase Armani, 'Clothing that is not purchased or worn is not fashion.' A good knowledge of fashion marketing can make the difference between a prototype that lingers in a dark storeroom and a garment that people really want to buy and wear.

Over the last two decades fashion has become a truly global business. Designers no longer work necessarily within manufacturing facilities and, as part of the knowledge industry, they need to be mobile and have the ability to communicate across cultures and business disciplines. Many brands like Gap, Zara and H&M which were just national brands a few years ago are now internationally recognized. Another major force influencing the fashion business is the growth of the Internet. The Internet has influenced the flow of creative ideas, the search for product information, the transparency of pricing and the management of supply chains amongst as well as how and where customers buy garments.

For the designer keen to start his or her own business, this book will offer a guide to most of the major decisions that will enable you to fulfil your creative

如果你对时装感兴趣或置身于时装业，想必已经意识到这一令人兴奋不已的领域充满着不断变化和创造力，它是全球性的商业活动。然而，只拥有时装设计技巧并不足以保证你能成功，即便你的设计非凡，还是有失败和破产的风险。对时装而言，具备营销知识是必不可少的，它可以为成功和减少失败的可能性来保驾护航。正如阿玛尼释义时装，“没人买、没人穿的时装不是真正的时装”。时装营销可以将陈列在黑暗库房的样品和人们真正想买、想穿的时装区分开来。

近20年来，时装业已确确实实发展成为全球性产业。设计者不必再局限于工厂中，作为知识产业的一部分，他们需要交流，需要拥有跨文化和跨业务间的交流能力。许多品牌如盖璞、Zara和海恩斯·莫里斯，几年前还只是所在国的国内品牌，而如今已发展成为全球知名的国际品牌。另一个对时装业影响巨大的力量来自互联网的发展。互联网影响了创新思想的传播、产品信息的搜寻、价格的透明度和供应链的管理，以及顾客如何购买和在何地购买时装。

对于试图开创自身业务的设计师来说，本书将提供对重大决策的指导，将帮助你挖掘创意潜能、获得经济效益。

potential and be a financial success. For the marketer who is interested in fashion, this book will help you understand the special way that marketing needs to be applied to the world of fashion. Established fashion businesses also need to remain competitive by asking questions such as:

◆ What are the major trends we should be monitoring?

◆ How should we set our prices?

◆ What is the most effective way to get our message across about the new product range?

◆ Which colour wash will be the most popular with buyers?

Fashion marketing finds answers to these and many other questions.

This book has a number of special qualities that make it essential reading for anyone involved in fashion.

◆ It deals with contemporary issues in fashion marketing.

◆ It has up-to-date examples of good practice. Over the past 35 years, all other major texts on fashion marketing have been centred on US practice. Fashion is now a global business and that theme is evident in all chapters in this revised edition.

◆ This book is exclusively about fashion marketing. It is not a marketing book with a few fashion examples among the anecdotes about motorcycles, industrial services and banking. It is all about fashion.

◆ There is a unique contribution on range planning which is a practical blend of sound design sense and commercial realism.

◆ There is a constant balance of theory and practice, with examples to illustrate key concepts. Where numerical concepts are included, there are clear worked examples to ensure that the ideas are easily understood and retained.

◆ Each chapter contains an introduction to set the scene and a summary of key points. There are over 50 diagrams to help to explain ideas and a glossary of the main fashion marketing terms is included.

对于那些对时装感兴趣的营销人员，本书将帮助你们了解时装界营销的特殊方式，既有的时装产业也需要通过提出以下问题来保持其竞争力。如：

◆ 我们需要监控哪些主要流行趋势？

◆ 我们如何定价？

◆ 发布新产品系列消息最有效的方式是什么？

◆ 最受购买者喜爱的色系是什么？

时装营销帮助解答了上述问题和其他问题。

本书还有一些特点，使之成为时装界人士的必读之作。

◆ 它论及的是当代时装营销。

◆ 它搜罗了行之有效的最新案例分析。近35年来，所有的其他时装营销实例都集中举出美国的案例。但时装目前已经走向全球化了，这一主题在本修订版本的各章中体现明显。

◆ 本书只涉及时装营销。并不是在众多关于摩托车、产业服务、银行业等的逸事中夹杂着几个时装营销的案例。一切都是关于时装的。

◆本书的独特贡献在于有一个长期的规划，能够把完整的设计理念和商业现实有效地融合。

◆ 有效地平衡理论与实践，通过实例阐释主要概念，大量概念出现时总是辅以清晰有效的实例，确保思想阐述地清晰易懂。

◆ 每一章前面有导言，阐述背景和主要观点。书中的50多张图表有助于对观点的解释，主要的时装营销术语汇编也附后给出。

◆ Included within each chapter is a guide to further reading. Keen fashion marketers will therefore be able to use this book as a foundation and springboard to becoming experts in specialist areas such as fashion marketing research or fashion public relations.

◆ 每一章后面有补充阅读材料。聪明的时装营销者会将本书作为将自己打造成时装营销研究或时装公共关系领域专家的基础或跳板。

◆ A coherent approach to fashion marketing is developed, based on the research, consultancy, working and teaching experiences of a team from a major centre of excellence in fashion marketing in the UK. What you will get is a systematic approach to fashion marketing, not hyperbole or speculation.

◆ 英国时装营销界的优秀人士基于研究、咨询、工作和教学经验提出了时装营销的合理方法。你得到的是时装营销的系统方法，并非夸张的描述和推测。

How this book is organized ／本书布局

Part A looks at the nature and scope of fashion marketing. In Chapter One the special ingredients that make for good fashion design, care for customers and commercial success are explored. All fashion enthusiasts know of some of the links between fashion and broader social change and Chapter Two identifies those links, showing how fashion marketers are able to anticipate and participate in the process.

第 1 部分内容涉及时装营销的性质和范畴。第 1 章中对造就优秀的时装设计、顾客至上和商业成功的特别因素加以探究。所有时装爱好者所知的一些时装与更广泛的社会变化之间的联系在第 2 章中加以阐释，并展示时装营销者如何预测和参与其中。

Part B is concerned with understanding and researching the consumer. In Chapter Three there is a detailed look at the consumer and what he or she wants from fashion, how ideas and brands are learned and how to paint a comprehensive and sound picture of the 'muse' for the fashion designer. Chapter Four deals with marketing research and shows how to investigate the preferences and behaviour of customers, distribution channels and competitors.

第 2 部分是关于了解和调研消费者。第 3 章详述消费者并弄清他对时装的需求是什么，如何创意和记住品牌内涵，如何勾勒出表达时装设计师灵感的完整又完美的效果图。第 4 章主要内容为营销调研，阐述如何调查消费者偏好、行为、分销渠道和竞争者。

Part C looks at target marketing and the fashion marketing mix. Chapter Five deals with choosing profitable markets to aim at and then gives an overview of possible action to meet customer requirements – the marketing mix. In Chapters Six to Nine, precise coverage is given to the design of marketing programmes to ensure that the right garments (Chapter Six) are correctly priced (Chapter Seven), available at the right time and place (Chapter Eight) and are properly communicated (Chapter Nine). The final chapter deals with planning and co-ordinating the whole fashion marketing process, and setting up a system that works for the consumer, offering good fashion design and delivering profits.

第 3 部分内容涉及目标市场营销和时装营销组合。第 5 章阐述选择可获利市场并加以定位，然后综述为满足顾客的需求可能采取的行动，即营销组合。第 6 章到第 9 章阐述营销方案设计，以确保合适的时装（第 6 章）的准确定价（第 7 章）并适时、适地（第 8 章）地投入市场，以及达成良好的流通（第 9 章）。第 10 章内容涉及整个时装营销过程的规划和协调，并建立起一个为消费者提供优秀的时装设计和产生利润的系统。

If, like us, you believe that consumers deserve good fashion design and that profits should flow to those who act systematically to make that happen, then join us for the challenge that is fashion marketing.

如果你同我们一样相信，消费者应该得到优质的时装设计，并且相信利润往往流向那些为之不懈努力的人，那么加入我们的行列，一起迎接时装营销的挑战吧。

The book's website ／本书网站

On the book's website, www.blackwellpublishing.com/easey, you will find invaluable on-line resources to support both teaching and learning – all downloadable free of charge. The website has the following features:

- For fashion marketing tutors, a full set of PowerPoint slides to accompany each chapter.
- Ideas and exercises for seminars.
- Access to sample assessment materials.
- Useful hyperlinks to relevant websites.

通过本书网站 www.blackwellpublishing.com/easey，你可以找到非常宝贵的可供教学和学习的网上资源，且均可免费下载。本网站有以下特点：

- 为方便时装营销教师使用，每一章都有全套幻灯片。
- 讨论课题的思考和练习。
- 有权使用样本评价材料。
- 链接至其他相关网站。

Contents
目 录

Part A
Understanding Fashion Marketing
第 1 部分　了解时装营销

Chapter One An Introduction to Fashion Marketing
第 1 章 时装营销绪论

The statistics reveal that fashion is a large global business sector going through a period of great change. It is the application of marketing that plays a crucial role in managing this growth and change. This book shows how marketing can be applied to fashion products and services.

This introduction looks at both fashion and marketing and how design and marketing work together in practice. An overview of the fashion marketing process covers the role of marketing in the fashion industry and the ethical issues raised by marketing in this context, with some practical examples of the work of fashion marketers.

数据显示，时装业是一个大规模的全球化商业领域，并且正经历一个巨大变革阶段。正是营销的运用对这种业务的增长和变化起着决定性的作用。本书内容主要讲述如何将营销学应用到时装产品及服务中。

本章主要阐述内容是时装和营销及如何在实践中将设计和营销结合到一起。时装营销过程综述引用一些时装营销人员的工作实例，对营销在时装业中所起作用以及在营销过程中所引发的伦理问题进行阐述。

1.1 What is fashion? / 什么是时装

1.1.1 Fashion is to do with change / 时装是随变化而改变的

Fashion essentially involves change, defined as a succession of short-term trends or fads. From this standpoint there can be fashions in almost any human activity from medical treatments to popular music. For the purpose of this book though, the concept of fashion will be taken to deal with the garments and related products and services as shown in Figure 1.1.

Figure 1.1 identifies some major categories of clothing along with their main usage situations, but this list is by no means exhaustive. Fashion marketers should take a broad view of their domain – fashion is not only about clothes.

The competitive ethos of the fashion industry revolves around seasonality. The industry has

时装本质包含变化，它被定义为一系列短期流行趋势或时尚。从医疗到流行音乐的任何一种人类活动中，时装无处不在。因此，本书将时装的概念定义为时装和相关产品及服务。如图 1–1 中所示。

从图 1–1 中，我们认识了时装的一些主要类型及其主要使用情境。但这个清单并不全面。时装营销者应该放眼至其整个领域——因为时装并不仅仅就指的是衣服。

时装业的竞争特点是应季而变。该产业将顾客在现实商品的消费中所获得的利益投入

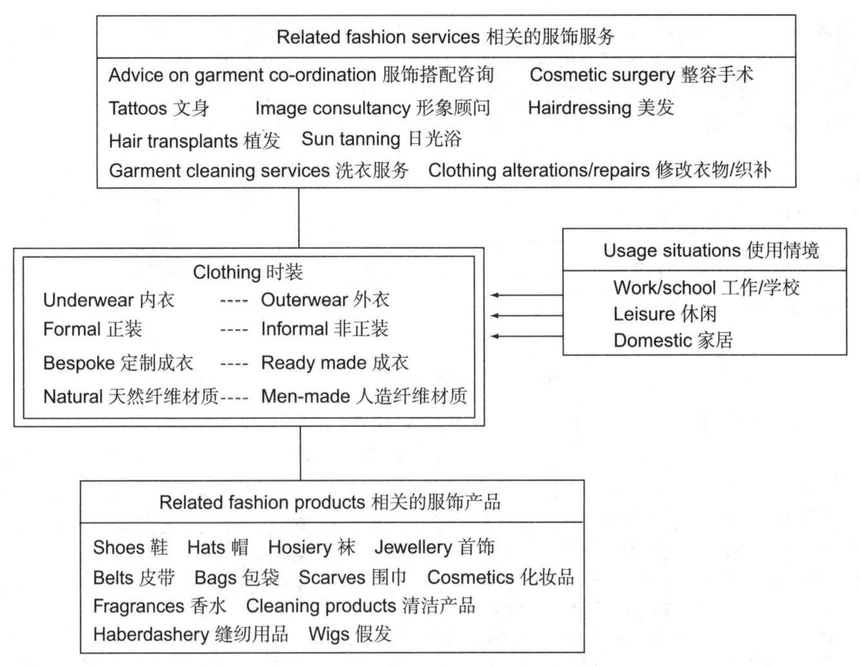

Figure 1.1 Fashion products and services. 图 1-1 时装产品和服务

a vested interest in developing new products for the customer at the expense of existing items: this process is known as planned obsolescence. Planned obsolescence is not confined to the fashion industry, it occurs in several other manufacturing sectors such as the electronics or automobile industries. While the concept of planned obsolescence can be criticized from several perspectives, many customers appreciate the continual change in fashion products and services. Unfortunately, the rate and direction of change are usually slower and less predictable than the fashion industry would like.

到开发新产品中，这个过程被称为“计划报废”。计划报废并不仅仅局限于时装业，还出现在其他制造领域，如电子业或汽车业。当计划报废这一概念可能受到质疑时，许多消费者意识到时装产品和服务在不断地变化。令人遗憾的是，工厂变化的速度相对较慢，变化的方向又不同于时装业的发展所预料的那样。

1.1.2 Fashion is about creating ／时装是关于创意设计的

In order for the change which is intrinsic to fashion to take place, the industry must continually create new products. Used in another sense, the term fashion means to construct, mould or make. Fashion, therefore, also involves a strong creative and design component. Design skill is essential and can be seen in all products from the made-to-measure suit to the elaborate embroidery on a cardigan. The level of

时装的本质是变化，时装业必须持续创造新产品以顺应这种变化。另一方面，时装的定义是绘制结构图、制板和缝制衣服。因此，时装包含大量的创意和设计元素。无论是定制的套装还是精致刺绣的毛衣，所有的产品都能够体现出设计元素的至关重要性。例如基础款式T恤，可可·夏

design can vary considerably from a basic item such as a T-shirt to the artistic creations of Coco Chanel, Christian Dior, Yves St Laurent or, in more recent times, Stella McCartney. To some the design of fashion garments can be viewed as an art in its own right, though this is a notion supported more in countries such as France and Italy than in Britain. The majority of garments sold do not come into this category, but the inspiration for the design of many of those garments may have come from works of art.

奈尔、克里斯汀・迪奥、伊夫・圣・洛朗或近期的斯特拉・麦卡托尼的艺术创作、设计水准有相当大的变化。对于某些时尚服饰的设计，从其本身来说就可以看作一件艺术品，相比较英国而言，在许多国家如法国和意大利，人们更加赞同此观点。虽然出售的大部分时装并不属于艺术品的范畴，但许多时装的设计灵感可能来自艺术品本身。

1.1.3 Fashion and marketing／时装和营销

The continual change, i.e. fashion, involves the exercise of creative design skills which result in products that range from the basic to the rare and elaborate. The creative design personnel provide part of the mechanism by which the industry responds to the need for change. At the same time the ability to identify products that the customer needs and will buy is also essential to the industry. Marketing can help to provide this additional knowledge and the skills needed to ensure that the creative component is used to best advantage, allowing businesses to succeed and grow.

时装持续的变化，包含了创意设计技巧的运用，从基本款时装到稀少并精致的高端时装的变化幅度来自这些技巧。创意设计人员提供部分技术，商家通过利用设计人员所提供的技术去适应由于变化所带来的市场需求。对于商家来说，预测消费者对该时装的需求及购买能力也是必要的。营销有助于提供附加知识和这种技能，附加知识和技能能用来确保创意元素得以最优发挥作用，保证企业的成功和成长。

1.2 What is marketing?／什么是营销

Marketing is a business philosophy or way of thinking about the firm from the perspective of the customer or the potential customer. Such a view has much merit as it focuses on the acid test for all business – if we do not meet the needs of our customers we will not survive, let alone thrive. Fashion firms depend upon customers making repeat purchases and the key to such loyalty is the satisfaction of customers' needs with garments which are stylish, durable, easy to care for, comfortable, perceived value for money and all the other criteria deemed relevant by the buyer. For this reason, fashion design personnel should readily appreciate the need to understand the customer's perspective. Most designers have a mental picture of a typical customer. Fashion marketers ask, how typical is that mental picture and does the 'customer' belong to a group of buyers that form a profitable prospect for the company Notice that the notion of seeing the business from the perspective of the customer does not preclude concern for profit. Indeed, if profit

营销是一种商业理念，或是一种站在消费者或潜在顾客的角度来考量公司的运作方式。这种观点有很多优点，因为它重视对所有商业进行严格的考验——如果没有满足消费者的需求，企业将不能生存，更不用说发展壮大了。时装企业依靠消费者不断消费或购买商品，而消费者对商品的忠诚度的关键是满足消费者对时装款式、耐用度、保养难易度、舒适性、合理的价格及其他符合购买者所认可的所有相关标准的时装产品需求。因此时装设计人员应该欣然接受这一需求，了解消费者的心理。

大多数设计师都在心中为典型顾客勾勒出了具体形象。时装营销人员则会质疑这种具体形象的典型程度以及这些所勾勒出来的顾客是否属于会为公司带来利润的顾客群体。要注意的是，从消

is not actively sought then the firm's ability to meet customers' needs in the long term will be greatly diminished.

费者的角度来看，企业也不能忽略利润。的确，如果看不到高额利润，公司长期满足消费者需求的能力将会大大减弱。

Marketing comprises a range of techniques and activities, some of which are highly familiar to the general public. Most people have encountered market researchers and all have seen advertisements. Other less public aspects include product development and branding, pricing, publicity, sales promotion, selling, forecasting and distribution. An overview of the range of fashion marketing activities is given later in this chapter.

营销包含一系列的技巧和活动，其中有些是被大众所熟知的。许多人都曾遇到过市场调查员并且所有人都看过广告。其他不为公众熟知的方面包含产品开发和品牌化、定价、宣传、促销、销售、预测和分销。本章之后会对时装营销一系列活动进行阐述。

Marketing is a management process concerned with anticipating, identifying and satisfying customer needs in order to meet the long-term goals of the organization. Whilst concerned with the organization's relationship with customers it is also concerned with internal organizational factors that affect the achievement of marketing goals.

营销是一个管理过程，为了实现一个经营组织的长期目标，这个过程与预测、识别和满足消费者需求相关。营销不仅涉及商家与消费者之间的关系，而且涉及公司内部会影响到营销目标的因素。

Is marketing a solution to all business problems? / 营销是所有商业问题的解决方案吗？

There are many views of what marketing is and what it does. To the zealots, marketing is the panacea for all business problems and can provide remedies for product failures or falling profits. Clearly, this is naive and does not recognize the interdependence of the many business and creative functions within organizations. Nor does this view fully appreciate the wider marketing environment that confronts all firms when they embark upon marketing activities.

人们对于营销是什么以及营销在做什么有许多种观点。对于营销的追捧者来说，营销是解决所有商业问题的良药，而且营销还可以针对产品失败和利润下降的状况提出补救方法。很明显，这种看法没有认识到众多业务间的相辅相成关系和组织中的创新作用，是不成熟的。

The best marketing plans and activities can be easily and quickly undermined by changes in the economy or in competitors' actions. Such changes cannot always be anticipated, although a framework for monitoring and anticipating change is discussed in Chapter Two. In the fashion industry, which is highly competitive and is characterized by change, the role of good fortune cannot be easily discounted. The fashion industry is well known for the high failure rate of new businesses and the regular price reductions on product lines that have not sold. Such failures are in part a reflection of the enormous risk of fashion, but some are also due to the inadequate or inappropriate application of the marketing process. It is the contention of the authors that, when properly applied, marketing will help to reduce some uncertainty in the fashion industry and cut down the number of business failures.

就算是最成功的营销规划和活动，也会被经济中的变革或竞争者的商业运作中的变化轻易、快速地破坏掉。尽管有专门监测和预测这些变化的系统，这些变化也常常不能被人们预料到，第 2 章将会探讨这部分内容。在时装业中，竞争十分激烈而且以多变著称，因此机遇的作用是不容忽视的。众所周知，新企业的高倒闭率和未售产品系列规律性降价。从某种程度上看，这些规律性反映出时装业经营存在的巨大风险，但有些倒闭是由于在营销过程中采取了不充分或者不适合的方法。作者认为合理地运用营销手段有助于降低时装业经营中的不确定性程度，并且减少企业的倒闭数量。

1.3 What is fashion marketing? /什么是时装营销

Fashion marketing is the application of a range of techniques and a business philosophy that centres upon the customer and potential customer of clothing and related products and services in order to meet the long-term goals of the organization. It is a major argument of this book that fashion marketing is different from many other areas of marketing. The very nature of fashion, where change is intrinsic, gives different emphasis to marketing activities. Furthermore, the role of design in both leading and reflecting consumer demand results in a variety of approaches to fashion marketing which are explored below.

时装营销是一系列技术和一种经营理念的运用，而这一经营理念是以时装和相关产品及服务的顾客和潜在顾客为中心，以求实现公司长远目标。本书的主要论点是时装营销不同于其他领域里的营销。时装的内在特性是变化，其本质使得营销活动有不同的侧重点。此外，在引导和影响消费者需求中，设计的作用导致产生了多种时装营销方式，这些时装营销方式将会在下章一一探究。

1.4 Fashion marketing in practice /时装营销实践

Within the fashion industry there is enormous variation in the size and structure of businesses serving the needs of customers. From a small business comprising a self-employed knitwear designer to major multinational corporations such as Liz Claiborne or Zara, diversity remains a key feature. With legislative changes and expansion of the EU, the gradual removal of trade barriers on a global scale and the growth of the Internet, the fashion industry is increasingly a global business. This implies considerable variation in the cultural, social and economic perspective of the participants. The consequence of these variations in size, experience and perspective is that the practice of fashion marketing is not uniform at a national level, let alone at an international one.

At the centre of the debate over the role of fashion marketing within firms resides a tension between design and marketing imperatives. Relatively few fashion designers have had formal training in business or marketing, although fortunately this situation is changing in the EU. Similarly, the formal training of marketing personnel can often lack an appreciation of the role of design in business. Training has tended to be separate and this, when coupled with the differing approaches of the two areas, causes divergent views. Design students were traditionally taught to approach problems

在时装业中，服务于顾客需求的商业结构和规模发生了巨大变化。从只有一个毛织品设计者的小公司到像里兹·克莱本或Zara这样的跨国公司，多样性一直是一个重要的特征。随着相关立法的改变和欧盟的扩张，全球贸易壁垒的逐渐消失和国际互联网的发展，时装业逐渐成长为一个全球化的行业。这其中也蕴藏了文化、社会、企业和经济前景方面相当大的差异。这些差异在规模、经历和前景发生了变化，而这些变化造成的结果是时装营销的实践在全国范围内都不能达到统一，更别说国际性的统一了。

在对时装营销作用的争论中，设计和营销必要性之间的侧重点处于争论的中心地位。相对来说，仅有为数不多的时装设计者参加过正规的商业或营销方面的专业训练，在欧盟这种情况稍有改善，但仍然很普遍。同样地，营销人员的正规培训常常缺乏对设计在商业领域中所起作用的高度评价，培训趋向于把设计和营销分离，所以当两个领域不同的方面结合时会产生不同的观点。设计

as though there were no constraints on time or cost so that creativity might flourish. The assumption of much of this training was that creativity flourishes when there is freedom from structural factors. Spontaneity, eclecticism and the willingness to take risks in challenging the status quo are some values central to traditional design training.

类的学生受到传统的教育，他们不用考虑成本和时间的限制去进行创作，因此他们的创造力很丰富。这些培训多数基于这种假设，即认为在完全不受时装结构因素限制的情况下，创造力才能丰富。面对现存的挑战，自发地、有选择地并且心甘情愿地去承担风险，已成为传统设计训练的核心价值观。

Marketing training, by contrast, embraces different values. Marketers are taught to be systematic and analytical in approaching problems. The foundation of a lot of marketing involves the setting of objectives and quantifying inputs and outputs, such as advertising expenditure and market share. Success, marketing students are taught, comes from careful research and planning, not spontaneity or ignoring market realities such as competitor price levels. Owing to a lack of training, marketing personnel often fail to understand the aesthetic dimension of a design or many qualitative aspects of product development.

相反，营销培训有不同的价值观。营销人员被灌输要系统地、分析地去解决问题。许多营销的基本原理包含营销目标的设定及量化投入和产出量，如广告支出和市场占有率。营销类的学生被灌输，成功是来自细致的研究和规划，而不是主动了解或者忽视市场的实际情况，如竞争者的价格水平。由于缺乏相关的培训，营销人员常常不理解一个设计作品的美学原理或没有考虑到许多产品开发中品质方面的问题。

The above outlines concentrate on differences in perspective between marketing and design personnel but naturally there are areas where they share common values. Good designers and marketing personnel both recognize the need for thorough preparation and the exercise of professional skill, both understand the importance of communication, although with differing emphasis on the visual and process components, and both tend to be in agreement about the functional aspects of clothing, such as whether a garment is waterproof or machine washable.

以上主要讨论营销人员和设计人员的观点的差异性，但是他们自然也会在一些方面持有相同的价值观。优秀的设计师和市场营销人员都能认识到完善的准备和专业技巧运用的必要性，而且都能懂得交流的重要性，尽管在视觉和实现过程中他们有不同的侧重，但是他们都认同时装的功能性。例如，他们都会关心一件衣服可以防水还是可机洗。

Starkly put, the designer may see the marketing person as one who constrains freedom and imagination, while the marketer may see the designer as undisciplined and oblivious to costs and profitability. Such views are stereotypes fostered by differing experiences and training, and which are often held by those who do not understand the perspective of both the marketer and the designer. This difference in perspective engenders a range of views about what fashion marketing ought to be. Two views of fashion marketing are shown in Figure 1.2. These views can be labelled design centred and marketing centred, and are detailed below.

诚然，有一个现象很明显，设计者可能会认为营销人员会限制他们的创作自由和想象空间，而营销人员则觉得设计者没有原则并且不考虑产品的成本和利润。这都是由于不同的经历和教育而产生的过时的理论，并通常被那些既不了解营销人员也不了解设计者的想法的人所赞同和持有。这个分歧导致了一系列关于时装营销到底应该是什么的观点的产生。时装营销的两种观点如下图 1–2 所示。这些观点可以被定义为设计中心论和营销中心论，具体内容如下所述。

View 观点	View of Design Centred 设计中心论	View of Marketing Centred 营销中心论
Sample statements 观点陈述	Fashion marketing is the same as promotion 时装营销等同于促销	Design should be based solely on marketing research 设计仅基于营销调研
Assumption 基本假设	Sell what we can make 出售我们能生产的东西	Make what we can sell 生产我们能出售的东西
Orientation 定位	Design centred 以设计为中心	Marketing centred 以营销为中心
Alleged drawbacks 主要问题	High failure rates Relies on intuition 高失败率，依靠直觉	Bland designs Stifles creativity 平凡的设计，扼杀创造性

Figure 1.2 Tow views of fashion marketing. 图 1–2 时装营销的两种观点

1.4.1 Design centred: fashion marketing as promotion / 设计中心论：时装营销等同于促销

According to this view marketing is seen as synonymous with promotion. Adherents of the view state that designers are the real force, and marketers should merely help to sell ideas to the public. Translated into practice this view tends to have all marketing activity carried out by either public relations or advertising departments or agencies. Customers and potential customers are seen as people to be led or inspired by creative styling that is favourably promoted. At the extreme, it is rationalized that the only people who can appreciate creative styling, in a financial sense, are the more wealthy sections of society.

Research within such a perspective is limited to monitoring the activities of others who are thought to be at the forefront of creative change, i.e. film directors, musicians, artists, etc. Many great fashion designers subscribe to this view and have run successful businesses based upon the above assumptions. The principal weakness of this approach is that it depends ultimately on the skill and intuition of the designer in consistently meeting genuine customer needs and consequently earning profit.

根据这种观点，营销被认为是促销的同义词。这种观点的支持者认为设计师是真正的主宰，营销人员仅仅有助于向公众推销理念。在实践中，这种观点倾向于认为所有营销活动的贯彻执行是通过公共关系或广告宣传部门或代理公司。顾客和潜在顾客被认为是被富有创意的款式牵着走或吸引的，富有创意的款式才是有力的促销。极端意义来讲，即设计中心论的支持者认为下面这种想法是合理的，即从财务方面来讲，只有可以接受富有创意的款式的顾客才是社会最具有价值的部分。

立足于这种观点的调查仅限于调查那些认为是在设计变化最前沿的人，例如电影导演、音乐家、艺术家等。很多成功的设计师也遵循这种观点，并且在预测的基础上建立了成功的事业。这种观点最主要的缺点在于它完全依赖于设计师在维持满足真正的顾客需求和最终获得利润方面的能力和直觉。

1.4.2 Marketing centred: design as a research prescription / 营销中心论：设计等同于一项调研指令

Here marketing is dominant and it regards the designer as someone who must respond to the

在这个观点中，营销占有主导地位，认为设计师应当是这样一些人：即必须

specifications of customer requirements as established by marketing research. Detailed cost constraints may be imposed and sample garments pretested by, for example, retail selectors who may subsequently demand changes to meet their precise needs. Several major retail stores still operate systems not too far removed from this, with merchandisers and selectors exerting considerable control over the designer. The result, according to many, is a certain blandness in the design content of garments available from such retail outlets.

对通过营销调研确认的顾客需求的事项作出回应。被要求精细地控制成本并进行样衣预算，例如零售部门可能有接二连三的需求变化以满足预期需求。很多大型的零售店的运营系统始终保持着由营销人员和买手为主导来管理设计师的方式。这种方式导致多数情况下在其零售店销售的商品缺乏设计感显得单调平庸。

It is argued that marketing constraints have strangled the creative aspects of design. Taking profitability as a measure of popularity, this restrictive prescription for design seems to work for many firms. Whether popular acceptance of fashion designs equates with good design is another matter.

这种模式通常会引发争议，因为有观点认为营销部门的限制扼杀了设计中创造力的发挥。只把利润率作为流行的衡量标准，而对于时装设计的流行认可等同于好的设计则不考虑在内，这种对设计的限制方法很多企业都在应用。

1.4.3 The fashion marketing concept ／时装营销观念

There is another way to view the relationship between marketing and design, and this is termed the fashion marketing concept. That good fashion design only requires sufficient promotion to succeed is a view applicable to a very limited number of businesses – usually those producing expensive garments for an elite market. The alternative view of fashion design as a function of marketing research fails to recognize either that many people do not know what they will like until presented with choices, or that their preferences change over time. For example, many who profess to hate a design seen on the catwalk may later come to like it when they try the garment themselves or realize that others have signalled acceptance. Good fashion design can challenge conventional views. It should be recognized that consumers vary in the conservatism they have towards fashion styles and also the speed and readiness with which they change their opinions.

用另外一种方式来看待营销和设计之间的关系，这称为时装营销观念。那种认为好的时装设计只需要充分地促销就能成功的观点仅仅能被极少数企业所接受，这些企业通常是那些面向奢侈品市场生产非常昂贵的时装的企业。另一种认为时装设计只是营销调研的一种功能的观点则没有认清下列两种事实：一方面是很多消费者在面临许多选择的时候，才会知道自己的偏好，另一方面是消费者的偏好会随着时间的流逝而改变。例如，很多表示不喜欢甚至厌恶时装秀中的设计的人很可能在试装后或者当大众都开始接受这种设计作品之后喜欢上这种设计作品。优秀的时装设计作品可以超越传统的观念。显而易见，消费者对于时尚款式的保守程度不同，他们改变自己观念的速度和意愿也各不相同（图 1–3）。

A simple model of the interrelationship of fashion design and marketing can be seen above.

以上所见是时装设计和营销的相互关系的简单模型。

In the matrix in Figure 1.3 it can be seen that low concern for customers, profit and design leads to failure. This occurs as a consequence of overestimating design ability while disregarding customers' preferences and the need for profit.

从图 1–3 的矩阵图中可以看出，当给予顾客和利润低关注度时，会导致设计出现失误。这种情况发生在过高评估设计能力但却忽视了顾客偏好和利润需求的时候。

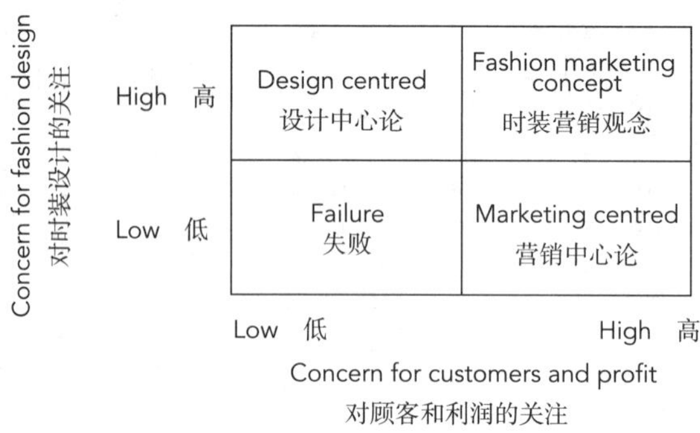

Figure 1.3 The fashion marketing concept. 图 1–3 时装营销观念

The fashion marketing concept attempts to embrace the positive aspects of high concern for design, customers and profit by recognizing the interdependence of marketing and design. If designers understand how marketing can enhance the creative process and marketing personnel appreciate that within the fashion industry design can lead as well as respond to customer requirements, progress can be made. Market researchers can establish the sizing information customers want on garments and can also analyse reactions to several provisional illustrations, but they cannot produce detailed styling specifications. Marketing as applied to the fashion industry must appreciate the role of design. Some major retailers such as Zara have developed information systems bringing designers, manufacturing teams and retail sales staff much closer together enabling customers to be offered fast fashion at affordable prices and achieving good levels of profit for the company.

This section has discussed a number of approaches to fashion marketing. Many companies have embraced the fashion marketing concept and have demonstrated equal concern for design, customers and profits. In recent years an increasing number of winners of major fashion awards have also achieved success not only in terms of design but also in terms of sales and profit. Thus the fashion marketing concept is not just a theoretical model, it does work in practice and this book sets out to develop it further.

时装营销观念中提到设计和营销之间的相互依赖关系，因此包含了设计、顾客和利润的积极因素。如果设计师明白营销能够强化设计过程，市场营销部门明白时装工业化的设计可以像回应顾客需求一样来引导顾客，这种交互关系的过程就可以实现。市场研究人员可以建立消费者所需的时装尺码信息，也可以对不同的设计草图分析其回应效果，但他们不能设计生产出具体的时装款式。时装业中的营销必须意识到设计的地位。一些大型零售商，例如 Zara 开发了信息系统，这些信息系统让设计师、制造商和零售人员更紧密地结合在一起，这样可以以消费者可承受的价格更快速地提供给顾客时尚产品，并为公司创造高额利润。

本节我们探讨了许多时装营销的方法。很多公司已经接受时装营销观念，并且表露出对唯设计论、唯顾客和利益论的担心。近年来，越来越多的时装大奖的获胜者不仅在设计上取得了成功，在销量和销售利润上也取得了成功。因此说，时装营销观念不仅是一个理论模型，它在实践中确实有效，本书将着手展开研究。

1.5 How fashion marketing can help the fashion industry 时装营销如何有利于时装业

The vast output and profits from the fashion industry come not from the designer collections seen on the catwalk but from items sold in high street stores. To put the impact of designers in perspective, one only has to note that the British Fashion Awards' Designer of the Year will often have annual earnings that amount to less than a day's sales for one large retailer in the Arcadia group. Even so, the designer collections are given extensive coverage in the fashion press where each season more than 250 collections are reviewed within a matter of weeks. Reporting and promotion of these collections are suffused within hyperbole, excitement and genuine enthusiasm by many who attend, the catwalk exhibitions being viewed with a range of perceptions from incredulity to sheer entertainment. However, few people see the direct link that some less experienced commentators assert exists between the garments on the catwalk and 'what we will all be wearing next season'. The influence of the designer collections on everyday apparel purchases is complex and will be considered in later chapters on the fashion consumer, product design and fashion promotion.

The main concern of fashion marketers is therefore the design and sale of garments to the majority of the public, for that reason, the techniques described in this book will concentrate on high street fashion rather than haute couture.

Many people in the fashion industry have aspirations to run their own business. Indeed, the industry is characterized by many small firms and regrettably many failures. This book embraces the fashion marketing needs of people starting their own business; it does not, however, extend to all the needs of small businesses, particularly the financial and legal aspects of new ventures. For the new entrepreneur the chapter on marketing research will provide a sound basis on which to start building a business plan. The marketing component of the business plan is covered in the last chapter of this book.

Medium and large businesses are also catered for. The need for co-operation and communication

时装业中的巨大的产值和利润并不是来自T台上时装秀中设计师的成衣作品，而是来自繁华商业街的店铺内所销售的时装。人们只要注意会发现，获英国时尚年度最佳设计师奖的奖金数额通常不如阿卡迪亚集团旗下一家大型零售店一天的销售额。即使如此，设计师成衣作品还是连篇累牍地被时尚媒体报道，每季都有多于250场成衣展在大约一周内接受检阅。由参加发布会的人发布的这些成衣的报道和促销信息充满着夸张、骚动和巨大的热情，人们对观看T台成衣展从抱怀疑态度到认为纯粹是娱乐，所持看法各异。但是，很少有人可以看出缺乏经验的评论员宣称的T台上的时装和“我们下一季将要穿着的时装”之间的直接关系。设计师成衣作品对日常时装销量的影响是复杂的，这点将会在时装消费者、产品设计和时装促销等后续章节中加以阐释。

因此，时装营销人员主要关注的是面向大众的时装的设计和销售问题，所以，本书中阐释的经营技巧将集中于繁华商业街的时装而不是高级定制时装店的时装。

置身时装业中，许多人都渴望经营自己的公司。的确，该行业具有诸多小公司的特点并具有许多令人惋惜的失败特征。本书涵盖了准备开始自己创业的人需要的时装营销知识，但是，它并不能包括小企业所需的全部知识，尤其是对新的风险企业中的财务和法律方面的知识。对于新的创业者，营销调研这章将提供从开始构建一个商业规划到所有环节的一个良好的基础。商业规划在本书的最后一章阐述。

时装营销对大、中型企业同样适用。分销部门各个层次在合作和沟通上的需

between the various levels of distribution in this sector is so important that manufacturer, wholesaler, importer and exporter will all benefit from understanding the structural aspects of the marketing of clothing and related products and services. Many of the principles and techniques described in detail as applicable to the UK are transferable to other markets. For example, UK mass media data are given in the chapter on fashion promotion, but criteria for designing campaigns and selecting media are also given; these criteria are readily transferable.

要是如此重要，以至于生产商、批发商、进口商和出口商都将从了解时装和相关产品及服务的营销组织结构方面而获裨益。许多被详细描述的适合英国的经营原理和经营技巧是可以移植到其他市场的。例如，在时装促销章节中提供了英国大众媒体的数据资料，这些标准数据都是很容易转为己用的，当然，设计大赛和自选媒体所提供的标准除外。

1.6 What fashion marketers do:five examples 时装营销者所从事的工作：5 个范例

To give an overview of the sort of activities that fashion marketing personnel engage in, five examples will be given. A key point to note is that job titles do not always accurately reflect what people do. In fact, few people are called fashion marketing managers, but many carry out functions that are fashion marketing, e.g. those with job titles such as selector, merchandiser, sales executive or public relations consultant.

这里将给出 5 个范例来概括时装营销人员所从事的几类工作。关键要注意工作头衔并不总是能准确地反映这个人所从事的工作。事实上，很少有人被称为时装营销经理，而许多拥有工作头衔诸如买手、零售商、销售主管或公共关系顾问的人履行的职能就是时装营销。

1.6.1 Fashion marketing research ／时装营销调研

A fashion marketing researcher may investigate the market shares of competitors and trends in those shares. Through a group discussion with potential consumers they may discover that a possible brand name has negative connotations and needs rethinking.

时装营销调查员可能要调查竞争对手的市场占有率和占有率的发展变化趋势。通过与潜在顾客进行小组讨论，调查员可能会发现一个原本合适的品牌名称有负面消极的含义并需要反思。

1.6.2 Fashion product management ／时装产品管理

A design manager may be concerned with producing a range of shirts for a major retailer. The shirts must co-ordinate with other garments such as jackets, trousers and ties, all of which may be provided by other manufacturers. The design manager must collect and pass on information to ensure that designers are adequately briefed. Later the manager will be required to sell the designs at a presentation to the retailer, usually in the face of fierce competition. The design manager's knowledge of the retailer's customers and an awareness of his or her own company costs will enable an effective marketing function.

设计部经理可能要考虑为一个大型零售商生产一系列衬衫。这批衬衫必须可以与其他生产商提供的衣服，像夹克、裤子及领带相搭配。那么这位经理就必须收集相关信息并且确保将这些信息清楚地传达给设计师。通常这些设计作品将在订货会上销售给零售商，这要面对激烈的竞争。设计部经理对零售商的顾客的了解和对自己公司成本的清楚认识将保证营销的有效运行。

1.6.3 Fashion promotion / 时装促销

A manufacturer of corporate workwear may have produced a range of clothes suitable for staff working in small independent restaurants. After careful research and planning the manufacturer may decide that a brochure is needed as part of the promotional effort. The brief to be given to the person preparing visual and textual material for the brochure will include an estimate of the number of brochures needed and a list of addresses – essential fashion marketing tasks.

一个已生产过一系列适用于独立经营的小餐馆员工工作服的团体制服生产商，在经过仔细的调研和计划后，可能会决定将这批时装做成产品手册作为促销活动的一部分。提供给人们配有图片和文字材料的手册，还有所需手册数量的估算和寄送地址清单——这是最主要的时装营销任务。

1.6.4 Fashion distribution / 时装分销

An owner of a retail outlet selling her own specially designed millinery wishes to expand. She needs to research a few options including franchising her business, obtaining concessions in selected department stores and linking with a leading womenswear designer to produce new complementary ranges each season. Marketing research and analysis of the status of the business along with the preparation of a future marketing strategy are the major fashion marketing activities needed here.

当一个自主设计独特造型女帽的零售店店主希望扩张自己的销售业务时，她需要调研几种可选择的办法，包括出售店铺的特许权，在目标商场中获得销售经营权，以及每季与一些知名女装设计师共同研发新的搭配产品系列。除了对未来的营销策略做准备工作以外，对公司现状的营销调研和数据分析是时装营销活动此时必须做的工作。

1.6.5 Fashion product positioning and pricing / 时装产品的定位和定价

A major retailer discovers that a competitor is selling imported silk lingerie similar in design and quality to its own, but at prices that are 20% lower. A fashion marketing decision must be made about the positioning and pricing of the product, taking into consideration the strategic goals of the company as well as the price sensitivity of its customers.

一家大型零售商的经营者发现竞争厂家正销售一款从设计和质量上都与自己的产品很相似的进口丝质女士内衣，但价格却比自己的产品低20%。这时，就要对这一产品的定位和定价做出一个时装营销决策，既要考虑公司的战略性目标，又要考虑顾客对价格的敏感度。

1.7 Ethical issues in fashion marketing / 时装营销中的伦理问题

The practice of fashion marketing is often criticized. These criticisms can be classified into two types, the micro-issues and the macro-issues.

Micro-issues concern particular products and services where consumers may feel that they have not been fairly treated or that they have been misled. Most customers have bought clothing that has fallen below expectations by, for example, coming apart at the seams or shrinking in the wash. These problems may occur due to poor quality control or at worst a

时装营销实践通常备受争议。这些争议可以分成微观问题和宏观问题两大类。

微观问题是有关某些产品和服务，顾客可能感觉他们没有被公正对待或者被误导。许多顾客买的衣服让他们大失所望，比如衣服开线或者洗后缩水。这些问题的发生可能是由于低劣的品质控制或是提供服务时对顾客冷淡的态度。令人遗憾的是，在时装业中的确存在部分商

callous attitude towards customers. Sadly, the view of customers as mere punters to be exploited does exist in some parts of the fashion industry but it is a short-sighted attitude as lack of repeat business, legal redress and negative word of mouth are all possible consequences. Given the number of items of clothing bought each year, however, some errors are inevitable and the issue really revolves around how the seller deals with the complaint. According to the fashion marketing concept we should be concerned about long-term consumer welfare as this is the key to building and retaining profitable custom.

家把顾客仅仅当成投注者加以利用的观点，但这是短视的看法，因为这将带来顾客重复购买次数的减少、法律赔偿和负面宣传。然而，鉴于每年时装采购的数量，一些错误是不可避免的，而且这类微观问题的确是围绕卖家如何处理这些抱怨和投诉的。按照时装营销观念，我们应该考虑长期的顾客利益，这是建立和保持盈利的关键所在。

The quick and fair correction of genuine errors reinforces the message to the customer that the retailer cares about long-term customer welfare. Unfortunately, some staff are placed in positions where their own interests may not coincide with those of the firm or the customer – those who work on a commission only basis, for example. Such practices should be condemned as they lead to an undermining of public confidence in the fashion industry.

对于确实存在的问题作出及时公正的整改会增强消费者对零售商的信心，因为这表明这个零售商在意长期的顾客利益。遗憾的是，有些员工将自己的利益置于可能与公司或者客户的利益相冲突之地，例如只关心客户所给回扣多少。像这种情况应该受到谴责，因为这样会破坏公众对时装业的信任。

Macro-issues are broader and emerge not from the conscious conspiracy of individuals or groups of individuals but as unintended or unanticipated consequences of certain activities.

宏观问题存在较广泛并且不仅仅暴露在个人或者团队的意识中，还是某些特定活动的不可预测的意外后果。

The most obvious example is the criticism that the bulk of the fashion industry is lacking in sensitivity to environmental issues in that it encourages a throw-away society, conspicuous consumption and unnecessary use of packaging. Marks and Spencer plc can lay claim to a serious attempt to address some environmental concerns with their 'Plan A'. The Marks and Spencer 'Plan A because there is no Plan B' involves a £200 million eco-plan to become carbon neutral by 2012, to extend their sustainable fabric sourcing and to set new standards in ethical trading. Other attempts to address such concerns, although on a relatively small scale, include the so-called 'environmentally friendly' or 'green' fibres and recycled wool.

最明显的例子是有评论认为大多数时装业缺乏对环境问题的敏感度，因为时装业倡导"浪费"型社会，鼓励人们炫耀消费以及产品的过度包装。玛莎百货（马克斯和斯班赛股份有限公司）宣称他们认真地尝试通过他们的"A 计划"来获得一些对环境保护的关注。玛莎百货的"A 计划，因为没有 B 计划"涉及一个 2 亿英镑的环保计划，即到 2012 年成为碳中立者，扩大他们的可持续的布料采购以及在诚信贸易中建立新的标准。尽管相对来说规模较小，但是对于环境保护的其他尝试性做法也在进行，包括采用被称为"环境友好"或"绿色"纤维材料和可回收利用羊毛。

However, the charge of encouraging a throw-away society is a problem that is likely to recur with sharper and move vehement focus in the future. The public response to the various anti-fur campaigns run by PETA, Lynx and others since the 1980s has reduced the market for fur products in many countries and has transformed a status symbol of the

然而，鼓励浪费型社会的费用还是个问题，这个问题将来很可能反复产生而且成为受关注的焦点。自从 20 世纪 80 年代以来，动物慈善组织、山猫组织及其他组织发起了多种反毛皮制品的活动，这些活动引起的反响减少了许多国家的毛皮产品

rich to an item of derision. 'Green' issues in fashion marketing are examined further in Chapter Two.

市场，并且令人们对皮草的态度发生了变化，从过去认为是富贵的象征到现在是对富贵的一种嘲弄。时装营销中有关“绿色”的议题我们将在第 2 章进一步探讨。

Another example of a macro-issue is the use of particular models to show garments in advertising material or on the catwalk. Critics allege that this can cause damage ranging from supporting an image of women as mere sex objects to acting as a contributory factor in dietary problems of adolescent females. The over-representation of young, tall and slim female models raises many issues, not least of which is the sensitivity of some promoters to the responses of the audience. The Madrid Fashion Week has banned models with a body mass index (BMI) of below 18.5; this is a BMI that is regarded as unhealthy by the World Health Organization. The use of wider ranges of body shapes and sizes has been effectively used by Dove in their campaign for real beauty. The non-response or excuse of 'We have to do it, because everyone else does it' from some fashion companies may reveal an unwillingness to research other less potentially harmful ways of promotion. In an industry with an abundance of creative talent, it is surprising to find such pockets of conservatism.

宏观问题的另一个实例是在广告中或走秀中运用模特来展示时装。批评家认为，无论将女性形象仅仅作为一种性吸引的手段，还是成为导致影响年轻女性饮食问题的助因，这种模特的应用都起了破坏性的作用。过度让那些年轻、高挑的模特做代言会引起很多问题，尤其是那些对这些模特的身材反应敏感的观众。马德里时装周不允许使用身体质量指数低于 18.5 的模特，身体质量指数低于 18.5 是世界卫生组织规定的身体不健康的最低标准。对体型和尺码选择的宽泛标准已经被有效地应用到了“多芬”真美选秀大赛中。有些时装公司对此不做回应或辩解“我们不得不这么做，因为别人都在这么做”，对这种理由的冷淡反应或借口可能就透露了他们不愿意去研究其他减少潜在伤害的促销方案。在一个拥有足够多创意人才的业界，你会惊奇地发现存在如此多的保守思想。

1.8 An overview of the fashion marketing process / 时装营销过程概述

Fashion marketing can be viewed as a process and Figure 1.4 illustrates that process. It also gives an indication of the structure of this book and how various parts link together.

时装营销可以看成如图 1–4 图解流程，这个图也反映出本书的整体结构以及各个部分是如何衔接在一起的。

All firms operate within a wider commercial environment that influences their activities. Changes in value added tax may inhibit demand for certain garments whereas a fall in unemployment may stimulate demand for workwear. These two simple examples illustrate how changes in the marketing environment can have significant effects on the operation of fashion firms. The marketing environment and how to analyse it are covered in Chapter Two.

所有的公司都要在一个对其工作有影响的广泛的商业环境里运营。增值税变动可能会抑制对某些时装的需求，但是失业人数的减少又可能会刺激对工作服的需求。这两个实例说明营销环境变化是如何有效影响时装公司运营的。有关营销环境和如何分析营销环境我们将在第 2 章阐述。

Central to the concept of fashion marketing is the role of the customer and Chapters Three and Four deal with understanding and researching the

时装营销观念的中心是消费者，第 3 章和第 4 章主要涉及对时装购买者的了解和研究。第 3 章讨论消费者的购买行为，尤其调

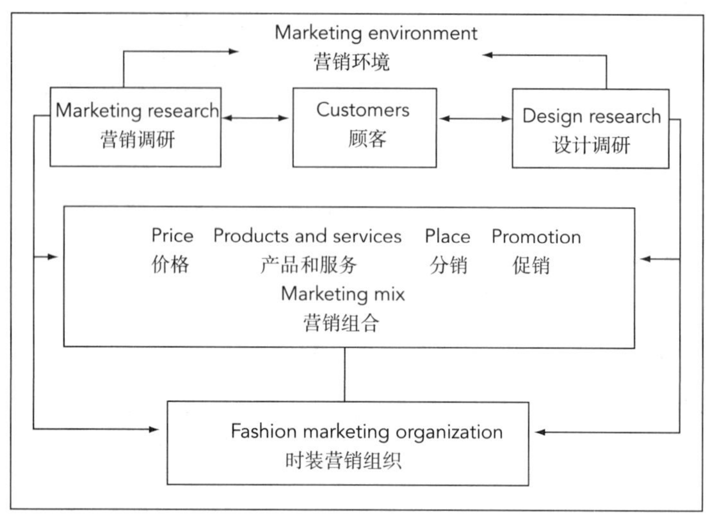

Figure 1.4 The fashion marketing process. 图 1–4 时装营销过程

fashion purchaser. In Chapter Three the behaviour of consumers will be discussed. In particular, there will be an examination of the reasons why people buy particular garments: what influences them and what criteria they use. Clothing may be an expression of how people wish others to see them, it may denote membership of a certain group or represent a particular lifestyle. To understand customers' aspirations and expectations about clothing fully, relevant psychological and sociological factors are examined in Chapter Three.

查了人们选购某款衣服的原因：是什么影响了他们，以及他们使用什么标准。服饰是人们希望他人如何看自己的一种外在表现，它也可能意味着某个团队的成员关系，或者象征某种特定的生活方式。为了能充分了解顾客的强烈愿望和期望，与其相关的心理和社会因素我们将在第 3 章验证。

Chapter Four takes the understanding of customers' behaviour one step further by looking at how data concerning this behaviour are obtained, namely marketing research. This research can also involve the study of competitors and analysis of the company's own marketing efforts.

第 4 章通过寻找所获得的有关消费行为的相关资料，也就是营销调查，进一步了解消费者购买行为。这个调研还要包括对竞争对手的研究和对本公司营销工作的分析。

In Figure 1.4 the term marketing mix is used to describe the combination of variables used by the fashion marketer to meet the needs of specific groups of customers known as target markets. The selection of target markets and the management of the marketing mix are discussed in Chapters Five to Ten of this book.

图 1–4 中的营销组合项目是用来阐述一个变量组合的，时装经营者用这个变量组合去满足某个特定的顾客群体，即被称为目标市场的顾客群体的需求。对目标市场的选择和营销组合管理我们在本书的第 5 章到第 10 章加以阐述。

Here is an example of how a variable may be adjusted using an example concerning price. A firm may decide to charge low prices and sell large quantities making a small profit on each item, but a large profit in total. A consequence of charging

这里引证一个用有关价格的样本来说明变量如何被调整的实例。某公司可能决定以低价出售大量商品，虽然从单位商品中获得了较少的利润，但是在总量上却获

low prices may be that certain outlets are selected because their image is compatible with low prices. The concept of the marketing mix and target marketing are dealt with in Chapter Five. The actual components of the marketing mix are known for the sake of simplicity as the four Ps, i.e. Price, Product, Place and Promotion, and these are covered in Chapters Six to Nine. The role of design research, integral to product design and development, is covered in Chapter Six.

Putting all aspects of the marketing mix together to achieve the goals of the organization is the most important marketing task. Activities must be planned, co-ordinated and implemented effectively, and the results monitored. The final chapter deals with fashion marketing planning.

得了较大利润。以低价出售的结果是某个折扣店被选中，因为其形象定位是与低价商品相一致。营销组合和目标营销的概念将在第 5 章讨论。简单来说，营销组合的组成实际可以看成 4 个 P，即价格、产品、分销和促销，这些内容将在第 6 章到第 9 章讨论。设计调研、整体产品设计和开发的作用在第 6 章进行阐述。

把销售组合的各个方面整合在一起去达成组织目标是最重要的营销任务。这些活动一定要经过规划、协调和有效地执行，并且要对结果进行监控。本书最后一章将讨论时装营销规划。

1.9 Summary / 小结

This chapter has introduced and defined fashion and marketing, and how fashion marketing:

- emphasizes the importance of design;
- aims to meet customers' needs;
- helps to achieve corporate goals.

There followed an examination of the practical side of fashion marketing:

- how fashion marketers work;
- the ethical issues.

The chapter concluded by:

- examining the business environment, and the place of fashion marketing within it;
- introducing the ideas of marketing research and consumer behaviour;
- outlining the concepts of target marketing and the fashion marketing mix.

本章介绍并定义了有关时装和营销的概念以及如何进行时装销售：

- 强调设计的重要性；
- 旨在满足顾客需求；
- 有助于实现企业目标。

下面是时装营销实践方面的测试：

- 时装营销者如何工作？
- 时装营销中涉及哪些伦理问题？

本章包括以下内容：

- 调查商业环境和时装营销场所；
- 介绍营销调研和消费者行为的理念；
- 描述目标营销和时装营销组合观念。

Further reading / 课后阅读材料

1.Baker, M.J. (2007), Marketing *Management and Strategy*, 4th Revised Edition, Palgrave MacMillan, Basingstoke.

贝克·M.J.（2007），《营销管理和策略》，第 4 次修订版，帕尔格雷夫·麦克米兰，贝辛斯托克 .

2.Barthes, R. (2006), *The Language of Fashion*, Berg Limited, New York.

巴特斯·R.（2006），《时装的语言》，贝尔格有限公司，纽约 .

3.Brassington, F. and Pettitt, S. (2006), *Principles of Marketing*, 4th Edition, Financial Times/ Prentice Hall, London.

布拉辛顿·F.，佩蒂特·S.（2006），《营销原理》，第 4 次修订版，金融时报 / 普伦蒂斯霍尔，伦敦 .

4.Costantino, M. (1998), *Fashion Files: Marketing and PR*, Batsford, London.
科斯坦蒂诺·M.（1998），《时装档案：营销与公共关系》，巴茨福德，伦敦.
5.Davis, F. (1994), *Fashion, Culture and Identity*, University of Chicago Press, Chicago, IL.
戴维斯·F.（1994），《时装、文化和身份》，芝加哥大学出版社，芝加哥，伊利诺斯州.
6.Hines, T. and Bruce, M. (2006), *Fashion Marketing, Contemporary Issues*, 2nd Edition, Butterworth-Heinemann, Oxford.
海因斯·T.，布鲁斯·M.（2006），《时装营销：当代伦理》，第2次修订版，巴特沃斯—海尼曼，牛津.
7.Jones, R. (2006), *The Apparel Industry*, 2nd Revised Edition, Blackwell Publishing, Oxford.
琼斯·R.（2006），《时装工业》，第2次修订版，威利—布莱克威尔出版社，牛津.
8.McDowell, C. (2003), *Fashion Today*, Phaidon Press, Oxford.
麦克道尔·C.（2003），《今日时尚》，菲登出版社，牛津.
9.Tomlinson, A. (1990), *Consumption Identity and Style: Marketing Meanings and the Packaging of Pleasure*, Routledge, London.
汤姆林森·A.（1990），《消费特征和风格：营销意义和快乐包装》，洛特列治，伦敦.
10.Tungate, M. (2005), Fashion Brands: *Branding Style from Armani to Zara*, Kogan Page Ltd, London.
唐盖特·M.（2005），《时装品牌：从阿玛尼到Zara的品牌风格》，柯冈佩奇有限公司，伦敦.

Chapter Two The Fashion Market and the Marketing Environment
第 2 章 时装市场和营销环境

2.1 Introduction / 引言

A market is a place for buying and selling, for exchanging goods and services, usually for money. The fashion market is unusual because until early in the twentieth century it was almost solely the domain of kings, queens, aristocrats and other important people. As will be seen, great changes, mainly due to technology and increasing globalization, mean that we now have a fashion marketplace open to everyone.

市场通常是指以货币的形式，买卖、交换商品和服务的地方。然而时装市场却是与众不同的，因为直到 20 世纪初期，时装还几乎是国王、皇后、贵族和其他上层社会的专属物。随着科技的发展和全球一体化进程的加速，我们可以看到显著的变化，如今的时装市场已经面向所有人开放。

Fashion can be a reflection of the time, from the utilitarian clothing of the war years to the yuppie look of the buoyant 1980s. Fashion also can be a reflection of individuals. Clothes are often chosen to reflect among other factors our age, gender, lifestyle and personality.

从战争时期的实用装到 20 世纪 80 年代轻松、活泼的雅皮士服饰就可以看到，时装成为时代的一个映象。时装也可以展现个人风格。对时装的选择体现出人们的年龄、性别、生活方式以及个性的不同。

Because fashion is both a reflective and yet creative discipline, it is necessary for fashion marketers to be aware of the factors surrounding the market and develop a broad understanding of the issues that can affect the garments that are seen in any high street store.

由于时装不仅是一种映象，还是一种创造力的训练，所以时装市场经营者有必要知道市场环境中的影响因素，并充分了解能影响繁华商业街的零售店所见的时装的仿版问题。

2.2 The development of the fashion market / 时装市场的发展

2.2.1 Origins of the modern fashion market / 现代时装市场的起源

Until relatively recently, fashion had always been élitist and was used by its adopters to show that they were above the common people. Even the inventions of the

直到最近，时装一直被精英人士用以显示他们较之普通大众更为优越之处。尽管 18 世纪和 19 世纪已发明了詹妮纺

eighteenth and nineteenth centuries; the spinning jenny, the water frame and the sewing machine have not had as great an effect on the market as have cultural changes and the explosion of the media during the twentieth century.

纱机、水力纺纱机和缝纫机，这些发明对市场的影响也不如 20 世纪所出现的文化巨变和媒体的爆炸性蓬勃发展带给市场的影响大。

The end of World War I, in 1918, really marked the start of mass fashion. Style began to be influenced by the fashion designers of Paris, Milan, New York and London. In the 1930s film personalities and later pop stars all played their part in spreading or even starting fashion trends.

1918 年，第一次世界大战结束，真正标志着时装大众化的开始。时装的款式开始受到巴黎、米兰、纽约、伦敦的时装设计师们的影响。20 世纪 30 年代，电影明星和流行歌手也都扮演了时装传播者，甚至引领了时装潮流。

Some fashion styles are more easily explained than others. World War II forced hemlines up because of a shortage of material. In the 1950s newer freer styles made corsets less and less necessary. However, other fashions are less easily explained and are regarded by some as merely a whim or the market just looking for a change.

一些时装款式较其他一些款式容易解释。如第二次世界大战时期，由于面料短缺，致使时装下摆底边上提。20 世纪 50 年代，时装款式的新潮和自由的发展趋势促使紧身胸衣越来越不必要。然而，有些时装较难解释，并被一些人认为只是一种奇想或只是为了寻求变化。

Technology played its part in advancing mass production methods, so that from the 1930s onwards ordinary people could buy copies of designer fashions from high street stores within weeks of the big fashion shows.

科技促进了规模化生产方式的发展。20 世纪 30 年代起，普通百姓在大型时装展览会后数周内就可以在繁华商业街的零售店里买到设计师的时装作品。

The media started to become an important influence in the late 1970s. People became more selective in what suited them, and magazines and books advised them on creating their own style. Designers could no longer dictate the styles as they had up to the 1960s. 'Street fashion' styles, developed by young people themselves in towns and cities, also affected designer clothes.

20 世纪 70 年代后期，媒体开始成为一个重要的影响因素。人们开始关注什么更适合自己。杂志和书籍也建议大家穿出自己的风格。直到 20 世纪 60 年代，设计师们不再像以前那样能够决定款式。“街头时装”款式即由城镇、城市里年轻人自发所形成的，“街头流行”时装款式也影响着品牌时装。

London was at the forefront of the fashion scene in the 1960s and early 1970s. Mary Quant was in her heyday and her clothing was famous the world over. It was the time of Carnaby Street, and Biba made famous by Barbara Hulanicki.

20 世纪 60 年代到 70 年代初，伦敦处于时装阵地的最前沿。玛丽・匡特正值巅峰时期，她的时装享誉全球。那是卡尔纳比街时代，芭芭拉・胡兰尼科将芘芭做成了名牌。

The influence of royalty on fashion made a comeback with the Princess of Wales in the 1980s as many women copied the lace and ruffles which she wore.

20 世纪 80 年代，由于许多女士仿效威尔士公主所着时装的饰带和皱褶，皇室对时装流行性的影响得以恢复。

While not the first to introduce lifestyle segmentation to the market, George Davies, then chief executive of the Next chain, is undoubtedly the best known. His retailing phenomenon, targeting a particular age and lifestyle group, exploded onto the

作为奈克斯特品牌首席执行官的乔治・戴维斯，虽说不是第一个提出将市场按生活方式细分的人，但无疑在当时是最知名的人。将销售对象按年龄、生活方式群体划分，对市场产生爆炸性影响。许多

marketplace and had many other high street retailers following suit.

Changes towards a healthier lifestyle advocated by the medical profession and the increase in leisure time have encouraged people to take up more sport, particularly jogging and aerobics. Membership of health clubs and gyms has increased in recent years. So the clothing from this and other activities has moved into everyday wear.

The future for the fashion industry is mapped out, perhaps more than at any time in its history. Influences from the demographic structure, concern for the environment and further adoption of new technologies are all inevitable. These factors could stifle designers if they are not careful or could offer them greater challenges than any they have had to face so far.

闹市的零售商纷纷效仿其做法。

一方面医疗界倡导人们朝更健康的生活方式改变，另一方面人们的休闲时间不断增多，人们有可能从事更多的运动，特别是慢跑和健美操。近年来，健身俱乐部和健身馆的会员与日俱增，因而健身形式和其他运动形式的运动时装成为大众的日常穿着服饰。

时装业的未来在此时比历史上任何一个时期更清晰地被描绘出来，来自人口结构、人们对环境的关心和未来对新技术的进一步采用这些方面所带来的影响都不可避免。如果设计师们对这些因素不加以认真考虑的话，就可能遏制其发展，或使设计师面临比以往更大的挑战。

2.2.2 Recent developments in the fashion market / 时装市场的最新发展

Consumer demand for clothing is now more fragmented and discerning. Retailers are wary of carrying high levels of stock, major demographic changes are occurring, and many different styles and fabrics are available. These have all resulted in the mass market for clothing being fragmented and are eroding the advantages of long-run manufacture.

Previously the UK textile industry had a reputation for being dictatorial and short on choice. This was blamed on the nature of the relationship between retailers and manufacturers. Clothing retailing was dominated by a few large groups who exercised enormous power in the wholesale market for garments and fabrics. Retailers emphasized basic garments with very little fashion content, and Marks and Spencer in particular set very detailed specifications for fabrics, making-up and quality. Manufacturers such as Courtaulds and Carrington Viyella geared their production to large volumes of basic fabrics for a few major customers. It became uneconomic to deal with orders that either were small or required much design detail. Competition among retail chains was over the price and quality of garments.

Since then the market share of the multiple retailers (such as Bhs, Debenhams and Marks and Spencer) has been affected firstly by the emergence of smaller specialist chains (Benetton, Next) then grocery supermarkets ('George' at Asda and Tesco).

目前消费者对于时装的需求越来越细化和有品位。零售商必须小心谨慎地时刻关注正运输的堆积如山的存货，重要的人口统计数据正发生哪些变化，有哪些不同款式和质地的商品可供选择。这些都导致了大众时装市场向细分方向发展，并将削弱长周期运转加工制造的优势。

以前的英国纺织业垄断性强、可选性较弱。这归咎于零售商和制造商之间的关系。时装零售业被那些在时装和纺织品批发市场行使极大权利的为数不多大集团所左右。零售商只经营那些很少有时装内涵的基本时装款式，尤其是玛莎百货对纺织品的缝制与质量有详细的规定。制造商，如：考陶尔兹、卡林顿·维耶勒把他们的产品定位于为为数不多的大客户提供大量的基本纺织品。如果针对那些小型的或者需要更多设计细节的小客户订货就不合算。连锁零售店的竞争体现在时装的价格和品质上。

从那时起，百货零售商（如：Bhs 百货公司，德本罕百货公司和玛莎百货）的市场份额受到接连出现的较小型的专门连锁店（贝纳通，奈克斯特）和杂货超市（阿斯达和乐购的“乔治系列”）的影响。敏特调

Mintel 2005 estimates that 'George' sales in 2004 (excluding VAT) were £1.07 billion and that non-specialist retailers of this type enjoyed an increase in sales of 13% from 2003 to 2004, with this rising trend continuing. Further European retailers (Zara, H&M) have also gained market share in the UK by importing low-cost garments. To avoid competing with the abundance of low-cost imports, the big retailers have responded by increasing the speed with which they introduce fashion and style changes. This, in turn, has forced suppliers to manufacture shorter runs of garments with higher design and fashion content. In some parts of the market there has been a distinct shift in retail competition away from an emphasis on garment price to non-price factors, such as design, quality and fashion. However, this non-pricecompetition has had only a limited success with even Marks and Spencer and its strong 'British Made' slogan, turning to importing more cheaply from overseas. Value retailers such as Matalan, Primark and TK Maxx, who have attracted the more price conscious shopper, have enjoyed considerable success in other sectors of the market (Table 2.1).

查公司 2005 年统计显示，"乔治系列"在 2004 年的销售额达到（不含增值税）10.7 亿英镑。这种非专门零售商的销售量从 2003 年到 2004 年增长了 13%，这种增长势头还在继续。另外欧洲的零售商（Zara，海恩斯·莫里斯公司）也通过进口低成本的时装获得英国市场份额。为了避免与大量的低成本进口商品的竞争，大规模的零售商加快进程促进时装款式的不断更新。这样，又会强迫供应商生产短期运转、设计考究、时装性强的时装。在市场的某些部分，出现了不以时装价格为中心的其他非价格因素，如设计、质量和时装性的零售竞争的区域轮换。然而，这种非价格竞争，只获得有限的成功，即使是玛莎百货大张旗鼓地打出"英国制造"的广告语，也转向更廉价的海外进口。价格零售商，如：玛塔兰、普里马克、TK Maxx 连锁店吸引了更多的关注价格的店主，在市场的其他方面获得了相当大的成功（表 2–1）。

Table 2.1 UK trade in clothing, 2001–2005 **表 2–1 2001 ~ 2005 年英国时装贸易** (£ million) 单位：百万英镑

年份 year	2001	2002	2003	2004	2005
进口 Imports	9160	9806	10341	10884	11543
出口 Exports	2592	2506	2713	2729	2679
贸易差额 Balance of trade	–6568	–7300	–7628	–8155	–8864
年度变化率 /% % change year on year	—	11.1	4.5	6.9	8.9

Source: HM Customs and Excise. © Crown copyright material is reproduced with the permission of the Controller of HMSO (and the Queen's Printer for Scotland).
资料来源：英国海关税费局。皇家版权材料经皇家文书局（和苏格兰皇后印刷商）允许方可复制。

2.3 The fashion market: size and structure／时装市场：规模和结构

2.3.1 Structure of the fashion market／时装市场的结构

Apart from technology, another reason why fashion is now available to the masses is that there are several levels at which fashion clothing functions, as shown in Figure 2.1:

◆ Haute couture houses are the major fashion houses of the world, run by recognized,

除科技原因外，另一促成时装走入大众群体的原因是时装在不同层面的作用，如图 2–1 所示：

◆ 高级定制时装店是由世界上公认的国际著名设计师经营的大型时装店。这

Figure 2.1 Levels of fashion. 图 2–1 时装层次

internationally famous designers. They show their collections at least twice a year and sell individual garments for thousands of pounds. For many designers the catwalk shows are essentially a publicity exercise for the many goods that are sold under their name such as perfume and accessories.

◆ Designer wear is shown at pret à porter. The move into ready-to-wear clothing by designers meant that they could offer their stylish designs and high quality to a wider audience. The garments are still highly priced, although in hundreds of pounds sterling rather than thousands. They are to be found in the designers' shops, independent stores and some of the more exclusive department stores. Designs are not unique, but are still produced in limited numbers and, although some garments are produced abroad, there is very strict quality control.

◆ Mass market or street fashion is the market area in which most people buy their clothes. New fashions can be in the high street stores extremely quickly and what the customers lose in exclusivity they can make up for in value for money. This is one area of the market that is undergoing many changes and this chapter will look at how it is being affected.

This three-tier view of the market is perhaps oversimplistic as there are many strata and price levels between the ones mentioned. Many customers do not stick to any one level when buying their clothes.

The more affluent will buy several haute couture outfits but turn to designer wear for every day. Women who mostly buy designer ready-to-wear may occasionally splash out on a couture dressfor a

些设计师每年至少两次展出其成衣，并且每件时装的售价约数千英镑。对于多数设计师来说，T 台秀场对于其名下的多数产品，如香水和饰品是必不可少的宣传演练之地。

◆ 设计师品牌时装通过高级成衣展示。由设计师设计的高级成衣进入市场意味着他们能够向更多的消费者提供设计时尚、质量上乘的时装。这类时装依然价格不菲，虽说不再需要数千英镑，但仍需几百英镑。设计师自营店、独立商店和一些专营店都属于这类时装店。设计虽然不是唯一的，但同一款式一直限量生产，即使有些时装会在国外复制生产，但在那里也有严格的质量控制。

◆ 大众市场或街头时尚店是多数老百姓选购时装之地。新时装可以在较短的时间内在繁华商业街的店铺买到。虽说消费者无法拥有某一款式的独享权，但从价格上来说还是合算得多。这一市场经历了许多变化，本章将着眼于影响这一市场的情况。

市场三层次论或许过于简单，因为在上述分类之间还有很多层次和价格水平。许多消费者在选购时装时，并不固守在某一层面。

过去，较为富裕的顾客一般会购买几身高级定制礼服套装，但现在转为选购设计师品牌时装作为日常着装。大部分购买设计师品牌高级成衣的女士可能偶尔会心

very special occasion. Those who generally only buy mass market clothing may still buy designer wear occasionally, if only from the discounted rail. In the early twenty-first century celebrity fashion icons have moved to mixing their outfits with some designer pieces and some from high street stores. At times it is difficult to identify the origin of our clothing and to decide who has the power in the marketplace. Is it the fibre and fabric industry that, after all,make the cloth for the garments? Is it the designers? Or perhaps the retailers are the power base in the market? Ultimately it should be the customer, but traditionally the fashion market has been one where the customer was dictated to and so merely followed along almost blindly.

The fashion flow chart in Figure 2.2 illustrates the flow of goods between the various participants in the marketplace. Later it will be seen that there is even more choice in deciding where the goods will be manufactured (see Section 2.5.2).

血来潮去订购一套高级时装以备特殊场合之需。那些一般仅在大众市场消费的顾客偶尔遇到设计师品牌时装打折，也会购买一两件。21 世纪初期，时装名人偶像已经发展到将不同层次的时装搭配起来。有时很难识别出时装的来源，也难以决定到底谁是市场的主宰力量。到底是纤维工业和纺织产业使面料成为时装的主要流行要素？还是设计师占主导作用？或许零售商才是市场的基本动力？最终应该是消费者，但是传统的时装市场中消费者是无权做主的，只是盲目地跟随潮流。

图 2–2 为时装流程图，该图显示出市场中商品在不同参与者之间的流动过程。后文将论述商品生产场所在决策中的多种选择（参见 2.5.2 节）。

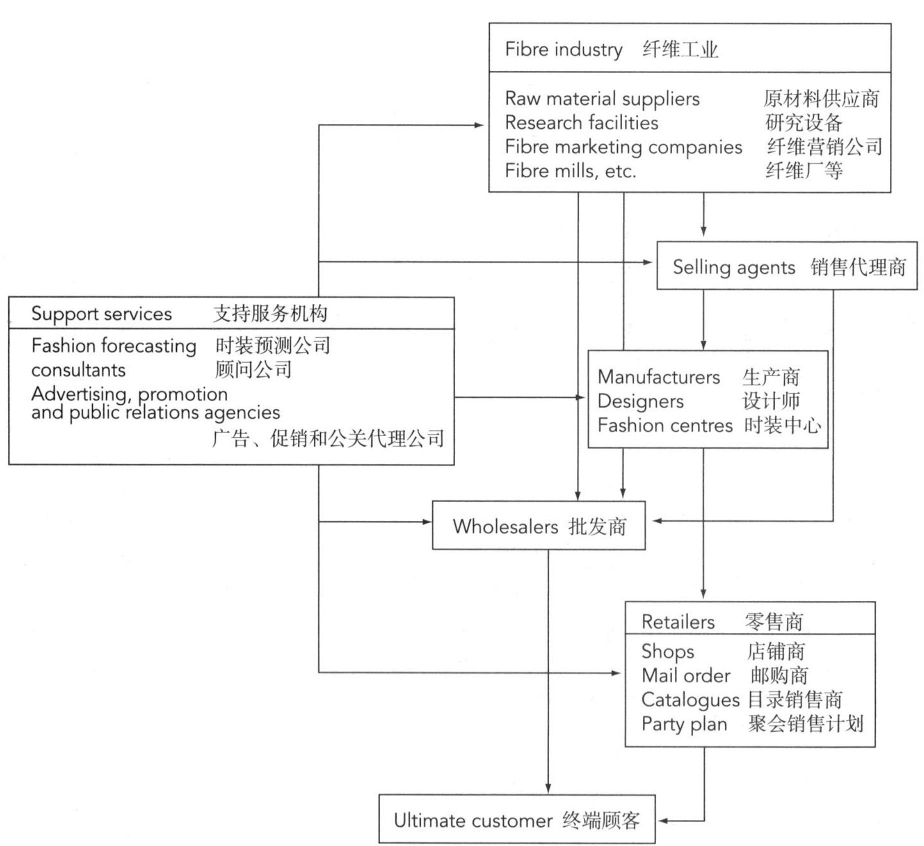

Figure 2.2 Fashion flow chart. 图 2–2 时装流程图

2.3.2 Size of the fashion market ／时装市场的规模

All three levels of the market have shown some growth in domestic clothing demand in recent years. Growth of the total UK market for clothing has grown by over 16% from 1994 to 2004 and retail sales for 2006 are predicted to be nearly 50 billion (Table 2.2).

这三种层面的市场显示出近年来英国国内时装需求的发展演变，从 1994 年到 2004 年全英国时装市场增长超过 16%，2006 年零售额预计约为 500 亿英镑（见表 2–2）。

Table 2.2 Some major developments in fashion

表 2–2 时装业的主要发展进程

Pre-nineteenth century /19 世纪前	Fashions only for the rich and powerful / 时装仅为权贵之人享用
1918 onwards / 自 1918 年起	Start of mass fashion / 大众时装的兴起
1930s /20 世纪 30 年代	Film personalities influencing popular clothing / 影星影响大众流行服饰
1939–1945 /1939 ~ 1945 年	World War Ⅱ – raised hemlines / 第二次世界大战——提高下摆
1950s and 1960s /20 世纪 50 ~ 60 年代	Freer styles, fewer control garments / 款式更随意、更少约束的时装
1970s to 1990s /20 世纪 70 ~ 90 年代	Growth of multi-nationals and mass media influence / 跨国公司的发展和大众媒体的影响
1990s /20 世纪 90 年代	Increase in branded and designer label goods / 品牌产品和具有时装设计师标记产品增加
2000 onwards /2000 年后	Growth of electronic shopping / 电子购物兴起
2002 onwards /2002 年后	Increasing influx of cheap foreign manufactured clothing / 廉价的国外加工时装大量涌入

UK imports now greatly exceed exports, having increased from £9.1 billion to £11.5 billion from 2001 to 2005 with the main traders being Hong Kong, China and Turkey (see Table 2.1). UK exports have remained steady at about £2.5 billion per annum over the same period with about 73% of this output going to other European countries. As less UK manufactured clothes are sold in the home market the proportion of goods being exported is actually increasing. The figures become more complex as UK manufacturers are developing their own production facilities overseas to take advantage of lower wages and production costs (Table 2.3).

这期间英国的进口额远远大于出口额，从 2001 年的 91 亿英镑增加到 2005 年的 115 亿英镑，主要的交易商是中国香港、中国内地和土耳其（见表 2–1）。英国的出口额趋于稳定，每年约为 25 亿英镑，约 73% 出口至欧洲国家和地区。英国加工的时装较少在国内销售，出口的比例却不断提高。由于英国的制造商正在利用海外工资和生产成本较低的优势研发自己的产品设备，因而数据较为复杂（见表 2–3）。

Table 2.3 Consumer spending on clothes
表 2–3 消费者在时装上的开支

	Consumer Expenditure at Current Prices in £ Million 消费者开支（时价，以百万英镑计）					
year 年份	2000	2001	2002	2003	2004	2005
Clothing 时装	31048	32103	33927	35689	37112	38067
Footwear 鞋类	4431	4719	5165	5466	5680	5661
Total 总额	35479	36822	39092	41155	42792	43728
% change on year 年变化率 /%	+6.3	+3.8	+6.2	+5.3	+4.0	+2.2

Source: Consumption, The Blue Book 2006. 资料来源：消费，2006 蓝皮书。

2.3.3 Employment in the fashion sector ／时装业的就业

Employment in the manufacturing of clothing textiles and leather production in the UK has now fallen to rank 24th out of the 25 categories of manufacturing industry recorded by the Government. Two main factors have reduced the numbers employed in the sector in recent years to only 132000 in 2006 (Table 2.4). New technologies have reduced the need for many workers, particularly in the more skilled areas of pattern cutting as much of this can be computerized. The computer systems still need to be manned by a skilled workforce, but retraining has to be done and still there will be redundancies.

The far more important factor has been the stiff level of cheap competition from abroad. With an inability to raise prices in the face of a depressed domestic market and crippled by large debts, many firms have had to make savage cuts in their labour force and investment plans as the alternative to going out of business. In the late 1990s many major UK clothing manufacturers suffered as their customers chose to source garments from cheaper overseas suppliers. The UK clothing industry is made up of small, medium and large manufacturers. The smaller manufacturers feed off the larger companies by offering specialist finishing services. As the larger retailers turn to overseas manufacturing or supplying, so the vulnerable smaller companies suffer. Table 2.5 shows the fortunes of the fashion industry in the context of the decline in manufacturing (Table 2.6).

政府报告显示，时装纺织品和皮革产品的就业已经在全英国 25 种制造业中下滑到第 24 位。两大主要因素造成近年来被雇用人数的减少，2006 年仅有 132，000 人被雇用（见表 2–4）。一方面是新技术减少了对工人的需求量，特别是像打板等这样的更需要技能的工作也被计算机化。计算机系统需要由技术精湛的工人操控，这部分人员留用，但依然有大量冗员被裁减。

更为重要的因素是来自国外的令人无法接受的廉价竞争。面对低迷的国内市场和重债缠身的现实，为了不至于停业，许多公司无力提高价格，不得不疯狂地裁员，减少投资计划。20 世纪 90 年代末，英国许多主要的时装制造业者受到重创，因为他们的客户选择从国外供应商提供的廉价的时装。英国的时装业由大、中、小制造业者构成。较小型的厂商为较大的公司提供专门的终端服务。由于较大的零售商转向国外加工和供货，因而，小型公司受损严重。表 2–5 显示制造业滑坡的时装业的情况（见表 2–6）。

Table 2.4 Recent decline in employment figures in textile clothing and footwear industries (in '000s, in June each year)

表 2–4 近年纺织时装和鞋类产业雇用量数字图（单位以千人计，每年 6 月统计）

年份	1998	1999	2000	2001	2002	2003	2004	2005	2006
被雇用人数	331	304	273	230	205	169	149	136	132

Source: ONS. 资料来源：英国国家统计局。

Table 2.5 Production output indices of total manufacturing industries and textiles, leather and clothing industries in the UK (index 2002 = 100, 2001, 2005)

表 2–5 英国整个制造业和纺织、皮革、时装业产品产量指数（指数 2002=100,2001,2005）

year 年份	2001	2002	2003	2004	2005
Total manufacturing industries 整个制造业	103.2	100.0	100.1	101.9	101.3
Textiles, leather and clothing 纺织、皮革、时装	108.1	100.0	98.1	87.0	83.2

Source: Monthly Digest of Statistics. 资料来源：统计汇编月报。

Table 2.6 Production of textile and textile products in UK, 2000–2006 (index 2003 = 100)

表 2–6 英国 2000 ~ 2006 年纺织品产量（指数 2003=100）

年份	2000	2001	2002	2003	2004	2005	2006
纺织品产量	122.4	107.2	99.7	100	98.1	90	89

Source:ONS. 资料来源：英国国家统计局。

2.3.4 The current role of London in the fashion business / 伦敦在时装业的潮流引领作用

Fashion centres of the world have always included London, even before the era of Carnaby Street and Mary Quant, but recently designers have been choosing not to show in London. Now that London Fashion Week no longer has the financial backing of the French Chambre Syndicale (the French organization that decides which fashion houses may join the ranks of the haute couturiers), the number of exhibitions has declined. With it no longer being a requirement to show in London, designers have taken the opportunity to save the expense of showing at yet another fashion week, instead concentrating on the ones which they feel will be most prestigious and best covered by the media.

This shift away from London is of concern to the industry, particularly for the knock-on effect that it will have on everything from employment to tourism. Cities which are taking a more prominent role in the fashion year are New York, Tokyo and, new to the list, Shanghai.

在卡尔纳比街和玛丽·匡特时代之前，世界时装中心一直包括伦敦，但最近设计者们不再选择在伦敦举办时装秀。由于伦敦时装周不再有法国时装协会（决定哪家时装店为高级定制时装店的法国机构）的财政支援，展览会数量大大减少。因为并非一定要在伦敦举行时装秀，设计师们抓住机遇，节约在一个个时装周举办时装秀的开支，集中精力于最具声望和媒体所关注的热点。

伦敦不再是时装秀的中心这一变化对于该产业至关重要，尤其对从就业到旅游的各个方面带来冲击。在时装岁月中起到越来越重要作用的城市是纽约、东京，新上榜的还有上海。

2.3.5 The British High Street /英国繁华商业大街

In contrast to Italy and most of the rest of Europe, UK has a much more consolidated market sector with only a few players as the big earners. Mintel (2005) stated that the top five UK retailers account for almost 45% of sales. The leading players by turnover being Marks and Spencer, Next, Arcadia Group (comprising Top Shop, Etam, Wallis, Dorothy Perkins, Burton, Miss Selfridge, Outfit and Evans), Matalan and Bhs. This dominance of the big players makes it hard for independent stores to get a foothold into the marketplace. It is hard to compete on price when dealing with high rents and cheap imported clothes.

与意大利和欧洲其他大多数国家不同，英国有为数不多的大赢家和更为稳固的市场机构。敏特调查公司（2005）指出前五强的英国零售商占全英总销售额的45%。营业额居前位的有玛莎百货，奈克斯特，阿尔卡迪亚集团（包括屋脊商店、艾格、沃利斯、多萝西·帕金斯、伯顿、塞尔弗里奇小姐、奥特维特和埃文斯），玛塔兰和 Bhs 百货公司。几大公司的垄断地位使独立经营店难以在市场中有一席之地。面对高租金和廉价进口时装，很难在价格方面具有竞争力。

2.4 Marketing environment /营销环境

Fashion is ultimately about change. Every season there are new fashions that lead to obsolescence of last year's clothes. Many of these changes are brought about by designers trying to create something new to satisfy customers, but others are because of influences beyond the control of designers or manufacturers. These are all gathered together in what is called the marketing environment, as shown in Figure 2.3. Some changes occur very slowly while others can affect the market much more quickly; some are within a company's control and others are way beyond it.

时装最终是涉及变化的话题。每一季都要有新款式，从而淘汰去年的式样。许多变化来自设计师设法创造出新的令客户满意的款式，还有一些并非出自设计师和制造商所能控制的款式。这些一并被称为营销环境，如图 2–3 所示。有些变化较为缓慢，可是其他的变化会对市场产生快速影响。有些在公司可控范围之内，有些也超出控制范畴。

2.5 Micro-marketing environment /微观营销环境

Factors which ideally are within companies' control are to a greater or lesser extent their suppliers, marketing intermediaries (which help to get the goods from the factory to the consumer) and the consumers themselves. For customers the providers of fashion may seem to have a variety of sources, for instance the designer who has the idea for the style, the manufacturer who makes up the garment or the retailer to whom the consumer goes to buy the garment.

在一定程度上，公司控制范围内的合理因素包括供应商、营销中介（帮助把产品从工厂送达消费者）和消费者自身。对消费者来说，时装的供应商拥有各种货源。比如，可以来自有时尚设计理念的设计师，或负责制造时装的生产商，或购买时装的零售商。

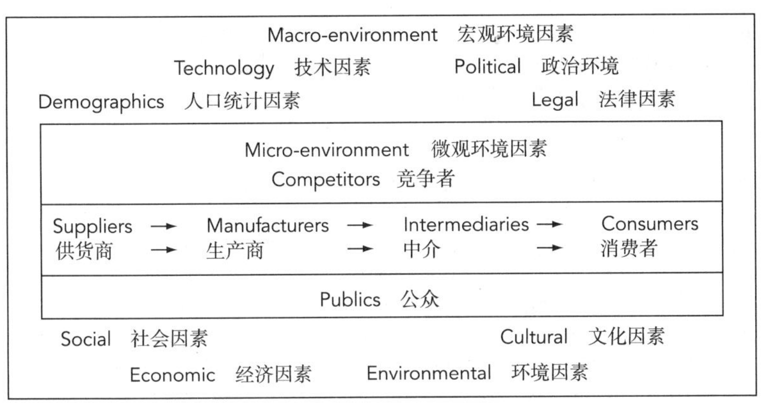

Adapted from Kotler, P. (1994), *Marketing Management*, 8th edn.,Prentice Hall International, New Jersey.
选自科特勒《营销管理》第 8 版（1994 出版），新泽西普伦蒂斯·霍尔国际出版社

Figure 2.3 The marketing environment. / 图 2–3 营销环境

2.5.1 Designers / 设计师

While Paris is often thought of as the fashion capital of the world in fact there are five main cities supplying designs and new ideas to the international market.

Paris is historically seen as the fashion capital and has the edge on many other cities as its fashion industry is taken very seriously by government and citizens alike. The haute couture designers are protected by the French Chambre Syndicale, which has strict codes of practice for any designer wishing to style him- or herself as an haute couture house. The main French designers are Yves St Laurent, Chanel (now run by Karl Lagerfeld), Christian Dior, Pierre Cardin, Jean Paul Gaultier, Sonia Rykiel and Christian Lacroix. The British are also making an impact in France, with Julian MacDonald and John Galliano securing senior designing roles in French fashion houses.

Milan is the other fashion capital of Europe, and Italians have always taken fashion very seriously. There are probably fewer well-known designers, such as Giorgio Armani, Franco Moschino, Muicca Prada, Emanuel Ungaro and Versace, now headed by Donatella, sister to the founder Gianni who was tragically murdered in 1997, but Italy is a country whose people and retail set-up, with many more independent stores, is a successful environment for young designers.

巴黎常被认为是世界时装之都的同时，其他五大城市也在为国际市场提供设计和新的理念。

巴黎在历史上就被认为是时装之都，由于政府和市民都重视巴黎的时装业，因而，相较于其他城市略胜一筹。高级时装设计者受到法国时装协会的保护，该协会为每一位渴望将自己打造成高级定制时装店的设计师制定严格的执业守则。法国最主要的设计大师有伊夫·圣洛朗、香奈儿（目前由卡尔·拉格菲尔德经营），克里斯汀·迪奥、皮尔·卡丹、让·保罗·戈尔捷、索尼亚·里基尔和克里斯汀·拉克鲁瓦。由于有朱利安·麦克唐纳、约翰·加利亚诺在法国时装公司一直稳坐首席设计之席，英国时装界也对法国产生影响。

米兰是欧洲的另一个时装之都。意大利也一直高度重视时装业。或许意大利只有少数几个像乔治·阿玛尼、弗兰科·莫斯基诺、缪西娅·普拉达、伊曼纽尔·温加罗和范思哲这样世界知名的设计师，范思哲 1997 年被谋杀，现在由创始人詹尼的妹妹多纳泰拉主管，但是意大利是一个百姓和零售机构建有许多自营店的国家，有一个对年轻设计师胜出有利的环境。

London is no longer the focal point of fashion that it once was, though it still produces many internationally influential designers. Many are quite small fish by international standards but others have their designs bought by the rich and famous from all over the world. Although London is no longer a major centre, the UK clothing industry is still significant and exports are actually growing in contrast to internal sales. The city also retains many successful designers such as Bruce Oldfield, Jasper Conran, Matthew Williamson, Alexander McQueen, Dame Vivienne Westwood, Paul Smith, Katharine Hamnett, Joseph Ettedgui, Rifat Ozbek, Amanda Wakely, Betty Jackson and Caroline Charles.

In America the major centre is New York. To a considerable extent American fashions are confined to the home market, although all the big names are known and bought internationally. American designers include Ralph Lauren, Calvin Klein, Oscar de la Renta, Marc Jacobs, Vera Wang and Donna Karan.

Tokyo, the centre of the Japanese clothing market, has a reputation for a distinct style and for almost a lack of colour. There has been considerable growth in recent years at the top end of the Japanese clothing market by designers, especially since 1981 when Comme des Garçons and Yamamoto took Paris by storm. This is a fashion city that is destined to continue to grow with such designers as Yohji Yamamoto, Comme des Garçons (Miss Rei Kawakubo), Issey Miyake, Junya Wantanabe and Kenzo.

The Middle East is now considered the sixth fashion terminus of the world, not because any designs come from here but because it is where the submerged 11% of the fashion industry goes. Much clothing is bought by women either within or while on holiday from such places as Dubai, the United Arab Emirates, Kuwait, Bahrain and Saudi Arabia.

The overall market pattern now is that designers either make for themselves or subcontract to British or overseas manufacturers. Likewise retailers have their own designers and make them up in their own factories, subcontract their own designs to home or overseas manufacturers, or buy garments designed and made up by other companies.

伦敦虽然依旧会产生许多具有国际影响力的设计师，但已不再像以前那样是时装界的焦点。按照国际标准，许多是相当小的新手公司，有些公司的设计已被世界上富有和出名的公司买断。虽然伦敦不再是主要的时装中心，但英国的时装业依然很重要，出口量相对于国内销量在显著增长。伦敦城还有许多成功的设计师，如：布鲁斯・奥尔德菲尔德、贾斯帕・康兰、马修・威廉姆森、亚历山大・麦克奎恩、维维安・韦斯伍德女爵士、保罗・史密斯、凯瑟琳・哈姆内特、约瑟夫・埃特狄、拉法特・奥兹别克、阿曼达・沃克利、贝蒂・杰克逊和卡罗琳・查尔斯。

在美国，主要的时装中心是纽约。虽然美国所有大品牌在国际上知名且能够买到，但在很大程度上，美国时装囿于本土市场。美国设计大师包括拉尔夫・劳伦、凯文・克莱恩、奥斯卡・德拉・伦塔、马克・雅各布斯、维拉・王、唐娜・卡兰。

东京是日本时装市场中心，日本时装以独特的款式和几乎没有色彩而享有盛名。尤其是 1981 年，川久保玲、山本耀司在巴黎风靡之后，近年来发展迅速，达到日本时装市场高峰。东京可谓时装城，由于拥有了像山本耀司、川久保玲、三宅一生、渡边淳弥、高田贤三这样的设计师，这座城市注定将继续发展。

中东目前被称为世界第六大时装终点站，并非由于某些设计作品来自这里，而是因为这里消费时装业 11% 的市场份额。许多时装被当地或来自迪拜、阿联酋、科威特、巴林、沙特阿拉伯等地度假的妇女买走。

目前，全球市场格局要么是设计师为自己设计，要么是将其设计转包给本国或国外的生产商的模式。同样，零售商有他们自己的设计师并且在自己的工厂加工或将其设计转包给本国或海外的生产商，或购买其他公司设计和加工的成衣。

2.5.2 International sourcing ／国际货源

The UK clothing industry is being squeezed further between the highly price-sensitive volume market which gets its supplies from low-wage economies and the quality end of the market which is increasingly supplied from Europe. The level of imports to the UK from the relatively high-cost producers on the continent has finally succumbed to pressure from other parts of the world and is decreasing.

Supplies come from three main sources:

1. UK, Europe and just beyond (Germany, France, Italy, Portugal, Eire, Turkey and more recently Romania) making up about 20% of UK clothing imports. Italy has traditionally been the major player here with Germany and France in close second place.
2. The Far East (Hong Kong, China, South Korea, Thailand, Taiwan, Malaysia, Indonesia and Mauritius). The two major players here are Hong Kong and China. They contribute, almost equally, to the 30% of clothing entering the UK from the Far East.
3. Asia (India, Bangladesh and Sri Lanka). These main three players contribute to more than 12% of UK clothing and accessory imports. Predictions that the reduction of quotas for Chinese goods would have a negative impact on these countries do not seem to have held true so far.

The greatest increase in supply has come from China and this is only expected to increase further now that quotas have been all but dropped to the UK and most of the rest of the world. However this does not seem to have affected UK exports suggesting there are different ranges of products being trade such as knitwear, rainwear and high-quality tailored items.

Imports from eastern European countries such as Romania have been seen to rise, as they have benefited from preferential access by the European Union (EU) in order to aid their economic restructuring prior to the abandonment of Multi-Fibre Agreement (MFA) quotas.

The days when Marks and Spencer used to boast that its garments were almost all produced in the UK, have long gone and they have suffered from criticism by some of the groups discussed later in Section 2.5.9.

英国时装业正处在双重压力之下，这双重压力一方面来自高价格敏感度市场，该市场从低工资经济地区得到货源，另一方面来自越来越多的市场上从欧洲供应的粗制滥造的产品。迫于世界其他地区的压力，进口到英国的欧洲大陆的相对高成本的生产商数量正逐渐减少。

来自三大主要货源的供给：

1. 德国、法国、意大利、葡萄牙、爱尔兰、土耳其和罗马尼亚，约占英国时装进口量的20%。传统上，意大利居第一位，德国和法国紧随其后居第二位。

2. 中国香港、中国内地、韩国、泰国、中国台湾、马来西亚、印度尼西亚和毛里求斯，最主要的两个是中国香港和中国内地。两者几乎平分秋色，占英国从远东时装进口量的30%。

3. 印度、孟加拉国、斯里兰卡，这三地的英国时装和服饰进口量超过12%。减少对中国产品的配额将对这些国家产生负面影响的预测目前还未应验。

货源量增长最大的来自中国内地，因为配额限制已经取消，这种增长还将继续。然而这并未影响英国的出口，依然有不同种类的时装可出口，如针织衫、雨衣、高品质西装。

来自东欧一些国家如罗马尼亚的进口在增加，这是因为他们得益于欧盟的优惠性进入条件。这些条件在取消多种纤维协定的配额之前，能帮助他们进行经济转型。

玛莎百货自诩其成衣都是英国制造的时代已经不复存在了，他们已经遭到其他社团的抨击，这个我们将在2.5.9节中阐述。

2.5.3 Manufacturers／生产商

In the late 1990s and early 2000s a gloomy picture was painted as a result of the move towards global sourcing. Several larger clothing companies such as J. Baird Ltd closed factories and others such as Dewhurst in the north-east of England who relied on a few major customers such as Marks and Spencer have suffered from this loss of business.

There has been a reduction in the clothing manufacturing industry in the UK and many foreign companies have changed from both designing and manufacturing to one of merely cut, make and trim (CMT) for other people's designs. Other parts of this chapter look at the way forward for the UK manufacturing industry. There is undoubtedly a role that it can play in the international sourcing market if it exploits the strengths of flexibility and quality and moves away from competing on price alone. It is in these areas that the UK is still exporting its fashions, although Table 2.5 illustrates the changing fortunes in the import and export of clothing. Clothing manufacturers have had to improve their manufacturing methods. There has been severe cost cutting in some areas coupled with an increased emphasis on good design in other areas.

从 20 世纪 90 年代末到 21 世纪初，由于转向全球性货源，时装业经历一段惨淡经营时期。几家较大规模的时装公司，如贝尔德有限公司停业，其他的像曾经依赖于像玛莎百货等几大客户的英国东北部的杜赫斯特公司，也遭受重创。

英国的时装制造业在下滑，许多国外公司从兼具设计与加工转向仅为其他人的设计进行单纯的裁剪、缝制与装饰（简称 CMT）。本章的其他部分将论述英国制造业的未来。如果不考虑价格的竞争，利用在灵活性和品质方面的优势，毋庸置疑英国在国际货源市场中，还是占有一席之地的。尽管图 2–5 表明时装进出口的情况已经发生变化，英国依然出口自己的时装。时装生产商必须改进加工方法，一方面要努力大规模降低成本，同时，另一方面要提高设计水平。

2.5.4 Marketing intermediaries／营销中介

These are the main channels that help to get the goods from the manufacturer to the consumer. A detailed consideration of marketing intermediaries is given in Chapter Eight. Their roles can be many and varied. The main ones are:

- retailers,
- agents,
- distributors,
- wholesalers,
- advertising agencies,
- market research agencies.

The intermediary having the greatest influence on the clothing market is the retailer group. British clothes retailing is unique in that 70% of garment sales come from only 17 retail chains. The larger chains have taken an increasing share of the growing clothing market at the expense of the smaller firms. In 2004 the Arcadia group (formerly Burton), which included Dorothy Perkins,

产品从生产商到消费者之间有几条主要渠道。营销中介我们将在第 8 章中进行详细阐述。营销中介的角色很多且形式多样。主要包括以下几种：

- 零售商；
- 代理商；
- 经销商；
- 批发商；
- 广告商；
- 市场调研商。

在营销中介中，对时装市场影响最大的就是零售商群体。英国的时装零售有其特征，那就是 70% 的成衣销售来自 17 家零售连锁店。较大规模的连锁店在时装市场的成长中不惜以牺牲小公司为代价，不断增加其

Top Shop, Top Man, Miss Selfridge, Wallis, Evans, Burtons and Outfit, had sales, estimated by Mintel, of £1527 million from their clothing outlets numbering more than 2000. Supermarkets have had an increase in the share of the clothing market; however, the largest market share still goes to Marks and Spencer despite the company's recent difficulties from which 2006 seemed to be a turning point. In Italy, by comparison, 95% of clothes are sold by single shops.

市场份额。据敏特调查公司研究机构统计，2004 年阿尔卡迪亚集团（原波顿），包括多萝西・帕金斯、屋脊商店、型男店、塞尔弗里奇小姐店、沃利斯、伊文思、波顿和奥特维特的销售额超过 2000 年，达到 15.27 亿英镑。超市中时装市场的份额也有所增长，然而，最大的份额还是玛莎百货，虽说该公司目前面临困难，2006 年似乎有了新的转机。在意大利，相比之下，95% 的时装是由独立经营店销售的。

On the whole, competition, particularly on price, has intensified since the 1990s. Customers are increasingly looking for value for money; but are not totally driven by price; they also want good design, comfort and quality.

总之，自从 20 世纪 90 年代，竞争尤其是价格上的竞争不断加剧。消费者一方面越来越多地关注物有所值，但并非完全受价格驱使，另一方面消费者还需要设计精美、穿着舒适和品质精良的时装。

Companies have had to rationalize and restructure to combat increasing competition, cheaper imports and changing customer expectations. In consequence, many womenswear multiples have been forced to segment markets more effectively, making their customers much more aware of the markets that are being catered for. This has led and will increasingly lead to a narrowing of product ranges.

于是这些公司不得不进行合理化改革并进行重组，以应对日益激烈的竞争、更廉价的进口货和不断变化的消费者期望。结果，许多女装连锁店不得不通过更加有效地细分市场，使顾客明白市场在迎合她们的需求。这逐渐导致了产品线的不断缩小。

Retailers always need to be aware of how demographic factors can affect their core 15- to 29-year-old customer and adjust their offering accordingly. Demographic changes often force retailers to reposition themselves in the marketplace as was seen a few years ago when Top Shop, suffering from a reduction in the number of 15–20 year olds, decided to increase the age of their target customer upward. Targeting certain groups in terms of age and, often as important, lifestyle will become ever more crucial. Research into market trends and close co-operation with chosen target groups can help retailers. As the 'middle youth' market of women in their forties continue their youthful interest in fashion, there are opportunities for some retailers to try to keep customers loyal for longer. Others, such as H&M, have professed concern that the presence of too wide a target market in their stores could alienate their core younger customers.

零售商始终需要了解人群统计数据的因素能怎样地影响 15 ~ 29 岁的核心消费群，并相应地调整货品。人口统计数据的变化常常迫使零售商在市场中重新定位自己的产品，这一点可以通过屋脊商店的案例说明。几年前，屋脊商店减少了针对 15 ~ 20 岁群体的时装，以提高目标消费者的年龄，结果损失较大。按照年龄来定位消费对象很重大，按照生活方式定位更关键。对于市场趋向的研究和与所选目标群密切合作对零售商有利。由于 40 岁左右的“中青年”妇女依然对时装保持着其年轻时的兴趣爱好，因而对于试图将顾客的年龄定位放大的零售商来说就有了很多机会可寻。但也有其他不这么想的，比如海恩斯・莫里斯对此心存疑惑，认为如果目标市场定位过宽，将疏远其核心年轻顾客。

2.5.5 Fashion predictors / 时装预测者

For the consumer it must be quite baffling to understand how each year designers, manufacturers

令消费者困惑的是每年设计师、制造商和零售商好像知道什么款式、什么颜色

and retailers all seem to know what styles and colours will be in fashion. The reality is that since the 1970s there have been companies who specialize in fashion prediction and act as consultants to interested parties in the fashion world.

将引领时尚。事实上，自从 20 世纪 70 年代，就有一些公司专门致力于时装预测或担当时装领域内相关团体的顾问。

Companies such as the Paris-based organizations Peclers and Promostyl, France, and London-based Worth Global Style Network (WGSN) sell their predictions on styles, colour and the market for the coming season or even further in advance for up to 18 months. There are at least 10 main organizations of this type in the world, although some specialize in specific markets such as childrenswear. Their predictions are not all identical, although there are usually many similarities between them.

如以巴黎为主的法国佩克乐思和普若斯塔公司，以伦敦为主的英国在线时尚预测和潮流趋势分析服务提供商（WGSN）销售的就是他们对于下一季或长达 18 个月在款式、色彩和市场所作预测的时装产品。全世界至少有 10 家这种大型组织机构，有一些仅针对特定市场，如儿童时装市场预测。他们的预测虽说有许多共同之处,但也不尽相同。

These predictions help manufacturers and retail buyers alike to make and stock the fashions; styles and colours that will be 'the fashion' for a coming season. However, at the end of the day the final decision rests with the customer in deciding whether to buy or not.

这些预测将同样帮助厂商和零售采购员生产和采购时装。这些款式和颜色将成为下一季的时尚导航。然而，最关键的还在于消费者选购与否。

2.5.6 Consumers／消费者

Once fashion was dictated to consumers and there was little choice but to accept what was on offer. The tables are beginning to turn and the consumer has more power to accept or reject fashions. Recognizing this, clothing producers are researching the market more to see what will be acceptable before filling the stores with goods that just end up being discounted at sale time.

以前，时装是被强制提供给消费者的，消费者只有很少的选择权，只能去接受所提供的货品。现在，形势发生了变化，顾客有更大的权力去决定接受还是拒绝这些时装。时装生产商已经意识到这个变化，正加大市场调研力度以在货品积压之前预见哪些是顾客愿意接受的，否则在销售期只得最后打折销售。

Consumers of all descriptions are more fashion educated and consequently more fashion conscious. They are demanding products that are designed to perform in special ways. Most want to express their personalities through their appearance and therefore their choice of clothing. The increasing numbers of working women want garments designed for their particular needs. They understand fashion cycles and they know when a style has become tired. Manufacturers must constantly research and develop new fibres, fabrics and uses for these to keep up with the consumer's higher level of ability to select from the vast choices on offer.

消费者接受的时装教育越来越多，他们的时尚意识越来越强，他们需要的产品是针对不同场合而设计的时装。大多数消费者试图通过容貌和服饰来展示其个性。越来越多的职业女性想要得到满足其特定需要的成衣。她们了解时装的流行周期，并懂得何时一种款式过时。生产商必须要不断研发新的纤维和纺织品并用来加工时装，以跟上顾客们在众多可选商品面前的高水平的选择力。

However, there are other changes in the marketplace affecting consumers' attitudes, values and priorities. They are suffering some degree of fashion fatigue. For some the desire to acquire is more muted and rather

然而，也有其他市场上的变化，影响着顾客的态度、价值观和选择的优先次序。人们有时会患一定程度的市场疲劳症。有一些人对拥有时装的欲望减弱，

than spending their income on fashion clothing they prefer to choose from a much wider range of products, services and leisure pursuits.

不愿把收入花在时装上面，而宁愿选择更广泛的产品、服务和休闲项目。

In the past, fashion styles, types of garments and advertising were all deeply influenced and directed by the interests and needs of the young consumer. Now that the increasing numbers of older consumers are becoming a market to be reckoned with, things must change or opportunities will be lost. The trend is towards people dressing more to please themselves. They won't be dictated to. People are more self-reliant and cautious and careful for their individuality. They are putting more emphasis on self. Recognition of the new fashion consumer may mean that the fashion models of today will have the opportunity of a longer career than they first imagined. Elle McPherson's modelling career saw no sign of ending as she entered her forties and Twiggy who started her modelling career in the 1960s is still popular, with the turn around of Marks and Spencer being largely attributed to using her in their advertising. To a small degree the shape of the fashion model is showing signs of change with more magazines producing features using size 16+ models. This trend probably started with the then somewhat voluptuous Sophie Dahl being heavily featured in fashion magazines and on posters, although now at a size 10 she has ditched the trend herself.

过去，时装款式、成衣种类和广告都深受到年轻消费者的兴趣、需要的影响和指导。现在，数量日益增多的年龄较大的消费者群体，成了需要认真考虑的市场消费群体，所以很多事情要随之改变，否则将错失良机。现在的着装趋势是人们更主要的是要取悦自我。消费者不会被强迫接受他们不喜欢的那些衣服。人们更加自立，更加谨慎，更强调个性化。他们在自己身上花费更多的心思。对于新的时装消费者的认识，意味着当代的时装模特将获得比他们最初想象的更长的职业生涯。艾莉·麦克弗森 40 岁时，还没有迹象表明她的模特生涯画上句号。崔姬从 20 世纪 60 年代开始了她的模特职业生涯，至今还广受欢迎。这在很大程度上归因于玛莎百货起用她作为其广告宣传的模特，使她成功转型。时装模特的外形也在一定程度上发生着变化，更多的杂志使用丰满型的模特。这一趋势的开始或许是由于当时性感的苏菲·达儿频繁出现在时装杂志或海报上，她现在是骨感型的，已经背离了以前的时尚偏好。

2.5.7 Competition within the fashion market／时装市场内的竞争

Consumers today are presented with a bewildering array of choice, yet it is probably in the clothing market more than any other that the consumer complains that he or she cannot find what they want. The clothing producers and retailers are working hard to correct this, but increasing competition and very small margins have made many firms wary of too much investment and experimentation. The high street stores have had to work much harder at tempting consumers and at times it seemed as if price cuts were their only weapon.

如今的消费者面临令人眼花缭乱的时装市场选择，却抱怨找不到他们所想要的时装。时装生产商和零售商辛苦地工作，试图改善这一状况，但是由于日益加剧的竞争和很少的利润，使得许多小公司在投资和实验项目中相当谨慎。繁华商业街的店铺不得不千方百计地吸引顾客，有时打折成了唯一的武器。

However, much of the major competition happens at the sourcing of goods rather than in the stores, as summarized in Figure 2.4. It has been mentioned that globalization and sourcing from wherever cheapest is increasingly becoming the trend, particularly among European competitors. This is enabling them to keep overall costs down, while offering merchandise of good design and quality.

然而，大规模的竞争往往在货源，而不是在商店，正如图 2-4 所示。全球经济一体化，特别是在欧洲的竞争者之间哪里便宜就哪里进货，已经成为一种趋势。这样在保证所售商品的设计和品质的同时，降低整个成本。

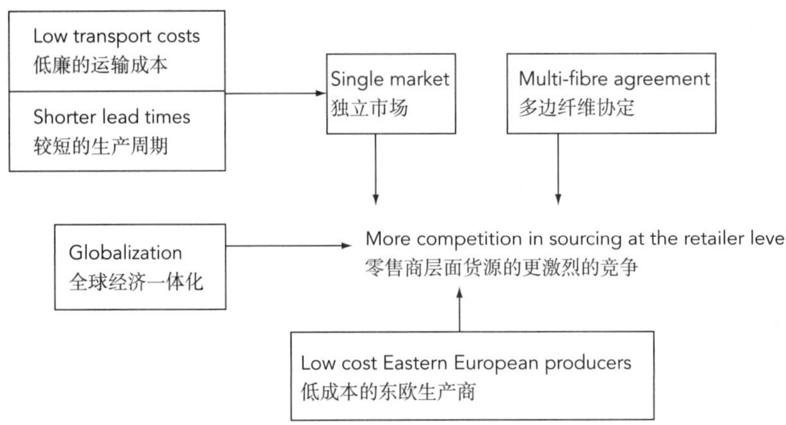

Figure 2.4 Competitive forces in fashion sourcing. 图 2–4 时装货源的竞争压力

Since the opening of the single European market, competition from continental clothing producers has increased further, partly because of lower transport costs and shorter lead times. With a single MFA quota for the EU, the highly concentrated and accessible British clothing market has become even more of a target than it was previously.

There are also concerns about increased low-cost competition from some eastern European countries whose pleas for special treatment of their exports to the EU are showing sings of success. Now that Poland, Hungary and the Czech Republic have joined the EU, they too have gained free access to this vital market as will Turkey which is a candidate country. The clothing industries in these countries, in conjunction with EU companies, have undergone major restructuring and re-equipping. This has enabled them to present some formidable competition.

自从欧洲单一市场开放以来，欧洲大陆的时装生产商之间的竞争日益激烈，部分是由低廉的运输成本和较短的生产周期所致。由于欧盟多边纤维协定配额，密集而且交通便利的英国时装市场比以前更容易成为目标市场。

也有一些关于不断升级的低成本竞争的担忧，这种竞争来自一些东欧国家，他们希望对欧盟的出口商品享受特殊待遇的要求有可能获准。由于波兰、匈牙利、捷克共和国已经加入欧盟，他们也已获得进入时装市场的自由通道，土耳其也是候选国。这些国家的时装业，和欧盟的公司一起，经历着重要的重组和重新装备，这将使他们之间出现难以应对的竞争。

2.5.8 Direct and indirect competition for fashion products / 时装产品的直接和间接竞争

Marketers have to realize that with increased choice consumers have many different ways to spend their money. In the western world people rarely need to buy clothes out of pure necessity. A woman does not merely choose between one dress and another; she also may choose between a new dress or hiring one, or making one or even to spend her money on something completely different like a handbag or entertainment. A man may choose between one jacket and another, or he may

营销人员必须意识到由于选择的多样性，顾客在消费过程中有许多不同的方式。在西方，很少有人出于单纯的必需而购买时装。女士不仅在两件裙子之间进行选择，她或许是在购买、租用一件裙子之间选择，甚至是将钱消费在完全不同的方面，如手提包或进行娱乐消费。男士可能在两件

choose between a jacket and some new golf clubs.

夹克衫之间选择，也可能在夹克衫和新的高尔夫球棒之间进行选择。

When consumers have to choose between similar goods such as one shirt or another, the garments, stores or manufacturers can be described as being in direct competition. However, when the goods are different, but perhaps fulfil similar needs, like the woman choosing between buying and hiring a dress, then the stores and manufacturers are deemed to be in indirect competition.

当消费者在相似的产品如两件衬衫之间进行选择，商店和生产商经历的就是直接竞争。当产品不同，但可能满足的需求相似，如女士选择购买或租用裙子时，商店和生产商就处于间接竞争。

2.5.9 Publics ／公众

There are many groups of publics that can affect a company's success, notably the financial institutions, unions and pressure groups to name but a few. The concept of fashion marketing publics is developed further in Chapter Eight within the context of fashion promotion.

有许多公众群体会影响一家公司的成败，主要有金融机构、工会、压力集团等。关于时装营销公众的概念我们将在第 8 章时装促销章节中进一步阐述。

Perhaps one of the most powerful groups to affect the fashion market is the media. A report in the fashion press after a designer shows a collection can have disastrous results. It is for this reason that some fashion editors have been criticized for having too much power and influence on the market. Whether true or not, much time and effort is spent between fashion editor and designer to try to maintain good relations between the two. It is hoped that this courting may result in a favourable article at a critical time.

或许，影响时装市场最为有力的群体之一便是媒体了。设计师作品系列发布会后，时尚新闻中的一篇报道足以带来极坏的后果。这也是一些时装编辑因对市场拥有过多权力和影响力而饱受争议的原因。无论真实与否，都要花费大量的时间和精力，以尽力维护与时装编辑、设计师的良好关系。人们希望能设法获得媒体支持，可以在评论的时候有篇对自己有利的文章。

While many national newspapers have strong fashion pages, the two most recognized fashion magazines in the UK are Vogue and *Elle*. Both are seen as essential reading for the woman or man who wants to know the important people and events in the fashion world. Powerful as these magazines are, neither has the overwhelming importance of the 92-year-old publication and premier daily newspaper for thewomen's fashion and retail industry in the USA as Women's Wear Daily, whose editor John Fairchild has long been regarded as a fashion guru.

许多国家级报纸都有整版的时装专栏，英国公认的两大时装杂志是《时尚》和《世界时装之苑》。这两大杂志的主要读者是那些想要追踪时尚界的名人和重大事件的人们。尽管这些杂志有较强的影响力，但也比不过具有 92 年出版历史、美国女性时装和零售业的第一要报《女装日报》的影响力，这一报纸的主编约翰・费尔柴尔德长久以来被称为时装教父。

Another force which seems to be having an impact is the pressure groups, concerned with the use of cheap labour and unethical practices. Anti-sweatshop campaign groups, in particular Labour Behind the Label, No Sweat and Tearfund have criticized manufactures whose production practices are deemed unethical. Their concerns have been taken up by the media and many retailers are now taking a much closer interest into the conditions under which their garments are being made.

另一具有影响的力量来自压力集团。他们关注廉价劳动力的使用和缺乏职业道德的行为。反血汗工厂运动团体，尤其是"商标背后的劳工""无血泪"运动团体等谴责那些在生产过程中存在的不道德行为。他们的关注得到媒体的支持，如今许多零售商对其成衣的加工条件给予了更密切的关注。

2.6 Macro-marketing environment / 宏观营销环境

Factors considered within the macro-environment affect not only the company, but all the other members of its micro-environment, namely its suppliers, consumers, etc. These generally have a much wider influence and their effects become apparent more slowly than factors within the company. Factors within the macro-environment are cultural and social, political and legal, demographic, technological and environmental (Figure 2.5).

宏观环境范围内的因素不仅影响公司，而且影响微观环境中的其他要素，如供应商、消费者等。这些因素一般有更广泛的影响力，其影响没有公司内部的诸因素那样明显。宏观环境因素指的是文化、社会、政治、法律、人口、科技和环境因素等（如图 2–5 所示）。

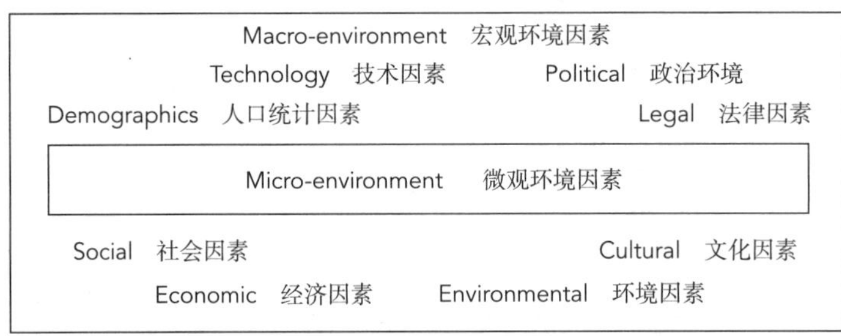

Figure 2.5 The macro-environment. 图 2–5 宏观环境

The inter-relationship of macro-environmental factors is most easily discerned in matters of world tension. Political, legal, social and economic matters become entwined to exert a great impact upon general levels of consumption. Consumer confidence was thought to have been dented by the Gulf War in 1991, which, although now over, has influenced consumer thinking. The war and terrorist activities in London have also affected the market as tourists stayed away for fear of terrorist action, which has particularly influenced more upmarket brands and retailers such as Jaeger and Austin Reed.

宏观环境因素之间的相互关系在世界紧张局势中最容易辨清。政治、法律、社会和经济问题交织在一起对大众消费水准产生巨大影响。1991 年的海湾战争削弱了消费者信心，虽然战争已结束，但仍影响着消费理念。伦敦的战争和恐怖分子的活动也影响着市场，因为游客害怕恐怖活动而不敢久留，这对那些像积家、奥斯丁瑞德等高档零售品牌的影响尤其大。

2.6.1 Political and legal / 政治和法律因素

Politics and law might seem a world away from fashion but both can have extensive consequences for manufacturers. With such globalized sourcing of suppliers, world political events can aid or hamper the acquisition of supplies. A new legal requirement, be it in the product or the methods of manufacture, can have a make or break effect for some companies.

政治和法律看上去似乎与时装互不相干，但二者却对时装生产商产生重要的影响。由于货源供应的全球性，世界政治局势可能促进或阻碍其货品征购计划。所以，一项新的法律规定，不论是产品方面或是生产方式方面，都将会起到至关重要的影响。

The General Agreement on Tariffs and Trade and the Multi-Fibre Agreement / 国际关税及贸易总协定与多边纤维协定

The Arrangement Regarding International Trade in Textile, popularly known as the MFA, is an international agreement that regulated imports of textile and clothing products into western industrialized countries from low cost, mainly developing countries. Operating under the auspices of the General Agreement on Tariffs and Trade (GATT), the MFA currently has 43 signatories, the EU counting as one. Until January 2005, under the system most imports of textiles and clothing into developed countries were subject to detailed quantitative ceilings, implemented through a combination of import and export licences. The MFA was therefore unique in international regulation of trade in industrial products in that it was a formal departure from the free trade principles of GATT. Especially as there is no regulation on exports from industrialized countries to low-cost producers and there are no regulations between the EU and USA.

Originally signed in 1973, the MFA has been renewed on several occasions, most recently in 1994 in Uruguay where an agreement was made to phase out the quotas over a 10-year period which ended on 1 January 2005. This regulated, gradual dismantling of three decades of protection for western textile and clothing industries has had a huge impact on the UK clothing market, probably even more so than for some of its other EU partner's countries for whom imports from developing countries as well as exports to them would grow. However during 2005 imports from China quickly grew by more than 100% for many items and so the EU set up its own quotas to control the influx of Chinese clothing and footwear. In a hurry to beat the deadline for new quotas, Chinese manufacturers speeded up imports and quickly exceeded their full years' quota. Consequently 75 million items of Chinese manufactured clothing were held in European ports until a resolution for their release was reached in August 2005. Whilst, many of the items were school uniform required by retailers for sales prior to the autumn school term, there was also a large amount of underwear leading to the dispute being called the 'Bra Wars'. These new agreed quotas will last unti 2007.

关于纺织品国际贸易的协定，如众所周知的多边纤维协定（MFA），是规范纺织时装产品从低成本地区，主要为发展中国家，进口至西方工业化国家的国际性协议。它在关税及贸易总协定（GATT）的支持下运行，目前已有43个签约成员，欧盟算其一。直至2005年1月，在该体系下，大多数发达国家的纺织品时装进口仍有数量限制。通过实施进出口许可证制度，多边纤维协定因此成为工业产品领域国际贸易法规的特例，与国际关税贸易总协定的自由贸易原则相悖。特别指出的是，没有关于工业化国家出口低成本生产国的任何法规，欧盟与美国之间也没有。

自1973年签订以来，多边纤维协定已修订数次，最近一次是1994年在乌拉圭，当时达成了一项协议，将在逾10年期间分阶段取消配额制度，直至2005年1月1日完全终止配额。这项保护了西方纺织品时装业长达30年之久的规定被强制逐步撤除，对英国时装市场造成了巨大的影响，甚至可能比其他一些欧盟伙伴成员的影响更大。对他们来讲，从发展中国家的进口和对其出口都将增加。然而，2005年，从中国进口的许多纺织服装商品量猛增超过了1倍，欧盟因此设立了自己的配额制度以控制中国时装和鞋的大量涌入。为在新配额期限之前尽快完成出口，中国生产商加快了速度并很快超出了他们全年的配额。随后，7500万件中国生产的时装都扣留在欧洲港口，直到2005年8月才对它们放行。其中有许多是零售商要在学校秋季学期到来之前提前销售的校服，也有大量内衣类产品，因此导致了被称作“内衣大战”的争夺。这些新通过的配额制度将持续至2007年。

Legal aspects: children's nightwear and other safety considerations / 法律方面：儿童睡衣和其他安全要求

All children's nightdresses and dressing gowns, including threads and trimmings, have to comply with British Standard BS 5722. Those which do not must be labelled 'keep away from fire'. While manufacturers had two years to comply completely with this standard, some were still taken unawares.

Hoods on children's coats and jackets can no longer be drawn by a cord for fear of strangulation or being caught in something such as a fairground roundabout, which could result in the child being dragged along by the cord.

所有儿童睡衣和睡袍，包括其加工所用的线和装饰物，必须遵从英国标准BS 5722［译者注：BS 5722是英国儿童睡衣织物的阻燃标准］。那些未包含在内的必须注明“远离火源”。尽管生产商要求按照此标准生产已有2年的时间，但仍有一些不知情者。

儿童大衣和夹克上的兜帽不能再使用绳带，以防勒到孩子或被游乐场旋转木马一类的东西绊住而可能导致孩子被绳子拖行的危险事故发生。

Minimum wage /最低薪金

The introduction of the minimum wage in 1995 undoubtedly affected UK clothing manufacturers. Labour costs in North Africa and the Far East showed a widening gap from UK labour costs and many British clothing manufacturers set up their own units abroad, initially favouring Morocco, Tunisia and Sri Lanka, and more recently moving further afield mainly to China. British and European manufacturers also have to conform to a more stringent set of legal obligations and working standards than many other countries.

1995年关于“最低薪金”的实行无疑影响了英国时装生产商。北非和远东地区的劳动力成本与英国劳动力成本相距甚远，许多英国时装生产商纷纷在海外建立工厂，早期比较偏爱在摩洛哥、突尼斯和斯里兰卡，到近期主要移至中国。英国和欧洲生产商也不得不比其他国家遵守更为严格的法律标准和工作标准。

Copyright /版权

Any design is the creative work of the designer – it is an original and priced as such. Imitation can be said to be the highest form of flattery, but it is unlikely that any designers who have had their creations copied would agree.

There are essentially two types of copying, either of a logo or of a design, as shown in Figure 2.6. Both are very frustrating and often it is too late to do anything about it when, or if, the copying is discovered.

任何设计都是设计师创造性的作品——它们本身是原创的和有价值的。据说仿造是推崇的最高级形式，但也未必所有设计师都允许自己的创作被复制。

仿造本质上有两种形式，如图2–6所示，一种是标志，一种是设计。这两种设计被仿都非常令人苦恼，因为发现某个地方出现仿品时，已经为时已晚，无计可施了。

Logo copying might be imitations of the Lacoste crocodile, Mickey Mouse T-shirts or the copy of a registered design feature such as the Levi's stitching marks. Copies of this type are an infringement of trademark and the perpetrator can be sued.

仿造标志就像冒充鳄鱼恤（Lacoste法国鳄鱼、crocodile中国香港鳄鱼）、米奇T恤或者像李维斯牛仔后袋双行弧形缝线标那样的注册设计标志。这类仿制品是违反商标法的，可能会被起诉。

Design copying can happen in one of two ways:

仿造设计有两种形式：一种是时装上

first, before the garment is on general release, the thief can sketch designs at a fashion show, or steal the design sketches, computer tapes or discs from the designer's place of work, or even steal the actual garments. This can mean that the copies get into the shops at the same time as or even before the original. Secondly, designs can be copied once they are already in the stores.

市之前，剽窃者在时装发布会上勾画下新款式或盗走设计稿、电脑录像带或碟片，甚至样衣。这意味着仿品将与正品同时甚至在正品之前进入店铺；另一种情况是，时装一旦在店铺售卖，设计就可能被抄袭。

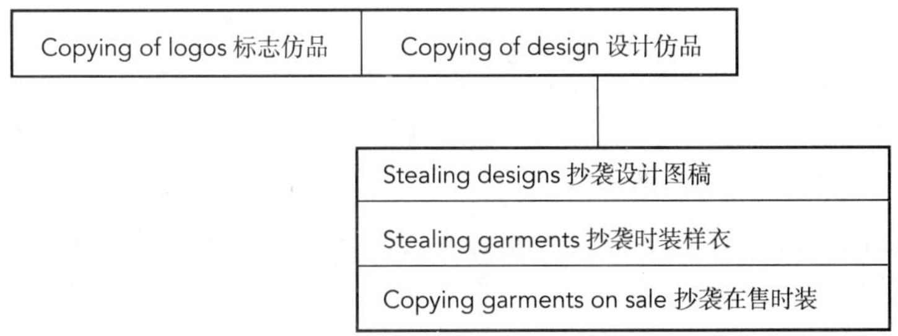

Figure 2.6 Copying of fashion. 图 2–6 时装仿品

Copies are usually cheaper and of inferior quality to the original and can give the original designer many problems. First, they will lose sales to the cheaper versions. At first sight the copies may not seem any different to the unsuspecting buyer who usually would go for the cheaper version. Frequently it is only after wearing the garment or more particularly washing it that the quality differences become apparent. Fabrics do not wash or clean as well and seams will not hold as well. These quality differences can lead the original designer to get an unjustly poor reputation among the consumers who think that they are buying original labels.

仿品通常比正品便宜，质量较差，给原创设计师带来诸多问题。首先，由于有较便宜的版本，正版销售量将减少。对于那些常去买便宜货的购买者，仿品往往第一眼看不出与正品有什么差别，经常是在穿了或者多次洗涤之后，质量问题才会凸显。面料洗涤性较差，接缝也不牢固。这些质量差异会导致原创设计师在那些认为自己购买了正版品牌的消费者中得到不公正的声誉差评。

Retailers could be criticized for encouraging this practice. Now that goods can be produced very quickly, high street stores pride themselves on having high fashion 'copies' available within their stores only days after they have been seen on the catwalks. Fashion magazines often have features, such as the *Sunday Times*' Style magazine's 'skinted and minted', showing their readers how to get a designer look at a fraction of the price by buying from high street stores. It is very difficult to decide at what point these items are blatant copies or merely following a fashion trend.

零售商助长了仿品行为的产生而可能受到批评或指责。目前这类仿品上市的速度很快，繁华商业街店铺自豪于他们看完发布会几天后便能在其店里买到高级时装的仿品了。时装杂志经常有专题，比如《周末时光》时装杂志的"平价与时尚"，就向杂志的读者展示了如何在繁华商业街店里花少量的钱而买到某个设计师设计款式外型的衣服。很难判断这些商品在哪些地方是公然的赝品或仅仅是追随潮流。

Copying of designs is not new. In 1975 the Fashion Design Protection Association was set up by Achilleas

抄袭设计并不新鲜。埃瑞拉时装公司的艾彻莱斯·康斯坦廷诺发现自己的

Constantinou of Ariella Fashion after he saw many of his designs in stores that he knew his company had not supplied. This was subsequently taken up by the British Clothing Industry Association (BCIA) who lobbied to get the Department of Trade and Industry to bring out the Copyright Designs and Patents Act in 1988. The aim of this Act is 'to protect creativity without restricting competition'. Designers are encouraged to claim copyright of their designs by signing and dating their original drawings. However, designs are often copied and sold in other countries without the designer ever knowing, although the effect might be felt in decreased sales and reputation. So these laudable efforts have not really solved the problem. Aside from the practical difficulties of time and cost in pursuing legal actions against the suppliers, there is still the problem of deciding when a fashion house is merely following a trend and when it is breaking the law.

One solution, used by Levi's, is to monitor the market outlets constantly, to make life harder for the counterfeiters. This may not be possible for a smaller company, especially when any monitoring has to be done internationally. Most of the copies are made abroad, to enable cheaper manufacture and avoid copyright laws. Another tactic used by Levi's is to tightly control the distribution of their red label tag stitched into all their jeans. They count out an exact number for their manufacturers and require exactly that number of pairs of jeans back from them, so preventing the manufacturer from producing overruns and selling them as originals.

Such is the problem that in November 1999 the Consumer Affairs Minister, Dr Kim Howells, attended the Sports Industries Federation 'War on Counterfeiting' conference in London. He pledged to 'Crack down on the "Mafia Gangsters" who peddle counterfeit sportswear costing the economy billions of pounds. Consumers need to know that fake goods are dangerous and damaging and rarely last as long as the genuine article'. Many companies are trying to do this crackdown themselves. Mulberry, the Bond Street producer of original leather handbag designs, took out 17 legal actions against retailers for copying their designs; only one reached court as the other 16 were all settled out of court. In all cases Mulberry won, either compensation or at least the withdrawal and destruction of stock.

许多设计作品都在公司并没有供货的店里出现之后，于 1975 年成立了时装设计保护协会。随后 1988 年，英国时装工业协会也游说贸易工业部出台设计版权法和专利法，该法旨在“不约束竞争的情况下保护创新”。法规鼓励设计师在自己的设计原稿上署名和签上日期以证明所有权归属。然而，某些设计作品还是经常会在设计师毫不知情的情况下在其他国家被抄袭和出售，甚至可能带来销售量减少和毁誉的不利影响。因此，这些值得称赞的努力并未真正地解决问题。除了对供应商采取法律措施时花费的时间和成本上的实际困难之外，判断一家时装公司是否仅仅是跟随潮流和是否违法也是一个问题。

李维斯使用的一种解决办法就是持续监控市场上的货品，使仿造者的日子不好过。特别是面向全球实施的监控，这对小公司来说不太可能。大多数仿品都在国外制造，可使生产成本更低并避开版权法。李维斯用的另一种策略是严格控制车缝在所有牛仔裤上的红色标签。他们统计出了生产商的确切数目并要求返厂牛仔裤数目精确，以阻止生产商泛滥生产并且当作原版售卖。

以一个事件为例：1999 年 11 月，消费事务部长科姆・霍韦尔斯博士参加在伦敦召开的运动工业联盟的“与仿造开战”会议。他在会上保证：“对那些散播价值数十亿英镑的运动时装仿制品的‘黑手党’严惩。消费者需要知道赝品是危险的、有害的，且不能像正品一样耐穿持久。”许多公司自己也在努力打击制售贩假者。玛百莉，邦德街上的原创皮革手袋设计生产者，采取了 17 个针对抄袭他们设计的零售商的法律行动；只有 1 个上了法庭，其他 16 个均为庭外解决。玛百莉赢了所有案子，有的得到赔偿，有的至少是收回并销毁仿品库存。

2.6.2 Technological ／技术因素

As in all areas of industry new technology is making great inroads to improve quality of life and increase speed and quality of manufacture. In the area of fashion and clothing there have been many inventions. Some have had only minor effects on the market, whereas others have or are about to revolutionize them.

在所有工业领域里，新技术正带来巨大的冲击，生活质量得以提高，生产的速度和质量也得以提升。时装和面料领域也有许多发明，有的在市场上影响甚微，然而有的却是带来革命性的影响。

Other innovations in fabric technology are in the introduction of a variety of different properties in fabrics. Available in stores is heat-sensitive hosiery to keep the wearer warm or cold; moisturizing hosiery and underwear with a built-in fragrance capable of surviving up to 40 washes.

面料技术方面的另一些创新在于实现面料的多种不同性能。商店里可以看到使穿着者暖和或凉爽的针织品；滋润型纺织品和洗涤 40 次仍有香味的内衣。

Fibres and fabrics ／纤维与面料

Lycra is not a fabric. The trademark Lycra is the property of theUS-based chemical company Du Pont and is an Elastane fibre that lends itself to whichever fabric it is mixed with. Lycra is therefore an additive that gives knitted and woven textiles the quality of lasting stretch and recovery. It was first developed in 1959 and its first real use in garments was in the 1960s in ski wear and men's cord trousers. It was really not until the 1980s that it took off in knitted garments.

莱卡不是面料，其注册商标的持有者是美属化学公司杜邦，莱卡是一种弹性纤维，并可将其混纺到其他任何面料中。因此，莱卡成为能赋予针织和机织面料持续拉伸和回弹力的添加物。它最早发明于 1959 年，真正在时装中使用是在 1960 年，用于滑雪装和男式灯芯绒长裤。直到 20 世纪 80 年代才应用于针织时装。

Lycra has become a household name associated with dancewear, swimwear, hosiery, cling-to-fit fashion separates such as leggings and vest dresses, in fact anything knitted. Lycra overcomes problems of fit and movement for body-hugging designs. Manufacturers obviously benefit from associations with a consumer recognizable brand in premium, superior quality garments and fabrics.

在舞蹈服、泳装、针织袜以及像紧身裤和打底衫等合体时尚单品中的运用，实际上包括所有针织类物品，莱卡变成了家喻户晓的名字。它解决了紧身设计的合体性和运动机能性的问题。生产商从这个在主流、高质量的时装和面料上明显可辨识的莱卡标志中受益。

Such is the swimwear market's reliance on Lycra that swimwear designers do not design their collections until they have received Du Pont's own fashion forecasts.

泳装设计者在拿到杜邦公司的流行预测后才开始自己的系列设计。这情形足以说明泳装市场与莱卡的联系。

Lycra is now being mixed with woven fabrics for outerwear and tailoring to take advantage of such benefits as improved appearance, better drape and less wrinkling. There is more development into adding Lycra to other cloth to create a wide diversity of fabrics. This has resulted in all kinds of finishes for fabrics using Lycra such as bubble, cire, shiny, matt, satin finish or printed.

如今，莱卡已混纺到外衣和套装的机织面料中，在改善外观、增加悬垂性、减少起皱等方面发挥其优势。在其他布料中加入莱卡制造更多种差异性面料，将大有前景。莱卡已经用于面料各种各样的后整理中，像起泡、蜡光、闪光、哑光、缎面等后整理或印花。

The development of Lycra into other clothing, notably sportswear, has led to the increase of interest and sales in sportswear for professional, hobby and leisure purposes.

莱卡在其他时装中的应用发展，特别是在运动装领域，已经提升了其利润和销售的增长，满足了专业性和舒适性的要求。

The clothing industry is extremely labour intensive, but installation of modern machinery fitted with the latest electronic controls is helping to improve productivity.

时装是劳动密集型产业，安装使用最新的电子控制的现代化机器设备有助于提高生产率。

In the sportswear clothing field there have been huge developments in energy transfer fabrics which transfer heat away from the body so allowing sportsmen and -women to remain cool during their activity.

在运动装领域，导热面料有了巨大的发展，它可以将热能从人体传导出去，以使运动者在活动过程中保持清爽。

Computers ／计算机

The dramatic increase in the use of computers has not passed by the fashion world, as shown in Figure 2.7. One of the main uses of computer systems is that of computer-aided design (CAD). The implication that this can have on the speed of transition of goods from design to the shop floor is quite phenomenal. It also has great implications for the employment sector in this industry. It may be the saviour of the UK clothing industry if it is accepted quickly enough.

在服装界，计算机应用的急剧增加势头并未终止，如图 2–7 所示。使用计算机系统主要是在计算机辅助设计（CAD）方面。它在提高产品从设计到上市的速度方面表现相当出色，而且对时装业的就业市场也影响颇大。倘若它能足够迅速地被接纳使用，没准儿会成为英国时装业的救星。

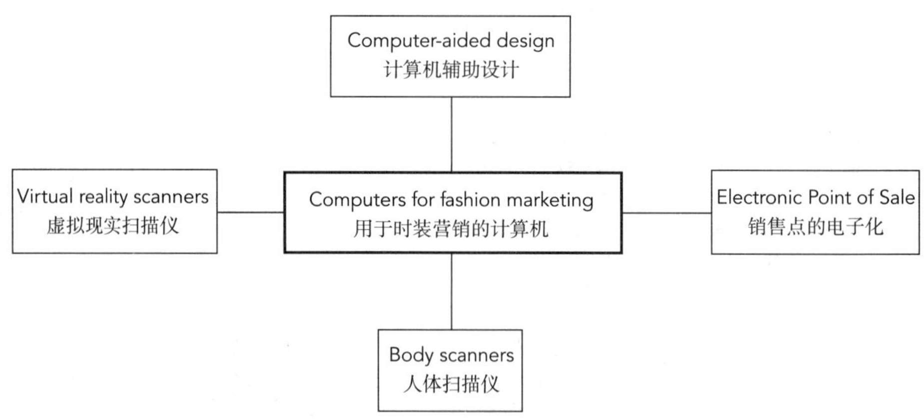

Figure 2.7 Computers in fashion marketing. 图 2–7 计算机在时装营销中的应用

A CAD system can perform a wide variety of tasks:

◆ The programmer designs a motif.

◆ The motif can be enlarged to any size, and duplicated to cover a piece of cloth. This can then be

计算机辅助设计系统应用广泛，可执行以下任务：

◆ 程序员设计一个图案；

◆ 这个图案可以被放大成任意尺寸，并复制到一块布料上，而且能在电

viewed on the computer screen to see how the design will look on the draped fabric.

◆ The fabric can be tried in different colourways.

◆ The fabric can then be printed either directly onto the fabric using a bubble jet printer, or for larger lengths of fabric a printing layout can be produced.

◆ The operator can then design a garment, perhaps a blouse, by selecting different sleeves, collar, yoke, length, etc.

◆ The software will then print out a paper pattern to any basic measurements given.

◆ It can also plan a layout for the pattern pieces to achieve the optimum use of the fabric.

There is no reason why all these tasks cannot be performed by one skilled computer operator; however, the question today must be whether we need to train designers or computer operators. Although in 1992 only 150 out of 9000 fashion companies in the UK were using these systems to design garments, this number has increased dramatically, particularly as the systems become more flexible and prices are reduced.

These programmes can dramatically speed up the time it takes for a garment to get into the stores. They are also very cost effective both in terms of time saved and in minimizing fabric wastage. Perhaps the biggest saving that these systems can offer is in the area of pattern making and grading.

Some high street retailers like to deal with designers using this system as they can easily ask for adjustments to be made without delaying delivery time. So decisions are made more quickly and the buyer has more choice and influence.

Made-to-measure has been used as a means of producing garments since the inception of clothing. Since the industrial revolution, standardized sizing has gained prominence as it brings affordable garments to many markets. With growing populations comes diversity, the need for flexibility and the desire for better fitting clothes for all, not just those who can afford it. CAD can take a customer's measurements and reproduce designs or patterns for many different garments, quickly and accurately. It also can grade patterns for different sizes.

A further development in technology for the clothing market is for use in the made-to-measure

脑屏幕上看到该设计在自然悬垂面料上的效果；

◆ 面料色彩可用不同的配色方式；

◆ 可直接用一个喷墨打印机对面料进行喷绘，而对长度较长的面料，也可制作出印花编排图；

◆ 接下来，操作员就能设计时装了，比如一件上衣，可选择不同的袖子、领子、育克、长度等自由搭配；

◆ 然后，软件会输出指定打印基本尺寸的纸样图；

◆ 为实现面料的最佳利用率，也可将裁片纸样编排成排料图。

为什么这些工作不能由一个技术熟练的电脑操作员来承担呢？理由是显而易见的。现在的问题是我们要训练设计师还是电脑操作员。尽管 1992 年英国 9000 家时装公司中仅有 150 家使用这些系统设计时装，但在计算机系统更加灵活、价格也降低之后，这个数字增长很快。

这些程序可明显加快时装上市的速度，能省时和降低面料浪费，也非常节约成本。它们提供的最大节约便是在打板和放码环节。

一些繁华商业街的零售商愿意与使用计算机辅助设计系统的设计师打交道，因为不必延迟交货时间，就可以很容易地做出相应调整。所以，决策做出得更快，而且买家有了更多的选择机会和影响力。

量身定制自时装业之初便是时装生产的一种方式。随着工业革命，标准化号型得以推广，并将大众买得起的时装带入众多市场。人口增长随之带来了差异性需求，这是对灵活性的需求，是所有人对更符合自己身体的时装的需求，而不仅仅是那些能负担得起的人。计算机辅助设计能快速精确地获得某位顾客的尺寸，并再次生成许多不同款式时装的设计和纸样。它也可以将纸样放缩成不同尺码。

对于时装市场来说计算机技术的更进一步发展是在量身定制市场中的应用，

market, where a system like a body scanner can be used to measure body size and shape within seconds to provide electronic tailoring.

如人体扫描仪系统能用于测量尺码和体型，在几秒钟内提供给电子裁缝。

In the future, virtual reality could transform the fashion business. There would be no need for supermodels or scrambles to get the front row at the fashion show. Designers could have the model they wanted parading around their salons, while clients could view whole couture collections in the comfort of their own homes.

未来，虚拟现实技术可能会改变时装业。那时，将不再需要超级模特或者发生争抢时装秀前排座位的场面。设计师们可以让他们想要的模特在沙龙里展示，而顾客则舒适地在自己家中观看整个时装系列发布。

Another major computerized invention for the retailer is EPoS (Electronic Point of Sale). This is very familiar in our supermarkets where bar codes are scanned to give the price. The bar codes can also tell the clothing retailer such information as size of garment, colour and how long it has been in stock. This information can then go into a central system that controls stock, and can, if necessary, rapidly reorder.

对零售商来说，另一个计算机发明创造是电子销售终端机。超市中常见，扫描条形码可显示价格。条形码也可以告诉时装零售商诸如时装尺码、颜色、仓储时间等信息。这些信息可进入控制仓储的中央系统；如果需要，还可以快速再订购。

Computerized links with suppliers are growing in importance, speeding up order processing and improving the accuracy of transactions. The use of computers and EPoS has become very important in retail success in data capture at the point of sale, management of the merchandise and links with suppliers. Those retailers who have invested in these systems will fare best in the future.

与供应商的计算机化链接日益重要，它可以加速订购流程，改善交易的精确性。计算机和电子销售终端机的应用在零售领域已非常重要，可成功实现销售终端数据的获取、商品的管理以及与供应商的链接。那些投资这些系统的零售商将会在今后得到最好的经营和发展。

Internet ／互联网

With 86% of all homes in the UK having Internet access in 2006, clothes shopping via the web is predicted to continue to increase from the estimated 4.1 billion or 1.8% of retail sales estimated by Mintel (2005). While most fashion retailers now have established websites, but there are mixed fortunes in terms of online purchases. The tactile dimension of clothing purchases, the salience of colour matching with skin tones and the variability in sizing are all factors that continue to inhibit the use of the Internet by some customers. In addition, many consumers still express concerns about the security of passing credit card details over the Internet. The body scanner mentioned above could be used to see whether the clothes available via a website will fit the consumer before a purchase is made. Companies that have been most successful such as Next use a multi-channel format of store, catalogue and website. Other

鉴于2006年英国86%的家庭装有互联网，预测指出，通过网络购买时装将在估计的41亿或敏特调查公司估计的零售量1.8%的基础上继续增长。虽然现在大多数时装零售商都已经建立了网站，但从在线购物来说喜忧参半。选购时装时的感觉、色彩搭配是否与肤色相称，以及尺码的可变性全都是影响某些消费者网络购物的不利因素。另外，许多消费者对在网上使用信用卡的安全性还表示担忧。上文提及的人体扫描仪可使消费者在购买前通过网络看到时装是否合体。像奈克斯特做得很成功的公司则使用店铺、产品目录和网站销售的多渠道模式。其他成功的例子都在那些以线上销售为特点的公司，像仿名人创意时装的Asos（译者注：Asos是英文"as seen on screen"的简写，中文意思就是"像银屏明星一样"。2000年6月网店开始营业，以经营模仿电影明

successes have been amongst those who specialize in selling online such as Asos with their celebrity inspired fashions or Figleaves with lingerie.

星穿着的时装和配饰为主）或以内衣闻名的Figleaves。

Television shopping ／电视购物

Still in its infancy, shopping via interactive television direct from the armchair has a similar potential to change how we buy clothing. However, growth of this area is limited by the same inhibitors as those connected with Internet shopping. Figures from Mintel (2003) estimate sales to be worth £395 million and only take a 2.7% share of the total home-shopping market.

早在其初期，直接坐在扶手椅里通过互动电视进行购物，这种购物方式改变了我们买衣服的方式。然而，这一领域的发展同样受到网络购物不利因素的制约。敏特调查公司（2003）数据统计销售额达 3.95 亿英镑，而整个居家购物仅占 2.7%。

Body scanners ／人体扫描仪

Body scanners are a way of collecting 3D data about a consumer's body shape and size. By standing, fully clothed, in a booth or pod, up to 3000 body measurements can be taken in a matter of seconds by cameras and lasers. Minutes later an accurate true to scale 3D body model can be produced. This technology is already being put to a variety of uses. Whilst mass production companies can now ensure that their garments more closely fit the average consumer, the greater benefits will be made by the made-to-measure market for which measurement is both quick and accurate. Retailers are also finding uses for this technology. Selfridges, on Oxford Street, London, offer body scanning in order to produce custom-fit jeans. The customer can choose the fabric, rise and leg style and be assured of a perfect fitting pair of jeans. In some Gap stores consumers can use the body scanner to help them find which brands and sizes will offer the best fit. There are even predictions that body scanners could eliminate the need for changing rooms. The one market where they could reap most benefits are in clothing purchased online. Internet sales still suffer from consumer dissatisfaction due to poor fit and consumers frequently do not bother to return goods that don't fit, they just don't bother shopping with that company again. In time consumers could have their own body scan on their computer they could 'try on' clothes from participating online retailers. Early efforts in this area have been made by some organization such as Landsend to offer 'My Virtual Model™'. An attractive mannequin can be programmed to assume a customer's shape,

人体扫描仪是用来采集消费者体型和尺码的三维数据的，被测者穿着完整，站立在一个棚里或舱里，多达 3000 项人体尺寸测量数据便可由摄像机和激光器在几秒钟内获得。几分钟后可生成一个精确真实的 3D 人体模型。这项技术已被运用至多个领域。同时，大批量生产的公司现在可以确保其时装更符合普通消费者的体型。量身定制市场将会得到更大益处，他们要求人体尺寸测量既快速又精确。零售商也在寻找这项技术的用途。在伦敦的牛津大街上，塞尔弗里奇店为生产出合体的定制牛仔裤，便提供人体扫描服务。顾客可选择面料、立裆长短和裤腿的款式，并保证得到一条完美合体的牛仔裤。在一些盖普店，顾客可用人体扫描仪帮他们找到最适合自己体型的时装和尺码。甚至有预言说，人体扫描仪将使试衣间消失。它们能获取最大好处的一个市场就是网络购衣。网络销售仍因衣服不合体而饱受消费者的不满，而消费者经常不厌其烦地退换不合体的时装，仅仅为了下一次从那家公司买衣服不要再如此麻烦。消费者可以及时在他们的电脑上看到自己的人体扫描，并从参与在线销售的零售商那里“试穿”衣服。在这一领域，一些机构已做了初步尝试，像兰德森德这样的老牌经销商提供的“我的虚拟模型”。一个可由程序实现的吸引人的人体模型能看到顾客的体型、肤色、发型和面部特征，顾客可在他们自己的模型上试穿衣服并检查不同

skin tone, hairstyle and facial features, and customers can try clothes on their model to check fit and co-ordination of different outfits. Clearly this is more fun than accurate but as a tool for getting the customer involved with the merchandise it is very effective.

套时装的合体度和协调性。比起精确性的特点，这明显更有趣，但作为一个让顾客与商品能相关联的工具，它无疑是非常有效的。

2.6.3 Demographics ／人口统计因素

This is the study of changes in the size and make-up of the population. While these changes occur slowly and can be predicted well in advance, only the foolish manufacturer ignores the effect they might have on business. The UK has begun to undergo a quite radical change in the make-up of its population and many of these changes will have strong repercussions on the fashion clothing market.

这是研究人口规模和组成变化的学科。当这些变化发生的比较缓慢并提前准确预测时，生产商不应忽略它们可能给生意上带来的影响。英国已经开始经历它的人口构成方面的剧变，这其中的许多变化都将在时装市场产生强烈反响。

Customer size ／顾客尺码

As a nation we are changing shape and businesses are being forced to cope with the larger customer. Adult obesity rates have almost quadrupled in the past 25 years and now 22% of Britons are obese, classed as having a body mass index of over 30, and three-quarters are overweight. The implications for the fashion industry are obvious in terms of sizes, stock levels and styling. Not only are people heavier but the average height for both men and women has increased by 10 mm. This has implications for all sorts of goods and services such as transport, furniture and clothing.

由于整个国民的体型都在改变，商业领域也被迫要应对更大体型的顾客。在过去的 25 年中，成人肥胖率几乎翻了 4 番，按体重指数超过 30 划分，现在 22% 的英国人肥胖，其中 3/4 超重。这在尺码、库存量和款式方面对时装业的暗示是明显的。人们不仅仅是变重了，男女的平均身高也增加了 10mm。这对诸如交通、家具和时装等所有种类货品和服务方面都是具有提示作用的。

Many clothing manufacturers are offering goods in a wider range of sizes or a more generous cut, although some have pandered to their customers' vanity and disguised the increase in size, Marks and Spencer have admitted that a size 12 made in the 1980s is not exactly the same as the equivalent size now. Even high fashion retailers targeting the younger consumer are realizing the need to cater for a broader range of sizes. Top Shop now offers a selection of their clothing up to size 16 and Next up to size 22, although availability is greater online or in the directory.

许多时装生产商提供的货品有更宽的尺码范围或者更大尺码的剪裁，尽管有的已经满足了顾客的虚荣心并隐藏了尺码的增加，玛莎百货已经承认 20 世纪 80 年代的 12 码和现在的 12 码不一样了。即使面对年轻消费者市场的高端时装零售商也意识到需要满足更大的尺码。屋脊商店现在的时装尺码选择已经增至 16 码，奈克斯特到了 22 码，这些尺码在线上销售和目录销售方面获得的可能性更大。

Apart from offering a wider range of sizes, some stores have a special own range in store, e.g. Bhs's range 'Extra', and H&M's range BiB. Many stores, including Marks and Spencer, also have petite ranges and New Look has a range for women over 5'70" There are also more retailers catering solely for the larger customer. High and Mighty, as the name

区别于提供更宽尺码范围，一些商家在店里有自己的特殊系列，例如，英国百货连锁店 Bhs 百货公司的“Extra”和海恩斯·莫里斯的“BiB”；许多店铺，包括玛莎百货，也有小尺码系列；而新外貌则对身高超过 5 英尺 7 英寸的女性有一个产品

suggests, is a growing chain for men. Dawn French has an upmarket store in South Molton Street in London for women sized 16 and upwards. If the trend continues the time may come when it is the size 10s who are complaining that they cannot find anything to wear.

系列；还有很多零售商也在独自满足大尺码的顾客，High and Mighty，正如名字所示，是大尺码中的一个连锁男装；Dawn French在伦敦的南莫尔顿大街有一家为穿16码及以上的女性开设的高档店。如果这种趋势继续发展，可能有一天那些穿10码的人就会抱怨他们找不到任何可穿的衣服了。

An ironic contrast, however, is the concern for people, particularly women, who try to stay extremely thin or have eating disorders. For them, stores are stocking jeans in sizes 6, 4 and sometimes even smaller.

然而，一个讽刺性的对比，就要涉及那些试图保持极瘦或饮食不规律者，特别是女性。为了她们，商家正在制作6码、4码甚至更小的牛仔裤。

Changes in the family ／家庭变化

The much quoted statistic of the family with 2.4 children has changed. In recent years it has fluctuated around the 1.8 mark. Couples are tending to marry later and start a family later. This gives them the opportunity to become more financially stable, to get further on in their careers and to have more disposable income to spend on their children, some of it on clothing. More exclusive children's clothing shops have, like many others, suffered during the recession of the early 1990s. However, there is still a substantial designer market for childrenswear whether the garments are bought as gifts from generous grandparents or as regular clothing by more financially indulgent parents.

之前大量引用的一个家庭有2.4个孩子的统计数字已经变了。近些年，这个数字一直在1.8附近波动。男女结婚和建立家庭越来越晚。这可使他们经济基础更稳固，事业发展更好，能有更多可任意支配的收入在他们的孩子身上，其中一部分是时装开销。像其他店一样，许多高级童装店在20世纪90年代初的不景气环境中举步维艰。然而，仍有一个坚固的童装设计师市场，生产有让慷慨的祖父母买来当作礼物的童装以及出手阔绰的父母买来当作常备品的童装。

With more people remarrying and starting a second family in their late thirties and early forties, there is a need for maternity wear for the more mature expectant mother, who may also be working at the time. Whilst the high street caters quite well for the younger mother within high street stores such as New Look and H&M, there are several successful companies who sell mainly via catalogue or online. JoJo, Maman, Bebe and Isabella Oliver offer more upmarket ranges with a high design element to cater for the more mature and more affluent mother to be. These mothers will also want to keep a youthful appearance consistent with their young children so there are other market opportunities for post-natal ranges. Further details about the role of the family in purchasing behaviour are given in Chapter Three.

随着越来越多的人再婚，在他们三四十岁的时候重新建立第二个家庭，那些仍在工作的更加成熟的准妈妈穿着的孕妇装是有市场需求的。同时，诸如新外貌和海恩斯·莫里斯一类的繁华商业街店铺都能很好地满足那些年轻母亲，有几个主要通过目录和网络销售的成功公司，如JoJo，玛曼，碧碧和伊莎贝拉·奥立弗都提供具有高感度设计元素的高级系列以满足那些越来越成熟和越来越富有的准妈妈们。这些母亲也希望和她们的孩子保持一致的年轻容貌，因此，针对产后妇女的着装也有另外的市场机会可寻。家庭购物行为规律的进一步详情将在第3章展开讨论。

Age changes in the population ／人口年龄变化

The British population is forecast to rise by less than

预测显示，2005年到2010年间，英

2% between 2005 and 2010, but the significant impact on the clothing sector is the large changes to the structure of the population. Not withstanding minor fluctuations, the long-term decline in the number of 15–24 year olds, high spenders on clothing, continues, albeit slowly. Table 2.7 illustrates how different age ranges will be affected.

国人口的增长将低于2%，但对时装行业的显著影响是来自人口结构的巨大变化。15 ~ 24 岁年龄段是时装高消费人群，其人口数量不可抵挡地长期小幅减少，虽然较慢，但一直持续。表 2–7 显示了不同年龄段的逐年变化情况。

Table 2. 7 Population trends (male and female), Great Britain (in '000s)
表 2–7 英国人口变化趋势（男性和女性） 单位：千人

Age range 年龄范围	% Change 变化率 /% 2000 ~ 2005	2005 ~ 2010	2010 ~ 2015
0 ~ 4	− 3.48	+ 2.15	+ 0.64
5 ~ 9	− 6.39	− 3.27	+ 2.15
10 ~ 14	− 0.72	− 6.36	− 3.34
15 ~ 19	+ 9.14	− 1.94	− 6.25
20 ~ 24	+ 11.39	+ 7.75	− 1.60
25 ~ 29	− 7.88	+ 10.77	+ 6.88
30 ~ 34	− 9.36	− 7.52	+ 9.79
35 ~ 39	+ 0.84	− 9.34	− 7.70
40 ~ 44	+ 12.98	+ 0.65	− 9.33
45 ~ 59	+ 5.57	+ 4.29	+ 6.91
60 ~ 64	+ 7.37	+ 20.58	− 8.33
65 ~ 74	+ 2.19	+ 7.56	+ 15.68
75 ~ 84	+ 5.41	+ 1.86	+ 8.10
85 以上	+ 5.08	+ 16.87	+ 12.15
Total 合计	+ 2.25	+ 2.34	+ 2.27

Source: Adapted from Government Actuary. 资料来源：选自《政府精算师》。

Children / 儿童

Over the past 15 years there have been fluctuations in the size of the population in different children's age bands. However, it is estimated that, despite the increasing trend for women to be older when they have their first chind

在过去的 15 年中，不同儿童年龄段的人口规模都有浮动。然而，预计表明，虽然女性第一次生育的时间越来越晚，或者甚至有与新伴侣拥有第

or even the move towards having a 'second family' with a new partner, there will be little growth in the children's market.

However, changes in the children's market can still present many opportunities for clothing and footwear demand for infants. Many retailers have recognized this and the market is very competitive. Retailers can best compete by offering good styles and designs with good value for money. The premium end of the market shows room for some expansion with many children's only label such as Miniman and Oilily, plus many adult designer labels offering diffusion children's ranges such as Baby Dior, Moschino, Armani, Ted Baker and DKNY.

The 10–14 years of age children's market remains underdeveloped in retail terms at present. Marks and Spencer have all but withdrawn their attempt to appeal to teenagers. Next fare better but sell most of the teen boys range online or via the Next Directory. The one apparent success with stand-alone stores was Tammy Girl a younger extension of the Etam range. Now under the control of Philip Green, owner of the Arcadia group and Bhs, Tammy would appear to have been demoted and is now only offered within the Bhs stores, reinforcing the opinion that this is a very difficult sector at which to win. The increasing interest in sportswear and sportswear labels would suggest that it is the sports outfitters that are best satisfying this group.

二个家庭的趋势动向，儿童数量的增长仍少得可怜。

即便如此，儿童市场的变化还是显现出婴儿服和童鞋的很多机遇。许多零售商已经认识到这一点，市场竞争激烈。零售商可通过提供高性价比的好款式和好设计来使自己拥有竞争力。这部分市场的稀缺为那些仅做童装的品牌，如米尼曼和欧莉莉，提供了扩张的空间，另外，许多成人设计品牌也在发展童装产品线，像迪奥童装，摩斯奇诺，阿玛尼，泰德·贝克和唐娜·卡兰。

目前，零售领域的 10 ~ 14 岁童装市场仍需开发。玛莎百货应有尽有但却收回了吸引十几岁年龄段顾客的品牌。奈克斯特进展好些，但大多数十几岁男童系列在网上销售或者通过奈克斯特产品目录销售。一个独树一帜的成功例子是艾格旗下的黛咪少女年轻系列。如今，在菲利普·格林，阿卡迪亚集团和包豪斯［译者注：Bhs（British Home Store）创立于 1928 年，是遍布英国繁华商业街的连锁店，主要销售时装和日常用品］的所有者的掌控下，黛咪少女将降级，仅在包豪斯店中出售，更加强了这类产品系列的销售难以成功的论调。运动装和运动品牌的持续升温说明最能满足这一群体的应该是运动用品。

Traditional core market aged 15–34 / 15 ~ 34 岁的传统核心市场

The traditional core market for clothing suppliers, that of men and women between the ages of 15 and 34, declined rapidly between 1990 and 2000 when stores for whom the lower end of this market was key, such as Miss Selfridge, suffered as they saw their customer base drop by about a twelfth. This age group has remained fairly steady since then. Whilst the high spending 15–34 year olds will continue to remain steady in numbers as a group until 2010, there will be a drop in the 30 year olds at the top end of this market. There may be some consolation in the fact that the 20-year-old group will grow slightly, although they also have most demands on their finances with mortgages and many are starting to have families.

时装供应商的传统核心市场，是年龄在 15 ~ 34 岁的男性和女性，这个市场在 1999 年到 2000 年间锐减，当时，像塞尔弗里奇小姐店这类服务于此年龄段下端的商家经营困难，因为他们的顾客年龄下落到 12 岁。从那时起，这个年龄段一直保持得相当稳定。直到 2010 年，高消费的 15 ~ 34 岁人群的数量都将持续稳定，而在这个年龄段的上端 30 几岁会有一个下降。事实上，可能令人稍感安慰的是 20 岁这个年龄段将会有轻微增长，尽管他们有还贷和建立家庭的要求。

The mature market / 中老年市场

In 2005 almost 56% of all inhabitants in Britain were aged 35 years or older. By 2010 the number of 45–54 year olds is expected to rise more rapidly than any other age group. Previously people of this age would have been grouped together with older consumers who traditionally spend less on clothing, particularly men, than consumers in their late teens, twenties and thirties. They bought fewer garments and often spent less per garment than younger people. But emerging from this group is the new 'middle youth' market as they are sometimes referred to, who have a greater interest in health, fashion and shopping, and whose members, particularly the women, are a potentially lucrative market for the retailer who can offer the right formula.

2005 年，英国居住人口中的有将近 56% 的年龄在 35 岁或以上。到 2010 年，预计 45 ~ 54 岁年龄段的人口数量将比其他年龄段都增长迅速。过去，这个年龄段的人会被划归到与更老的人群一组，比起年轻他们 10 岁、20 岁、30 岁的消费者，传统上他们在时装上的开销很少，特别是男性。他们比年轻人买衣服数量少，每件衣服花费也更少。但是，从这个年龄段显露的是新“中青年”市场，就像他们有时提到的，这群人对健康、时尚和购物有极大的兴趣，他们其中的成员，特别是女性，对那些报价合乎常理的零售商来说就是个潜在的有利市场。

Going against this tradition of being the lowest spenders on clothing, in recent years, the spending of the 55–64 year olds has risen dramatically, particularly that of women. This increase is expected to continue as they benefit from inheritance money from older relatives.

近些年，出现了与 55 ~ 64 岁年龄段时装消费最低的传统认识相反的现象，他们的花销显著增加，特别是这个年龄段的女性。人们期待这种增长能持续，就像他们能从年长亲人的遗产中受益一样。

Most older groups, particularly towards the higher end of the age bracket, are not as interested in fashion as in comfort and quality of clothes. They buy fewer and lower priced items than younger people. However, price is now becoming less significant and service levels are of increasing importance. There are now more magazines aimed at them and a somewhat improved choice of merchandise in the shops. Such people are influenced in their fashion attitudes by their growing affluence and are more aware of different styles. This is mainly due to having been brought up in the post-war boom years. Retailers aiming to serve this older market are responding with updated classic ranges, particularly for women. There is, however, still an opportunity to stimulate more menswear sales to older consumers by updating ranges and retail presentation.

大多数年长群体，特别是年龄层的上端，更关注时装的舒适性和品质，而非时髦。比起年轻人，他们购买得更少也更便宜。然而，现在价格的意义已经不那么重要，服务水平正变得越来越重要。越来越多的时尚杂志以他们为目标市场，商店里也有一些可进一步选择的商品。日渐富足的生活使这些人的着装态度也受到影响，从而有意识地选择不同款式。这主要归因于战后繁荣时期成长的一代。定位于服务这个年长者市场的零售商正以最新的经典系列做出回应，尤其是对女性。与此同时，通过更新产品和销售推广方式刺激年长的男性顾客的时装消费也是个机会。

2.6.4 The social and cultural environments / 社会和文化环境因素

These can cover a wide range of issues, but are basically the society-wide influences, values and changes that can affect the market.

这些因素能涵盖的问题范围很广，但基本上是作用于市场的全社会影响、价值观和变革。

Leisure activities ／休闲活动

Changes in the amount and types of leisure activity have resulted in a move away from formal codes of dress to much more casual styling. The increased amount of leisure time that many people have, due to shorter working hours, more electronic help in the home and convenience foods, has led to a need for more clothing to wear in these leisure hours.

Leisure wear, particularly in the guise of sportswear, has become a style to wear during the whole day for most ages and socio-economicgroups. Nearly everyone wears some form of sportswear, be it T-shirts, sweatshirts, jogger bottoms or polo shirts. Tracksuits and trainers are almost a social uniform, in some parts of the market, for many daily activities such as shopping, housework, looking after children, dog walking and of course sports activities themselves.

休闲活动数量增加和种类变化已经引起了规范正统时装向更休闲着装风格化的转变。由于工作时间变短，家里越来越电器化，饮食方便快捷，许多人开始有越来越多的休闲时间，从而引发了在这些休闲时间要有更多休闲时装的需求。

休闲装，特别是运动装，已经变成大多数年龄段和各社会经济阶层的人全天可穿着的一类时装。几乎每个人都有一些运动装形式的衣服，比如T恤、运动衫、慢跑裤或polo衫。某些种类的运动服和运动鞋几乎是社会性制服，许多像购物、做家务、照看孩子、遛狗，当然还有体育活动本身，这些日常活动中均可穿着。

The role of work ／职业角色

The market for menswear and womenswear is very different in terms of the occupational status of consumers. As far as the 'working wardrobe' is concerned a wearer's occupation influences both his or her garment needs and how much they can actually spend. Changes over time in the occupations that comprise the labour market can therefore have a major effect on the overall size and composition of the domestic clothing market. The relationship between the structure of the labour market, socio-economic groups and purchasing is developed further in Chapter Three.

男装和女装市场因消费者的职业身份不同而有很大差别。提到“工作服”，穿着者的职业不仅影响他或她需要的时装，还影响他们实际能支出的置装费用。职场，包括劳动力市场，随时间产生的变化对主流时装市场的外衣尺寸和面料成分具有重要影响。劳动力市场构架、社会经济阶层和购买力之间的关系将在第3章展开论述。

The past 20 years has seen a gradual increase of working women to now make up just over 70% of the workforce. Less free time, more disposable income and a need for clothing for work all have implications for the clothing market. Although many of these women work part time, it is still be the case that working women have less free time in which to shop, but more disposable income. The desire to dress smartly, along with the desire for financial status, results in more spending on clothes for different occasions.

过去20年中，职业女性逐渐增多，如今已占到劳动力的70%之多。空闲时间减少，更多可自由支配的收入以及工作时的着装要求，所有这些都对时装市场有所启示。虽然许多女性都是做非全日制的工作，可职业女性越来越少闲暇时间去逛商场，结果使可支配收入越来越多。伴随职业女性经济地位提高的需要，得体着装的需求使得因购买应对不同场合穿着的时装要花费更多。

Women in supervisory jobs tend to spend well above the national average on their wardrobe. While there are still very few women in professional and higher managerial jobs, they do tend to spend more on their outerwear than the national average for women and are a small and highly lucrative market.

从事管理层工作的女性置装开销比一般人要多。即使从事专业领域和高级管理工作的女性不多，但比一般女性在外出着装上的花费要多的职业女性仍是一个小的高端市场。

Economically inactive women spend well below average on clothing but cover a broad spectrum of ages, purchasing power and reasons for not working, for instance they may be students, pensioners, unemployed or women whose husbands have well-paid jobs.

For working men there has been a long-term shift from blue-collar to white-collar work, which one might think would stimulate consumption. Now that the UK is enjoying high levels of employment and the steep rise in unemployment during the recession is over, sales of formal workwear have not returned to their previous levels. This is partly due to fashion changes, but pressure on the finances of many of its core customers can also be a strong contributory factor.

无经济能力的女性时装花费低于平均水平，但在年龄、购买力和不工作的原因方面却各有不同，例如，她们可能是学生、领养老金的老人、无业人员或那些丈夫收入颇丰的女性。

对职业男性来说，从蓝领升到白领需要很长时间，但可能会被认为能刺激消费。即使英国正处于雇用高峰期，经济萧条期失业率的急剧增长也已结束，职业装的销售却并未回到以前的水平。部分是由于流行的变化，但核心顾客群身上的财务压力也是一个主要因素。

Seasonal factors / 季节因素

Clothing producers and retailers have always found that demand for their goods is subject to the vagaries of the weather and the seasons. New ranges are introduced at certain times of the year in the expectation that the weather will be as normal. In the past few years the weather has been quite 'unseasonal' on many occasions. Summers have either arrived early and lasted longer than expected or even appear not to have arrived at all. Winters have been milder and suppliers have often found themselves with the wrong stock for the weather. This has led to a loss of profits either through lost sales due to shortages of clothing or through heavy discounting to get rid of leftover end-of-season stock. When viewing figures seasonally, it is necessary to look at several years together to avoid the bias of the extreme vagaries of the weather although as a trend we are buying less heavy overcoats and more summer wear.

Clothing sales are generally very low in January and February with only around 6% of the total annual consumer sales. Childrenswear is particularly weak here, whereas in September sales of school clothing make this month the second most important sales period for childrenswear. June is far more important than September for menswear and womenswear. This is the beginning of summer and the holiday season when around 10% of womenswear is bought, with menswear sales just slightly lower.

The largest amount of clothing is bought in December with 17% of total annual spending taking place. A large part of these sales is for gifts. This month is especially important for menswear as men very often receive clothing as gifts. Even the high volume of sales in the January sales in no way matches the bumper sales period before Christmas.

时装生产者和零售商总是发现他们商品的需求会受制于天气和季节。新系列发布在每年人们期待的那个特定时期，天气也会一如往常。过去几年中的天气在很多情况下相当“不合时宜”。夏天不是太早到来并比预期持续的更久，就是根本没来。冬天也越来越暖和，供应商们经常发现自己的应季货品备错了库存。不管是因货品短缺造成脱销，还是为避免季末库存积压而大幅度打折，都导致了利润损失。当看季度数据报表时，有必要一起看一下几年之内的，以避免天气的极度非正常变化，虽然我们的厚重外套买得越来越少、夏装买得越来越多已成趋势。

1 月和 2 月的时装销售量一般都非常低，仅占年度消费总量的 6% 左右。童装销售尤其薄弱，然而 9 月童装的销量却让这个月成为童装销售期的第二个重要月份。对于男装和女装市场，6 月远比 9 月重要得多。这是夏天和假期的开始，大约 10% 的女装在该月购买，男装略低。

时装购买量最大在 12 月，占全年花销的 17%。其中有大部分是礼品。这个月份对男装市场尤其重要，因为男性常会收到的礼物是衣服。甚至 1 月销售的高销量也无法与圣诞节前销售缓冲期的销量相提并论。

2.6.5 'Green' and ethical issues / "环保"和社会道德问题

As many consumers are accepting the concept of conserving and recycling in other areas such as washing powders and paper, so they may soon be questioning the need for constant renewal and replacement of clothing to follow fashion. To the environmentalist an industry that advocates continual change and ensures inbuilt obsolescence in its products is far from attractive.

To satisfy the environmentally conscious consumer the pace of fashion changes must slow down. The emphasis needs to shift from short-term fads to durable styles, comfort, quality and real innovations in fabrics and style that add to garments. There is already pressure to develop 'green fabrics' with demand for more organic cotton and an increased use of hemp but 'green clothing' is also likely to become an increasingly important issue. There will be a need for the recycling of fibres and fabrics, and production of biodegradable clothing.

Since successful companies need to recognize and anticipate consumer needs and desires, research and development into these environmental issues should be happening now.

Aligned to the concern of fabrics themselves is a concern over manufacturing conditions now that so many garments come from countries where wages are low and working conditions can be bad.

Green issues: the response of retailers

There have been several attempts to launch environmental clothing ranges by labels such as Esprit and Claus Steilmann, but the high-profile attempts by some parts of the fashion industry to become greener have yet to have any significant impact. At the retail end of the business, the major chain stores are examining how they can run their stores in a more environmentally friendly way. Most of their efforts may appear minor, but in total they could be quite significant.

Environmental efforts include:

◆ the use of recycled paper for till rolls;

◆ using recycled plastic and actually recycling garment overbags;

◆ recycling hangers and not offering them to the customer, but returning them to the clothing manufacturer to use again;

许多消费者正接受诸如洗衣粉和纸张等其他领域的资源保护和循环利用的理念，因此他们会很快质疑有无必要为跟随时尚而不断更新和替换时装。环境论者看来，一个拥护不断变化并确定在产品中加入了废弃物的工厂是完全没有吸引力的。

为迎合有环保意识的消费者，时装变化的步调必须减缓。重点需要从短期的时髦品转到耐久的时装，以及赋予时装舒适、优质的面料和款式的真正革新。随着有机棉和麻纤维使用需求增多，开发"绿色面料"已经势在必行，但"绿色时装"也很可能变成一个日益重要的问题。纤维和面料的循环利用和可生物降解时装的生产都会成为一种需要。

鉴于成功的企业需要认识并预测消费者的需要和欲望，因此现在应该针对这些环境问题进行研究和改善。

既然有那么多时装都来自工资低、工作环境恶劣的国家，所以关注面料本身的同时也应关注制造条件。

环保问题：零售商的反应

埃斯普利特和克劳斯・斯丹曼等一些品牌曾尝试将环保时装系列投放市场，但时装业的某些商家为更环保而做出的颇为高调的努力并未收到任何显著的影响效果。在商业链条的零售终端，主要的连锁店正考察如何用更利于环保的方式经营他们的店铺。其中大多数努力看起来很微小，但总体上他们收效明显。

环保性的尝试包括：

◆ 收银台小票卷纸用再生纸；

◆ 用再生塑料袋和循环使用的时装包装袋；

◆ 不提供衣架给顾客，而是循环使用衣架，并将其返给生产商再次利用；

◆ using less packaging: Marks and Spencer now use virtually no extra packaging for most of its garments, a far cry from when jumpers were all packed in cardboard and cellophane;

◆ using fewer hardwoods for fittings in store design;

◆ using more energy efficient transport, etc.

Hoechst, a European polyester and fibre manufacturer, was the first fibre company to gain a certificate under EMAS, the European Eco-Management and Audit Scheme. The review of its environmental practices led to a comprehensive report on energy and water consumption, production emissions and recycling.

Marks and Spencer, in particular, are taking environmental concerns into account. They are aiming to keep abreast of such issues and take them into consideration in their buying decisions and operational areas.

◆ 少用包装：玛莎百货现在的大多数时装很少使用额外包装，与夹克都用硬纸和玻璃纸包装的做法大相径庭；

◆ 店铺设计的装置尽量少用硬木材；

◆ 采用更节能的运输方式等。

赫克斯特，欧洲一家涤纶和纤维生产商，是第一家获得欧洲环境管理与审查机构（EMAS）认定的纤维公司。对它环保实践的审查后生成了一份关于能源和水资源消耗、生产废料和循环利用等的全面报告。

应特别指出的是，玛莎百货正将环保事务纳入考虑范畴。他们与时俱进，并在采购计划和操作领域里顾及环境因素。

Second-hand clothing ／二手时装

In some high street shopping centres charity shops seem to be almost as common as new clothing shops. The huge increase in the number of these and second-hand clothing outlets can be explained in many ways. As people buy more new clothing the second-hand clothing shops are an obvious place for them to dispose of their unwanted fashions from last season. Economic reasons could lead us to assume that lack of money means that the only clothing some people can afford is from the second-hand market. Or it could be that more environmentally conscious people are preferring to buy second hand and so recycling clothing rather than always buying new. The retro look of the late 1990s meant that second-hand clothes shops were a good source of desirable genuinely fashionable items.

One 'new' trend for the 2000s, partly fuelled by its popularity at red carpet events such as the Oscars, is vintage clothing. Be it a 1950s Dior dress or a 1970s Vivienne Westwood T-shirt, period pieces by well-known designers are becoming much sought after. Top Shop on Oxford Street, London, has a whole floor devoted to vintage clothing and several of London's famous markets such as Portobello Road are good hunting grounds for second-hand/recycled/vintage clothes. Many new websites have been launched devoted to the buying and selling of garments from another era. Ebay, whilst not exclusively selling clothing and accessories, plays a big part in this desire for recycled fashion.

在许多繁华商业街购物中心，旧货店几乎和新装店一样常见。旧货店和二手时装折扣店的大幅增加原因可从许多方面给予说明。由于人们购买的新衣服越来越多，对他们来说能将不想要的上一季的时髦货处理掉，二手时装店无疑是首选之地。经济方面的原因就是有些人因为囊中羞涩只能付得起二手时装的价格。或者，对很有环保意识的人，比起买新衣服他们更愿意购买二手时装和循环利用的时装。回头看 20 世纪 90 年代末，二手时装店是淘稀缺时髦货的好去处。

受红地毯流行趋势影响，像奥斯卡颁奖礼的红毯时尚，21 世纪初的一个新趋势便是古董服饰。20 世纪 50 年代的迪奥裙装，或者 70 年代薇薇安・韦斯特伍德的 T 恤，知名设计师当年的单品正越来越吃香。伦敦牛津大街上的屋脊商店有一整层卖古董服饰，几家伦敦知名的商场，像波特贝罗路，则是猎获二手时装 / 循环穿用时装 / 古董服饰的好去处。许多新的网站也已致力于其他时期时装的买卖。易趣虽然不专卖时装和服饰配件，但有很大部分是卖循环利用的时髦服饰。

Environmentally friendly fabrics ／环保型面料

During the late 1980s, when there was a sudden focus on environmental issues, the textile industry was forced to improve its processes as a result of increased legislation. It had become evident that environmental damage was being caused by gaseous and liquid emissions from the industrial processes of many producers, including textiles.

New legislation covers, among other things, the wet processing activities such as dyeing and finishing. Already, many firms are spending large sums to reduce gaseous emissions from their processes and are investing in systems for recycling dyestuffs and other chemicals and even water.

There is much misinformation in the media that natural fibre fabrics are best, leading many people to think that natural fibres are good for the environment and synthetics are automatically bad. Most of this thinking is based on negative perceptions of the chemical industry. Although natural fibres biodegrade more easily, some give off toxic gases as they do so. Some processes for making synthetic fibres are actually friendlier to the environment than those for making natural fibres, especially when energy and water usage are taken into consideration.

It is not only the manufacture of the fabrics that is of concern, but how they biodegrade after disposal. Germany's leading clothing producers have been working on a range of biodegradable garments.

While the textile industry is usually blamed for the unfriendly emissions and wastage, it is arguable that the clothing manufacturers and fashion designers should really be blamed. They are the ones who dictate that strong dyed fabrics are required or non-crease products that need to be made from the thermoplastic properties of synthetics. The clothing and textile industries need to integrate their efforts for the future.

Whilst the consumer does not often consider the manufacturing processes, the desire for organic products, popular among food stuffs, has also moved into clothing. The use of organically grown natural fibres fulfils the needs of those with sensitive skin who react to chemicals and those with a greater environmental conscience.

20 世纪 80 年代，对环境问题的关注陡然显现，纺织业鉴于日益增加的相关立法不得不改善其作业流程。很明显，纺织业环境污染由许多制造业的工厂排放的气体和液体废物引起。

新的立法涵盖了印染和后整理等操作。许多工厂已经在减少生产过程废气排放方面花费了很多，投资购买染料、其他化学制剂甚至水等可循环利用的系统。

媒体上有很多关于天然纤维最棒的错误信息，使得许多人认为天然纤维有益于环境，而人造纤维不好。大多数持这类观点者均基于对化工行业的负面理解。虽然天然纤维更易降解，但有的也会释放有害气体。一些合成纤维的生产过程比天然纤维的更环保，特别是将能源和水资源利用的因素考虑在内。

不仅要关注面料的生产，面料废弃后的降解过程同样需要注意。德国领先的时装厂商已开始致力于可降解时装产品线的开发。

尽管纺织业常因污染物排放和资源浪费饱受指责，但时装厂商和时装设计师是否真的应该受责备仍存争议。他们指出，印染面料是需要的，制造防皱产品也需利用合成纤维的热塑性能。纺织行业和时装行业需要齐心协力应对未来。

虽然消费者并不常常考虑生产过程，但在食品领域流行的对有机产品的需求也转移到时装界。有机长成的天然纤维的使用满足了那些对化学品有不良反应的敏感肤质人群的需求，也满足了那些环保意识强烈的人群的需求。

Fair trade ／公平贸易

With such a large proportion of clothing imported from overseas, concerns are growing regarding the working conditions within factories in some Asian countries. Large organizations such as Marks and Spencer and Nike have been accused of outsourcing to factories using the so-called 'sweatshop' labour. Often employing children, long working days in potentially unsafe and uncomfortable conditions are demanded in return for very low pay. Companies need to be able to reassure their customers that goods are manufactured ethically and fairly by closely monitoring the factories that supply them.

鉴于从国外进口的时装所占比例之大，因此对一些亚洲国家工厂工作环境的关注也在增加。像玛莎百货和耐克一些大企业已经因外购工厂使用所谓的“血汗工厂”劳动力而受到控告。血汗工厂经常使用童工，延长在危险的不适环境中的工作时间，而付给工人的工资极低。企业需要通过密切监控他们的供货工厂，以使其顾客消除疑虑，保证所生产货品是合乎职业道德和光明正大的。

Some smaller organizations use overseas labour not for their low wages and ability to mass produce, but for the special skills that people can offer in hand-made garments.

一些小的企业使用海外劳工不仅因为他们的低廉工资和能从事批量化生产，还因为一些有特殊技艺的人能提供手工制作的时装。

'Green' fashions ／“绿色”时装

Green fashion can be viewed in several different ways. On a simple level there is a growing movement against labels and conspicuous consumption. Some people are shying away from dressiness and are returning to basic clothing. Basics are usually part of traditional workwear – they have a high degree of functionality, and are simply cut and built to last. Doctor Marten boots and denim jeans are items of clothing that could be considered to be following the green ethos of less consumption as they are classic items that will not date and will only need replacing when they have worn out. Some of these views are shown in Figure 2.8.

绿色时装被认为有几种不同的形式。从简单层面上讲是正在兴起的反标签和炫耀性消费运动。有的人羞于时髦的穿着而回归基本款服饰。基本款通常是传统工作服的一部分——它们有高度的功能性、剪裁简单、穿用持久。马丁博士的靴子和牛仔就是这类时装，它们遵循少消费的绿色理念，因为它们都是不会过时的经典时装，只需在穿坏时替换即可。这类观点如图 2–8 所示。

In the late 1980s we also had the 'ecology look'. Fabrics were natural in both feel and colour. T-shirts available from the designer shop to the local chain store were adorned with environmental messages. Coming at a time when consumers had had enough of overt consumerism and the Yuppie look, the ecology look fitted in nicely as a contrast to the structured silhouettes and wide shoulders of the previous fashion.

20 世纪 80 年代末，我们还有“生态服装”。面料在手感和色彩上都是天然的。从设计师品牌到当地连锁店，可买到的 T 恤上都装饰了环保广告词。当消费者受够了明显的消费者主义，雅痞装时代来临，这类装束有较合体的原生态造型，与之前强调廓型和宽肩的潮流截然相反。

The controversy over who is to blame for the less environmentally friendly fabrics, designer or textile manufacturer has not gone unnoticed by some designers. Most denim producers have replaced traditional chemical finishing by using pumice stone to achieve a stonewashed fabric finish. These new fabrics

把责任归咎于使用和生产不环保面料的纺织厂商的论战已经引起某些设计师的注意。大多数牛仔生产者已经将传统的化学后整理替换成了用浮石达到石洗面料的处理效果。这些新的面料和工艺流

Figure 2.8 How 'green' can you be in fashion? 图 2–8 你能在时装上多“环保”

and processes will cost the consumer more. As with many environmentally friendly products there is a conflict of interest. Consumers and retailers seem to want new, environmentally sustaining products but are reluctant to pay for the additional cost involved.

Friends of the Earth have produced ranges of 'green' fashions using unbleached, undyed cotton. This satisfied the ecology issue but not the fashion issue, and sales have been rather limited. They were avoiding the issue by not using any processes rather than finding 'green' solutions to enable fabrics to be used for fashion items.

The next logical stage is for designers to now take these issues on board. Many, such as Katharine Hamnett, are concerned about the fabrics they use and are developing more environmentally friendly fabrics. It has taken time for these to 'trickle down' to appear in the garments stocked in high street shops and they still do not constitute a large part of what we buy. One company, Edun, set up by Bono and Alison Hewson aims to offer a clothing line for people with a social conscience. They use organic fabrics, made up in environmentally friendly factories with ethical working conditions.

Paris held the first 'Ethical Fashion Show' in 2004 offering a platform for ethical and environmental designers around the world to showcase their clothing and accessories. Now an annual event, up to 50 designers show to the increasing number of distributors who want to sell designs that are ethically produced and environmentally friendly.

Another environmental concern for consumers is the risk of skin cancer that depletion of the ozone layer

程会让消费者花费得更多。与许多环保产品相伴而生的就是利润上的冲突。消费者和零售商似乎都想要新的环保持续型产品，但谁也不情愿为增加的额外费用埋单。

地球之友已经用未漂白、未染色的棉生产出“绿色”系列时装。这满足了生态时装论，但非时尚论，因而销售相当受限。相比找寻用于各类时装的服用面料的“绿色”方案，他们未用任何处理过程就避开了问题。

对于设计师，接下来的符合逻辑的阶段就是现在要接受这些问题。像凯瑟琳·哈姆内特，许多公司已经开始关注他们使用的面料并正在开发更利于环境的面料。这些“穿石之滴水”，出现在繁华商业街店铺的时装库存中，需花费不少时间，而且，它们仍不能占据我们购买的时装的大部分。一家由波诺和艾莉森·亨森创立的名为艾顿的公司，致力于为具有社会意识的人群提供时装系列产品。他们使用有机面料，是在环保工厂里，合乎道德的工作条件下生产的。

2004 年，巴黎举办了第一场“道德时装秀”，为全世界的道德主义和环保主义设计师们提供了一个平台来展示他们的时装和饰物。现在每年一次，多达 50 位设计师面向那些日益增多的想要售卖道德化加工和环保主义时装的分销商们做展示。

消费者的另一个环境关注点是皮肤癌的危险，臭氧层的损耗和阳光的过度暴露

and excessive exposure to the sun may bring about. New ranges of beach and swimwear offering UV protection of up to 97% are being seen at holiday resorts, offering even more opportunity for Lycra.

会引发此类病症。在旅游胜地，人们所见沙滩装和泳装的新产品系列提供高达 97% 的 UV 保护，这也给莱卡提供了更多的良机。

2.6.6 Economy / 经济因素

General economic factors such as income, employment and home ownership have just as great an effect on the clothing industry as on other product groups. Consumer expenditure on new clothing is very dependent on the general state of the economy measured by the gross national product (GNP), their employment status and their disposable income. There are many other factors that influence the shape of the market for clothing and footwear. Consumer spending is influenced by some economic factors mentioned above while lifestyle changes that occur, such as getting married, having children, children leaving home and retirement, all alter people's requirements and aspirations for clothing and footwear. Clothing is one area where in recent years there has been price deflation, sales growth in volume is exceeding sales growth by value, people aren't buying less clothes but the clothes are becoming cheaper. In the 1960, households spent on average 10.3% of their income on clothing. This fell to less than 6% in the late 1990s and have more or less stayed at that figure ever since. This relatively low figure can be accounted for by the ability of manufacturers and retailers to source from around the world and constantly respond to competitive pressure on prices.

与其他类工业产品一样，普遍的经济因素，如收入、工作和房屋所有权等，也对时装业影响很大。消费者购置新衣的支出正是取决于经济的普遍水平（由国民生产总值衡量）、工作地位和可支配收入的情况。也有很多其他因素影响时装和鞋的市场模式。消费者开销也受上面提及的生活方式改变等经济因素的影响，比如结婚、生子、孩子独立和退休，所有这些都会改变人们对时装和鞋的需求和渴望。近些年，时装是价格降低的领域之一，销售增长的数量超越了销售增长的价值，人们没有少买衣服可是衣服却变得更便宜了。20 世纪 60 年代，家庭收入支出在时装上平均为 10.3%。20 世纪 90 年代末，下降到不足 6%，自那时起，便在这个数字上下徘徊。这个相对较低的数字可归咎于生产商和零售商资源全球化的能力增强，以及对价格竞争压力的持续反应。

Recession versus 'feel good factor' / 经济衰退与“利好因素”

In the late 1980s and continuing into the early 1990s the UK was in a recession that was mirrored throughout the world. Increasing unemployment and high interest rates led consumers to be wary of spending more than was necessary. This in turn led to more frugal spending on clothing and a partial rejection of fashions that require a total new look, causing a move towards more classic styles that will last beyond the next season.

By the late 1990s there was discussion in the media of a 'feel good factor' in the economy, but this did not necessarily reach the clothing stores, many of which had somewhat lost their direction and positioning in terms of consumer needs. In the new millennium people may feel the benefit of low inflation rates, easily available credit and a consumer confidence that their standard of living will stay the same or get better. This can lead to

从 20 世纪 80 年代末一直到 90 年代初，英国经历了全世界范围的经济衰退。上涨的失业率和高利率使得消费者花钱更加谨慎。随之导致了时装上更多的节俭性开支，以及对那些需要全新形象的时尚潮流的部分抗拒，这引发了向能穿用不止一季的更多经典款式的消费转移。

到 90 年代末，媒体上有关于经济“利好因素”的讨论，但这并未必然延伸到时装店铺，许多店家都多少迷失了经营方向，按照顾客需求的营销定位。新千禧年中，人们可能感受到了低通胀率、便利信贷、坚信生活水平会保持或更好的消费信心带来的好处。但这并未引起

more spending but with clothing, and the price deflation experienced in the market, more items purchased do not necessarily relate to more spending overall.

时装开销的增加，加之市场上的价格降低，即使购买再多的时装也未必与总消费额的增加有联系。

Unemployment ／失业

Local spending power can be greatly influenced by unemployment, which varies considerably from region to region within the UK. The retail sector of whole towns can be devastated by the closure of a large local employer.

失业问题对当地消费能力影响很大，在英国各个地区的失业情况差异很大。整个城镇的零售业可能因一家当地大型雇用单位的倒闭而崩溃。

Home ownership ／自置居所

Home ownership has been increasing steadily since the end of World War II. However, as interest rates rose, the cost of mortgages greatly increased for a time, putting pressure on owner-occupied households. Even as rates began to fall again, consumer caution and the switch to saving spare cash may not result in the anticipated increase in spending. With average house prices having risen more than two and a half times over the past 10 years, homeowners have gained in confidence as they have seen the price of their house rise (Table 2.8). Coupled with relatively low interest rates homeowners have been able to spend more on themselves. They are more willing to access the equity in their homes by remortgaging. Conversely high house prices mean that it is hard to get a foothold onto the property ladder for first time buyers. They are having to save hard for a deposit and then take out large mortgages to buy even the most modest property.

自第二次世界大战末以来，自置居所数量一直稳定增长。然而，随着利率上扬，抵押成本一时间大幅增加，给房屋居住自用的家庭带来了压力。即使利率开始再次下降，消费者的谨慎和转而存储多余现金的做法也不能使消费开支有预期中的上涨。在过去 10 多年里，房屋价格已经涨了 2.5 倍还多，房屋所有者获得了信心，就像他们看到自己房子的价格涨了一样（见表 2–8）。与相对较低的利率相联系，房屋所有者们已经能在自己身上多花费一些。他们更期望通过再次抵押房子而获得资产净增。相反地，对于首次买房的人，高房价意味着很难在财富阶梯上找到立足之地。

Table 2.8 House price increases 1997–2006 (index 1997 = 100)
表 2–8 1997 ~ 2006 年英国房屋价格上涨情况（指数 1997=100）

Year 年度	Standard Price 标准价格	Index 指数
1997	68042	100.0
1998	71704	105.4
1999	81595	119.9
2000	84293	123.9
2001	90590	133.1
2002	106195	156.1
2003	129450	190.3
2004	157091	230.9
2005	162783	239.2
2006	177962	261.5

Source: Adapted from Halifax UK House Price Index. 资料来源：选自《英国哈利法克斯房屋价格指数》。

Credit cards /信用卡

There is concern that consumers and their willingness to take out personal loans and credit will follow the pattern of the 1980s. At that time consumers were more willing to borrow when their homes rose in value and were confident to extend their personal loans in the knowledge that their assets were appreciating in value faster than the rate of inflation. However, as the rise in interest rates caused depression of the housing market, and the value of some properties fell, the banks, so willing to lend in the 1980s, restricted credit. Spending on plastic cards has increased over four times the amount spent 10 years ago, although this does include debit as well as credit cards. Usage of store cards as consumers have realized the high interest rates being charged or as they are converted into store credit cards, likes Marks and Spencer, where purchases can be made in other stores using a Marks and Spencer credit/store card.

有一种观点认为，消费者办理个人贷款和信用的意愿将遵循20世纪80年代的模式。那时，消费者当看到房屋涨价时更愿意借贷，并有信心增加个人贷款，因为他们认为自己的资产增值将比通胀率增长更快。然而，20世纪80年代的利率上扬引起房屋市场的不景气，一些财富贬值，银行则十分乐意受限信贷。信用卡消费比10年前增加了4倍多，尽管这包括了借方的信用卡。当消费者认识到所负荷的高利率或当他们转向店铺信用卡时，店铺信用卡开始使用，如用玛莎百货的信用/店铺卡也能在其他店里购物。

The rest of Europe does not have the same love of credit cards and willingness to go into debt as the British, having a much greater reluctance to take on the high levels of debt as seen in the UK.

欧洲其他国家并不像英国人那样钟爱信用卡消费和自愿负债度日，对在英国见到的那种高额借贷也不愿接受。

European Monetary Union /欧洲货币联盟

In January 1999, 11 of the 15 EU members at that time joined the European Monetary Union (EMU) and now have a single currency – the Euro. Currently, the UK Government does not feel that the economy fulfils the five economic tests set out by the Maastricht Treaty, and so UK membership is still on hold. The likely addition of the UK to the EMU in the next few years will mean that stores will trade in the Euro. UK retailers will gain the chance to trade more easily in a wider European market although this will also mean more competition. It will be possible for EU consumers to easily buy throughout Europe and the world via the Internet.

1999年1月，15个欧盟成员国中的11个加入了欧洲货币联盟（简称EMU），并有其独立的货币——欧元。现如今，英国政府感觉本国经济未满足《马斯特里赫特条约》设立的5项经济测试标准，因此，英国仍坚持不加入欧元区。接下来几年里如果英国加入欧洲货币联盟，那意味着商家将在欧洲进行贸易。英国的零售商将有机会在更广阔的欧洲市场更便捷地做生意，当然，这也意味着更多的竞争。对欧洲消费者来说，将有可能通过网络在全欧洲和世界范围内便利购物。

Exchange rates /汇率

Both exports and imports are greatly affected by the strength of the pound. Since the late 1990s sterling was particularly strong, making imported clothing cheaper and hampering clothing exports by increasing their costs in foreign markets.

出口和进口都很大程度上受英镑实力的影响。自20世纪90年代末，英镑尤其强劲，令进口时装更便宜，而由于海外市场自身成本的增加则限制了时装出口。

2.7 Trends in the marketing environment ／营销环境中的趋势

Trends are relatively slow-moving changes in the marketplace that can occur for a variety of reasons, and businesses ignore them at their peril. Sometimes trends are business led and sometimes consumers lead the way. General fashions can change very quickly and go from one extreme to another whereas trends in clothing fashion tend to be slower and build upon themselves rather than ignore what went before.

趋势是市场中相对缓慢的变化，可由许多原因引起，因此商家往往会忽视自己正身处险境。有时趋势受控于商家，有时由消费者引领。时尚可以变化很快，从一个极端到另一个极端，而时装时尚趋势变化较慢，是在自身基础上发展建立的。

2.7.1 Styles and consumer preferences ／风格与消费者喜好

While there probably will always be people who are interested in high fashion there has been a noticeable move away from status and image dressing. Consumers still demand fashion, but they are requiring more understated styles that combine realism, comfort and practicality.

Changing work and lifestyles, with more time for leisure pursuits, are speeding the change from formal wear to a more casual look and sportswear. There is an increasing blur of divisions between active wear and fashion. Sometimes the sports store and boutique seem to be carrying almost the same merchandise.

The explosion in sportswear sales has been accompanied by a sharp rise in demand for other casual garments. Sales of conventional jumpers and cardigans have suffered a severe contraction as casual knitwear such as T-shirts and sweatshirts have grown in popularity.

Demand for womenswear is as crucial as ever to the health of the domestic clothing market. Demographic changes have already been mentioned and these will quickly affect the relevant markets. First, the upper end of the children's market should be considered. Secondly, customers in their late forties and fifties represent a great opportunity.

These changes and the long-term weather pattern are encouraging lighter weight clothing and trans-seasonal clothes, where many people no longer have a winter and summer wardrobe, but use the same clothes year-round. There are two distinct shifts in clothes labelling. Many manufacturers are continuing to manufacture or source under their own brand, such as Dorothy Perkins, Next or Karen Millen. Other stores are using and promoting the clothing designers themselves or bringing in strong brand

尽管可能一直有人关注前沿时尚，但仍与现实中的身份和形象着装相距甚远。消费者仍需要时尚，但他们更需要综合了现实性、舒适性和实用性的朴素款式。

休闲时间增多带来的工作和生活方式的变化，加速了正装向休闲运动装的转变。介于运动装与时装之间的界限越来越模糊。有时，运动装店和那些潮流店看上去几乎卖同样的东西。

运动装销量的暴涨伴随着其他休闲时装需求的急速增加。传统夹克和开襟毛衫的销售正面临严重收缩，因为像T恤、运动衫一类的休闲针织衣正越来越流行。

对于主流时装市场，女装需求一如既往地至关重要。人口的变化在前面已经提到，很快会对相关市场产生影响。首先，儿童市场的上端应被关注。其次，四五十岁这个年龄段的顾客里蕴藏着巨大商机。

这些变化和长期不变的天气模式对轻薄时装和跨季节时装提出了要求，人们不再有冬装衣柜和夏装衣柜，而是全年穿用同样的衣服。时装标签上有两个鲜明的变化。许多生产商继续做自己品牌或生产其他品牌的时装，像多萝西·帕金斯，奈克斯特或者克伦·米雷顿。其他商家正起用和

names, particularly in the area of sports clothing. Some of these issues concerning taste preferences and seasonal aspects are developed further in Chapter Six in the context of product development.

推广他们自己的设计师，或加盟强势品牌，特别是在运动装领域。关注品位喜好和季节因素的一些观点将在第6章产品开发章节展开论述。

2.7.2 Manufacturing ／生产

Retailers are increasingly under pressure to carry less stock in the interests of greater efficiency, and to offer the customer more choice, more often. This means that suppliers are required to deliver shorter runs of merchandise more frequently than in the past.

零售商常常处于日益增加的压力之下，要降低库存以更高效地获利，又要提供给顾客更多的选择。这意味着供货商需要比以往更频繁地缩短商品运营流程。

Too many manufacturers have also been taking a back seat and relying on retailers to keep them in touch with customers' demands. In the future the most successful manufacturers will be those who invest in market research, design and technology.

太多生产商处于默默无闻的地位并依赖零售商以保持与消费者需求的联系。今后，最成功的生产商将会是那些对市场调查、设计和技术进行投入的生产商。

2.7.3 Trends in fibres and fabrics ／纤维和面料趋势

Performance and versatility are becoming increasingly important. Customers are beginning to seek out specially engineered high-tech, high-performance fibres and fabrics such as Lycra and the tactile fabrics and ask for them by name. They are looking for fabrics to fulfil not only a fashion or style function, but also a clearly defined performance need.

性能和多功能性变得日渐重要。顾客开始想要获得经过特殊设计的那些高科技、高性能的纤维和面料，比如莱卡和触觉面料，并会通过名称去寻找它们。他们寻找的面料不仅仅要时尚或风格化，而且还要有一个明确界定的功能。

Polyester and cotton are still the most widely used fibres, either on their own or as the dominant (50% or more) fibre in a blend; however, natural fibres are still more popular, and it is expected that their use, often for reasons of cost and handling properties, will rise further. Polyester is gradually losing ground and more cotton-rich blends are being used. Wool is still popular but for cost reasons it is again bought more as a blend than a pure fabric.

涤纶和棉仍是使用最广泛的纤维，或单独运用，或在混纺中充当主要成分（50% 或以上）；尽管天然纤维较为流行，但受成本和手感特性原因所限，人们预期未来混纺面料的使用会大大增加。涤纶渐行渐远，越来越多的富棉混纺被使用。羊毛依然流行，但出于成本原因，买混纺羊毛的比纯羊毛的更多。

The main area of development in fabrics is still in blending stretch Elastane yarns. They are being applied to a much wider range of fabrics either for fashion effect in body-hugging styling or for comfort and recovery in outerwear and tailoring.

面料开发的主要领域一直是混纺弹性纱。不管是为获得紧身合体的时尚造型还是令外衣和套装舒适、保型好，它们正被大范围应用到织物中。

Microfibres such as superfine polyesters and polyamides in new forms and applications, especially in blends with other fibres and knitwear, are likely to remain the main area of interest for some time to come.

超细旦纤维比如超细涤纶和锦纶以新形式和新用途，特别是与其他纤维混纺在针织物中，很可能今后一段时间内仍是主要的收益点。

Changes in the pattern of shopping ／购物模式的变化

Despite current government policy to limit the increase in out-of-town developments, the trend is towards large drive to shopping malls and complexes. This shopping trend is supplemented by the growth in catalogues and may be joined by a move towards electronic shopping.

目前政府的政策要限制增加城外开发区（译者注：城外开发区意味着更多的人依赖汽车，对老年人和残疾人造成很多困难），这个趋势就是朝向购物中心和百货店的大规模运作模式发展。这种购物趋势可以通过邮购商品目录来达到增长，还可以融合动态的电子购物。

2.8 Summary ／小结

◆ This is a time of change for the clothing market. The companies who survive will be the ones who initiate change and adapt. There is not much scope for those who are slow and lag behind. In the medium term there seems little prospect of a return to the high rates of growth in clothing sales seen during much of the 1980s.

◆ 对时装市场而言这是一个变革的时代。存活下来的企业是那些主动应变并适应变化的，而缓慢滞后的企业则机会甚少。20 世纪 80 年代所见的时装销售高增长率看来不易企及。

◆ Unless they can offer the discounted prices and high value that customers are looking for, many companies will find that they can only survive by moving away from these price-sensitive parts of the market into segments where quality, design, variety and quick response to changes in fashion and consumer tastes matter more than price. Although now with an expectation of low prices, it will be hard for customers to accept much in the way of price increases as spare income has already been allocated to other things. If anything they are moving the other way, demanding more quality and styling from retailers whilst still keeping prices low.

◆ 除非公司能提供顾客所寻找的物美价廉的时装，否则要想生存，只能远离这些价格敏感的市场领域，转而专注到其他环节，像时装的品质、设计、多样化以及针对时尚和消费品位变化做出的快速反应比价格更重要。因而不用太指望低价，因为多余的收入已经投放到其他环节上了，但对消费者来说，接受价格上涨十分困难，不管在其他环节上公司有何种转换，消费者仍然要求零售商的时装更优质、更时尚，同时保持低价位。

◆ In terms of clothing people are growing older later and there will be opportunities for producers and retailers who can meet the demand from older and more discerning customers who are looking for the current fashion styling in their clothing but adapted more closely to their needs such as better quality, more comfortable styling and well-informed friendly service.

◆ 就时装而言，随着人们渐渐变老之后，对于那些能满足老年人需求和比较挑剔的消费者的生产商和零售商来说就有了诸多机会。这些消费者在时装中寻找时下流行的样式，而且接受更加贴近其需求，例如品质上乘，款式比较舒适、服务又快又好的时装。

◆ The market is not changing very much in overall size but there will be major demographic growth in certain areas. Age bands offering significant scope for sales are among the young adults (20–24) and 45–54 year olds.

◆ 市场总体规模变化并不大，但在某些区域会有很大的人口统计学上的增长。针对销售所给出的明显范围的年龄带是介于年轻成人（20 ~ 24 岁）和 45 ~ 54 岁者。

◆ There is an increasing interest in designer labels

◆ 设计师品牌利润的日益上涨，导致

resulting in more diffused lines and more mixing of labels and clothing at very different price points.

产生了更宽泛的产品线、品牌的更多混合，以及不同价格点的时装。

◆ Garments manufactured overseas are dominating the UK High Street. To compete the UK has to offer a quick response, meaning low stock levels for the retailer, especially as the seasons become less distinct and retailers want to offer more frequent seasonal ranges.

◆ 海外生产的时装正主宰着英国的繁华商业街。为应对竞争，英国不得不做出快速反应，对零售商来说就意味着低库存量，特别是季节交替变得越来越模糊，而零售商想提供更频密的季节性时装时。

◆ Customers are choosing to buy their clothes from wherever suits them best, be it high street stores, out of town shopping malls, supermarkets, catalogues or via the Internet.

◆ 消费者正从最适合自己的某个地方购买时装，可能是繁华商业街商店、城外购物中心、超市、产品目录或者通过互联网购买时装。

◆ Fashion is moving into an era where marketing techniques will be more influential than ever before. Clothing producers need to be far more aware of consumer needs. To a large extent fashion still leads, but consumers are beginning to exert more leverage in the issue. No longer will they merely wear what is dictated to them. The customer is becoming king.

◆ 时装业正进入一个营销技术比以往任何时期更具影响力的时代。时装生产者要十分关注消费者需求。很大程度上，时装本身仍是主导，但消费者开始施加更多的杠杆作用。他们将不再给什么就穿什么。顾客为王。

Further reading ／课后阅读材料

1.Blythe, J. (2006), *Principles and Practice of Marketing*, Thomson, London.
布莱斯·J.（2006），《营销理论与实践》，汤姆森出版，伦敦.

2.Brassington, F. and Pettitt, S. (2005), *Essentials of Marketing*, Prentice Hall, Harlow.
布拉辛顿·F.，佩迪特·S.（2005），《营销要领》，普兰提斯·霍尔出版，哈洛.

3.Hines, T. and Bruce, M. (2001), *Fashion Marketing: Contemporary Issues*, Butterworth-Heinemann, Oxford.
海因斯·T和布鲁斯·M（2001），《时装营销：当代问题》，巴特沃斯—海涅曼出版，牛津.

4.Mintel Reports: Value Clothing Retailing (May 2005); Clothing Retailing (July 2005); Keynote Reports: Clothing Manufacturing (May 2006); Clothing and Footwear Industry (March 2006).
明特尔报告：《时装零售价值》（2005年5月）；《时装零售》（2005年7月）；主题报告：《时装制造》（2006年5月）；《时装和鞋业》（2006年3月）.

5.Oldroyd, M. (2003/2004), *CIM Coursebook Marketing Environment*, Butterworth-Heinemann, Oxford.
奥尔德罗伊德·M.（2003/2004），《营销环境CIM教程》，巴特沃斯－海涅曼，牛津.

Part B
Understanding and Researching the Fashion Purchaser

第 2 部分　了解和调研时装买方

Chapter Three The Fashion Consumer and Organizational Buyer
第 3 章 时装消费者和团体购买者

3.1 Introduction /引言

This chapter is concerned with the behaviour of fashion consumers and organizations that purchase fashion products and services. The relevance of fashion buyer behaviour is examined and links with marketing research, market segmentation and the marketing mix are established.

本章主要探讨时装消费者和团体购买者在购买时装产品及其服务时的行为特点，分析了消费者的购买行为，将其与营销调研和市场细分相联系，确定营销组合的策略。

An outline of consumers' decision-making is given. The types of decision made by consumers are described and the stages in the decision process are discussed. From the perspective of the buyer as a problem solver the chapter then focuses on the consumer as an individual. The main psychological variables relevant to fashion consumption are identified and outlined. For example, an understanding of the perceptual process allows us to comprehend more easily why some fashion promotional messages are more effective than others.

首先给出的是消费者购买决策的过程，阐述了消费者作出购买决策的类型以及决策过程的各个阶段。从购买者的角度将其看作是个体，定义了时装消费相关的心理变量，例如从感性方面分析为什么有些促销信息比其他的信息更有效。

Fashion goods enable people to show identification with, or separation from, certain social groups. Clothing can be a symbol of belonging or alienation. To understand the fashion consumer, the broader social forces that help to shape individual buying behaviour are assessed. These social dimensions include the family, social stratification, opinion leadership and cultural factors. Some people are more ready to adopt new fashions than others, and the study of diffusion and opinion leadership helps us to understand why this occurs and what may be done to facilitate the process.

时装可以体现人们的身份，并且时装能使特定的社会群体相区分。时装也是归属或者脱离于某个群体的标志。为了解时装消费者，需要对形成个人购买行为的多个社会因素进行评价分析，这些因素包括家庭、社会阶层、意见领袖和文化因素等。有些消费者易于接受新时尚，对传播者和意见领袖进行研究有助于了解其中的原因以及如何加速某种行为的发生。

Fashion firms not only sell to fashion consumers, they also sell to other firms in the industry. An obvious form of organizational buying is sales within the fashion distribution channel and this is described in Chapter Eight. Another area of organizational buying of relevance is that of the corporate consumer, for instance the purchase of uniforms and distinctive clothing as part of a company's image. The nature of organizational buying will be outlined, and differences and similarities with consumers will be highlighted.

时装企业不仅将产品销售给一般消费者，同时也将产品销售给其他公司，第 8 章中会介绍在时装销售渠道中团体采购的形式。与团体采购相关的就是公司的消费者，例如公司购买体现企业形象的职业装或者带有识别性的时装。文中也会分析团体采购的特点，以及其与个体消费者购买行为的异同。

3.2 Why study the fashion buyer? / 为什么研究时装消费者

A central component of the definition of fashion marketing is satisfying customers' needs profitably. To achieve that it is necessary to understand consumers, their needs and wants, and how they will respond to various marketing efforts.

Everyone interested in fashion marketing brings a particular quality to their studies, i.e. their experiences as a fashion consumer. That experience is a mixed blessing. The benefits are that concepts from consumer behaviour can be understood and readily applied to one's own clothing purchases. The main drawback is the temptation to generalize and assume that all other fashion consumers behave as we do. The unfortunate fact is that the study of fashion marketing will probably change buying behaviour and make the expert fashion marketer atypical. Greater knowledge of products and promotional processes coupled with enthusiasm for fashion mean that there is a dislocation from typical consumers. Interestingly, many serious market research companies exclude marketing personnel as survey respondents because of their tendency to be atypical.

As will be seen when looking at social processes in consumer behaviour, people tend to live within fairly narrow social networks. They interact with others of similar social status and sets of interests. For fashion marketers, the danger is that these narrow social networks reinforce 'world views' of what is good about fashion and this becomes the explanation of what all consumers want. The key point is that opinions should never be accepted without question and that fashion marketing decisions should be based on evidence about the market, and not just on introspection.

Each consumer is unique and that is a good reason to trust sound marketing research rather than hunches

时装市场营销定义中的核心就是有效地满足消费者的需求，为了实现这个目标，企业必须了解消费者，以及消费者的需求和愿望，同时观察他们对不同营销行为的反应。

每个人对时装营销都有着很大的兴趣，这也便于对他们进行研究，例如他们的购买经历。了解他们从消费行为中的获益并且将这些应用于个人时装购买的研究，其前提就是要假定所有的消费者都按照我们的期望发生购买行为。不幸的是时装营销的研究有可能改变消费者的购买行为，从而使得专业的时装营销人员无法发挥专业能力。掌握有关产品和促销的大量知识，并且对时尚抱有激情，也就意味着脱离了大众的消费群。有意思的是，很多营销调研公司并没有把营销人员看作是调研对象，因为他们都属于专业人士。

当分析消费行为中的社会阅历时，我们会发现人们通常倾向于在较小的社交圈内生活。他们会和那些有着相近社会地位和兴趣的人们交往。对于营销人员来说，最大的威胁就是这种狭小的社交圈会加深消费者对时装的认知，并且这也会成为多数消费者的共识。关键之处在于我们不能理所当然地接受这种观点，因为时装营销决策是以市场为基础的，而不是自我分析得来的。

每个消费者都是独立的，来自市场调研的声音要远远比个人动机的直觉判

based on the extrapolation of personal motives. As a starting point for marketing research hunches are useful when they are regarded as ideas to be tested. Therefore we can ask:

'Do many people share this view?'
'How many?'
'Do they have any other views that are more strongly held?'

For example, a fashion designer may be inspired by the reflection that business travel for the female executive would be enhanced by a small range of light flexible garments that do not crease. This inspir-ation may come from the designer or from his or her friends. The next stage is to determine via marketing research, how many women engage in business travel and of those, how many feel that the current clothing market does not meet their precise requirements. Chapter Four provides detailed coverage of marketing research techniques used to measure the behaviour of the fashion consumer.

断更为可靠。作为营销调研的第一步，当直觉被看作是一种想法并且进行检验的时候，它是非常有用的。因此我们需要知道：

"是不是很多人会分享这个观点？"
"有多少人？"
"他们是否持有其他的观点？"

例如，一个时装设计师可能会受女性执行官商务旅行时对时装轻便和无褶皱的要求所影响，这种灵感可能来源于设计师，也可能来源于设计师的朋友。下一步就是借助市场调研分析多少女性会有商务旅行的需要，以及她们当中有多少人认为现有的市场无法满足她们的需求。第 4 章会阐述研究时装消费者购买行为时的一些市场调研技巧。

3.2.1 The role of consumer behaviour in marketing ／市场营销中消费行为的作用

Consumer behaviour provides a range of concepts to help fashion marketers think about their customers, and marketing research provides the techniques to measure those concepts. Consumer behaviour is also closely integrated with all other aspects of fashion marketing, but most notably with the selection of target markets and the development of marketing mixes. An overview is given in Figure 3.1.

消费行为中的很多方面都有益于营销人员去了解企业的顾客，同时市场调研也提供了多种方法对这些方面进行检验。消费行为和时装营销的其他方面如目标市场的选择、营销组合的决策等是紧密相关的，图 3–1 是一个基本的概况。

3.2.2 Consumer behaviour and target marketing ／消费行为和目标市场

As mentioned earlier each consumer is unique. Besides bespoke tailor-ing and couture items, most fashion marketing is concerned with the provision of standardized garments aimed at particular groups of consumers. All consumers are different from other consumers, but, and this is not contradictory, they are similar to some other consumers. The marketing of volume clothing demands that groups of consumers with similar needs be identified and then supplied with similar products. Chapter Five considers the nature of target marketing further, but for the moment the links with buyer behaviour will be noted.

If the total market for clothing is considered it can easily be seen that it really comprises many smaller segments, each with specialized needs. Obvious bases

如前所述，每个消费者都是独立的，除了高级定制和高级成衣外，多数时装营销侧重的都是为特定团体的消费者提供标准化的时装产品。所有的消费者都不是完全一样的，然而他们和其他某些消费者又具有相似性。大批量时装的销售取决于具有相似需求的消费团体的具体需要，企业会向他们提供相似的产品。第 5 章会进一步分析目标市场的特点，在此主要分析消费者的购买行为。

纵观时装市场，它由众多细分市场组成。每个细分市场都有其特定的需求。细分的指标有年龄、性别和收入等。当

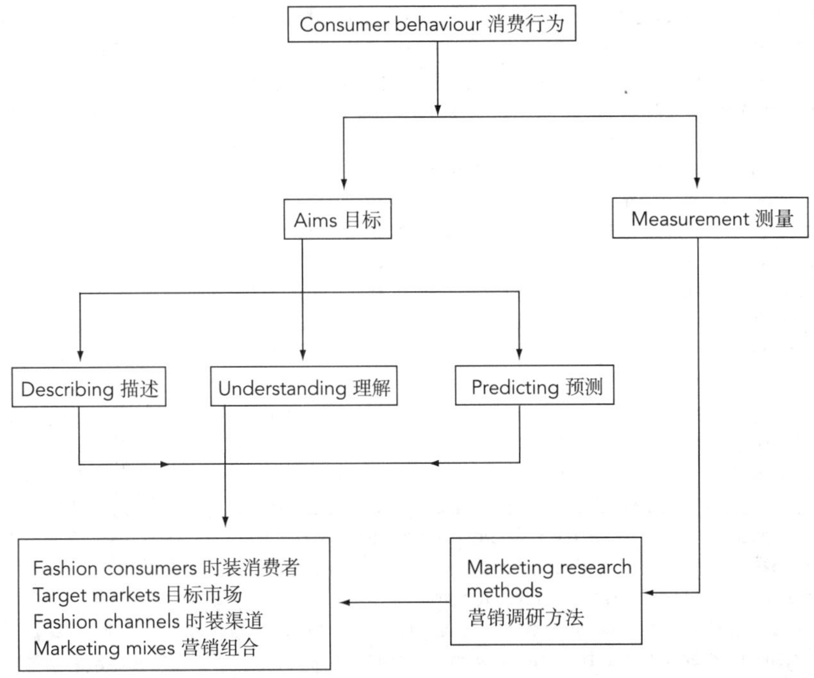

Figure 3.1 The role of consumer behaviour in fashion marketing.

图 3-1 时装营销中消费行为的作用

for the segments include age, gender and income. Less obvious, but as important, may be segments based on psychological or social characteristics that are common to significant numbers of consumers. For example, consumers differ in their levels of aspiration and also in the relationship they see between clothing and the achievement of social mobility. Throughout the twentieth century there were times when conspicuous consumption became a widely used mechanism for emphasizing new distinctions that emerged from changes in wealth and occupational structure. For example, the power dressing phase of the 1980s was followed by the 'dress-down Friday' phase of the 1990s and was succeeded by some companies reintroducing smart dress codes for work in the early 2000s. Socially aspirant groups will often seek clothing to support and reinforce their changing status. The fashion designer of the twenty-first century must meet these needs in a way that engages these social aspirations, yet is sensitive to the prevailing values concerning overt displays of wealth and social distinction. It is the understanding of these types of consumer needs that is the essence of consumer behaviour and the subsequent identification of suitable target markets for fashion firms.

然，较为隐性的但很重要的指标还有个人心理和社会角色等。例如，消费者的欲望不同，在人际关系中他们的着装和社会成就也有差异。在 20 世纪的一段时期里，炫耀性的消费被看作财富和职业结构的衡量标准。例如，20 世纪 80 年代的穿衣影响了 20 世纪 90 年代的“星期五便服”，并且在 21 世纪被很多公司重新设计为工作时穿着的时髦时装。追求社会地位的群体购买时装时会选择那些彰显自身身份的时装。21 世纪的设计师必须要满足消费者对社会地位的追求，同时要关注时装所象征的财富和社会身份。对于时装企业而言，了解这类消费者的需求是研究消费行为并且选择恰当的目标市场的关键所在。

Changes in social structure, or demographics, as identified in Chapter Two, cause new market threats and opportunities and therefore different targeting imperatives. For example, the increasing interest in environmental issues has been accompanied by a whole range of views from ardent advocates to strident opponents. Numerous research studies undertaken between the late 1980s and 2007 have demonstrated that the majority of consumers are concerned about environmental issues. However, there are also large differences among social groups in terms of how much extra they are prepared to pay for products in support of those beliefs. Within the fashion market, consumers can be categorized according to attitudes held on environmental matters. Clearly, if significant numbers with purchasing power are active supporters of environmental issues, then they probably would be most interested in recycled or recyclable fabrics and fibres and in long-lasting clothing that is manufactured and can be cared for in an environmentally friendly manner.

Investigation of consumer behaviour is sometimes designed specifically to identify particular groups of consumer with fashion interests and buying behaviour in common. The later section on lifestyles will outline one such approach to market segmentation.

第 2 章里提到的社会结构或人口特征的变化，产生了新的市场威胁和机会，进而出现了不同的目标市场。例如，对环境问题的关注形成了一批热情的拥护者和坚决的反对者。从 20 世纪 80 年代到 2007 年间很多研究表明，大多数消费者都关注环境问题。但是社会群体中的人们愿意付出多少钱购买产品以支持自己对环境问题的看法，这点上却存在着较大的差异。在时装市场中，可以将消费者按照他们对环境问题的态度划分为不同的类型。毫无疑问，如果多数具有较强购买能力的消费者都积极关注环境问题的话，他们自然会对那些使用可循环利用的纺织材料及纤维生产的耐用性强的时装感兴趣，而且这些时装对环境都是无害的。

有的时候，消费行为的调查主要侧重的是特定团体消费者在时装偏好和购买行为上的共同点。后面的章节中将着重介绍针对生活方式进行市场细分的步骤。

3.2.3 Consumer behaviour and the marketing mix / 消费行为和营销组合

The study of consumer behaviour not only provides a framework for identifying consumer needs and target markets, but it also enables the anticipation of consumer responses to marketing action. When studying the consumer the interest lies not only in describing what is the case, but also in predicting future behaviour.

The marketing mix is the combination of elements that a fashion marketer offers to a target market. It comprises decisions made about products, prices, promotion, services and distribution that are assembled in a coherent manner to represent the firm's offering to the consumer. A detailed discussion of the marketing mix is given in Chapter Five. For the present a consideration of links between consumer behaviour and some elements of the marketing mix will be given.

有关消费行为的研究不仅是为了区分消费需求和目标市场，同样也是为了预测消费者对于营销活动的反应。研究消费者的时候不仅要关注现在的情况，还要预测未来的消费行为。

营销组合是时装营销人员向目标市场提供的所有要素的组合，包括产品、定价、促销、服务和渠道等要素的组合以体现企业向消费者提供的产品或者服务。第 5 章中将对营销组合进行具体的论述，也会分析消费行为和营销组合各要素之间的关系。

Consumer behaviour and products / 消费行为与产品

Products are bought because they meet needs. These needs may be mainly physiological such as the

由于满足了消费者的需求，所以消费者才会购买产品，这些可能是生理方

requirement for warmth or may include social needs such as the desire to be thought sexually attract-ive. A psychological need, for example, may relate to vanity and self-image and be manifest in a desire to perceive oneself as smaller or larger than reality. Styling skill can create garments that emphasize or reduce the aspect size as wished, but a limited amount of 'psychological sizing' also can play a part. For example, a well-known bra manufacturer produces its leading brand with labels that are one size larger. The assumption is that some consumers derive satisfaction and confidence from a size label that flatters aspirations or a particular self-image. A similar situation exists with the sizing of boxer shorts where it is well known that very few men want the label small when buying or receiving underwear. Another example relates to perceptions and garment sizing where some women desire to see themselves as a smaller size and manufacturers respond accordingly by classifying what is really a size 18 dress as a 16.

面的需求，如保暖，或者是社会需求，如异性吸引等。而心理需求则和虚荣、自我相关，最明显的就是期望自己看上去比现实更娇小或者更丰满。可以强调搭配技巧或者调整时装的尺寸，但有些时候，心理错觉产生的尺寸变化也会起到一定的作用。例如，一家知名的内衣制造商生产的顶级品牌产品吊牌上的尺码会标注大一码，企业认为有些消费者会从满足自己欲望，并且修饰个人形象的产品的尺码标上得到一种满足和自信。拳击短裤的尺码标注也一样，因为很少有男性想购买或者穿一件小尺码的内裤。另一个例子就是有些女性希望自己看起来娇小一些，于是制造商就把真实尺寸为 18 码的时装标注为 16 码。

It is not the contention of this book that such examples are to be advocated. Indeed, we would argue that much time and effort is wasted at the retail level and that the net effect upon the consumer is probably counterproductive. When market researchers claim that the majority of British women do not accurately know their own bra size, one wonders whether this ignorance is not perpetuated by the absence of an industry standard on sizing.

这本书并不倡导以上这些方法。事实上，我们在零售环节浪费了大量的时间和精力，也没有达到预期的目标。市场调研的结果显示，大多数英国女性并不了解自己的内衣尺寸，此时有人会想知道这种现象会不会因为工业标准号型的出现而结束。

Consumer behaviour and promotion ／消费行为与促销

The promotion of fashion items requires an understanding of consumers' media habits so that the correct media can be chosen. Understanding consumer behaviour enables the selection of appropriate promotional messages. For example, fashion photography often seeks to reflect a particular lifestyle that the consumer can identify with and then perceive the product as a vehicle to the attainment of that lifestyle. The use of celebrities in advertisements also enables fashion firms to reach certain target audiences and influence consumers via the process of identification. Further consideration of the use of celebrities in fashion promotion is given in Chapter Nine.

在进行时装产品的促销时，企业需要了解消费者接触媒体的习惯，这样才能选择恰当的媒体。了解消费者的购买行为有助于设计恰当的促销信息。例如，时装摄影通常会力求表现一种能被消费者感知的生活方式，并通过产品来体现这种生活方式。广告中使用名人同样也可以使时装企业接触到目标消费者，并且通过对名人的识别来影响消费者的行为。第 9 章里将进一步论述时装促销中选用名人的具体情况。

Consumer behaviour and price ／消费行为与价格

Price for many people is a major indicator of quality. Style and design are sometimes difficult to judge,

很多消费者认为价格体现的是产品的质量。对于未经专业培训的消费者而

especially for the untrained. Therefore some consumers take surrogate indicators of quality and in particular price. An understanding of the perceptual process and how consumers learn about prices and value is helpful in constructing a pricing policy.

言，产品的款式和设计是很难评价的。因此，很多消费者将价格作为时装质量的一个评价标准。在进行产品定价时，深入了解消费者对产品价格和价值的认知是非常有用的。

Consumer behaviour and distribution ／消费者行为与渠道

The choice of an appropriate distribution channel and designing elem-ents within that channel should be based on an understanding of the fashion consumer. Knowing when, where and how consumers wish to buy are fairly obvious applications. Understanding and matching self-images and store images and creating particular store atmospheres to encourage certain moods need research and ideas from consumer behaviour.

了解时装消费者之后，才能选择恰当的营销渠道并且设计相关的要素。知道消费者在什么时间、什么地点以什么方式购买产品是非常重要的。了解个人形象和店铺形象，并且懂得将两者相匹配以创造特殊的店铺氛围，就需要研究消费者的消费行为和想法。

3.3 Fashion consumer decision-making ／时装消费者的购买决策

One main way of examining consumer behaviour is to take the view of the consumer as a problem solver. The requirement for clothing, however it is driven, is seen as a problem for the consumer to solve, usually by exchanging money with a seller. The problem-solving perspective raises many questions that will be addressed; they concern the types of decision fashion consumers must make, the various stages of the decision process consumers progress through and major factors that influence those decisions.

将消费者看作是问题的解决者，是了解时装消费者购买行为的一种主要的方式。通常情况下，消费者与卖家进行交易来购买时装，解决自己的需求问题。同时又会给卖家带来新的问题，例如，营销人员需要分析消费者购买决策的类型，消费者购买决策过程的各个阶段，以及影响消费者作出决策的主要因素。

3.3.1 Types of consumer decision ／消费者决策的类型

It is tempting to see the purchase of a garment as just one decision, to buy or not to buy. However, it can be useful to break the larger decision down into several separate decisions that collectively comprise the buy or no buy decision. For instance, consumers must decide the following matters:

- How to find out about new styles?
- What style, colour and size to buy?
- Where to buy from?
- How to pay?
- Which bills to pay promptly?
- When to buy?
- How many items to buy?

人们很容易把购买时装看作是一种决定，即买或者不买。然而，买或者不买其实是由很多个不同的决定共同影响的。例如，消费者需要做出以下决策：

- 如何获得新款的时装讯息?
- 购买什么款式、颜色、尺寸的时装?
- 从哪里买?
- 怎样支付?
- 哪些提货账单需要立即支付?
- 什么时候去买?
- 买多少样?

◆ Will any accessories need to be purchased?
◆ Whether to shop alone or accompanied?
◆ Whether to try the garment on?
◆ Whether to order an out of stock size or colour option?
◆ Which sales assistant to approach for help?
◆ What to do if the product is unsatisfactory?
◆ What will be the reaction of significant others to the purchase?
◆ Whether or not to purchase online or mail order?
◆ If buying online or mail order, how to arrange delivery?

◆ 需要购买其他配饰吗？
◆ 单独去商店还是有人陪伴？
◆ 是否试穿这件衣服？
◆ 是否需要订购缺货款的颜色和尺码？
◆ 寻找哪个时装导购获得帮助？
◆ 若对产品不满意应该怎么做？
◆ 购买后有什么其他反应？
◆ 其他人对购买货品的评价如何？
◆ 是否该通过网络或邮购来购买？
◆ 如果通过网络或邮购来购买，如何安排发货？

If fashion marketers see consumer decisions as a series of smaller related problems to be solved, then the benefit comes in terms of planning activities to ensure that the consumer is helped when help is needed. For example, a consumer may not be bothered about trying a blouse on if she knows she can easily exchange it later for another size if needed.

如果营销人员能够把消费者的购买行为看作是相关联的一系列问题时，那么就可以在消费者需要帮助的时候给予帮助并且使消费者获益。例如，如果消费者知道在购买衬衫之后不合适可以调换尺码的话，她就会觉得试穿是件麻烦的事情。

Alternatively, another customer may dislike the whole process of shopping for clothes and appreciate speedy service with advice and nearby displays of matching accessories. Marketing research is necessary to determine which decisions are important to the particular target market of the fashion firm.

另一方面，有些消费者不喜欢购买决策的过程，而愿意听取导购的建议选购配套的饰品。了解哪些决策对时装企业特定的目标市场是至关重要的，必须经过深入的市场调研。

3.3.2 Consumer involvement ／消费者参与

Another way to look at consumer decisions is the level of involvement the consumer has in the decision. Consumers differ considerably in terms of their interest in fashion. Even those people who are very interested in fashion may be more interested in some types of garment than in others. A common way consumer theorists have classified consumer decisions is into high- and low-involvement purchases. This classification, in part, reflects different theoretical paradigms, although some significant attempts at synthesis have emerged over recent years.

另一个观察消费者决策过程的方法就是消费者参与决策的情况，消费者在时装方面的喜好大不相同，即使那些对时尚很感兴趣的人们，他们也只是对时尚的某些方面有兴趣而已。研究消费者的学者将消费者的决策分为高度参与购买和低度参与购买两种类型，尽管近几年有些学者在尝试将这两种类型相结合，但在某种程度上而言，这种划分体现的还是不同的理论模型。

The level of involvement depends on the person, the purchase object and the time and place of purchase. For one consumer, the purchase of a pair of socks may involve considerable deliberation and visiting several stores to make comparisons in order to obtain a product that meets fairly precise specifications in terms

消费者参与决策的程度取决于个人以及他们购买的商品、购买的时间和地点。对某些消费者来说，买一双袜子可能都要经过深思熟虑，并货比三家，直到买到一双颜色、尺寸、面料都非常符

of colour, size and construction. For another consumer, the purchase of socks may be relegated to a simple commodity purchase undertaken with little conscious thinking through and they may be selected along with other low-involvement purchases in a supermarket.

合要求的袜子；而对另外的消费者而言，买一双袜子则会是一个极为简单的过程，他们不会经过细心的思考，就会以低度参与购买的方式在超市里购买到袜子。

The implication for fashion marketers is to find out the level of involvement of the target market or markets and design the marketing mix accordingly. A central issue is the provision of marketing information to consumers who may or may not want or use it. A connection between low-level involvement and impulse buying can be shown and this has a bearing on the relative proportion of the promotional budget that goes on in-store promotions rather than on advertising. If consumers do not really pay much attention to information about some fashion products, but simply make decisions in the store, it would be more productive to concentrate promotional efforts in-store.

这些对时装营销人员的启示就是要研究目标消费者参与购买的程度，并且制定恰当的营销组合策略，最关键的就是向消费者提供一些他们关心或者需要的销售信息。可以发现低度参与购买和冲动购买是有关系的，这对店铺促销而非广告的预算比例是有一定影响的。如果消费者不关注时装商品的信息，而只是在商店里做出简单的购买决策，那么企业就应该重视店铺里促销活动的策划。

3.3.3 The decision process ／购买决策过程

As shown earlier, the consumer decision to buy may be seen as a series of smaller decisions. It also can be shown as consumer progression through a number of discrete stages. Most models of consumer behaviour use the stages or near equivalents as shown in Figure 3.2.

如前所述，消费者的购买决策可以看作是由一系列的小决定组成的，也可以看成是消费者在一系列间断的过程中的不断进步。多数消费行为模型都是按照图 3–2 所示的过程或者近似的方式表现的。

The various phases will be briefly outlined. First, problem recognition occurs when a consumer becomes aware that a need for clothing arises. This may be triggered by garments wearing out, comments from others about how unfashionable existing garments are, a change of social status prompting or facilitating

下面简单介绍各个阶段的情况。首先就是需求认知，也就是消费者有了购买时装的需求，这可能是因为衣服破旧不能穿了，其他人认为自己穿着不时尚，社会地位改变了，需求欲望或者品味改

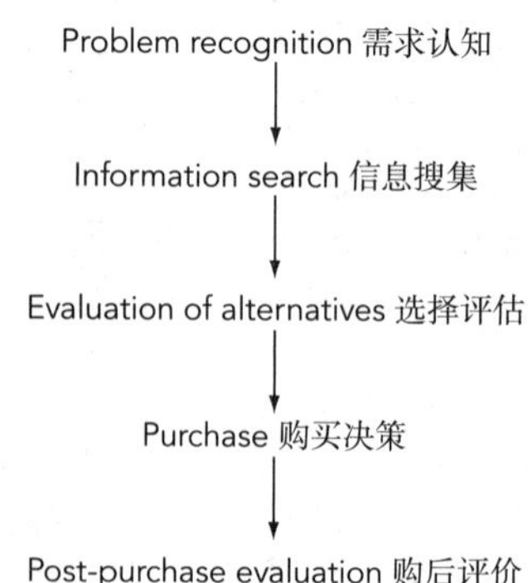

Figure 3.2 The consumer decision process. 图 3–2 消费者购买决策过程

purchase or a change in aspirations or taste. The extent to which fashion marketers are able to influence problem recognition is fiercely debated.

Whether marketers create needs is the question often asked. Blackwell et al. (2006) argue that marketers do not create needs, they show consumers better ways of satisfying pre-existing needs. For example, high-status needs can be satisfied by any number of different purchases or activities. The fact that a fashion advertiser captures the imagination of some consumers and secures purchases probably has more to do with the understanding of those needs and careful design of a message than the creation of the needs in the first place. Many powerful social forces operate in society of which advertising is only one and one not often held in very high regard. Advertising both reflects and influences societal values towards consumption. If it were truly able to create needs and exert such a powerful influence then it has been an outstanding failure in the world of fashion.

Having become aware of a need, the consumer reflects on the situation and can decide to proceed with the purchase process and collect information, defer the purchase or conclude that the problem is insign ificant or cannot be solved. In deciding to proceed, the consumer reviews information already held in memory. This includes knowledge of brands and stores where solutions may be found. Inexperience or unsatisfactory prior purchases may cause external information sources to be consulted. External sources include personal sources such as friends, neutral sources such as a television programme on eveningwear, or fashion marketing sources such as a window display or a poster advertisement. These three main external types of information sources are usually regarded with different degrees of credibility by the consumer.

When sufficient information is held by the consumer about pos-sible solutions then evaluations take place and a choice is made. The nature of the evaluations varies from individual to individual. Some consumers have extensive repertoires of buying criteria, whereas others have limited and often vague mechanisms for making decisions. The process of making an evaluation may involve the mental ranking or rating of alternatives or simply eliminating items that fail to meet a certain threshold. At times consumers can suffer what is

变了。然而时装营销人员在多大程度上能够影响消费者产生购买需求，这是个极富争议的问题。

人们经常问营销人员是否能够创造市场需求，布莱克威尔（2006年）等人认为营销人员不能创造市场需求，他们只是向消费者提供了满足现实需求的方式。例如，任何消费或者购买活动都可以满足高地位人群的消费需求。事实上，作为时装广告商而言，他们会先了解消费者的期望，深入分析消费者的需求以确保一定的购买量，并且借助这些信息组织广告的内容，这相比创造市场需求而言更加重要。在众多强有力的社会因素中，广告只是其中的一个因素，并没有引起太多的重视，广告影响着社会大众在消费方面的价值观。如果消费需求真的可以创造并且具有很大影响力的话，那么这将会是时装行业一个巨大的失败。

当意识到有消费需求的时候，消费者就会对这种需求做出反应，会考虑购买产品并且收集信息、推迟购买或者认为这个需求无关紧要，就不能通过购买来满足需求。在此决策过程中，消费者回忆那些已有的相关信息，包括品牌信息以及哪里可以购买到这些产品。没有经验或者之前购买不满意的消费者通常会从外部寻找一些信息，这些信息可能来自朋友，晚礼服相关的电视节目，或者营销方面的信息如橱窗、海报等，消费者对这三个主要的信息来源有着不一样的信任度。

当消费者掌握了足够信息的时候，他们会对这些信息进行评价，并且做出选择。每个人对信息的评价标准不一样，一些消费者熟知购买评价的标准，然而另一些消费者则只了解有限的评价标准，而且不懂得如何做出购买决定。对信息进行评价的过程可能会涉及心智水平、对多个方案的排序或者简单地去掉那些不能满足最低要求的项目。有时

described as information overload where there are too many possibilities or too much information has been presented. An awareness of consumer information needs and the provision of information in an appropriate manner via facts and advice from sales staff or brochures can help the consumer to make a choice. The decisions made by a consumer at the time of purchase have been mentioned earlier and the sales effort to influence purchase is covered in Chapter Nine.

候，消费者会因为信息负荷过重而苦恼，因为过多的信息会带来多种可能性。依据实际情况以及销售人员的建议或者宣传手册，采用恰当的方式观察消费者的信息需求，并且提供信息给消费者会比较有利于消费者作出选择。在购买的时候消费者是如何作出决策的在前文已讲过，影响消费者购买的销售策略将在第9章阐述。

After a purchase consumers may engage in a process of evalu-ation of the product and to an extent their own efficiency as a consumer. Systematic evaluation is most unlikely except where items are bought primarily for their functional characteristics, such as hiking boots where protection and durability may be closely scrutinized. The extent of evaluation seems related to how socially conspicuous the item is, how central the product is to the self-image of the consumer, the particular consumer orientation and also to the purchase price. For most consumers, the evaluation can involve seeking comments from others perceived to be significant.

购买产品之后，消费者会参与到商品评价的过程中，以行使消费者的权利。如果消费者购买的是登山鞋，他们首先会关心产品的功能性特点如保护性、耐穿性等，而不会对产品进行综合性的评价。对商品进行评价似乎和该商品带来的社会属性、商品所体现的消费者的个人形象、消费者的个人定位以及商品的价格有着一定的关系。对大多数消费者来说，评价过程中也会从他们认为重要的那些人那里获取意见。

Fashion marketers should be interested in this post-purchase behaviour as it can relate directly to repeat purchases, the level of customer complaints and word-of-mouth communications about the firm. The law of effect in psychology states simply that behaviour that is rewarded is likely to be repeated. Satisfied customers are likely to become regular customers. The goal of fashion marketing is to move customers along the continuum from the promiscuous to the insistent, as shown in Figure 3.3.

时装营销人员应该关注消费者的购后行为，因为这直接关系到以后的重复购买、消费者的投诉情况以及对公司的口碑传播。心理学理论表明，如果消费满意的话就会产生重复购买行为，感到满意的消费者极有可能成为回头客。时装营销的目的就是促使消费者从偶然购买转变为持续性的购买，如图3-3所示。

Careful monitoring of customer complaints can lead to the early correction of faults and avoidance of some future complaints. Sensitive handling of genuine complaints can also help retain goodwill and avoid negative word-of-mouth communication. As research indicates that consumers are more likely to pass on negative rather than positive information about products, onae dissatisfied customer may lead to many

对消费者的投诉及时处理可以提早修正错误并且避免日后的抱怨，灵活处理正面的评价有助于获得良好的声誉，并且避免负面的口碑传播。正如调查表明，消费者更倾向于宣传产品的负面信息而不是正面信息，一个不满意的消费者有可能导致很多人对店铺以及品牌产

Promiscuous –will shop around for the best deal 偶然购买——选购特价商品
Occasional –will sometimes buy from us 偶尔购买——有时会从我们这里购买
Loyal –will usually buy from us 忠实购买——经常从我们这里购买
Insistent –will only buy from us 持续购买——只从我们这里购买

Figure 3.3 Types of customer. 图 3–3 消费者的类型

more with negative attitudes towards the store or brand.

The above discussion of the decision process has shown the need to consider factors beyond the immediate concerns of the consumer when trying to understand and predict the behaviour of the fashion consumer. The factors to be considered may be grouped under the broad headings of psychological and sociological factors. Psychological factors are taken from the study of individual behaviour while sociological factors are based on the understanding that much consumer behaviour takes place as part of a group process and involves social interaction and patterns of influence. Figure 3.4 illustrates the main explanatory variables related to the decision process.

生负面评价。

以上关于决策过程的论述表明，在试图理解和预测时装消费者的行为时，必须考虑消费者最关心的方面，可将要讨论的因素按照心理和社会标准进行划分和归类。心理方面的因素主要源于对个人行为的研究，而社会性因素则将大多数消费者的行为看作是一个团体的共性，同时也涉及了社交以及相互影响的模式。图 3–4 说明的是与决策过程相关的因素。

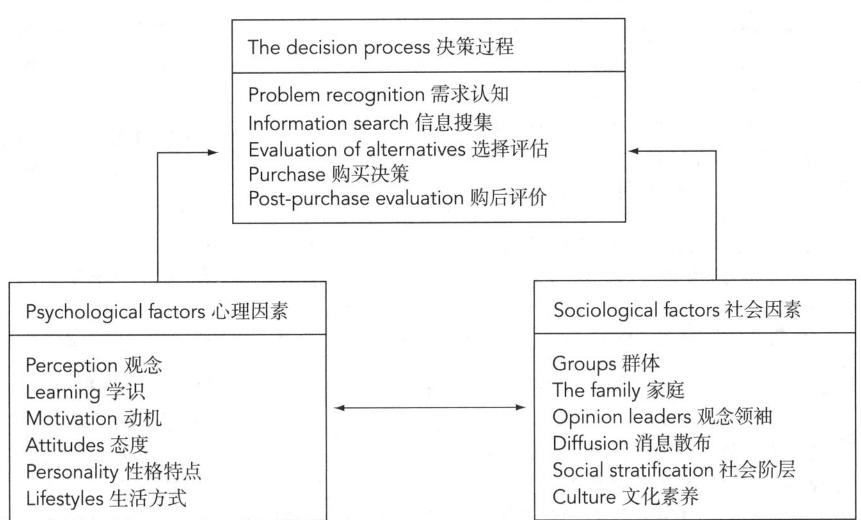

Figure 3.4 A model of consumer behaviour. 图 3–4 消费行为模型

3.4 Psychological processes ／心理过程

3.4.1 The buyer's perceptual process ／购买者的感性认知过程

Perception is the process whereby buyers select, organize and interpret simple stimuli into a meaningful and coherent picture of the world. To explain this process further, a distinction between sensation and perception must be made. Sensation refers to the responses of our sense organs to simple stimuli, whereas perception is the psychological consequence of sensation. An analogy would be to compare a photograph with a painting: the photograph is the

认知是一个过程，在这个过程当中购买者将简单的刺激因素进行选择、组织并诠释为一幅有意义的、与之内在关联的图景。为了更进一步地解释这个过程，必须区分“感觉”和“认知”的不同。“感觉”是指我们的感觉器官对简单刺激的反应，而认知是指感觉在心理上产生的结果，这类似于拿照片和油画作比

'reality', whereas the painting is a very personal view of 'reality'.

较，照片是“现实”的，而油画是对“现实”的个人看法。

For the fashion consumer, the stimuli presented in a busy fashion store are a bewildering array of sensations that must be made sense of. The consumer goes through a number of stages in the perceptual process that can be seen as steps in filtering and distilling marketing stimuli into a unique marketing experience. The stages in this perceptual filtering and distilling process are:

- selective exposure;
- selective attention;
- selective distortion;
- selective retention.

对时装消费者而言，一个生意兴隆的时装店给消费者的印象是一种混乱的感觉。在感知的过程中，消费者要经过几个阶段，然后才能将营销刺激一步步过滤和筛选进而形成独特的购买体验。过滤和筛选感知的过程包含以下步骤：

- 选择性接触；
- 选择性关注；
- 选择性扭曲；
- 选择性记忆。

Selective exposure / 选择性接触

Age or income can impose some constraints on the exposure to certain stores or media, as can the more deliberate choice by the consumer. This process, where there is a narrowing of the opportunities for experience of the total range of marketing stimuli, is known as selective exposure. Examples of marketing stimuli subject to selective exposure are the fashion page in a daily newspaper, advertisements, brochures and store window displays. The task for fashion marketers is to ensure that the correct media and location for retail outlets are selected to maximize the opportunities for selective exposure.

年龄和收入会影响消费者接触店铺或者媒体的类型，同样也会影响消费者深思熟虑之后作出的决定，同时消费者也很少有机会来体验所有的营销刺激，这个过程称为选择性接触。举例来说，选择性接触营销刺激包括消费者对报纸时尚版、广告、画册以及店铺橱窗陈列的关注。时装营销人员的任务就是选择恰当的媒介以及零售终端的选址，从而增加消费者选择性接触的机会。

Selective attention / 选择性关注

Selective attention is the next stage, and the range of possibilities is further narrowed when the consumer pays attention only to some marketing stimuli and not to others. Consumer factors that determine consumer attention to marketing stimuli are existing attitudes, attention span, emotional states, motives and expectancy. The last point is illustrated by the following well-known saying (Figure 3.5):

选择性关注是第二步，如果消费者只关注某些营销刺激而不关心其他，那么发生行为的可能性就会变得较小。决定消费者关注营销刺激的因素有观念、关注范围、情感状态、动机和期望，最后引用下面一句言论对此进行说明（图3–5）：

Many people will have 'read' the above statement and not have noticed the double use of the word 'time'; they will have perceived what they expected

很多人“读过”上面的这句话，但是还没注意到与“时间”有关的词用了两次，他们相信他们所期望看见的，而

A stitch in time 及时缝一针，
time saves nine 免得日后缝九针。

Figure 3.5 图 3–5

to see rather than the reality. Existing attitudes and prejudice similarly influence how we perceive marketing messages. Items which are promoted as designer label or sale items may attract attention or may even be screened out by the consumer depending on prior attitudes. Thus the importance of determining consumer predispositions, via marketing research, before designing marketing messages is underlined.

Some factors under the control of the fashion marketer can influence whether the marketing message gains the attention of the consumer. The size and intensity of a message (i.e. very loud) plus novelty, contrast, repetition and movement can all enhance the chances of gaining attention. Thus advertisements in the first 10% of a magazine such as *Company* or *GQ* have a higher potential readership than the latter part of the same magazine. Similarly, a black and white advertisement in a glossy magazine, which is surrounded by colour advertisements, stands a good chance of gaining attention because of the contrast.

不是现实。现有的看法和偏见同样会影响我们如何看待营销信息。以设计师标签促销或者销售的产品往往会吸引消费者的注意，按照之前的态度，消费者也会对产品进行筛选。所以在设计营销信息前，通过市场调查了解消费者的喜好是非常重要的，这点需要强调一下。

时装营销人员所掌握的一些因素会影响消费者对营销信息的关注度。信息的多少、密度（比如信息复杂），还有信息的新颖性、对比性、重复性、变动等都会增加消费者的关注度。因此在*Company*、*GQ* 等杂志中前 10% 的广告比起同一本杂志后半部分的广告而言会引起更多消费者阅读。同样，光板纸杂志中黑白广告和周围环绕的彩色广告有着一定的对比，所以会更容易引起消费者的注意。

Selective distortion／选择性扭曲

Having gained the consumer's attention the next perceptual filter for the marketer to penetrate is selective distortion. Consumers interpret stimuli in a manner that is consistent with existing attitudes. The perceptual process operates in such a way as to enable and maintain a coherent view of the world; too many contradictions to existing views make the management of everyday life irksome. That is not to say that changing consumers' perceptions is impossible, just that before embarking upon change marketers need to discover the starting points and the strength with which existing views are held. An example of the distorting effect of the perceptual process is easily noted when considering the stereotypes that are brought to bear in judging garments by country of origin. To most British consumers the labels 'Made in France' or 'Designed in Italy' have connotations of higher design content and quality than an item made in a developing country. These connotations can have such an influence that they may, and often do, override the judgements that would emerge in a blind test.

当受到消费者的关注之后，营销人员下一步的感知筛选就是了解消费者的选择性扭曲，消费者通常会根据已有的看法来理解营销刺激。感知过程就是使建立内在联系成为可能并且能够维持，对现有观点的看法不一致给人们的日常生活也带来了麻烦。当然这并不是说不可能改变消费者的认知，只是营销人员在着手改变之前需要找出改变的出发点以及人们凭借什么而产生现有观念的。感知过程中的扭曲很容易得到解释。举例来说，当人们评价时装的板型好坏时通常会查看产品的生产地。对大多数英国消费者来说，标注“法国制造”“意大利设计”的时装比起发展中国家制造的产品而言有着更高的设计含量和品质，这些暗示可能产生一种影响，那就是在盲测的时候消费者可能并且通常会推翻已有的评价。

Selective retention／选择性记忆

The final perceptual filter is selective retention. This refers to the phenomenon of consumers remembering

最后一个阶段是选择性记忆，这里指的是消费者以自己极其主观的方式记

information about fashion marketers and their products in a highly subjective way. An important aspect of perception is that the consumer interprets information in terms of current priorities and concerns to such an extent that the individual in effect rewrites their personal history. The main driving force behind this selective retention is a need for consistent and, sometimes, easy explanations for our feelings and past behaviour. In this process good and bad aspects of some items may become exaggerated with, for example, nostalgia for some so-called golden age of fashion when there was 'real pride and skill in tailoring, unlike today'. The close associations that many people have between blue jeans and youth have been recognized by the jeans manufacturers in the targeting of middle-aged consumers with the use of suitable music in advertisements to evoke the nostalgia.

住时装营销人员以及产品的信息。认知的一个重要方面是消费者会根据已有的优先次序和关注的事物来理解营销信息，以至于每个人都会重新梳理自己的记忆。选择性记忆背后的主要推动力是始终不变的需求，有的时候这也很容易解释我们的感觉和过去的行为。在这个过程中，某些产品好的或者坏的方面都会被夸大。例如，对所谓的时尚业黄金时代的怀旧情绪被描述为“与现在不同的值得骄傲的、高超的裁缝技术”。牛仔裤生产商已经意识到蓝色牛仔裤和年轻人之间的密切联系，在针对中青年目标消费者的广告中通常会配上恰当的背景音乐来唤起人们的怀旧情绪。

3.4.2 Learning ／学习

The fashion consumer is not born with a knowledge of fashion brands, of criteria for judging garments, a knowledge of stores or prices, preferences for certain styles or fabrics or even how to care for garments. All this information has to be learned. Consumer learning is any relatively permanent change in buying behaviour that is a result of practice or experience. Two main sources for consumer learning are the family and peer groups. However, much learning occurs through consumer experience with fashion marketers, their products and promotional methods.

Many explanations of consumer learning are given in the marketing literature, most of which can be classified as association learning or cognitive learning. Although the two main types of theory compete to explain behaviour, neither category is sufficient to explain all learning that occurs. The following discussion presents aspects of both approaches.

时装消费者并不是天生就了解时尚品牌，懂得判断衣服好坏的标准、店铺或价格信息，偏好某些款式或者面料，以及懂得衣物保养的，这些方面需要通过后天学习才能知道。消费者的后天学习是由实践和经验导致的在购买行为上发生的变化，他们学习的对象主要是家庭和同龄群体，然而很多学习也是在与营销人员交流、了解企业产品以及促销的过程中完成的。

营销学中阐述了很多有关消费者学习的内容，基本上可以归纳为关联学习和认知学习。虽然这两种说法都在解释消费者的学习行为，但是任何一个都不能用来解释人们的所有学习过程。以下讨论这两种说法的特点。

Association learning ／关联学习

Association learning occurs when a marketing stimulus and the consumer response are repeatedly paired. Much low-level learning such as brand names occurs at this level. A key explanatory theory for this type of learning is known as the law of effect. When behaviour is rewarded, it will tend to be repeated and when it is punished or not rewarded, it will tend to diminish in frequency. Therefore we have a simple explanation

当营销刺激引导消费者产生重复性的反应时就产生了关联学习，低层次的品牌名称的学习就属于此，这种学习最佳的解释就是众所周知的效果率。当某种行为受到鼓励时，此行为会不断地重复发生；当某种行为得到惩罚或未得到鼓励时，此行为则会慢慢地消失，如此

for repeat buying and brand loyalty. The consumer who buys a particular brand of shirt and finds that it meets his criteria in terms of being stylish, comfortable, durable and value for money will tend to buy the same brand again. The main lesson for fashion marketers is to identify the relevant buying criteria of the consumer and produce products to meet those criteria. Another consumer who finds that the skirt she purchased three weeks ago is starting to come apart at the seams will probably avoid buying another skirt from that supplier. Yet, another customer may learn to avoid certain shoe shops as the sales assistants, paid primarily by commission, all compete to serve the customer and do not allow adequate time for browsing.

我们便可以解释重复购买和品牌忠诚度形成的原因。当消费者购买某一品牌的衬衫时，发现款式新颖、穿着舒适、经久耐穿、物有所值，能够满足自己对衬衣的选购标准，那么他还会再买同一品牌的衣服。这对营销人员的启示是了解消费者购买时装的标准并且生产适合的产品满足这些标准。另一个例子就是当消费者发现她三个星期前买的裙子接缝处开裂时，她很可能就不会再从零售商那里买裙子了。然而，另外一些顾客可能不会去某些鞋店买鞋，因为这些鞋店聘请的导购是按佣金拿工资的，他们都争着为顾客服务，让顾客没有充足的时间看鞋子。

An interesting aspect of association learning is the notion of shaping behaviour. This notion allows marketers the opportunity to influence consumers and help them learn more complex forms of behaviour. By selectively rewarding closer and closer approximations to the final goal sought by the marketer, consumer learning is modified. In the section in Chapter Seven on pricing the link between sales discounts and consumer behaviour is described. Some consumers learn, because of regular retailer action, to defer purchase until sale time, as they are rewarded by lower prices.

关联学习一个有趣的方面是形成购买行为的方式，这就给营销人员提供了机会去影响消费者，帮助他们学习更为复杂的行为模式。当营销人员有选择性地实现自己的目标时，消费者的行为也会被改变。第 7 章中关于价格的部分将阐述打折销售与消费行为的关系。一些消费者知道企业定期的促销计划，于是就会选择在打折的时候购买，从而能够从低价销售中获利。

Shaping behaviour, when effectively planned, permits the fashion retailer to alter behaviour in other ways. Suppose the retailer introduces a new range of cotton underwear with Lycra, the goal is to encourage the consumer to buy several pairs. To launch the range and encourage a trial with minimum risk and maximum reward a coupon offering a discount may be offered. The consumer who buys the product receives another coupon as well, this time of lower value than the initial coupon. The second coupon should induce another purchase at reduced cost, but without coupon support. If the product performance meets expectations, then the beginning of brand loyalty has been shaped. It should be stressed that the main reward should come from the product and not the coupon, otherwise the consumer learns something else, only to buy from the retailer when an incentive is offered.

如果能够有效地实现计划，那么培养消费行为的时候零售商就可以通过不同的方式来改变消费者的行为。假设零售商向消费者介绍一种带有莱卡的新款内衣，目的是鼓励消费者多买几件，在发布新品的时候就可以尝试发放折扣券以实现低风险高回报。购买产品的消费者同样也会得到另一张优惠券，这张优惠券要比前一次的优惠券面额低，第二张优惠券可以吸引消费者在本店以优惠价格购买另一个商品，但是不再赠送优惠券。如果这个产品满足消费者的期望，那么逐渐就会形成品牌忠诚度。需要强调的是，主要的收益应该来自产品本身而不是优惠券，否则消费者就会了解其他信息，并且只会在有促销的时候才购买商品。

Cognitive learning / 认知学习

Cognitive learning theories approach the problem of consumer learning by assuming consumers reason and reflect upon the relationship between marketing stimuli and consumer response. Clearly all consumers do think about some purchases in detail and may engage in mental processes to try to reach a reasoned conclusion before purchasing. Inexperience, previous dissatisfaction, expense and high-involvement clothing items are most usually linked with cognitive learning. The cognitive approach concentrates on the thinking through of different courses and the identification of the decision criteria and rules used by consumers. Knowing how consumers make connections between product features and their buying criteria is obviously helpful for marketing staff in order to provide the right information at the right time. The concentration on the information processing aspect of learning will be developed further in Section 3.4.3.

认知学习旨在解决消费者学习的问题，其前提是假定消费者会对营销刺激和他们的反应的关系有所认识。很明显，所有消费者都会仔细分析消费行为的细节，并且想尽量在购买之前得出一个合理的结论。缺乏经验，对前次购买不满意，或者购买昂贵的时装，进行高度参与购买等都属于认知学习。认知途径集中在思考不同的过程和确定消费者做出决定所依据的标准、原则，了解消费者如何决定产品特性与其购买标准之间的联系对市场营销人员大有帮助，进而才能在合适的时间向消费者提供适合的信息。关于认知学习的信息处理过程将会在 3.4.3 部分中进一步分析。

3.4.3 Consumer attitudes / 消费心态

Attitudes are a learned orientation or predisposition to a given situ-ation, person, object or idea resulting in a tendency to respond favourably or unfavourably. There are three main components to an attitude: the cognitive, affective and conative. The cognitive dimension refers to knowledge or information possessed about the fashion product, service, image, store or prices; the knowledge possessed by the consumer may not be accurate or complete, but it is what is believed to be the truth by the consumer. The affective dimension is concerned with consumer feelings about fashion marketing offerings and is measured in terms such as like and dislike or good and bad. The conative aspect provides the behavioural aspect of attitudes and is usually expressed in terms of an intention, or not, to buy within a specified time. Thus a consumer may know of a new range from Missonia and of the colours, prices and sizes available; the consumer may like the new range and moreover intends to purchase a new sweater within the next seven days.

心态是学习的指导思想，或者是对给定的情况、人物、事物或想法形成的一种赞同或反对的倾向态度。心态主要由三部分组成：认知的、情感的和意动的。认知范围包括掌握的有关时装产品、服务、形象、店铺或价格方面的知识和信息，消费者掌握的知识可能并不准确或者不完整，但这是消费者确信的事实。情感方面涉及消费者对时装产品的感觉，常用诸如喜欢与不喜欢或好与坏来衡量。意动方面指的是心态所体现的行为，常被描述为一种在规定时间内买或者不买的意图。因此一名消费者会从蜜桑妮的新品系列中了解色彩、价格及可供选择的尺码等信息，消费者可能会喜欢新系列，也可能会在接下来的七天时间里买一件新的针织衫。

Fashion marketers are interested in consumer attitudes as they are seen to be closely linked to behaviour. A simple model of the link between attitudes and buying behaviour is shown in Figure 3.6.

时装营销人员对消费者的消费心态很感兴趣，因为他们认为这与消费行为紧密相关，消费心态和消费行为之间的关系可以用一个简单的模型来表示，如图 3–6 所示。

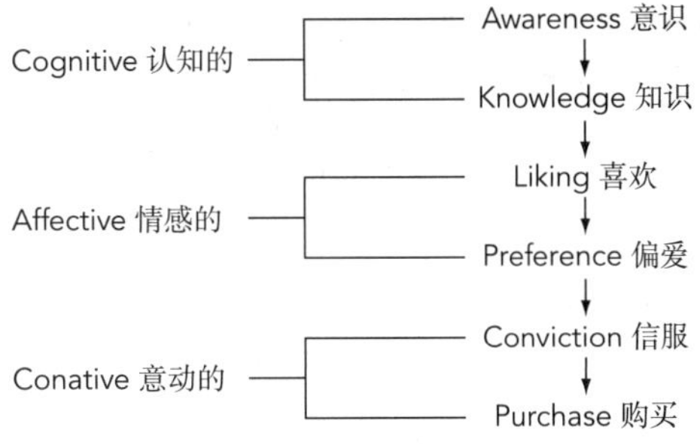

Figure 3.6 Attitude components and buying behaviour. 图 3–6 心态的组成要素与购买行为

The model below oversimplifies matters somewhat as it is argued that sometimes attitudes emerge or become manifest after purchase. Other writers contend that liking may precede knowledge in certain circumstances. Several attitude theories offer competing explanations for the same phenomenon. It is clear that predicting behaviour from simple measurements of attitudinal components is a problematic and contentious area. Numerous studies have shown that positive attitudes towards fashion products do not always result in higher sales. The work of Ajzen and Fishbein (1980) suggests that the crucial factors to consider are the measurement of the attitude towards the act of purchase and the identification of normative beliefs. For example, a consumer may like the designs of Jean Paul Gaultier and have very positive attitudes towards the designs and cut of the garments. However, the same consumer may not buy because of negative attitudes towards the price or a belief that his or her close friends may not like the styling. Techniques for measuring attitudes are described in Chapter Four.

When considering the point that attitudes emerge and/or change after purchase, it should be noted that post-purchase experience with garments can lead to attitude change, both positive and negative. Festinger (1957) proposed that there is a tendency to seek consonance or harmony of thoughts, feelings and behaviour. Post-purchase doubt over a new garment or dissonance then becomes a motivating state of affairs and the consumer acts to reduce dissonance. Dissonance can be reduced in a number of ways, including:

◆ changing behaviour (e.g. exchanging the garment for another colour);

上面的模型对某些方面进行了简化，因为有时消费者的想法在购买的时候才会表现出来或变得更加清晰。有些作者认为，在某些情况下，对商品的喜欢要先于对商品的了解。关于心态的几种理论对同一现象的解释出现了相互矛盾，很明显，从个人态度方面的要素预测消费行为是一种存在质疑和争论的方法。众多研究表明，对时装产品持有正面评价并不会一直产生较高的销售量。阿杰恩和菲什宾（1980 年）的著作中指出需要考虑的关键因素是对购买行为的衡量和对信念的识别，例如，一位消费者可能喜欢让·保罗·高缇耶设计的衣服，非常欣赏他的设计理念和时装的剪裁。尽管如此，同样的消费者可能因为价格昂贵或者自己的朋友不喜欢这种款式而不购买这件衣服。测试消费心态的方法将在第 4 章中讲述。

考虑到消费者的态度会在购买后出现改变，我们应该注意到购买后的感受可能会导致产生正面以及负面的评价。费斯廷格在 1957 年提出寻求想法、感觉和行为的共鸣或协调是一种趋势，购买之后消费者对衣服产生疑问或者衣服与自身需求不一致，然后这种不一致就会激发消费者感情上的因素，使得消费者发生行为减少这种不一致的程度。对比，有若干个不同的方法，包括：

◆ 行为改变（例如更换衣服的颜色）；

◆ changing attitudes (e.g. deciding that the brand is perhaps not as good as previously thought);

◆ revoking the decision (e.g. asking for a refund);

◆ seeking extra consonant information (e.g. asking a friend for reassurance of the wisdom of the choice made);

◆ avoiding dissonant information (e.g. not visiting other shops in case a lower price is seen for the same item).

A considerable amount of the early research on attitudes was conducted in the USA at the Universities of Yale and Columbia. Much of this research still provides a useful framework for the practising fashion marketer, and its findings are useful in the design of advertising efforts. Some of this work has been incorporated in Chapter Nine.

◆ 态度的改变（例如认为这个品牌或许没有之前想得那么好）；

◆ 撤销购买决策（例如要求退款）；

◆ 寻求额外的一致信息（例如询问一个朋友以确定购买决策是明智的）；

◆ 避开不协调的信息（例如不去其他商店，以免看见同样东西以更低的价格出售）。

大量早期对消费观念的研究是在美国耶鲁大学和哥伦比亚大学进行的，多数研究到现在都能够为从事时装营销的人员提供一个有用的框架，其研究结果对广告的设计也大有帮助，部分内容已并入第 9 章讲述。

3.4.4 Consumer motivation ／消费者动机

Motivation is the inner force that drives and energizes consumers towards goals. Motivation incorporates need arousal, causing the drive that leads instrumental behaviour to reduce the drive.

动机是驱使和激励消费者完成购买目标的内在力量，动机包括唤醒需求，以产生有益的行为降低驱动力。

Consumer motivation is a complex matter to understand for many reasons. First, motives are inferred, a consumer motive cannot be seen or observed; what is noted is behaviour and then an assumption about the underlying behaviour is made. An important distinction should be made between merely describing behaviour and explaining behaviour. Saying, for example, that a customer buys low-cut tops, because she is the sort of person who likes to reveal her cleavage is mere description, whereas, for example, a particular purchaser of a Prada jacket may be said to be satisfying status needs, especially if the brand name is prominently shown on the garment.

由于各种原因，消费者动机是一个复杂的问题。首先，动机是臆测出的，消费者的动机是不能用眼睛看到的，能看见的只是消费行为，然后是对潜在行为作出的设想，对描述行为和解释行为这两方面应该进行明确的区分。例如，一位顾客想买低胸上衣，因为她是喜欢露出乳沟的人，这只是一个描述；反之，购买普拉达夹克衫的顾客则是为了满足个人对社会地位的需求，尤其是当商标出现在时装上显眼位置的时候。

Motivation is a complex concept as similar motives may find expression in different behaviour. Just as in the example above, a status-seeking consumer bought a Prada jacket, other people will seek different brands or may find non-fashion products or activities to satisfy status needs. Furthermore, people may buy the same product, but for different motives. Another purchaser of a Prada jacket may do so primarily for warmth and protection (a physiological motive) or for social motives, e.g. to be accepted by a particular group of friends.

动机是一个复杂的概念，因为不同的行为中能找到类似的动机，正如以上的例子，满足地位需求的消费者会买普拉达的夹克衫，其他人则会购买不同的品牌，或者买一些不时尚的衣服或者参与一些活动来满足自己对地位的需求。此外，人们也会因为不同的动机购买同样的商品，购买普拉达夹克衫的另一个消费者也许首先考虑的是夹克衫的保暖和防护功能（一种生理动机）或者因为社会动机，比如容易得到特定群体中朋友的认可。

Motives may change over time with, for example, a change in social status. The arrival of a child is often accompanied by a change in motivation towards clothing purchases for most women. Another consideration is that many motives may simultaneously affect purchasing behaviour. Sometimes the motives operate to make the consumer positive towards the clothing item, whereas at other times there can be motive conflict. An example of motive conflict could be a person attracted to the purchase of a coat that will satisfy status needs, but at the same time repelled as the coat may not be warm enough to satisfy a physiological need.

动机会随时间而改变，例如社会地位的改变。对大多数女性来说，买衣服的动机会随孩子的出生而改变。另外需要考虑的是很多动机有可能同时影响购买行为，有时候动机会让消费者对购买的商品产生正面的评价，而有的时候则会产生与动机相反的评价，举个例子来说，因为一件外套能够满足消费者对社会地位的需求，消费者会产生购买动机，但同时相反的评价是这件外套不暖和，不能满足生理上的需求。

There are several ways of classifying motives and these are described below. Motives can be placed along a continuum from rational to emotional. Buying a waterproof hat clearly has a strong rational element; an evening dress costing several thousand pounds that will be worn only once is obviously near the other end of the continuum. Another question to consider is whether the consumer is conscious of all the motives impelling choice. Freudian theory likens the personality to an iceberg where people are only partly aware of their motives. Many consumers may be unaware of or unwilling to admit to some of the motives that cause them to buy or avoid certain garments. It is easier for many people to assert that an item was bought because it looks nice than to admit that it was bought to impress others. The measurement of consumer motivation is problematic and some qualitative techniques for measuring motives are outlined in Chapter Four.

动机有几种分类方法。动机可以置于理性至感性转变的过程之中，购买一项具有防水功能的帽子明显是基于很强的理性因素，花几千英镑买一件只穿一次的晚礼服则很显然是同一个体的另一端反应即感性。还有一个需要考虑的问题是，消费者能否意识到所有的动机都能促使其做出选择，弗洛伊德学说把人性比喻成冰山，人们只能意识到部分动机。很多消费者可能没有意识到或者不愿承认某些让他们产生购买或者不购买衣服的动机，对很多人来说，让他们承认购买某件商品是因为商品好看，而不是因为给别人留下好印象要容易得多。如何测试消费动机还是一个疑问，第 4 章中会简要阐述测试动机的一些定性技巧。

A widely cited classification system for motivation was developed by Abraham Maslow. Maslow, a psychologist, stated that motives were organized in a hierarchy and that only when lower-level needs were satisfied did higher-level needs become important (Figure 3.7).

亚伯拉罕·马斯洛曾提出了一个广泛应用的动机分类体系，作为心理学家的他认为动机是按照级别组织起来的，只有当满足了较低层次的需求后，较高层次的需求才会变得重要（图 3–7）。

Figure 3.7 Maslow's hierarchy of needs. 图 3–7 马斯洛的需求层次

Thus the consumer on a limited income will be concerned with perhaps the functional aspects, such as warmth, of low-cost clothing before matters of social acceptance assume importance. Social needs include the need to belong and be accepted by others. Esteem needs are the need for the consumer to think well of themselves and have others hold a high opinion of them. Self-actualization, for Maslow, was the desire to grow psychologically and it embraces creativity and achievement. For one person knitting needles and some wool may enable self-actualization, whereas for another the participation in the design process by suggesting colours or styling aspects of a garment enables self-actualization. Some clothing purchases may satisfy needs at more than one level, e.g. a Barbour waxed jacket may satisfy the need for warmth and protection from the elements as well as enab-ling acceptance by a group who are similarly dressed. The translation of product features into specific benefits related to motives is a key selling task and this is described in more detail in Chapter Nine.

因此收入有限的消费者或许会关注商品的功能方面，例如廉价衣服的保暖性，而较少考虑时装的社会属性。社会需求包括归属感或者被别人认可；尊重需求是指消费者自我感觉良好，并且别人对自己也有很高的评价；在马斯洛看来，自我实现是对心理成长的渴望，它包含自身的创造力和成就。对某一个人来说，针织品和毛织品都能实现自我价值，而对另一个人来说，参与到一件衣服的设计、提供颜色和款式方面的建议，才能实现自我价值。购买时装可能会同时满足多个层次的需求，例如巴伯尔防水夹克衫可以保暖，而且具有防护性，同样也会被一个有着近似穿着的群体所接受。把商品的特点转换为和动机相关的特殊利益是一项重要的营销任务，这部分在第 9 章中有更详尽的讲述。

3.4.5 Consumer personality ／消费者个性

Personality is the particular configuration of qualities that make a person unique. Two main approaches to personality will be considered, psychographics and the self-concept.

个性是一个人区别于他人的特殊的品质，有两种主要的方式形成人的个性，分别是消费心态和自我意识。

Earlier approaches to consumer behaviour concentrated on consumer personality traits and tried to discover consumer types. The hope was that having identified certain types of consumer, buyer behaviour could be predicted and fashion products could be produced and promoted accordingly. Unfortunately, the correlation between personality type and buying behaviour was very small and this approach was succeeded by one which based consumers not on traits, but on activities, interests and opinions (AIOs). This is known as psychographics or lifestyles. Typically consumers are asked a large number of questions, usually based on a Likert scale, as described in Chapter Four, of general and specific questions relating to AIOs. Examples of such questions are 'I believe regular exercise is essential for good health' (general) and 'I go swimming at least once a week' (specific). The answers to these questions are then analysed together with demographic, purchasing and media data about consumers to derive distinct groupings, or types who have AIOs in common. Some interesting analyses

之前研究消费行为的方法主要集中在个性的具体特点上，并且试图明确消费类型，以期识别消费者的消费模式，预测购买行为，并且生产和销售相对应的产品。遗憾的是，消费者的个性类型与购买行为之间并没有太大的关系，这种方法能够取得成功的基础不是研究消费者的特点，而是分析他们的行动、兴趣和观点（AIOs），这就是我们所知道的消费心态学或生活方式。通常会以第 4 章中李克特量表的形式提问典型消费者很多与 AIOs 相关的一般问题或者特殊问题，此类问题有“我认为常运动有利健康”（普遍）“我每周至少游泳一次”（特殊）。然后结合统计学、购买以及媒介数据将消费者分为不同的小群体或者具有相同 AIOs 的人群。人们已经将以生活方式划分的群体和地理人口统计联系起来进行了相关的分析，

have been undertaken linking clothing lifestyle groups with geodemographics and this work will be discussed later in this chapter.

本章后续也会继续阐述。

These lifestyle groups are given names and can be the basis of target marketing efforts or used as a platform for advertising copy design or store design. The major drawback to lifestyle analysis is the lack of theoretical underpinning or measures of reliability or validity of much of the work undertaken. Evidence suggests that general lifestyle analysis is less useful and that research is best conducted into specific products and related areas such as health, beauty and fashion. Some labels given to the groups are plainly insulting to consumers, such as apathetics or dowdies, and at worst are little more than promotional aids for advertising agencies trying to sell their services to retailers and manufacturers. Recent work by Mintel and TGI on fashion lifestyles in Europe examined the incidence of eight lifestyle categories (Big Spenders, Label Admirers, Well Dressed, Stylish, Fashion Conscious, Shopaholics, Individualists and Practical) across four EU countries (UK, Germany, France and Spain). Marked differences were found between Germany and France, for instance where Germans were over-represented as Big Spenders and Label Admirers, whereas French consumers were over-represented as stylish and fashion conscious. The clear implication of this research for retailers is that the influence of culture means lifestyle marketing is perhaps not easily transferred across national boundaries. When done systematically, lifestyle analysis can offer real insights into buying behaviour, but there is no consensus on methodologies and the technique is expensive and needs to be undertaken continuously.

这些有着不同生活方式的群体会被重新命名，以作为制定目标市场策略的基础或者作为广告设计或店铺设计的参考。生活方式分析的最大缺陷是缺少理论支持，缺少对所进行的工作的可靠性和实用性的评定。各种迹象表明，对普遍生活方式进行分析的用处不大，最好是和具体的产品或者相关方面如保健、美容和时尚结合起来分析。给予这些群体的标签如冷漠、懒散等有的时候会冒犯他们，最差的情况也就是广告代理公司进行促销宣传试图销售他们的服务给零售商或者制造商而已。敏特调查公司和 TGI［译者注 TGI：即“目标群体指数”，可反映目标群体在特定研究范围（如地理区域、人口统计领域、媒体受众、产品消费者）内的强势或弱势。其计算方法是：TGI 指数 =（目标群体中具有某一特征的群体所占比例 / 总体中具有相同特征的群体所占比例）× 标准数 100。］最近关于欧洲时尚生活方式的研究划分了八种类型的生活方式（异常挥霍、名牌崇拜、穿着体面、时髦、具有时尚意识、购物狂、个性、实用），覆盖了欧洲地区的四个国家（英国、德国、法国、西班牙），德国和法国存在明显的差异。例如，德国挥金如土者和名牌崇拜者占多数，而法国的消费者则是时髦、具有时尚意识者占多数，这项研究对零售商有一个清晰的暗示，即文化的影响意味着生活方式营销也许不会很难移植到不同的国家。通过系统的研究，对生活方式的分析使得我们对购买行为有一个清晰的认识，但在研究方法上没有达成共识，研究方法花费高而且需要持续性地进行。

Analysis of the self-concept is another major strand of research from the area of consumer personality studies. The dimensions of the self-concept include:

自我概念的分析是研究消费者个性特点时忽视的一个方面，自我概念的研究包括：

◆ the self-image, which is how the person sees him- or herself;

◆ 自我形象，指一个人如何看待自己；

◆ the ideal self-image, which is how the person would like to see him or herself;

◆ 理想的自我形象，指一个人希望如何看待自己；

◆ the social self-image, which is how the person thinks others see him or her;

◆ the ideal social self-image, which is how the person would like others to see him or her.

In addition, the self-concept is influenced by situational factors such as who the 'others' are and the context of buying. Thus there seem many 'selves', although there is an enduring sense of continuity and sameness that provides coherence for the consumer and this is known as identity. It should be noted that consumers do not always accurately perceive themselves or the reactions of others towards them. The main tool for measuring the self-concept is the semantic differential scale and that is described in Chapter Four.

For the fashion marketer, the self-concept represents a promising area as clothing is an obvious way in which a consumer may express him- or herself and show how they would like others to judge them. Consumers buy clothes both to maintain and to enhance the self, depending on the ascendency or salience of the self versus ideal self-image. Self-images are affected by many factors, but most notably by age and social class. Perceived opportunities and/or the lack of opportunities can influence not only images of the self, but also the value placed upon the self, namely self-esteem.

◆ 社会自我形象，指一个人认为其他人如何看待自己；

◆ 理想的社会自我形象，指一个人希望其他人如何看待自己。

除此之外，自我形象受外界环境的影响，例如“其他人”指哪些人，以及购买的过程是怎样的。尽管持续性的感知和相似性能够体现消费者的一致性，但依然会有很多个“自身”这样的词汇，这就是我们所说的“身份”。值得注意的是，消费者并不是一直都能准确地感知自身或者感知其他人对自身的反映。测定自我概念最主要的方法就是语意上的差别量表，这将在第 4 章中讲述。

对时装营销人员来说，自我概念呈现的是一个期望的现象，就像穿着是体现消费者的最直接方式，也会体现他们希望别人如何评价自己。消费者购买时装既是为了体现自我，也是增强自我的形象，这取决于与理想的自我形象相比自我形象本身的优越性和突出性。影响自我形象的因素很多，最明显的就是年龄和社会地位。能够察觉到机会或者错过机会不仅会影响自我形象，而且会影响置于自身形象之上的价值,即自我尊重。

3.5 Sociological aspects of consumer behaviour ／消费者行为的社会属性

Consumers are social creatures, who form groups and interact in relation to goals. Consumer behaviour when viewed from a sociological perspective is more than a simple aggregation of individual acts, for the patterns and processes of both individual acts and wider social changes are profound in their impact on fashion marketing. Several social dimensions of consumer behaviour will be examined and these relate particularly to the process of influence over choice and to the basis for segmenting markets.

消费者是社会的产物，他们组成团体并且在达成目标的过程中相互影响。从社会学的角度看人们的消费行为不只是简单的多个行为的组合，因为每个人的行为发生的模式和过程以及社会变化对时装营销产生的影响是深远的。文中将会讨论几个消费行为方面的社会要素，这些要素对购买选择有着一定的影响，同时也是市场细分的基础。

3.5.1 Social groups ／社会群体

A group may be defined as two or more people who bear a psychological relationship to one another and who interact in relation to a common purpose. People do not just form groups, they form groups for reasons

群体可以定义为相互具有心理关系且为共同的目标相互影响的两个或多个人。人们不仅是组成群体，他们组成群体的原因是想得到社会需求的满足，也

such as to satisfy social needs, for mutual protection and enhancement or to check attitudes and perceptions. The price of group membership is conformity to norms, a norm being a shared expectation of behaviour. Norms are essential to groups as they enable stability and provide a framework within which identities may be expressed and common goals can be pursued.

是希望相互保护和提高以检查自己的态度和看法。群体中的个人对价格的看法与准则相一致，这是一个分享期望行为的准则。对于群体而言，这个准则是必须的，因为在描述身份的时候会确保稳定性并且会提供一个框架，进而能够实现共同的目标。

For many aspects of life there is uncertainty and groups provide a mechanism to check that uncertainty. This checking function is apparent in clothing purchases where the advice and support of friends is sought to check, among other things, the appropriateness of styling of garments and whether the items represent good value for money. Group members do not usually dress identically, but for specific occasions there are norms or unwritten rules about the range of garments and stores that would be considered acceptable. For example, a group of friends may all visit an Escada store (Figure 3.8), but not necessarily buy the same items within that store. The young man whose friends usually wear blue denim clothes doesn't turn up to meet his friends wearing a suit without the anticipation of a little teasing.

鉴于生活的许多方面都存在不确定性，群体提出了一种方式来检查这种不确定性。在购买时装时，这种检查的作用显而易见，当衡量一件衣服的款式是否合适以及商品是否物有所值的时候，人们通常都会征求朋友的意见和支持。群体成员通常不会穿着统一的时装，但在特定场合有一些规范和不成文的规定，即哪一类的时装或者店铺是被认可的。例如，一群朋友去逛艾斯卡达的店铺（图3-8），他们并不需要在店内购买相同款式的时装。穿着牛仔服的年轻人很少与穿西装的那些朋友见面，因为可能会被嘲笑。

The mechanisms of maintaining conformity are rewards for compliance and punishments for deviance.

保持一致的方法是遵守则奖励、违反则惩罚。多数的监管都是通过非口头

Figure 3.8 Escada store. 图 3-8 艾斯卡达店铺

Much of the control is exercised by non-verbal means or joking and teasing. These methods allow group members to retain dignity and comply without the great risk that would follow from blunt verbal demands. Norms for dress are most explicit for formal occasions where the expectations may be printed on invitations. Many workplaces have dress codes, although these vary in specificity from the rigidly prescriptive uniform through the broad list of exclusions to the vague hints about dress related to status within the organization.

The anticipation of the reactions of others can be a key factor in the choice of clothing. Consumers may not accurately anticipate those reactions or may lack confidence and rely upon friends to advise and accompany them on shopping trips. Everybody differs in their social needs and those with the highest needs will tend to conform the most. The discussion so far has concentrated on face-to-face groups where conformity is often greater.

Consumers also belong to many groups that are not face to face; they also may aspire to belong to certain groups and still further wish to distance themselves from others. Everyone belongs to automatic groups by virtue of age, gender, race, religion, etc. and with membership come sets of expectations of how one ought to dress. Two women may both have legs that are flattered by short skirts, but if one woman is in her fifties and the other in her early twenties, the social influences and pressures to conform may be markedly different.

Groups that individuals identify with are known as reference groups and as noted they can be positive, negative or aspirational. An example of negative reference group influence may be a young man not buying a well-known brand of boot because he thinks they are worn by skinheads and racists. Aspirational reference group influence is most apparent when people apply to join new organizations – for instance most people take care over their job interview outfit. Similarly, parents sending children to school for the first time will make an effort to dress their child in a way that will enable him or her to be accepted quickly. Reference group influence is important not only for styles of fashion products, but also for endorsements and rejections of particular brands. Teenage purchases of trainers are influenced by what brands are regarded as 'in' and what is considered 'out' by the reference group.

的方式或开玩笑和取笑来进行的，这些方法容许集团员工保留自尊和顺从，也不会因为遵守那些生硬的口头要求而遭受风险。在正式场合的着装要求会清晰地印在邀请函上。尽管从严格的特定制服到列出的一些不恰当的着装，以及模糊着装所体现的个人在组织中的地位，这些方面是具有不同特点的，但是许多工作场所依旧有穿着要求。

在选择时装时，他人的反应是一个关键的因素。消费者不能准确预测别人的反应，因此会依赖朋友的建议并且和他们的朋友一起购物。每个人的社会需求不同，但是最高需求却是趋于一致的。以上讨论针对的是面对面的群体，对于他们来说遵守规范往往更重要。

消费者还属于很多非面对面的群体，他们渴望加入某些群体但又希望与他人保持距离。因为年龄、性别、种族、信仰等因素会把每个人自然地归属于一个群体，群体成员则会制定出一套着装规范。两名女性穿短裙时，腿会显得很美。但如果一个五十多岁，而另一个只有二十出头，她们受到的社会影响和压力可能会明显不同。

识别个人的群体被称为参照群体，这个群体会被描述为正面的、负面的或是有雄心壮志的。参照团体产生负面影响的例子如下：一个年轻人不购买某知名品牌的长靴，因为他认为这靴子应该是光头仔和种族主义者穿的。当人们申请加入新的群体时，有雄心壮志的参照群体的影响是显而易见的，例如大部分人都会认真对待面试时的着装。同样，第一次送孩子去学校的父母也会重视孩子的穿着，以使得他们能够很快地被接受。参照群体不仅对时尚品的款式有影响，而且会影响人们接受或者排斥某些品牌。青少年购买运动鞋的时候，会受到参照群体认识的影响，如哪些品牌是时尚的，哪些品牌是落伍的。

3.5.2 Opinion leadership ／意见领导力

Opinion leadership refers to the degree of influence exerted where a consumer is faced with a choice. Many people discuss clothing and fashion advertising as a normal part of social interaction. The influence of others is accepted under certain circumstances. When little information about garments or stores is possessed or when the information is out of date, consumers seek information from others. Opinions are also sought where products are highly visible such as outerwear or where the garment involves risk because it may be expensive, go quickly out of fashion or simply prove unpopular with significant others. Opinion leaders exist in all groups and indeed the role may change according to the issue facing the group; one person may exert much influence over the choice of where to dine, whereas another group member may have sway over which are the best clothing stores to visit.

Celebrity influence is a particular type of opinion leadership. Evidence on celebrity influence shows that it is most powerful when the celebrity selected has credibility, is attractive, is trustworthy and is likeable. The enduring involvement of many leading fashion houses with clothing celebrities at the Oscar Awards is testimony to their belief in the power of such influence. Further examples of celebrity influence and their use in fashion promotion are discussed further in Chapter Nine.

There are many reasons why people try to influence others about fashion products and services, as shown in Figure 3.9. There may be genuine concern for the well-being of a friend and advice is given on obtaining value for money by visiting particular stores. The influencer or opinion leader may talk about fashion products because he or she is fascinated by the design or fabrics used. Sometimes a fashion message via advertising or public relations may prompt discussion and generate much media coverage. Dolce & Gabbana, Sisley, Puma, Benetton and Wonderbra have all used advertisements at times that have provoked strong public reactions. At other times opinion leaders may talk about clothing as a way of establishing self-worth by claims to superior knowledge or taste. In addition, the opinion leader may discuss an item of clothing as a way of reducing his or her dissonance (see earlier).

Fashion marketers often hope to use opinion leadership

意见领导力指的是当消费者面临选择时所受影响的程度。许多人把讨论衣服和时装广告作为社交活动的一部分，在某些情况下会接受别人的影响。当对时装、商店信息了解很少或不知道信息什么时候过期的时候，消费者通常会从他人那里获取信息，同样也会获取一些看法，即什么地方能够买到外套，什么地方买衣服会存在风险，例如衣服价格贵、很快会过时、大多数人不喜欢等。任何群体中都有意见领导，并且这个角色会根据群体所面临的问题不同而变化；一个人在选择何处就餐时可能会有较大的影响力，而另一个人则会在决定哪一个时装店是最好的时候摇摆不定。

名人的影响是意见领导力的特殊类型。证据表明，若所选择的名人是有信誉的、迷人的、值得信赖的和可爱的，这样的影响是最有效的。许多顶级时装屋持续支持参加奥斯卡颁奖礼的名人，就说明了这种影响的程度。名人效应和在时装促销中应用的实例将在第 9 章中进一步讲述。

为什么人们试图在时装产品和服务方面影响他人？这有多个原因，如图 3–9 所示，当中有些可能是真正关心朋友的幸福，并且会逛一些特色商店给朋友提供物有所值的建议。影响者或者意见领袖可能会谈论一些时装产品，因为他们被产品的设计或所使用的面料所吸引。有时通过广告或公共关系所传播的一条时尚信息很可能会引发激烈的讨论或者媒体报道。杜嘉班纳、希思黎、彪马、贝纳通和神奇胸罩等品牌有时也会进行广告宣传，而且也引起了强烈的公众关注度。其他时候，意见领袖则会以提出一些专业的知识或者品位来建立自我价值的方式谈论时装。除此之外，意见领袖还会把讨论一件衣服作为减少不合群的一种方式。

时装营销人员希望利用意见领导力

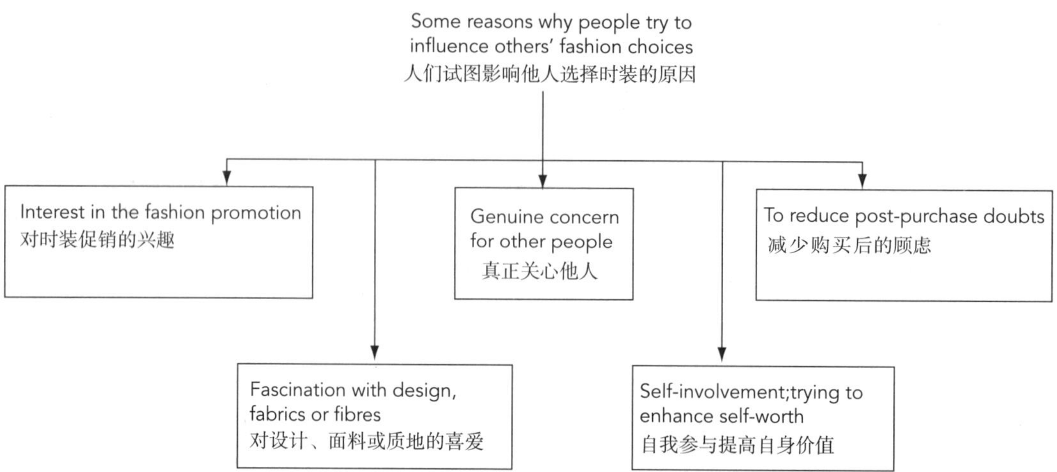

Figure 3.9 Opinion leadership. 图 3–9 意见领导力

as a way of encouraging the diffusion of a product range. If opinion leaders can be identified and targeted with promotional efforts, then the hope is that the message will be distributed via word-of-mouth communications. Fashion media personnel perform an important role in the word-of-mouth process and the marketing efforts directed at them will be discussed in Chapter Nine, particularly with regard to public relations, trade fairs and exhibitions.

来扩充产品系列，如果能够确定谁是意见领袖，并且有针对性地进行促销，那么信息就会通过口头传播的方式散布出去。在这个口头传播的过程中，时尚媒体工作者发挥着重要的作用。第 9 章将讨论他们所制定的营销策略，特别是关于公共关系、交易会和展览会。

3.5.3 The family ／家庭

The family is the basic social group and the main mechanism by which social values and aspirations are transmitted. The family is important to the fashion marketer because families share finite financial resources and media exposure, and they make some purchases either collect-ively or in anticipation of the reaction of other family members. Paying attention to the role of the family is important when it is realized that the person buying the item of clothing may not be the wearer. For example, about half of all male underwear in the UK and a significant proportion of knitwear for men are purchased by women.

Families, as defined by government statisticians, are persons related by blood, marriage or adoption who reside together. It is tempting to view the family as in decline when newspaper headlines about divorce rates are considered. However, the family remains a strong institution in British society, most people get married

家庭是最基本的社会群体，是传播社会价值和期望的主要途径，家庭这一因素对时装营销人员而言至关重要，因为家庭成员共用经济资源并且关注相同的媒体，他们通常会一起购买或者根据其他家庭成员的反应来决定是否购买。当意识到衣服的购买者并不一定是穿着者的时候，就知道了家庭的重要性。例如，在英国大约一半男性的内衣和大部分的男性针织时装都是女性购买的。

政府统计人员把家庭定义为有血缘、婚姻或收养关系的居住在一起的人。当注意到报纸上有关离婚率的新闻时，人们会认为家庭的数量正在减少。然而，在英国社会中家庭仍然是强有力的机

and the majority of those do not get divorced. Over the long term, divorce is a factor that has had a major influence upon the lives of many people and is often accompanied by a reduced purchasing capacity for either or both former marriage partners.

构，结婚的人当中大多数都不会离婚的。从长远来看，离婚对多数人的生活会产生较大的影响，随之发生的是前婚姻一方或双方购物量的减少。

The family life cycle is an attempt to classify people according to the age of the head of household, marital status, and the age and number of children. Early models of the family life cycle, by Wells and Gubar, omitted the occurrence of divorce and made the assumption that everyone followed the same route from birth to old age, namely single, married without children, married with children, etc. Later models of the family life cycle have recognized the role of divorce, but there is still a need to account for the extent of cohabitation, the number of people who remain single all their lives and alternative lifestyles.

家庭的生命周期是根据户主的年龄、婚姻状况及孩子的年龄和数量进行分类的。威尔斯和古芭早期提出的家庭生命周期模型没有考虑离婚的问题，并且认为每个人从生到老都是一样的，即单身、已婚没有孩子、已婚有孩子等。后来建立的家庭生命周期模型意识到离婚这一现象，但也有必要说明同居的情况、终生保持单身的人口数量以及另类的生活方式。

Modelling the progress of people through time via the family life cycle is useful for two major reasons. People at the same stage of the life cycle may, because of similar demands upon income, constitute target markets for companies. The fashion retailer Next grew dramatically during the early 1980s by recognizing and responding to a demographic change connected with the family life cycle. Further, knowledge of how many people are at a certain stage in the life cycle enables predictions for future demand. For instance, knowing the marriage rate and the fertility rate, some fairly accurate estimates can be made about the number of births over the next few years. This information is vital for manufacturers of baby clothes and stores such as babyGAP and Gapkids.

通过家庭生命周期来模拟人的成长过程之所以有用，主要有两个方面的原因。处于生命周期同一阶段的人们会构成企业的目标市场，因为他们的收入水平相近。时装零售商奈克斯特在20世纪80年代初期得到了快速的发展，是因为它意识到与家庭生命周期相关的人口结构的变化并及时采取了有效的策略。进一步而言，了解处于生命周期某一阶段的人口的数量就可以预测未来的市场需求。例如，根据结婚率和出生率可以较准确地预测出未来几年的新生儿数量，这样的信息对于像盖璞婴儿装和盖璞幼儿装这样的童装生产商来说是极其重要的。

Family decision-making is important for fashion marketers, for it is important to know how decisions are made and who exerts influence over the clothing decisions made by families. Three stages of the purchasing process are relevant: initiation, information search and purchase decision. It may be within a family that the female notices that an item of clothing needs replacing, and she also may collect information via reading magazines or clothing catalogues to narrow the choice. In the same family the male may be the sole wage earner and he may be the person sanctioning the purchase. If such a pattern of decision-making were typical for the target market, then there would be clear implications about which media should be used for advertising.

家庭决策对时装营销人员来说同样很重要，因为他们需要知道决策是怎样制定的，以及谁会影响家庭对服装购买的决策。购买过程的三个阶段是相互关联的，包括提议、搜集信息和决定购买。在一个家庭中，女性往往会注意到需要购买新的时装，她会翻看杂志或者产品目录以缩小购买选择的范围。男性则可能是家庭中唯一有收入的人，他可能会赞成购买。如果这种决策方式在目标市场中是较为普遍的，那么就会启发商家来决定选择何种媒介进行广告宣传。

Family decisions can be classified according

家庭决策可以根据丈夫或妻子对特

to the degree of influence that husbands and wives exert for given product choices. Four types can be considered: husband-dominated, wife-dominated, joint and autonomic. Joint refers to equal influence and a shared decision and purchase. For example a couple may shop together to purchase a new suit for the husband. Autonomic refers to an equal number of decisions made, but those decisions are made separately. Autonomic decisions are perhaps best illustrated by gift purchases, where a female may buy some jewellery herself, but also receives other items purchased by her husband. The factors related to joint decision-making are higher-priced items and where the couple is younger. Whether young couples are more egalitarian or simply less knowledgeable about one another's needs is a matter to be determined by longitudinal research.

Family decision-making requires more research, in particular into the role of children in influencing clothing purchases. Changes in the level of participation in the labour market by married women and relative earnings of males and females mean continuous research is necessary in this area. Discovering the actual level of influence within families is problematic as influence is not always accurately discerned by the participants or even revealed to market researchers. The gender of the interviewer, the presence of the other party, and vanity and modesty from both partners can conspire to make this important research task very difficult to undertake.

定产品选择的影响力来分类，有四种类型：丈夫主导、妻子主导、共同决定和自主决定。共同决定是指具有同等影响，一起做出决定和购买，例如夫妻一同外出购物，为丈夫买一件西装。自主决定指所做决定的数量相同，但这些决定是独立产生的。购买礼物能够很好地解释自主决定，女性为自己购买珠宝，但同时还会收到丈夫购买的其他礼物。当购买高价商品，或者购买者是年轻夫妇的时候，通常都会是共同决定购买的。年轻夫妇是否追求平等或者对另一半的需求知之甚少是纵向研究需进一步解决的问题。

需要进一步对家庭决策进行研究，尤其是孩子对所购服装决策的影响。已婚女性参与职场的程度，以及男性和女性相对收入的变化暗示着还需要对家庭决策进行深入的研究。发现家庭成员的实际影响程度是很难的，因为他们自身往往都不能准确地看出这种影响，市场调研人员自然也很难了解。面谈者的性别、其他人的存在以及双方的虚荣、谨慎等因素凑在一起，使得这项重要的研究工作很难进行。

3.5.4 Social stratification ／社会阶层

All known human societies are stratified. Stratification refers to div-isions of people according to their economic position in society, whether they are aware of that position or not. In the UK the main method of determining social stratification or social class is based on occupation. The most widely used system in the fashion market is the National Readership Survey using A, B, C1, C2, D and E. Table 3.1 gives a brief outline of this system.

This system is not the only system nor is the basis of classification uncontradicted, but it is the most widely used system and can be useful in explaining some of the vagaries found in fashion purchasing. A thorough exposition and critique of theories of social class is beyond the scope of this book; however, its impact is undeniably pervasive. A simple model of the influence of social class is that a person's position in the social structure, as determined by occupation, is associated with purchasing power, sets of aspirations and constraints and

众所周知，人类社会是分阶层的。阶层是根据人们在社会中的经济地位而进行的划分，不论他们是否意识到。在英国，划分社会阶层主要依据的是职业。时装市场应用最广泛的是按照全国读者调查得到的 A、B、C1、C2、D 和 E 等级来划分的，表 3–1 对这个体系进行了简单的描述。

这个体系并不是唯一的，也并非毫无疑问，但它是应用最为广泛的，并且在解释时装购买过程中的一些变幻莫测的问题时是很有用的。对社会阶层进行深入分析和论述超出了本书的范围，然而，不可否认其影响是普遍的。社会阶层影响的一个简单例子就是一个人在社会结构中的地位是由

Table 3.1 Socio-economic groups 表 3–1 社会经济群体

Class 等级	% 占比	Description 描述
A	4.0	Upper middle class 中上层阶级 Higher managerial, administrative and professional 高级管理、行政和专业人士
B	21.9	Middle class 中产阶级 Intermediate managerial, administrative and professional 中级管理、行政和专业人士
C1	29.0	Lower middle class 中下层阶级 Supervisory, clerical or junior managerial, administrative or professional 监管、文秘或初级管理、行政或专业人士
C2	20.7	Skilled working class 熟练工人阶级 Skilled manual workers 熟练的操作工人
D	16.2	Working class 工人阶级 Semi–skilled and unskilled manual workers 半熟练或不熟练的操作工人
E	8.1	Those at the lowest level of subsistence 生活在最低层的人 Includes most pensioners and the unemployed 包括大多数退休及无业人士

Source:National Readership Survey(NRS Ltd) January to December 2006.
来源：全国读者调查，2006.01 ~ 2006.12。

membership of social groups, all of which lead to patterns of consumption. The process is not only one way, as how somebody's income is spent can be relevant to some of the causal factors. Savings can be one factor in social mobility, though how particular clothing purchases, in themselves, influence social class is both less clear and less powerful.

The links between clothing purchases and social class are less clear than in the past. Photographs from the 1920s and 1930s reveal that clothing was an easy way to depict class. Hats, in particular, were markers of social status. Nowadays, because of the fragmentation of styles, the range of choice available and the change in classes themselves, clothing is no longer an unambiguous guide to class. Socio-economic groups have all changed, partly on account of the changing occupational structure of the country – while far fewer workers are employed in large-scale manufacturing operations, the service sector has grown dramatically. To give one stark example, in 1907 over 7 million people worked in production industries in the UK and in 2007 the figure was

职业决定的，而这种地位与购买力、一系列欲望、约束以及群体成员相关，所有这些因素决定了消费类型。这并不是独立的，因为人们如何消费是有原因的。储蓄是社会流动性的一个影响因素。无论购买时装的行为有多特殊，其对社会阶层的影响依旧不会很明显，而且影响也不会很大。

与过去相比，购买时装和社会阶层之间的联系变得不那么明显了。从 20 世纪 20 年代到 30 年代的照片可以看出，时装是体现社会阶层的基本方式，尤其是帽子成为了社会地位的重要标志。现在，由于风格多样化，购买选择更多，而且随着社会阶层的变化，着装已不再是社会阶层的明显标志。社会经济群体都发生了变化，一方面是因为职业结构的变化，从事大规模制造业的操作工人比以前少得多，服务行业却得到了快速的发展。举一个鲜明的例子，1907 年在英国有超过 700 万人从事生产领域的工作，而到了 2007 年人数只有 300 万左右。在 20 世纪，更好的卫生保健、教育条件及生活水平改变了社会

around 3 million. The provision of better health care, education and higher standards of living through the twentieth century have changed all social classes. Class differences at the beginning of the twenty-first century are not the same as the class differences that prevailed a hundred years ago, but that is not to argue that a convergence of class values, attitudes and behaviour has occurred.

阶层。21 世纪初社会阶层的差别与一百年前盛行的社会阶层差别大不相同，但那不是讨论由此出现的社会阶层的价值、态度及行为。

Class remains a significant discriminator of consumer behaviour. Although it is not a linear relationship, there is a link between class and income, and the prospects of increases in income. People do not wear rank overtly via their clothing as in the armed forces, but ways are found by many to indicate status. Within social classes, distinctions can be made between creative professional people such as advertising copywriters and accountants in how they dress. The former may tend to favour less formal attire at work whereas the latter tend to dress more conservatively.

社会阶层仍然是消费行为的主要的识别符号。社会阶层与收入及收入预期的增长有关，尽管它们之间并不是线性关系。人们不会像在部队里一样通过着装来体现等级，但许多人依旧发现了能够象征地位的着装方式。在社会阶层内部，可以通过着装来区分哪些人从事的是富有创新性的工作，如观察广告编辑与会计师的穿着，前者工作时一般喜欢随意的着装，而后者的穿着则较为保守。

Many working-class people may reach their earnings peak early in their career, whereas many middle-class occupations have incremental salary scales. Such experiences, coupled with different entitlements to, and discretion over, holidays, pensions schemes and other 'perks', are associated with different 'world views'. The daily experience of work impacts on these views where, for example, a manager may exercise discretion and make decisions, and a manual employee may work to a rigid work schedule almost like a robot. Workplace tasks, rules or norms may place restrictions upon clothing that can be worn depending upon a person's position. Where uniforms have to be worn it is usually the lower levels that wear them – even the Japanese companies excuse their senior managers from the need to wear overalls. In consequence, clothing worn during the person's leisure time may be chosen to express a distance from, or affinity to, work identity. Class differences are evident in media use, store selection, ownership and use of credit cards and bank accounts, and annual expenditure on clothing and footwear per person.

许多体力劳动者在他们职业生涯的早期就达到了收入的高峰，而中产阶层的薪酬则是逐渐增加的，以这样的经验和不同的权利来确定假期、养老金计划、额外津贴等是与不同的“世界观”有关系的。日常的工作经历对他们的观念都会产生影响，例如经理会行使酌情权并且做出决定，而体力劳动者则像个机器人一样按照严格的时间表工作。工作内容、制度和准则会限制他们的着装，他们必须根据自己的地位选择恰当的着装。通常情况下，较低层次的工人必须穿制服，甚至日本企业以此作为高级管理者不必穿制服的理由。结果是，业余时间可以选择不同于或近似于工作身份的着装。社会阶层的差异在人们使用的媒介、商店选择、信用卡以及银行账户的所有权及使用权、每个人在时装和鞋品消费的年度支出方面表现得很明显。

3.5.5 Geodemographics / 地理人口统计

Related to social class is a newer system of classifying consumers based upon where they live. A small number of proprietary systems exist based upon the census and categories of neighbourhoods. One such system is ACORN, which stands for A Classification Of Residential

与社会阶层有关的一个新的方面就是根据居住地对消费者进行分类，也存在着少许建立在人口普查和地区划分基础上的专用体系。ACORN 就是这样的体系，它代表居民区的 A 级，

Neighbourhoods and is owned by CACI; Pinpoint is another. These systems are derived from statistical analysis of census variables to discover residential areas, usually census enumeration districts comprising about 150 households and approximately 450 people, that are distinct in composition.

The census data can be linked to survey data on purchasing behaviour and information on media usage. Knowing the postcode of a respondent, the market researcher can determine the geodemographic category. ACORN has 5 categories and 17 related groups. The categories are Wealthy Achievers, Urban Prosperity, Comfortably Off, Moderate Means and Hard Pressed. Among the categories in Urban Prosperity category there are groups known as Prosperous Professionals, Educated Urbanites and Aspiring Singles. The owner of the ACORN system is CACI and the hyperlink is: http://www.caci.co.uk.

Geodemographic data have been used by marketers for target marketing, media planning, setting sales targets by area, forecasting, market testing and selecting new locations for outlets. Among fashion firms, the heavy users are the mail order firms, although retailers such as House of Fraser are involved. Geodemographics presents a promising future for marketing, especially when demographic data are interlaced with psychographic data. However, a number of major criticisms can made of geodemographics. First, it relies on census material that, at best, will be at least one-year-old when it is first used and up to 11 years old before the next census material is readily available. The owners of these systems claim they are able to update their databases to take account of changes in the housing mix and local economies. The systems are in competition and currently are much more expensive than data from secondary sources. Geodemographics is not equally predictive of buying behaviour across all product categories. A geodemographic category is a composite of a number of variables such as class, age, ethnic origin and housing amenities, and critics assert that it is either social class sub-division by another name or a statistical artefact looking for a theory.

An interesting recent development is the combination of geodemographics with lifestyles, particularly those focused on fashion segments.

归CACI所有，Pinpoint则是另一个体系。这些体系源于对人口变量的统计分析，并且会以此来发现人们的居住地，通常人口普查是按照大约150户家庭或者大约450个人来确定区域并且进行数据统计的。

人口普查的数据和购买行为的调查资料以及媒体使用方面的信息相关，掌握了对媒介信息做出反应的人所在地的邮政编码，市场研究人员就可以确定地理人口统计的类型。ACORN有5种类型和17种相关团体，5种类型分别为：富有的成功者、都市中的富裕人群、相当富有的人、中等富裕者和经济拮据者。都市中的富裕人群是富有的专业人士，受过教育的城市居民，有抱负的单身等群体。ACORN归CACI所有，其链接为：http://www.caci.co.uk。

地理人口统计数据被营销者用于目标市场、媒体策划以及确定各区域的销售目标，也会用于市场预测、销售测试和新店铺选址。时装企业最大的客户是需要邮购订单的企业，即使是弗雷泽百货公司之类的零售商也包括在内。地理人口统计在市场营销中有着重要的作用，尤其是综合考虑人口统计数据与心理方面的数据时。然而，人们对地理人口统计也存在一些负面的评价。首先，统计的依据是人口普查材料，最好的情况也是在一年后才能得到数据，而在11年后才会有另外一份人口普查材料可用。虽然这些体系的所有者声称他们可以根据住房情况和当地经济的变化更新他们的数据库，但是对此还是有争议的，目前来说地理人口统计的费用要比二手资料的获取昂贵得多。地理人口统计并不能对所有商品的购买行为作出预测，一个地理人口统计的分类是由一些变量诸如阶层、年龄、民族和住房设施组成的，并且评论家声称它既是社会阶层细分的另一名称，又是寻求一种理论的统计假象。

近期一个有趣的发现就是将地理人口统计与生活方式，特别是与那些关注时尚的人的生活方式相结合。“益百利”与“特

One commercial system developed by Experian and TNS has categorized every adult in the UK into 1 of 20 female and 15 male categories called the Mosiac Fashion Segments. The categories are based on attitudes and shopping behaviour in relation to fashion and these are linked to the census and location data. An example of a female is 'Annabel' a type 12 female described as 'best-dressed fashionistas', aged 18–25, often living with parents, interested in designer labels, quality and style and shopping at River Island and Independent Stores. A male example is 'Stephen' a type 6 described as 'a mainstream father' aged 35–46 who shops at Next and Debenhams, he doesn't rate brands and quality is not a high priority for him, but he does like to spend money on clothing for his children. The actual profiles available give much more detail than that above and readers can access the full dataset via the hyperlink: http://www.business-strategies.co.uk/.

恩斯”开发的一个商业系统已经将英国的每个成年人都归类于了 20 种女性和 15 种男性中的一类，称为“默赛克”服装细分系统。这种分类是以和时装有关的态度和购买行为为基础，和人口普查和地区统计信息相关的。举个例子，属于类型 12 的称为“安娜贝尔”，她们被认为是“穿着最佳的时尚达人”，年龄在 18 ~ 25 岁之间，一般和父母同住，对设计师品牌感兴趣，关注质量、款式，通常会购买“瑞沃艾伦”的产品，或者会在一些特色店购物。属于类型 6 的男性被称为“斯蒂芬”，会被描述为“主流老爸”，他们年龄在 35 ~ 46 岁之间，通常会在奈克斯特和德本汉姆斯百货店购物，他们不推崇品牌，也不优先考虑质量，但是非常喜欢为他们的孩子们买衣服。真实的例子比上述内容的描述更加清晰，读者可以通过下面的链接获取全部数据：http://www.business-strategies.co.uk/。

Fashion marketers obviously need better tools for analysis and planning, and geodemographics combined with fashion lifestyles represents a significant advance, but it is not a panacea or even a clear successor to alternative methods of analysis. To ask some obvious questions, why should the type of dwelling have any bearing on the purchase of clothing? Does the buyer of a leather coat live in an inner city flat, an affluent suburb or a rural setting?

很显然，时装营销人员需要掌握更好的分析和策划方法，地理人口统计和生活方式相结合提供了一个很重要的启示，但是它不是万能药，也不是能够改变分析方法的替代者。问一些简单的问题，为什么居住类型与购买时装有关？皮衣的购买者是居住于市区公寓、富饶的郊区还是乡村？

3.5.6 Diffusion of innovation / 创新的传播

An innovation can be defined in a number of ways. Innovation can be anything that is new to the company, so it could include 'copying' a method of merchandising or a new style of garment. An innovation also can be taken to mean anything that has been taken up by only a small proportion of the market, usually 10% or less, or an item that has only been on the market for a short time. For the purposes of this discussion an innovation will be taken as anything the consumer perceives to be new, thus it could include an 'old' product introduced into a new market.

创新可以用多种方式定义，创新可以是任何对于公司来说新的东西，所以它可以包含复制一种营销方法或者一件时装的款式。创新也可以被认为是被小部分市场接受的任何事物，这个市场份额通常是 10% 或小于 10%，或者是上市不久的一件新品。为了此处讨论的需要，创新在此被看作是任何消费者认为的新事物，所以它可能会包含一个引入到新市场的“旧”商品。

Obviously different individuals will adopt new fashion products with differing degrees of enthusiasm

很明显，不同的人会以不同的热情和在不同的时间接受新的时装产品，创新

and at different times. The process by which the acceptance of an innovation is spread by communication to members of a social system is known as diffusion. Diffusion refers to how an innovation is spread among consumers (groups) over time, whereas adoption refers to individual acceptance of new products. Rogers (1983), after an extensive literature review, proposed a scheme whereby consumers are classified on the basis of the time when they adopt any innovation. Rogers' scheme is obviously arbitrary with regard to percentages, and therefore ideal types are presented in Table 3.2. The scheme is based on the common-sense notion that most users do not adopt the innovation simultaneously. Another way of looking at the issue is to conceive the process as being segmentation over time.

者接受的过程会在社会体系内的成员间通过交流进行扩散，这就是传播。传播强调的是一种创新随着时间是如何在消费者（群体）之间散布的，而接受指的是个体对新产品的认可。经过广泛的文献检索，罗格斯（1983）提出一个新的方案，这种方案是根据消费者接受创新的时间来将他们分类。从比例的分配来看，罗格斯的想法显然有些武断，因此表 3–2 给出了理想的分类情况。这一方案的产生是考虑到大多数顾客不会同时接受某一项创新。另一个看待此问题的方法就是将这一过程按照时间进行分段。

Instead of trying to find characteristics of the above five groups, modern research efforts have focused on the differences between innovators and non-innovators. In practice this means researchers have combined innovators and early adopters and compared them with the rest. Innovators tend to be more open-minded, inner- rather than other-directed, and younger rather than older. They also tend to be higher than non-innovators in terms of income, education, social mobility, and reading magazines and newspapers. Non-innovators tend to watch more television and perceive more risk in the purchase of new products than do innovators.

现今研究的焦点是创新者与非创新者的差别，而不是试图找到上述 5 个群体的特点，实际上这意味着研究者已经将创新者和早期采纳者结合起来和其他人进行比较。创新者思想更加开放，自主且不受人支配，并且更加年轻。他们在收入、教育、社会流动性和阅读杂志和报纸的数量上比非创新者要高，非创新者更喜欢看电视，并且会先于创新者意识到购买新商品的诸多风险。

There is only limited, and contested, evidence of the super-innovator, i.e. a person who is an innovator across several unrelated product areas. As with opinion leadership, the evidence suggests there is moderate overlap depending on product interests. Therefore we may find an innovator for fashion products to be an innovator for other aspects of appearance, but not necessarily for food or electronic items.

只有有限并且有争议的迹象表明超级创新者的存在，即一个消费者，他可能是多个不相关产品领域的创新者。与意见领导力一样，证据表明，其在对感兴趣的产品方面会有些重叠。因此我们或许能够找到时装产品的创新者，同时他们也是其他领域的创新者，而不一定是食品或者电子产品的创新者。

Table 3.2 A classification of adopters of innovations

表 3–2 创新接受者的分类

Innovators 创新者	2.5%
Early adopters 早期适应者	13.5%
Early majority 早期接受者	34%
Late majority 后期接受者	34%
Laggards 不接受者	16%

There is often a tendency to equate the innovator and the opinion leader. They may indeed be the same, but there are differences, as shown in Table 3.3. Opinion leaders are active since they tend to communicate with others, positively and negatively, about their purchases.

有时也会有一种将创新者与意见领袖等同的趋势，或者他们两者确实相同，但也会存在区别，如表 3–3 中所示。意见领袖是活跃的，因为他们易于与他人就购物进行积极的或者消极的沟通。

Table 3.3 Comparison of opinion leaders and innovators

表 3–3 意见领袖与创新者的对比

	Acceptor 采纳者	Rejector 拒绝者
Active 积极的	Opinion leader 意见领袖	Opinion leader 意见领袖
Passive 消极的	Innovator 创新者	Innovator 创新者

Fashion marketers are interested in the factors that influence the rate of diffusion, so that appropriate marketing action may be taken to overcome obstacles of speed during the process.

The main factors that influence the rate of diffusion are:

◆ Relative advantage: The more immediate and important the benefits, the faster the rate of diffusion in terms of lower cost or long product life.

◆ Compatibility: The innovation must match cultural values, beliefs and expectations. An example of a compatibility issue, when first introduced, was the Next Directory, one of the first major paid-for catalogues. More recent examples compatibility concerns are ethical use of labour and the use of sustainable raw materials in garment manufacture.

◆ Possibility of trials: The ability to try on garments or easily exchange those that cannot be tried on, i.e. mail order items, is a key factor.

◆ Observability or communicability: Ease with which information about an innovation is transmitted.

◆ The complexity of the innovation: The more complex, in terms of understanding and use, the slower the diffusion. Newer synthetic fabrics or garments that have complicated care or cleaning requirements are examples.

◆ Perceived risk: The greater the risk the slower the diffusion. Risk can be financial, physical or social. In addition, a perception may exist that a delay in purchasing will lead to lower prices.

◆ Type of target market: Some groups are more willing to accept change than others, e.g. the young,

时装营销人员对影响传播速度的因素感兴趣，因为适当的营销措施能够克服传播过程中影响速度的障碍。

影响传播速度的主要因素有：

◆ 相对优势：速度越快，获取利益越重要，低成本或生命周期长的产品就会被传播得越快。

◆ 兼容性：创新必须符合文化价值，信念和期望。有关兼容性的一个例子就是当奈克斯特的工厂店初建的时候，第一个需要付费的就是产品目录。很多时装制造商都开始关注用工的道德感以及原材料的可持续利用问题。

◆ 试穿的可能性：指的是能否试穿时装或者很容易退换那些不能试穿的时装，如对于邮购订货来说这点就很重要。

◆ 观察性和传播性：创新方面的信息传播的容易度。

◆ 创新的复杂性：过于复杂的、难以理解和运用的术语通常传播得较慢，例如新型合成材料或者用此生产的时装洗涤保养的要求。

◆ 意识到的风险：风险越高的信息传播得越慢，风险可能是经济方面的、生理方面或者社会性的。另外，较晚购买的话产品的价格会较低一些。

◆ 目标市场的类型：有些群体相比于其他群体而言更容易接受一些变化，例

the affluent or the highly educated.

如年轻人、富裕的人或者受过良好教育的人。

◆ Type of decision: Depends on whether the purchase of the innovation is an individual or a collective decision.

◆ 决策类型：取决于某种创新购买是个人发起的还是群体的意见。

◆ Marketing effort: The rate of diffusion is not completely beyond the control of the firm selling it. Greater promotional spending can speed the diffusion process.

◆ 营销策略：传播的情况并不会完全超出公司销售产品的范围。推广费用高会加速传播的速度。

Knowledge of diffusion of innovation may aid planning, particularly concerning setting targets over time and forecasting. The diffusion process is directly related to the product life cycle concept discussed in Chapter Six. The key roles of the innovator and early adopter are examined from the perspective of product planning in Chapter Six and in relation to promotion in Chapter Nine.

创新传播的知识能够协助营销人员进行策划，尤其是最后确定目标市场以及进行市场预测的时候。传播的过程与产品生命周期理念在第 6 章会介绍。从产品企划的角度来说，创新者和早期接受者的作用会在第 6 章分析，他们与促销的关系会在第 9 章阐述。

3.6 The organizational buyer ／团体购买者

The discussion so far has concentrated upon the retail consumer of fashion. It should be remembered that a significant amount of fashion marketing effort is directed at organizations, be they manufacturers or retailers, who buy to sell on, or companies who purchase garments for consumption by their staff. All of the concepts discussed so far have a bearing upon organizational buying, for organizational buyers are still humans with needs and attitudes, who also conform to social norms like consumers. However, there are some differences that do influence behaviour and these points will be addressed.

至此讨论的对象都是时装零售消费者，我们应该知道其实很多重要的营销策略也是针对团购组织的，他们可能是制造商或者零售商，他们先采购然后再销售，或者是那些给自己员工采购时装的企业。之前所讲的理念都是针对零售消费者，团体采购者也是具有需求和消费态度的自然人，像普通消费者一样，他们也必须遵守社会规范。然而，也有很多其他影响消费行为的因素，这点将会在后续介绍。

It is argued that because organizational buyers buy in bulk, are better trained and better informed, are accountable for their decisions and are often part of a buying team they are more rational than consumers. Organizational buying usually involves more formality with regard to explicit buying criteria or vendor rating systems and unlike most consumer buying, there is often negotiation over products and prices. Given the greater concentration in fashion retailing that has occurred in recent years (see Chapter Eight), organizational buyers are subject to personal forms of promotion, more so than consumers who receive mass communications and have impersonal relations with suppliers.

团体购买者采购商品的量都比较大，他们很有经验，掌握多方面的信息，并且要对自己的决定负责。通常他们属于采购团队，比普通消费者更有理性。团体采购的时候需要遵循明确的采购标准或者会对卖家进行排序，与大多数消费者的购买不同之处是，团体购买者可以和商家针对产品以及价格进行协商。近几年大家对时装零售有了更高的关注度（见第 8 章），团体采购者更多倾向于听取促销员的建议，而个人消费者则会从多种渠道获取信息，与供应商之间并没有直接联系。

The preceding arguments support the view that

更多的观点都认为团体购买者是比较

organizational buyers are more rational. However, there is another perspective that argues otherwise. Because organizational buyers are spending someone else's money they may be less careful than the consumer would be with his or her own money. Fashion is concerned with personal taste and the consumer needs only to be certain about his or her purchases, whereas the organizational buyer faces greater uncertainty in the anticipation of the needs of an assortment of others. This multiple responsibility for buying can, under some circumstances, lead to careless action, as personal accountability may be diffused via committees or teams. The extent of supplier loyalty displayed by retailers and manufacturers could be taken as being counterindicative of a more rational approach to buying than that of the consumer who shows no loyalty to any brand or retailer.

理性的，当然也有相反的看法。因为团体购买者花费的是其他人的钱，所以他们并不会像普通消费者一样谨慎地消费。时尚侧重的是个人的品位，而消费需求则和消费者个人的实际购买有关，团体购买者在预测需求的时候面对着很多的不确定性。因为团体采购者承担着很多责任，在某些情况下，可能会导致他们采取不谨慎的行动，同时每个人的责任也会通过组织或者团队进行传播。零售商和制造商对供应商的忠诚度可以认为是对理性采购的负面暗示，而不像有些消费者对品牌和零售商没有任何忠诚度。

Clearly the arguments about relative rationality cannot be easily resolved, but the point to note is that both types of buyer are influenced by psychological and sociological processes which are expressed in buying decisions. Key structural factors that enable fashion marketers to determine specific approaches to organizational buyers are developed further in Chapters Six to Nine, where the relationships between the organizations are explored in relation to the marketing mix.

很明显，相对理性是很难解释的一个观点，但需要指出的是两种类型的购买者在表达购买决策时都会受到心理以及社会因素的影响。促使时装营销人员决定研究团体购买者的方法的主要因素将会在第6章到第9章分析，同时也会比较团体购买者和组织之间的关系对企业营销组合的影响。

3.7 Summary / 小结

This chapter has introduced the concept of buyer behaviour in the fashion market. It has dealt with:

- ◆ the importance of understanding buyers;
- ◆ how individual customers make decisions;
- ◆ what types of decision they must make;
- ◆ psychological influences on customer decision-making;
- ◆ how fashion marketers classify customers and sociological influences;
- ◆ a comparison of organizational and consumer buying.

本章主要介绍了时装市场中购买行为的概念，具体内容包括：

- ◆ 认识购买者的重要性；
- ◆ 个体消费者是如何做出决策的；
- ◆ 消费者应该做出何种决策；
- ◆ 影响消费者决策的心理因素；
- ◆ 时装营销人员是如何将消费者和心理因素分类的；
- ◆ 团体购买者和个体消费者购买的对比。

Further reading / 课后阅读材料：

1.Ajzen, I. and Fishbein, M. (1980), *Understanding Attitudes and Predicting Social Behavior*, Prentice Hall, Englewood Cliffs, NJ.

艾奇森·I.，费希本·M.(1980)，《认识态度和预测社会行为》，普伦蒂斯霍尔出版公司，恩格尔伍德·克利夫斯，新泽西 .

2.Blackwell, R.D. *et al*. (2006), *Consumer Behavior*, 10th Edition, Thomson Business and Economics, Mason, OH.

布莱克威尔・R.D 等 .(2006),《消费者行为》, 第 10 版, 汤姆森商业和经济学, 梅森出版, 俄亥俄州 .

3.East, R. et al. (2008), *Consumer Behaviour*, Sage, London.

伊斯特・R 等 .(2008),《消费者行为》, 赛奇出版公司, 伦敦 .

4.Evans, M.J. *et al*. (2006), *Consumer Behaviour*, John Wiley and Sons, Chichester.

埃文斯・M.J. 等 .(2006),《消费者行为》, 约翰威利父子出版社, 奇切斯特 .

5.Festinger, L. (1957), *A Theory of Cognitive Dissonance*, Stanford University Press, Stanford, CA.

费斯廷格・L.(1957),《认知失调》, 斯坦福大学出版社, 斯坦福, 加利福尼亚 .

6.Peter, J.P. and Olsen, J.C. (2008), *Consumer Behaviour and Marketing Strategy*, 8th Edition, McGraw-Hill, London.

彼得・J.P., 奥尔森・J.C.(2008),《消费者行为与营销策略》, 麦格劳希尔出版集团, 伦敦 .

7.Rogers, E.M. (1983), *Diffusion of Innovations*, 3rd Edition, The Free Press, New York.

罗杰斯・E.M.(1983),《创新的传播》, 第 3 版, 独立出版社, 纽约 .

8.Schiffman, L.G. and Kanuk, L.L. (2007) *Consumer Behavior*, 9th Edition, Pearson Prentice Hall, Upper Saddle River, NJ.

谢夫曼・L.G. 卡努克・L.L. (2007),《消费者行为》, 第 9 版, 培生普伦蒂斯霍尔出版公司, 新泽西 .

9.Solomon, M.R. (2007), *Consumer Behavior*: *Buying*, *Having*, *and Being*, Prentice Hall, Harlow.

所罗门・M.R.(2007),《消费者行为: 采购》, 普伦蒂斯霍尔出版公司 .

10.Solomon, M.R. and Rabolt, N.J. (2004), *Consumer Behavior: In Fashion*, Prentice Hall, Upper Saddle River, NJ.

所罗门・M.R., 罗伯特・N.J.(2004),《时装消费者行为》, 普伦蒂斯霍尔出版公司, 新泽西 .

Chapter Four
Fashion Marketing Research
第 4 章 时装市场营销调研

4.1 Introduction ／引言

The purpose of this chapter is to provide an introduction to some of the main concepts and decisions involved in the research process, as well as the main techniques used in survey research.

Most adults in the UK have had some experience of marketing research, usually through contact with the 'lady with the clipboard' in street surveys. As such, the main emphasis of this chapter will be on the decisions that must be made as part of survey design; from the definition of the research problem to the design of the questionnaire and data collection. The application of marketing research to product development and fashion forecasting international marketing research issues and the impact of the Internet will also be considered.

本章主要介绍调研过程中涉及的主要概念和定义，以及调查研究的主要方法。

英国大多数成年人都经历过营销调研——在街上通过问卷进行的调查。本章的重点是调研设计中如何进行决策，包括调研问题的确定，以及问卷设计和数据统计，也会阐述营销调研在产品开发、趋势预测和国际营销问题研究等方面的应用，以及网络对营销调研的作用。

4.2 The purpose of marketing research ／营销调研的作用

4.2.1 What is marketing research? ／什么是营销调研

Kotler (2000) defines marketing research as 'the systematic design, analysis and reporting of data and findings relevant to a specific marketing situation facing the company'.

科特勒（2000）把营销调研定义为“系统地设计、收集、分析和报告与公司所面临的特定的营销状况有关的数据及发现的调查研究结果”。

It is often asked whether there is a difference between market research and marketing research. The difference is in the scope of an investigation, as shown in Figure 4.1. Market research is used to refer to research into a specific market, investigating such aspects as market size, market

市场调研和营销调研是经常容易混淆的两个概念。区别主要在调研内容方面，如图 4–1 所示。市场调研主要指的是针对某一特定市场的调查，包括市场规模、市场趋势、竞争者分

Figure 4.1 Comparison of market research and marketing research.

图 4–1 市场调研和营销调研的对比

trends, competitor analysis, and so on. Marketing research is a much broader concept, covering investigation into all aspects of the marketing of goods or services, such as product research and development, pricing research, advertising research, distribution research, as well as all the aspects of market analysis covered by market research.

析等。营销调研是一个广义的概念，包括市场上产品和服务的所有方面，如产品研发、价格调研、广告调研、渠道调研以及市场调研所涵盖的市场分析方面的内容。

4.2.2 Why is information necessary? / 为什么信息是必需的

In today's fierce market economy the risks faced by businesses are great. Aggressive competitors pose serious threats for both large and small businesses in the constant fight to maintain and increase their market share. To maximize opportunities the successful business person must make the right decisions at the right time. The consequence of making the wrong decision can be financial ruin.

Without the gift of clairvoyance, such decisions are problematic. An understanding of the market and the needs and wants of your consumers now and in the future are rarely based on intuition alone. Sound market information provides the basis for marketing decisions. Marketing research, properly designed and implemented, will provide this information.

在如今竞争激烈的市场经济环境下，各行业都面临着很大的风险。或大或小的企业都会受到强有力的竞争对手的威胁，它们不断在维持和扩大企业的市场份额。为了创造更多的机会，成功的商人必须能够在正确的时间做出正确的决策，一系列错误的决策会给企业带来经济上的损失。

如果没有超强的洞察力，企业所作的决策就有可能存在问题。从来没有谁会依靠直觉来了解市场的需求、现在和未来消费者的需求和欲望，可靠的市场信息会为营销决策提供资料，而这些信息的获取需要有效地设计和进行营销调研。

4.2.3 Marketing research as part of a marketing information system / 营销调研是营销信息系统的一部分

The wealth of information flowing into a company has to be organized so that it reaches the right people. Successful companies operate marketing information systems (MIS) to gather accurate, up-to-date information, analyse it and disseminate the results to appropriate decision-makers in time to allow the company to maximize its opportunities and to avoid potential threats. Along with other information producing departments within the company (sales, accounts, etc.), marketing research can assist management in the decision-making process across the full range of marketing activities, from description of a market segment to prediction of future trends.

流入公司的大量信息必须通过整理之后才能送至合适的人，成功的公司使用营销信息系统收集准确的、最新的信息，进行分析并且将结果及时汇报给决策者，以便扩大公司的营销机会，避免潜在的威胁。在整个营销活动中，营销调研得到的信息和公司内其他的信息收集部门（销售、会计部门等）获取的信息共同用于营销决策，包括细分市场的描述以及未来趋势的预测等。

4.2.4 The scope of marketing research / 营销调研的范围

There is no area of marketing activity to which the techniques of marketing research cannot be applied. Marketing research can provide information on the size and structure of a specific market as well as information about current trends, consumer preferences, a competitor's activities, advertising effectiveness, distribution methods and pricing research. Marketing research also plays a vital role in the development of new products and new advertising and promotion strategies. It can also monitor performance following implementation of those strategies.

The techniques used in the collection of marketing information depend largely on the nature of the research problem, but will vary from the well-known street interview carried out by the 'ladies with clipboards' to more sophisticated techniques such as projective techniques used in such areas as motivation research.

营销调研方法对任何的营销活动都适用。营销调研可以提供市场规模和某一特定市场结构方面的信息，同时也会提供当今潮流、消费者的特点、竞争者的市场活动、广告效果、分销策略以及价格方面的信息。同样，营销调研在新产品开发和新广告企划以及促销策略制定方面起着重要的作用，同时也需监控这些策略的执行情况。

营销信息收集的方法主要取决于调研问题的类型，但是它与众所周知的通过“笔记板女士”完成的街头调研方式完全不同，是一种更为精确的方法，例如动机调研时的投影技法。

4.2.5 Types of research / 调研方法

Although marketing research techniques can be applied to all areas of marketing, not all techniques are appropriate to every situation. Broadly speaking, there are two types of research: qualitative and quantitative.

Qualitative research uses techniques such as group discussions, individual depth interviews, projective techniques and observation. The information obtained

尽管营销调研的方法适合营销的任何环节，但并不是所有的方法都适用于任何情况。广义而言，有两种调研的方法：定性研究和定量研究。

定性研究运用分组讨论、个别深度访谈、实验法和观察法。获取的信息主要是现实情况是怎样的，

attempts to find out the 'how' and 'why' of a situation, rather than 'how many'. Analysis may be difficult owing to the depth and complexity of the data collected and so it should be carried out by experienced and trained researchers. Qualitative research is invaluable for basic exploratory studies, new product development and creative development studies.

为什么会是这样的，而不是有多少信息。收集的资料复杂多样，分析就会比较困难，因此必须由有经验的并且经过培训的调研人员进行调研。定性研究对于基础的考察研究、新产品开发和创新研究来说是非常有用的。

Quantitative research provides information to which numbers can be applied. Quantitative research is the best-known face of marketing research and its main survey method is what most people recognize as marketing research.

定量研究得到的是数据信息，它是营销调研最主要的方面，其中应用最多的研究方法就是人们所讲的营销调研。

4.3 An overview of the marketing research process／营销调研过程的概述

The collection of information is a process that must be planned. There are many different areas in which planning decisions need to be made, so good organization is vital.

信息收集的过程是需要计划的，很多方面都需要进行详细的计划和决策，因此有效的组织和安排是至关重要的。

4.3.1 Stages in the research process／调研过程的各个阶段

Research procedures will vary depending on the nature of the research problem, but in general, the process of marketing research can be seen to be made up of a number of stages. They are:

1. Define the research problem and set the research objectives.
2. Design the research. This includes:
   (a) data sources;
   (b) select the sampling method;
   (c) select the data collection method;
   (d) design the data collection form (questionnaire).
3. Test the research design (pilot).
4. Collect the data.
5. Analyse the data and interpret the results.
6. Present the findings.

调研过程根据调查问题的特点而有所不同，一般而言，营销调研过程有几个阶段。它们是：

1. 确定调研问题和调研目标。
2. 市场调研设计，包括：
   （a）资料来源；
   （b）选择抽样方法；
   （c）选择资料收集方法；
   （d）设计资料收集方式（调查问卷表）。
3. 检查调研设计（测试）。
4. 收集资料。
5. 分析资料并且说明结果。
6. 提交报告。

4.4 Problem definition and setting research objectives／确定问题和锁定调查对象

Defining the research problem is the most critical step in the research process. Unless the problem is accurately defined, the information collected will be of limited or no use. Careful thought and discussion about the problem, the information needed to address the problem

确定调研问题是调研过程中最为关键的一步，只有准确地确定调研问题，收集到的资料才会有用。对问题仔细考虑和分析，必须提前准备要分析的问题所需要的资料以及明确

and the relative value of the information collected should take place before anything else. A structured, systematic approach to decision-making will also enable management (or the commissioner of the research) to set the objectives of the research. In other words, what is the problem and what do we want to find out to try to solve it? This preliminary planning is important as it has implications for the design of the research and the quality of the information collected.

所收集信息的价值。一个有组织的、系统的营销决策方法同样便于管理者（调研专员）确定调研对象。换句话说，就是问题是什么以及我们想找到什么样的方法解决这个问题？这个初步计划是重要工作，因为它事关调查设计和信息收集的质量。

4.5 Research design ／调研设计

There are three types of research design: exploratory, descriptive and causal. The choice of research design will depend on the problem previously defined.

调研设计有三种类型：探索性研究、描述性研究和因果关系研究，调研设计主要根据先前确定的调研问题而定。

4.5.1 Exploratory research ／探索性研究

This is most useful in the early stages of research, particularly if the researcher is not familiar with the subject area. There is no formal structure to exploratory research as the researcher needs to look at a wide range of information sources without being restricted. The aim of exploratory research is to uncover any variables that may be relevant to the research project as well as an investigation of the environment in which the research will take place.

在调研早期这种方法是最有用的，尤其是调研人员对调研问题不太熟悉的时候。探索性研究没有具体的框架，调研人员需要看很多资料，探索性研究的目的是发现那些和调研计划相关的变量并研究将要进行调研的环境。

4.5.2 Descriptive research ／描述性研究

The purpose of descriptive research is to provide an accurate description of the variables uncovered by the exploratory stage. This could be used to investigate the market share of a company's products or the demographic characteristics of the target market (age, gender, income, etc.). Data are usually obtained from secondary data sources or from surveys.

描述性研究的作用是对探索性研究得到的变量进行准确的描述，这种方法可以用来调查企业产品的市场份额或者目标市场的人口因素（年龄、性别、收入等），一般是通过二手资料和调研资料来获取相关数据。

4.5.3 Causal research ／因果关系研究

Causal research is used to determine the relationship between variables, e.g. the relationship between advertising and repeat purchases.

因果关系研究用来确定变量之间的关系，例如广告与重复购买之间的关系。

4.6 Data sources ／资料来源

Data come from two sources, primary and secondary.

资料来源有两种方式，一手资料

Secondary data sources consist of information that has already been collected for other purposes and primary sources of information are those used for the purpose of collecting information specifically for the current research project.

和二手资料。二手资料包括为其他目的而收集的资料，以及为目前调研项目而专门收集到的信息资料。

4.6.1 Secondary sources ／二手资料

These provide the researcher with a starting point for data collection. It may be possible to solve the research problem either wholly or in part by using secondary data. This reduces the cost of a research project as secondary data are cheaper than collecting primary data. Secondary sources of information, are in the main, fairly accessible, although some sources may remain confidential and others may be too expensive to acquire.

Secondary sources can be separated into the two types as shown in Figure 4.2. Internal sources are those that generate information within a company or an organization, e.g. sales figures and accounts information. External sources are those that generate information outside a company or an organization. These are by far the more numerous, and some examples of external sources are listed below:

二手资料是调研人员资料收集的起点，运用二手资料可以全面解决调研问题或者解决部分问题，这样就降低了调研项目的成本，因为二手资料比起一手资料来说花费的成本相对较少。尽管有些资料是机密的，而其他资料的获取成本可能较高，但是获取二手资料相对容易。

如图 4–2 所示，二手资料的来源可以分为两种：企业或者组织的内部资料，例如销售数据，财务信息等；外部资料是公司或组织以外的信息，有很多方面。下面列出了外部资料的来源渠道：

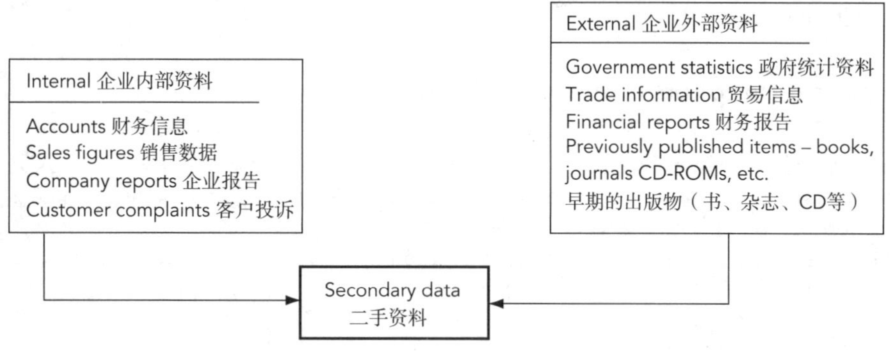

Figure 4.2 Sources of secondary data. 图 4–2 二手资料的来源

◆ *Government statistics*: Census data, family expenditure surveys, trade and manufacturing trends.

◆ *Trade information*: Trade press, e.g. Fashion Weekly, Drapers Record; trade associations, e.g. CBI, trade surveys, company reports and competitors' accounts.

◆ 政府统计数据：户口普查资料，家庭消费调查，行业发展趋势。

◆ 贸易信息：贸易出版物如时装周刊、零售商的记录，贸易协会例如英国工业联合会信息、贸易调查资料、公司报告和竞争者的财务报告等。

◆ *Financial institutions*: Many major banks publish

◆ 财务资料：主要银行的区域

reports on regional and national industries.

性或全球产业的财务报告。

◆ *Commercial research*: Many market research companies undertake continuous research and omnibus surveys covering an extremely broad range of topics, including consumer, media and retail (e.g. Taylor Nelson Sofres, NOP, Ipsos-RSL). Various market reports are available, from, Mintel, Keynote and Retail Intelligence, for example.

◆ 商业调查资料：大多数营销调研公司都长期开展调研活动，调研内容涉及领域很广，包括消费者、媒体和零售商——例如泰勒·耐斯特·斯夫托［译者注：简称 TNS 市场研究公司，是市场信息的全球领导者］、NOP、Ipsos-RSL［译者注：Ipsos 是世界著名的市场研究机构集团，RSL 是其下属独立的市场调研机构］。企业可以从敏特、主旨（Keynote）以及零售情报调查公司获取各种各样的报告。

The use of secondary data sources, also called desk research, can be very time consuming because there is such a lot of information available, including CD-ROM and 'online' data. Keeping the objectives of the research in mind will help to ensure that time is spent efficiently.

获取二手资料的方法也称为案头调研，因为信息量太多所以非常耗费时间，包括 CD 光盘和在线资料等，调研人员始终要把调研目标记在心里，这样才能事半功倍。

4.6.2 Primary sources ／一手资料

Most marketing research projects will involve the collection of more up-to-date information than is available from secondary sources. Primary sources of information may include consumers, designers, buyers, manufacturers, retailers, and so on, depending upon the research problem.

大多数营销调研计划都会要求收集最新的数据资料，而不只是容易获取的二手资料。一手资料的信息内容主要包括消费者、设计师、采购者、制造商、零售商等的情况，主要取决于调研的问题是什么。

4.7 Practical sampling methods ／实用的抽样方法

In designing research a major decision that the researcher must make concerns the selection of a sampling method. Sampling is a very important tool in marketing research. It involves selecting a small number of people from the larger survey population whose characteristics, attitudes and behaviour are representative of the larger group.

在调研设计中，对调研人员来说最重要的是确定抽样的方法。抽样是营销调研中的一个重要工具，它指的是从较大的调研总体中选择少数的人员，这些人员代表的是调研总体样本的消费者特点、消费态度和消费行为。

Before selecting the sample, however, the researcher must first define the research population from which to draw the sample. Exploratory research can help to define the population to include all the players and variables that are relevant to the survey.

然而在确定抽样之前，调研人员首先必须确定从哪些样本中进行抽样，探索性研究有助于确定需要调研的对象和变量。

For some surveys, particularly if the survey population is small or concentrated in one geographical area, it may be possible to take a census, which is a useful method in some business surveys. More commonly a representative sample is interviewed as this reduces both the time and the cost of the research.

对于有些调研而言，尤其是如果调研总体数量较小或者集中在一个区域的话，就需要进行人口普查，对于某些商业调查来说这是很有用的方法。一般都推荐选择具有代表性的样本，这样可以节约调研的时间和成本。

4.7.1 Deciding sample size ／确定样本大小

Deciding how many people to include in your sample is as important a decision as how they should be selected. Factors such as cost, time and staff availability, level of accuracy required, data collection method and location of the population all play a part in deciding sample size. In reality, cost-effectiveness is the most important factor in deciding how many should be contacted in the research, followed by time and staff availability. If it is decided to select a large number for the sample, there may be insufficient staff available to contact the respondents within the time constraints of the survey, so a smaller sample size may be accepted as a compromise.

确定调研样本中有多少人与如何选择样本一样重要。成本、时间和可用的人员，调研要求的准确性、资料收集方法、人口的聚居区域等因素在确定样本大小的时候都起着重要的作用。事实上，成本效益对确定样本大小是很重要的，接下来才是时间和可用的人员。如果确定要选择一个较大的样本，但可能会因为人手不够的原因而在调研的期限内不能及时联系被访者，此时需要作出妥协以选择较小的调研样本。

When selecting a sample it is important that there is a high level of confidence that the sample is representative of the research population as a whole. The sample must be large enough to provide accurate results, without being so large as to increase research costs unnecessarily. It is possible to calculate confidence levels for different sample sizes and there are several texts that cover this adequately (see Further reading at the end of this chapter).

当选择样本时最主要的是保证选择的样本能够很好地代表调研总体样本的情况，样本数量应该足够大以保证调研结果的准确性，但是不能太大而增加不必要的调研成本。调研人员首先可以对不同样本的可靠性进行评估，书中对此也进行了充分的分析(见本章后续内容)。

4.7.2 Choice of a sampling method ／抽样方法的选择

The two main types of sampling method – probability methods and non-probability methods – are shown in Figure 4.3.

有两种主要的抽样方法：随机抽样法和非随机抽样法，如图 4–3 所示。

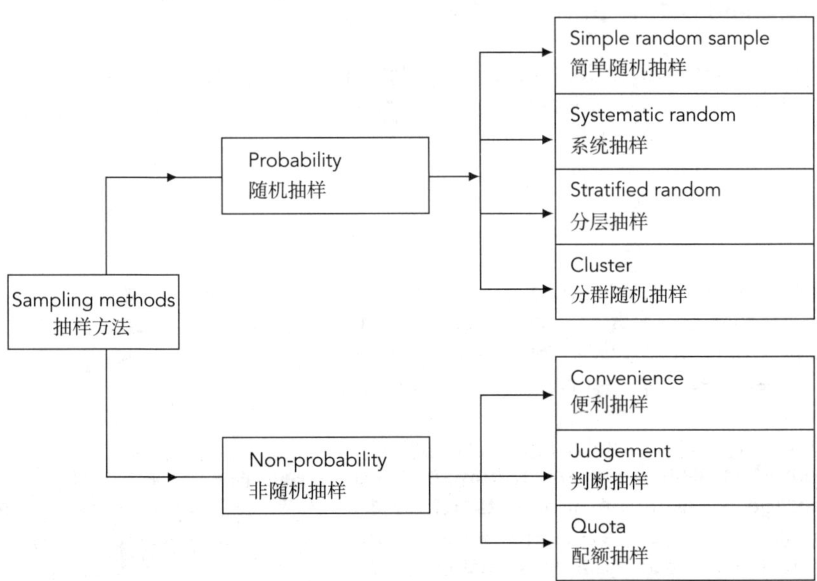

Figure 4.3 Types of sampling method. 图 4–3 抽样方法的类型

Probability methods /随机抽样法

Statistically speaking, these are the best types of sampling method as each respondent has a known chance of being selected, so bias is minimized. They also allow the accuracy of the results to be estimated statistically. Sometimes probability sampling methods are referred to generically as 'random sampling' methods. In fact, this refers to a specific type of very precise probability sample. There is often some confusion over the use of the term 'random'. Selecting people in the street at random is not technically random sampling, but more often refers to selection of respondents by interviewers for quota sampling.

从统计学来看，这些都是很好的抽样方法，因为每个调查者都有被选中的机会，从而调查的误差就很小。运用这些方法可以对调查结果进行系统的评估。有时候，随机抽样法也就是一般意义所说的“任意抽样”法。实际上，这指的是非常精确的随机抽样法中的一种特殊形式，有时候会和“任意”这个词汇混淆。随机在街上选择行人并不是技术层面所讲的任意抽样，但更多的时候指的是从配额抽样中选择被调查者。

The main types of probability sample are simple random sampling, systematic random sampling, stratified random sampling and cluster sampling.

随机抽样的主要形式有简单随机抽样、系统抽样、分层抽样和分群随机抽样。

Simple random sampling Items can be selected from the sampling frame by using the lottery method, e.g. taking numbers out of a hat. In the UK, ERNIE the computer selects Premium Bond winners, and does so by using simple random sampling. Random number tables are generated by computer and often used in marketing research.

简单随机抽样 从抽样范围中按照彩票抽奖法抽样。例如，从帽子中任意选择数字。在英国，用摇奖机选择有奖证券中奖者，就是采用的简单随机抽样法。营销调研中也会用到计算机生成的随机数据表。

Systematic random sampling With larger samples it is more convenient to divide the population by the sample size to calculate the sampling interval (n). A random starting point is selected using random number tables and every nth time after that is selected.

系统抽样 样本数量较多时，确定调查样本比较便捷的方法是根据样本大小计算出样本间隔。运用随机数据表，按照一定的间隔确定样本选择的起点。

Example If the sample size is 50, and the population size is 3000, then the sampling interval is calculated as:

$$n=\frac{3000}{50}=60$$

实例：如果样本大小为50，总体样本为3000，样本间隔就是：

$$n=3000/50=60$$

If the random number picked from the tables was 35, for example, then the first item selected from the sampling frame would be 35. Every 60th number after that would be selected until a sample size of 50 was achieved.

例如，如果数据表中选取的数字是35，第一个从样本范围中选择的就是35。间隔60个分别选取样本，直到样本数量达到50。

As the first number w as selected randomly, this method is sometimes called a 'quasi-random' method.

第一个数字是随机选取的，这种方法有时也称为准随机抽样。

The advantage of these methods is that they are relatively simple to carry out and sampling error and confidence levels can be calculated statistically. The main disadvantage is that samples may be produced

这些方法的优点是很容易操作，可以从统计学角度对抽样误差和样本的可靠水平进行评价，最大的缺点是选择的样本有

that do not reflect the characteristics of the survey population. For example, if a sample of students were drawn from a list of all students at a university, it is possible that all the students in the sample might be design students. This is clearly not representative of the student population as a whole.

Stratified random sampling One way to try to overcome this type of sampling error is to use stratified random sampling. This is used when it is felt that different groups within the population have characteristics that are likely to lead to different types of answers. The population is divided into distinguishable groups (strata) who have similar characteristics. Stratification factors should be as relevant as possible to the survey (e.g. consumer surveys are often stratified by age, gender, socio-economic group, and so on). A random sample is then taken from each stratum.

There are two main methods used to stratify samples. First, with a uniform sampling fraction (proportionate sampling), or secondly, with a variable sampling fraction (disproportionate sampling).

Proportionate and disproportionate sampling If all the strata are equally important to the survey, a proportionate sample would be taken, i.e. the same number selected from each stratum. Frequently, some strata are more important to the research than others. For example, if you were conducting a survey into the purchase of outsize garments (size 18+), it would be reasonable to assume that most of these items would be purchased by those who were larger than size 16 rather than those who were not. It is logical that more of these people should be included in the sample. In other words, a disproportionate sample would be taken. If a proportionate sample were taken, too few of the people who took larger sized clothes would be included in the survey and it would be difficult to extrapolate the results to the general population with any degree of accuracy.

Cluster sampling Cluster sampling is a variation of stratified random sampling and may be used when the survey population is concentrated in a relatively small number of groups (clusters) that are considered typical of the market in question. A random sample of these clusters is then taken. A random sample of units from within these clusters is then taken. If the number of units within a cluster is small, a census may be carried out. In a national survey of specialist bridal wear retailers, for example, sales areas could be identified by geographical

可能不能反映调研总体样本的特征。例如，如果从一个大学生的列表中选择样本的话，就有可能出现样本中所有的学生都是设计类学生，很明显这些样本就不能代表总体样本。

分层抽样 要避免以上抽样方法所产生的误差就需要采取分层抽样法。这种方法适用于总体样本中不同的群体具有同样的特点，那就是他们的回答可以分为不同的类型。将总体样本分为不同的群体（分层），每一个群体有着共同的特点，分层的要素尽量与调研有关（例如，消费者调研通常按照年龄、性别、社会阶层等划分），然后在分层中进行随机抽样。

分层抽样有两种主要的方法。第一，使用统一的抽样比率（比例抽样法）；第二，使用分段变量抽样法（非比例抽样法）。

比例抽样和非比例抽样 如果所有的分层对市场研究都同等重要的话，就需要采取比例抽样，例如，从每个分层中选择同样的数字。通常情况下，相对于其他样本，有些分层样本对市场研究更为重要。举例来说，你在做一项有关大号时装购买的调查（尺码18+）时，就应该认为购买这类产品的应该是那些比 16 号体型稍胖的消费者而不是其他人，逻辑上来说样本中应该包括这些人中的大部分。换句话说，就需要采用非比例抽样。如果采用比例抽样的话，调研中那些穿大号衣服的人可能就很少，从而要获得准确的预测结果就会比较困难。

分群随机抽样 分群随机抽样是分层抽样的一种变化，当调研的总体样本集中在少数的分层样本，并且这些分层样本是市场中的典型群体时就需要采用这种方法。如果群体中单位数量少的话，就需要进行人口普查。例如在对婚礼服零售商进行全国性的调查时，就需要根据地理区域和选择的随机样本对销售区域进行划分，在

region and a random sample of these taken. Within each selected sales area, all or a sample of the store managers would be interviewed.

选择的销售区域中对全部店长或者某个店长进行访谈。

There is a problem with cluster sampling that occurs if the clusters are not sufficiently representative of the survey population. For example, in a small geographical area, it is likely that it will consist of people with similar housing, incomes and lifestyle. Although cluster sampling can be more cost-effective than some other methods of probability sampling, there is a danger that sampling error will increase if the clusters are not carefully defined before the first stage of sampling.

如果分群不能代表总体样本的话，分群随机抽样就会出现问题。例如，在一个小的地理区域，可能就会包含那些有同样的房屋、收入和生活方式的人群。尽管分群随机抽样相比随机抽样的其他方法具有更好的成本效益，但在第一阶段如果没有认真地确定分群的话，抽样的误差就会增加。

Sampling frames When using probability sampling methods it is necessary to use a sampling frame. This is a list of every element in the survey population. The sample is drawn from this list. A sampling frame is essential for probability-based techniques, as each element must have a known chance of selection, and so must be included in the sampling frame. According to Webb (1999), a sampling frame must have the following characteristics:

样本架构 在使用随机抽样的方法时有必要使用样本架构，它是调研总体样本每一个分组的列表，样本就是从列表中选取的。样本架构对随机抽样非常有用，每个分组都有可能被选中。根据 Webb（1999）的说法，样本架构必须有以下特点：

- Each element should be included only once.
- No element should be excluded.
- The frame should cover the whole of the population.
- The information used to construct the frame should be up-to-date and accurate.
- The frame should be convenient to use.

- 每个分组只出现一次；
- 所有分组都必须包含在内；
- 样本架构包括了整个总体样本；
- 构建样本架构时用到的资料应该是最新的，并且是准确的；
- 样本架构应该便于使用。

Examples of sampling frames include electoral rolls, the telephone book, the Royal Mail's lists of postcodes and other similar databases.

样本架构包括选民名册、电话簿、英国皇家邮政编码列表和其他类似信息。

In practice, most sampling frames are not perfect. Not everyone with a telephone is in the phone book, for example. Finding a sampling frame that is suitable for your research can occasionally prove difficult.

事实上，大多数样本架构都是不完整的，因为并非每个有电话的人都会出现在列表中，找到适合你的调研样本架构有的时候是很难的。

Non-probability methods / 非随机抽样法

With non-probability sampling methods, some element of judgement enters the selection process. The extent to which judgement is used, and therefore the element of bias introduced, varies in these methods. Non-probability methods do not require a sampling frame and the chance of each unit being selected is unknown. Statistical estimates of

采用随机抽样法，需要考虑一些判断性的要素，什么时候需要判断以及考虑误差因素，在非随机抽样方法中这点是有所不同的。非随机抽样不需要抽样架构，每个单位

the size of the sampling error cannot therefore be made.

The methods are convenience sampling, judgement sampling and quota sampling.

Convenience sampling Items are selected that are close or easily available. This is useful in the exploratory stage of research, giving the researcher a 'feel' for the subject. Despite being very cheap and quick to carry out, the level of error and bias with this method is likely to be very high and so it should be used with caution.

Judgement sampling Items are selected by the researcher that are felt to be representative of the survey population. This method attempts to be more representative than convenience sampling. Experts also may be consulted for advice on which items are likely to be more appropriate for the survey. For example, in a survey of textile manufacturers, a staff specialist such as a product developer may provide useful advice on which manufacturers would be suitable for selection.

Quota sampling This is the most likely non-probability method to produce a representative sample as items selected are based on known characteristics of the population.

Example Assume that your survey population has the following characteristics:

Age: 16–29=26%; 30–64=58%; 65+=16%
Gender: Male=48%; Female=52%

If we wanted to interview 150 people who were representative of the above population in terms of the two quota controls (age and gender), we would calculate the quotas as shown in Table 4.1.

This is more conveniently represented as shown in Table 4.2.

A survey's accuracy of representation can be increased by narrowing the bands and including more characteristics, e.g. social class. Interviewers are then allocated a number of interviews (quotas) with specific types of respondent.

The advantages of quota sampling are that it is relatively quick to carry out and easy to administer from a fieldwork point of view. It is also cheaper to use than probability sampling methods. The disadvantages of quota sampling involve problems of bias and sampling errors. The responsibility for selection of respondents

能否被选中是不确定的，因此也不能对抽样误差的情况进行统计分析。

这些方法包括便利抽样、判断抽样和配额抽样。

便利抽样 指的是选择那些容易接近的或者容易获取的样本。在调研的探索阶段这是非常有用的，能够使调研人员很快地了解调研项目。除了费用很低以及获取速度很快等优点以外，采用这种方法时误差和偏差水平有可能会很高，因此使用时要谨慎些。

判断抽样 指根据调查人员的主观经验从总体样本中选择那些被判断为最能代表总体的单位作为样本的抽样方法。这种方法选取的样本比便利抽样的样本更具代表性，一般会遵循专家的建议确定哪些样本比较适合调研项目。例如，对面料生产商进行调查，内行人员如产品研发人员就会给出哪些生产商是适合选择作为抽样的建议。

配额抽样 是非随机抽样中使用最为广泛的一种抽样方法，选择的代表性样本是以总体样本的特点为依据的。

实例：假设你的总体样本有以下特点：

年龄：16 ~ 29=26%，
30 ~ 64=58%，65+ =16%
性别：男性 =48%，女性 =52%

如果我们准备根据两个配额控制要素（年龄和性别）访问总体样本中的 150 个代表人员时，就可以计算出如表 4–1 所示的配额表。

表 4–2 的描述则更为简单方便。

可以通过缩减分段或者包含更多的样本特点来提高调研的准确性，例如社会阶层这一要素，再根据回答情况将被访者分为若干个不同的小组。

配额抽样的优点是操作起来速度快，并且从实地研究的角度看更容易管理。其缺点是会产生误差或者偏差，因为是调查人员选取被访问者的，这就可能产生误差。另外的问题是配额

Table 4.1 Quota sampling frame (A)

表 4–1 配额抽样架构（A）

Age 年龄	16 - 29 16 ~ 29 岁	30 - 64 30 ~ 64 岁	65+ 65 岁以上	Total 总数
MALE 男性	16 - 29=26% 16 ~ 29 岁占 26%	30 - 64=58% 30 ~ 64 岁占 58%	65+=16% 65 岁以上占 16%	73
	Male 男性 =48%	Male 男性 =47%	Male 男性 =48%	
	26% of 48% of 150=19 26% × 48% × 150 ≈ 19	58% of 48% of 150=42 58% × 48% × 150 ≈ 42	16% of 48% of 150=12 16% × 48% × 150 ≈ 12	
	Quota 配额 =19	Quota 配额 =42	Quota 配额 =12	
FEMALE 女性	16 - 29=26% 16 ~ 29 岁占 26%	30 - 64=58% 16 ~ 29 岁占 58%	65+=16% 65 岁以上占 16%	77
	Female 女性 =52%	Female 女性 =52%	Female 女性 =52%	
	26% of 53% of 150=20 26% × 52% × 150 ≈ 20	58% of 52% of 150=45 58% × 52% × 150 ≈ 45	16% of 52% of 150=12 16% × 52% × 150 ≈ 12	
	Quota 配额 =20	Quota 配额 =45	Quota 配额 =12	
TOTAL 总数	39	87	24	150

Table 4.2 Quota smapling frame (B)

表 4–2 配额抽样架构（B）

Age 年龄	Male 男性	Female 女性	Total 总数
16–29 岁	19	20	39
30–36 岁	42	45	87
65 岁以上	12	12	24
Total 总数	73	77	150

lies with the interviewer, which may introduce bias. There is the added problem that there is no probability mechanism with quota sampling, so the sampling error cannot easily be calculated.

抽样没有随机性，因此抽样的误差就很难衡量。

Quota samples are often used in surveys where fine degrees of accuracy are not required, for instance in product testing for preference between products.

配额抽样通常适用于那些对精确性要求不高的调研活动，例如对产品的喜爱度进行测试。

Although many companies who provide continuous research services use probability sampling, the majority of *ad hoc* marketing research is conducted using quota samples. If this method gave consistently biased or misleading conclusions, it would not be used.

尽管很多提供长期调研服务的公司采用随机抽样的方法，但大多数比较特别的营销调研都采用的是配额抽样法。如果这种方法不断产生误差并且误导结论的话，就不要采用了。

4.8 Primary data collection methods ／一手资料的收集方法

The researcher should not rely on the use of secondary data alone to answer the research problems. Not all secondary data are available to the researcher as some may be unavailable, for example in confidential reports, and other data may simply be too costly to acquire. The information that is available may be out-of-date or not sufficiently detailed to solve the research problem. Usually, primary data need to be collected.

The four main approaches to primary data collection – observation, focus groups, experimentation and surveys – are shown in Figure 4.4.

调研人员不能单纯地使用二手资料来回答调研的问题，他们也不可能获取所有的二手资料，例如要获取一些机密报告和其他的资料可能费用就很高。能够获取的资料有可能是过时的或者不足以解决调研问题的，通常这个时候就需要收集一手资料。

获取一手资料的方法有四种：观察法、焦点座谈法、实验法和调查法，见图 4–4。

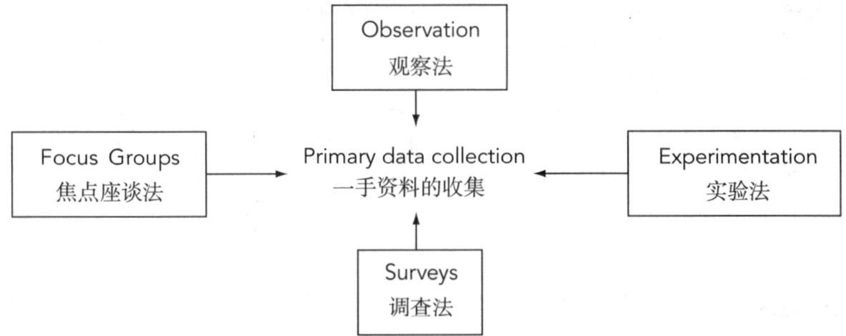

Figure 4.4 Approaches to primary data collection. 图 4–4 一手资料的收集方法

4.8.1 Observation ／观察法

There are occasions when it is more useful to observe behaviour than to interview the respondent about it. Observation is usually used to complement other research methods in marketing research, rather than being used alone, as this method can identify patterns of behaviour, but cannot provide information on the reasons behind that behaviour. There are a number of methods available for the observation of behaviour, as follows.

通常有这样的情况，就是观察人的行为活动比亲自访问调查者更有用。观察法通常是用来辅助营销调研中的其他方法的，而不会被单独使用，这种方法可以识别人的行为模式，但是不能了解产生某种行为的原因。观察行为的方法有很多，具体如下：

Personal observation ／贴身观察

The researcher observes behaviour and records it as it occurs. The skill and the objectivity of the researcher play a key role in the collection of unbiased data. The audit data are collected by taking an inventory of certain products or brands at the premises (at home or office) of

调研人员边观察行为边记录。要获得没有偏差的资料，调研人员的能力和客观态度就起着重要的作用，审计方面的数据可以通过现场（在家或者办公室）观察某些产品或者品牌的

the respondent.

This type of ethnographic research (observing respondents in natural settings, e.g. observing fashion buyers at trade fairs) is particularly useful in fashion marketing research. Methods such as accompanied shopping can provide insight into the processes by which decisions are made. Using this method the researcher would accompany the respondent on a shopping trip, often following a prior discussion of the process in the respondent's home, observe the respondent and often use direct questioning to gain insight into underlying reasons for certain behaviour, e.g. why certain products attracted the respondent's attention. This is a useful tool for store layout research and evaluation of point-of-sale displays. Wardrobe analysis is another observational method employed by many image consultants. Here existing garments and accessories that constitute a respondent's wardrobe are examined. This is combined with information on work and lifestyle needs to provide advice on how best to build on existing outfits and to expand the wardrobe to obtain a desired image. Some companies also offer this service online.

情况来获取。

这种人类学研究法（在自然环境中观察被调查者，例如在交易会上观察时装采购商）在时装市场调研中非常有用。陪同购买的方法可以深入了解购买决定的过程。采用这种方法时，调研人员需要全程陪同被调查者完成购买活动，一般是在被调查者家中与其讨论后才决定陪同的，直接观察被调查者并且直接询问了解其发生某种行为的根本原因，例如为什么被调查者对某些产品感兴趣，这种方法对商店陈列调查和售点展示评估都是有用的。衣橱分析是观察法的另一种形式，主要选择大量的形象顾问进行观察，这里调查的是在被调查者的衣柜里有哪些时装和配饰。这就需要结合工作和生活方式等方面的信息给消费者建议以进行恰当搭配，以及如何增添衣柜里的时装来达到预期的造型，有些公司会提供这种在线服务。

Mechanical observation／机器观察法

Recording devices may be used either in laboratory settings or in natural settings. In the laboratory, devices such as the psychogalvanometer are used to measure the respondent's level of perspiration (and so the level of arousal) following exposure to an advertisement or other stimuli. Other devices include the eye-movement camera that detects the movement of the eye over an advertisement, identifying the visual aspects of the advertisement that gain attention. In natural settings, in-store video cameras may be used to record behaviour, with the film being used later for analysis such as researching store layout.

在实验室或者自然环境下可能会使用一些有记录功能的装置。在实验室里，心理反应监测器主要用来测试被调查者在看到广告时或者受到刺激条件下的出汗情况（被触动的程度），其他的包括眼动仪（眼球运动监视器）主要测试的是被调查者在看到广告时眼球的移动情况，以及识别广告引起注意的视觉因素。在自然环境中，可以用店内摄像机来记录被调查者的行为，随后再使用拍摄到的影像资料对商店陈列进行调查分析。

4.8.2 Focus groups／焦点座谈法

The focus group (also known as the group discussion) is a form of qualitative research. The group usually consists of between 6 and 12 respondents who discuss products, services, attitudes or other aspects of the marketing process. The discussion is led by a skilled researcher called a group moderator, who guides the discussion, following a checklist of topics. The group usually meets in an informal setting, often someone's home, and the

焦点座谈法（也称为小组座谈法）是定性调查法的一种形式。调查小组包括 6 到 12 个被调查者，他们会讨论产品、服务、观念或者营销活动的其他方面。讨论由经验丰富的调查人员主持，主持人负责依照讨论题目的列表组织活动。小组人员通常在非正式

group members are paid a small sum for attending. These discussions can take several hours to complete and are often used as a preliminary to survey research. It is also possible to conduct online focus groups via the Internet (see Section 4.14).

场合见面，通常是某个人的家，讨论组人员需要支付很少的参加费用。这些讨论可能需要几个小时的时间完成，通常在调查研究之前进行，同样也可以通过网络进行在线焦点座谈会（见 4.14）。

4.8.3 Experimentation ／实验法

According to Kotler (1994), this is the most scientifically valid type of research. Here, matched groups of respondents are subjected to different treatments and the difference in the responses is observed. All variables outside the scope of the research are controlled and as such, the observed responses are taken to be as a result of the difference in treatment of the group. Experimental research seeks to identify cause-and-effect relationships that are central to marketing work.

根据科特勒（1994）的观点，实验法是最科学且有效的调研方法。选择的被调查小组处于不同的环境下，从而调研人员可以观察他们不同的反应，由此可以监控研究领域以外的所有变量。这样一来，被观察者的反应就可以当作是因为小组处于不同的环境下而造成的结果。实验法调研主要是为了寻找营销工作的中心，即原因和结果之间的关系。

4.8.4 Surveys ／调查法

Survey research is the most well known of the research approaches and is widely used for descriptive research. Surveys collect information from a representative sample of the survey population on such topics as consumer behaviour, attitudes and beliefs, as well as buying intentions. The strengths of these beliefs, attitudes and intentions are measured and the results extrapolated to the population as a whole.

调查研究法是调研方法中最为大众所熟知的，在描述研究中使用极为广泛。从调研总体中的代表样本中获取调查的信息，内容包括消费行为、看法和信念，以及购买意图等。对这些信念、看法和购买意图的程度进行测试，测试结果用来推测整体样本的情况。

4.9 Data collection methods ／资料收集的方法

If a survey is to be conducted, there are a number of methods available for the collection of data and each has its relative advantages and disadvantages. The three main traditional methods are by personal interview, telephone interview and mail questionnaire. Online data collection methods will be discussed later in the chapter.

进行一项调研的时候，可以用到的收集数据的方法很多，每一种都有其相对的优点和缺点。三种主要的传统方法有个人面谈法、电话询问法和邮寄问卷调查法。在线数据收集方法在本章后面讨论。

4.9.1 Personal interview ／个人面谈法

Face-to-face interviewing is still the most widely used method of primary data collection in the UK, although telephone interviewing is becoming increasingly popular. This method is labour-intensive and costly, but is more likely to result in a satisfactorily completed questionnaire than any of the other methods. This is particularly true if the questionnaire is long or complicated or covers

在英国尽管电话询问法日益普及，但个人面谈法仍是使用最为广泛的一手资料收集法。这种方法耗费大量人力并且费用高，但是比其他方法更容易得到满意的问卷调查结果。如果问卷内容多且复杂或者包含敏感话题的话，这种方

sensitive subjects. Respondents have the opportunity to build a rapport with the interviewer, who can elicit full and accurate answers to questions without biasing the responses.

法更为有效。被调查者和访问者之间会建立一种默契，访问者会引导被调查者给出完整和准确的答案而不会误导被调查者的反应。

In a personal interview there is the opportunity to show supporting material, such as examples of a product or still photographs from advertisements. Open-ended questions can also be included in the questionnaire design as the interviewer is present to record the answers verbatim.

在个别访谈时，调研人员有机会向被调查者展示如产品或者广告商那里拿到的画册等资料，问卷设计中也可以设置开放式问题，因为访问者是现场逐字记录问题的答案的。

The interviewer or fieldworker also plays a vital role in the selection of respondents for interview when using quota sampling. This, however, may introduce bias into the survey.

采用配额调查法选择被调查者时，访问者或者现场调查员起着重要的作用，然而这样可能使调研产生误差。

There is another type of personal interview, the depth interview, which belongs to the realm of qualitative research. Typically, these interviews can last for over an hour. The interviewer does not have a questionnaire as such, but uses a less structured interview schedule. This may consist of either a series of open questions that must be asked as they are written or a checklist of topics for discussion, as with the focus group. The interviewer must be very highly trained in the art of asking unbiased questions, and usually, the interviews are recorded for transcription and analysis later. This method is particularly useful and is a rich source of information if the subject of the survey is of a personal or embarrassing nature.

另外的一种个人访谈法是深度访谈，属于定性调查法，一般都需要超过一个小时的时间。访问者不用调查问卷但会有一个简单的访谈计划，计划中包括一系列边问边记录的开放式问题，或者要讨论的问题列表。访问者必须经过很好的训练，不会问及一些有误导性的问题，通常在访谈之后会对访谈记录进行分析。这种方法是非常有用的，对于个人隐私或令人尴尬一类问题的调查可以获取丰富的信息。

Increasingly technology has made data capture easier for fieldworkers. CAPI (Computer Assisted Personal Interviewing) using laptops has meant that the large amounts of paper questionnaires no longer have to be carried by interviewers. Progress in wireless technology has allowed some market research companies to equip their fieldworkers with XDAs (small hand-held devices, similar to palmtops) for the administration of short face-to-face questionnaires. The questionnaires are sent directly to the XDA and allow for fast data capture and subsequently, fast turnaround of data to the client.

不断发展的技术使得现场访问者获取的资料更为容易。计算机辅助个人访谈使用的是笔记本电脑，这样访问人员就不需要携带大量的调查问卷了。无线电技术的发展使一些调研公司可以给他们的现场调查人员安装 XDAs（一种小的手提式的设备，近似于掌上电脑）来监控短时间的面对面问卷调查，问卷调查直接装在这个设备上，可以快速充分地获取资料，随后把这些资料转交给客户服务部门。

4.9.2 Telephone interviewing ／电话询问法

The development of CATI (Computer Aided Telephone Interviewing) has greatly increased the extent to which telephone interviewing is undertaken. Interviewing is done from a central location, cutting the costs of fieldwork considerably, providing the sample size is

计算机辅助电话访谈的发展扩大了电话调查可以触及的范围，访问在一个中心位置进行，如果调查样本足够大的话，使用这种方法就会大大地缩减现场调查的费用，但样本较少时这种方法

large. It is not a cost-effective method for small samples. With the increased demand for immediate information, particularly for commercial omnibus surveys, CATI is ideally suited for the provision of a very fast turnaround of data as the results are recorded and processed as the questions are answered. The sample also can be drawn from a wide geographical spread, as the fieldworkers do not have to travel.

并不节约。随着对即时信息需求的不断增长，尤其是对商业综合性调查来说，计算机辅助电话访谈技术对于提供快速的资料来说非常适合，进行提问时就可以记录和整理结果。样本可以从人口普查数据中提取，现场调查人员就没有必要跑来跑去了。

There are disadvantages to this method of data collection. It is difficult to establish a rapport with the respondent by telephone, which is partly why this method is not successful for the researching of personal or embarrassing topics. Many respondents are fearful of 'sugging', selling under the guise of marketing research, and expect the interviewer to try to sell them double glazing and the like. With a disembodied voice it is also easier for a respondent to refuse or end an interview prematurely. The telephone interview demands the use of very structured, precoded questionnaires that may be completed quickly without having to rely on examples of supporting material. An ideal telephone interview will last no longer than 15 minutes, on average.

用这种方法收集资料也有不足，因为很难与被调查者之间建立一种默契，这也就是为什么这种方法对于个人隐私和令人尴尬的问题调查时不容易取得成功的原因。大多数被调查者都害怕被欺骗，在营销调研时都会假装，他们希望调查人员能重视他们，同时空洞没有吸引力的嗓音可能会导致被调查者拒绝接受调查或者会提前结束访谈。进行电话访谈时调研人员要特别严谨，需要准备一份预先拟好的问卷调查表，这样可以较快地完成调查并且不需要任何辅助材料，一个理想的电话访谈的时间不应超过 15 分钟。

4.9.3 Mail (postal) questionnaire ／邮寄问卷调查法

If the survey population is widely dispersed, it may be more useful to send the questionnaire by mail than to have an interviewer call on the respondent. Mail surveys also have the advantage of a reduction in field staff, and if there is a high response rate, the cost per questionnaire is low. A high response rate is more likely if the survey population consists of members of a special interest group (e.g. keep-fit enthusiasts) and the questionnaire relates to their area of interest. Otherwise, a response rate of 30–40% is not uncommon. The advantage over the telephone interview with this method is that the questionnaire can be lengthy and ask for detailed information.

如果被调查的人员比较分散的话，比较有用的方法是邮寄问卷调查法而不是打电话访问被调查者。邮寄问卷调查法的优点是可以减少调研人员人数，如果问卷回收率高，那每一份问卷的成本就会很低。如果调研对象包括一些特殊的群体时，问卷问题的设计就需要紧密联系他们的兴趣，这样问卷回收率就会高些。当然问卷回收率在 30% ~ 40% 之间是属于正常的。与电话访谈相比，邮寄问卷调查法的问卷设计内容可以多一些，也可以问及一些具体的问题。

The disadvantages (apart from the low response rate) are several. A mail questionnaire has to compete with the increasing amounts of junk mail that pour through our letterboxes. If there is a high non-response rate then the cost per questionnaire is high, particularly if a reply-paid envelope is included. There is no guarantee that the selected respondent will actually complete the questionnaire, and in spite of careful design, the control of the question sequence is removed. If the respondent

邮寄问卷调查也有一些不足的方面（除了回收率低之外）。邮寄的问卷需要和投递到我们信箱的那些垃圾邮件相竞争，如果问卷回收率低而且包含回寄邮票时，单个问卷的成本就会很高。没有谁能确保选择的被调查者会认真地完成问卷，不管问卷设计是否仔细，回答问题的顺序是很难控制的。如果被调查

does not understand any of the questions, there is no interviewer present to clarify the problem. There also may be a long time lag between sending out the questionnaires and receiving completed forms.

者不理解某些问题，调查人员也不可能亲自到场解释。同样，邮寄出问卷到收回完成的问卷会是一个很漫长的过程。

4.10 Questionnaire design ／调查问卷的设计

Questionnaire design is an aspect of research in which many people automatically assume expertise, even those without prior research experience. The questionnaire is a vital part of most surveys and great care must be taken with its design. To the novice, the problems inherent in designing a questionnaire tend not to become apparent until the pilot stage of the survey.

问卷设计是市场调研的一方面，在这个过程中大多数人都需要懂得专业知识，甚至是那些先前没有调研经验的人。问卷是大多数调研中最为关键的环节，必须特别认真地进行问卷的设计。对于初学者来说，直到进行试调研时才会发现问卷设计中存在的问题。

Many factors will affect the design of the questionnaire, such as the nature of the data required (qualitative or quantitative) and how the questionnaire is to be administered (by personal interview, telephone, mail or other self-completion, or whether electronic instruments will be used). However, most questionnaires tend to lie between two extremes: first, the highly structured questionnaire used, for example, in telephone interviewing, where the question wording is fixed and responses are limited; and secondly, an unstructured interview schedule used in qualitative research, which consists of a list of topics to be covered, with the actual wording of the questions left to the trained interviewer.

问卷设计有很多影响因素，例如获取资料的性质（定性的或者定量的），如何进行问卷调查（个人访谈、电话调查、邮寄问卷调查还是自行完成，或者是否使用先进的电子设备）。然而大多数问卷不会脱离这两种形式：第一，例如在电话调查中使用的结构性强的问卷，提问用词严谨，答案有限；第二，定性调查中通常使用结构松散的访谈计划表，包括一系列要问及的题目，那些需要用词准确的问题设计就交给经过训练的调查人员来完成。

A well-designed questionnaire will provide the researcher with complete, accurate and unbiased information using the minimum number of questions and allowing the maximum number of successfully completed interviews.

好的问卷设计应该给调查人员提供完整的、准确的并且没有误导性的信息，问卷中的问题不宜过多，这样的话就可以回收大量的完成较好的问卷。

4.10.1 The decision areas ／问卷问题中的决策区间

Questionnaires are notoriously difficult to construct, but Tull and Hawkins (1997) suggest that a convenient way of tackling the design is by breaking up the task into a number of decision areas, namely:

- preliminary decisions;
- question content;
- question wording;
- response format;
- question sequence;
- questionnaire layout;

众所周知，调查问卷是很难构建的，但是塔尔和霍金斯 (1997) 提出最方便的方法就是把问卷设计的任务分成若干个决策区间，称为：

- 初步确定；
- 问题的内容；
- 问题的用词；
- 回答问题的形式；
- 问题设计的顺序；
- 问题的排列；

◆ pretest and revise.

◆ 预测和修正。

Preliminary decisions ／初步确定

These include decisions on what information is required, who will be included in the survey and how they will be contacted.

这主要是确定需要哪些信息，谁将会参与调研以及他们之间是怎样相互关联的。

Question content ／问题的内容

This section is concerned with the content of individual questions: what to include, rather than how to phrase the question. Points to consider include the following:

Is the question necessary? The first decision to be made here is whether or not the question is actually necessary. If the question is not necessary for the purposes of meeting the survey objectives, then leave it out.

How many questions are needed? If the question is necessary, one must take care that the information you elicit will answer the question without ambiguity. For example, if you asked a respondent: 'Do you think woollen trousers are comfortable and warm to wear?' and the response was 'No', would that mean woollen trousers were uncomfortable or did not keep the respondent warm? Rather than ask double-barrelled questions, it is better to use one question for each point of information required, so you would ask: 'Do you think that woollen trousers are comfortable to wear?' and 'Do you think that woollen trousers are warm to wear?'

Has the respondent the information to answer the question? Sometimes respondents are asked questions on subjects about which they are not informed. A husband may not have the necessary information if asked how much his wife spends a month on clothing, for example. Some respondents will attempt to answer questions without being adequately informed, which will affect the validity of the results.

Is the respondent able to articulate the response? Even if the respondent has the necessary information to answer a question, they may not always be able to articulate their responses successfully. If asked to describe the type of person who might wear a particular fragrance, many respondents would find difficulty in phrasing their answers. It is easier for the respondent if they are presented with a set of alternatives from which they can choose the response that they feel to be the most appropriate. Using aids such as descriptions and

这部分主要指的是每个问题的具体内容包括什么，而不是如何表述问题。需要考虑以下几点：

这个问题是必需的吗？第一个要做的决定是这个问题是否真的有必要，如果问题对于达到调研目标没有用的话就舍弃掉。

设计多少问题？如果这个问题是必需的，你就必须注意你所给出的信息不会造成问题的答案模棱两可。例如，如果你问一个调查者：“你认为羊毛裤舒服并且保暖吗？”答案是“否”，难道这说明羊毛裤穿着不舒服或者它不保暖吗？与其提问两个相关联的问题还不如单独设计每个问题，你可以这样问：“你认为羊毛裤穿着舒服吗？”和“你认为羊毛裤保暖吗？”两个问题。

回答者是否有足够的信息回答问题？有时回答者会被问及一些他们并不熟悉的问题，例如一个丈夫是不会知道他的妻子每个月在时装方面的消费是多少的。有些回答者试图在不知情的前提下回答问题，这就会影响到问卷结果的有效性。

被访者是否可以给出明确的回答？即便回答者掌握了必要的信息回答问题，但是也不可能一直都会清楚地表述他们的答案。如果问题是要描述用特殊香水的是什么样的人时，多数回答者都会发现很难说清楚他们的答案。比较容易的做法是给回答者提供一套选项，他们可以从中选择适合的答案。使用一些辅助材料如说明书

pictures makes it easier for the respondent to answer the questions, and so complete the interview.

Asking questions beyond the memory span of the respondent Asking questions about behaviour over a long time span may not produce accurate information. For example, asking the respondent how much they spent on tights in the last year would result in an answer that was pure guesswork. Asking how much they spent on tights in the last fortnight would be more likely to provide accurate information.

或者图片的话，回答者就会比较容易给出答案，从而也就完成了访谈。

问及一些超出回答者记忆范围的问题。问及关于长期行为的问题可能不会得到准确的答案。例如问被访者他们去年在紧身内衣消费上花了多少钱时，他们的答案可能都是估计的，但是问他们在前两个星期紧身内衣消费上花了多少钱时，可能会得到准确的答案。

Question wording / 问题的用词

Great care must be taken with the wording of questions. This is of particular importance when conducting cross-cultural or international marketing research. Decisions about question wording include:

- Does the word mean the same to all respondents?
- Some words such as 'dinner' and 'tea' mean different things in different parts of the country. Words should be chosen to mean the same to all respondents.
- The use of vague or ambiguous words also should be avoided. For example, 'Are you a regular purchaser of nylon tights?' is not specific enough. How often is 'regular'? This may mean different things to different respondents.

Are the questions loaded? Some words or phrases should not be used in questionnaire design as they are likely to result in bias. Emotive words or phrases invite particular responses; for example, 'Are you in favour of sending money to help the poor, starving people in Africa?'

必须特别注意问题的用词，尤其是当进行跨文化或者国际市场研究时。确定问题的用词包括：

- 这个词对所有的被访者是否有同样的意思？
- 一些词如“晚餐”和“茶”在不同国家的不同区域其含义是不同的，应该选择那些对所有被访者意思都一样的词汇。
- 应该避免使用模糊的或者模棱两可的词汇。例如，“你会经常购买尼龙紧身内衣吗？”这个问题就不明确，“经常”指的是多久？这对不同的被访者指的是不同的意思。

问题是否有偏见？有些词汇和短语因为可能会产生偏见，所以在问卷设计中不能使用。感性的词汇或短语会促使被访者做出特殊的回答。例如“你喜欢用钱帮助那些非洲饥饿贫穷的人吗？”

Response format / 回答问题的形式

There are a number of types of response format that may be used. The most commonly used are dichotomous, multiple-choice and open-ended formats. Most questionnaires contain a mixture of these.

Dichotomous Only two responses are allowed, such as 'yes' or 'no', 'male' or 'female'. A neutral 'don't know' category is sometimes included. The advantages are that these questions are quick to ask and the responses are easy to record and analyse. The disadvantages are

可以使用很多不同的回答问题的形式。最常用的是二选一（是非题）、多项选择题以及开放式回答，大多数调查问卷都是以上形式的组合。

是非型 只有两个答案可供选择，“是”或“否”，“男性”或“女性”，有的时候也会用“不知道”这个选项。优点是问这个问题速度快，并且访问

that they do not allow for any shades of meaning to be included in the responses, and many questions would have to be asked to derive information of any detail by using this format alone.

者容易记录和分析，缺点是可能不会包含被访者作答的所有内容，许多问题选择这种方式提问主要是想获得具体信息。

Multiple-choice Here the respondent is presented with a choice of several possible answers to the question. Frequently, the list of choices is shown to the respondent on a card. The order of the alternative answers should be rotated to avoid bias. Again, the questions are quick to ask and the responses are easy to record and analyse. This format also allows for more shades of meaning and the respondent has more freedom of choice in the response. The difficulty of this format is that it is difficult to ensure that the list of possible responses is complete.

多项选择型 这种形式会给被访者提供几个可能的答案让其作答。通常选项会显示在一张卡片上，答案的顺序应该设计合理避免误导回答者。这种问题回答速度快并且访问者容易记录和分析，这种形式有很多变化，回答者会自由地选择答案。这种形式的难点是所列举出的答案是否包含了所有可能的情况。

Open ended The respondent has complete freedom of choice in the response given with this format. This format is often used where little information exists to construct a multiple choice list, or when great detail is required. The advantage is that the information produced is extensive and is free from any bias of suggested answers. The main disadvantage is that the responses are slow to record as they must be recorded verbatim. This can lead to interviewers selecting what they think are the most important points, resulting in bias. These responses are also difficult to analyse as coding frames must be constructed for each question after the fieldwork has taken place. Coding of responses at a later stage requires grouping of responses, which can lose some shades of meaning.

开放式回答 回答者回答这种形式的问题有充分的自主性，在没有足够的信息形成多种选项答案或者是需要具体详细的信息时通常会采取这种形式。优点是得到的信息内容广泛，不会受到给定答案的影响。最大的缺点是记录答案速度慢，调查者必须逐字记录。采用这种形式的话，访谈者会选择那些他们认为重要的问题，可能答案会产生误解，进而也很难对答案进行分析。因此在进行现场调查前，必须对问题进行编码，后期再对编码回答进行归类，这样就不会产生误解了。

Question sequence ／问题设计的顺序

The questions need to be organized logically to avoid introducing error or bias. Generally, you should move from general questions that the respondent finds easy to answer, to more specific or difficult questions about attitudes or behaviour.

In some surveys it is possible to ask classification questions, which may appear personal or embarrassing, at the end of the interview. If a quota sample is being used, some of these questions will need to be asked at the start of the interview, as they may form part of the quota control. To overcome this, showcards may be used, e.g. with age or income bands (Figure 4.5).

必须按照逻辑性组织问题，避免产生误解。一般而言，应该尽量少设计那些回答者容易作答的一般性问题，而多设计一些针对看法和行为的更为精确和复杂的问题。

在一些研究中，有可能会问及一些分类性的问题，这些问题可能在访谈的时候会涉及个人隐私或者使人尴尬。如果采用的是配额抽样法，有些问题就需要在访谈开始的时候完成，因为这些问题可能会形成配额控制的一部分。为了解决这些不足，可以使用卡片，例如按年龄和收入分段（图4-5）。

(A) 15~24
(B) 25~34
(C) 35~44
(D) 45~54
(E) 55+

(A) under £5000 p.a. 5000英镑以下
(B) £5000–£9999 p.a. 5000 ~ 9999英镑
(C) £10 000–£14 999 p.a. 10000 ~ 14999英镑
(D) £15 000–£20 000 p.a. 15000 ~ 20000英镑
(E) £20 000+ p.a. 20000英镑以上

Figure 4.5 Sample showcards. 图 4–5 卡片样例

Questionnaire layout /问题的排列

The overall aim is clarity. There are some procedures that can aid clarity. These include ensuring that all questions are numbered; filter questions (ones that may be omitted in certain situations) should be clearly marked; instructions to the interviewer should be in block capitals; arrows or visual aids may be used.

整体目标很明确，有些步骤可以使问卷更清晰易懂。这些方法是保证所有问题都有编号，筛选型问题（有些情况下可以省略的问题）应该清楚地标注，提示信息应该用大写字体，可以使用箭头或者视觉辅助信息。

Pretesting (pilot) and revision /预测和修正

The questionnaire must be thoroughly tested, using respondents similar to those who will take part in the final survey. This is known as the pilot stage and is vitally important to the reliability and validity of your survey results. Once this has been done, any modifications needed can be made, and the questionnaire tested again.

认真地进行问卷测试，选择那些将会参与最终调研的人员进行测试，这称为预测阶段，对于调研结果的可靠性和有效性是非常重要的。一旦完成了问卷测试，就可以进行调整和修正，再进一步对问卷进行测试。

4.11 Attitude measurement and rating scales /态度测量和评价量表

These are used to quantify the strength of a response. The two scales most commonly used in attitude measurement are Osgood's semantic differential scale and the Likert summated rating scale.

这主要是用来量化回答问题的情况的。态度测量时会用到两个评价量表，奥斯古德的语义区分量表和李克特的总加量表。

4.11.1 Types of attitude scale /态度量表的类型

Attitudes are measured in scales. The main types of scale are as follows.

按照量表测量态度分类，主要有以下的类型。

Nominal scales /名词量表

These classify individuals into two or more groups, e.g. male/female, agree/disagree.

这种形式把个体分为两个或多个小组，例如男性/女性，同意/不同意。

Ordinal scales / 顺序量表

These rank individuals according to certain characteristics, e.g. Yves St. Laurent fragrances according to preference:

- Opium
- Paris
- Rive Gauche, etc.

指根据不同的特点将个体进行排序。例如根据喜爱程度对伊夫·圣·洛朗的香水进行排序：

- 鸦片；
- 巴黎；
- 塞纳河左岸等。

Interval scales / 区间尺度

These scales have regular calibrations, for example see Figure 4.6.

这种量表是有刻度的，如图4–6所示。

Figure 4.6 Interval scale. 图4–6 区间尺度

The advantage of this scale is that it can be used to measure the strength of a particular attitude. It also allows the use of statistical measures such as standard deviation, correlation coefficients and significance testing.

这种量表的优点是可以测量某种态度的强度，也可以应用统计测量如标准偏差、相关系数以及显著性检验。

Ratio scales / 比例标尺

These scales have a fixed origin or zero point, which permits the use of all arithmetical functions, e.g. measurement of length or weight. Measurements of market size, market share and number of consumers are also examples of ratio scales.

这种标尺有固定的起点或者是零点，可以运用数学函数来进行计算，例如测量长度或者重量。市场规模、市场份额和消费者的人数测算都属于比例标尺测算的实例。

As previously mentioned, the most widely used attitude scaling techniques are the Likert and semantic differential scales.

如前所述，态度测量中使用最广泛的技术是李克特的方法以及语义区分量表法。

4.11.2 The Likert scale / 李克特量表

Respondents are asked to indicate their level of agreement or disagreement with a series of statements about a subject or an object. The statements used are identified as either positive or negative, and scores are allocated for particular responses. The list of possible responses is usually:

- strongly agree;
- agree;

被访者根据一系列有关某个话题或者实物的描述表明他们赞同或者不赞同的程度。描述被区分为正面的或者负面的，某些特殊的回答会给定分值。可能的回答如下：

- 非常同意；
- 同意；

- don't know/neutral;
- disagree;
- strongly disagree.

The Likert scale is not an interval scale, so it is not possible to infer that 'strongly agree' is twice as strong an attitude as 'agree'. The scores achieved by individual respondents are only relative to those achieved by other respondents. Likert scales are popular as they are easy to construct and give reliable information about the degree of respondents' feelings.

- 不知道 / 中立；
- 不同意；
- 非常不同意。

李克特量表并不是一个间隔标尺，也不可能将非常同意认为是同意的双倍程度，每一个回答者的分值确定与其他人的回答只是相对而言的。李克特量表应用普遍，因为很容易根据回答者的感受程度构建或者给出可靠的信息。

4.11.3 The semantic differential scale ／语义区分量表

This is another widely used technique in marketing research. A series of bipolar (opposite) adjectives of descriptive phrases are presented to the respondent at opposite ends of a five or seven point scale. Respondents are asked to indicate where on the scale best describes their feelings towards the subject or object. An example is shown in Figure 4.7.

这是市场调研中使用较为普遍的另一种方法，提供给回答者一些描述性的双极形容词量表（或者形容词的反义词），以相对的形式给出 5 个或者 7 个量点。提问哪个位置量点最恰当地描述了回答者对某个话题或者实物的感受，图 4–7 给出了实例。

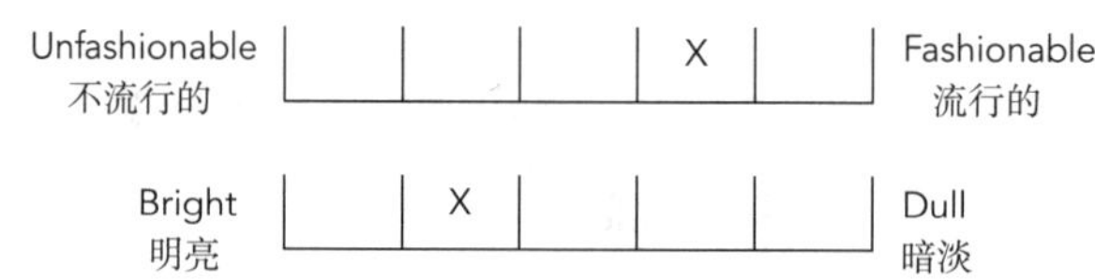

Figure 4.7 An example of the semantic differential scale. 图 4–7 语义区分量表

Semantic differential scales have been successfully used for such investigations as corporate image, brand image and product image. It is often difficult for consumers to articulate their feelings in these areas, and the semantic differential scale offers them an easy way of expressing themselves. These scales are widely used in marketing research as they obtain information about consumer behaviour that may not be obtained with the same degree of success by direct questioning.

在企业形象、品牌形象和产品形象调研中可以很好地使用语义区分量表法。一般来说消费者很难说清楚他们对这些方面的态度，语义区分量表法给消费者提供了很好地描述他们想法的方式。这种量表法在市场调研中应用广泛，因为运用这种方法获取的消费者消费行为方面的信息比直接询问获取的信息更有用。

4.12 The role of marketing research in new product development ／营销调研在新产品开发中的作用

Marketing research has a vital role to play in ensuring that new products launched onto the market are successful ventures, rather than dismal failures. The

营销调研对确保产品成功入市有着重要的作用，营销调研对新产品开发的作用主要表现在以下方面：

main input that marketing research makes into the new product development process is in the areas of:

- idea generation;
- evaluating and developing new product concepts;
- evaluating and developing new products;
- pricing new products.

These inputs are similar in the development of fashion.

Since the late 1970s, there has been an increase in the number of stores developing their own product lines. Specialists called product developers create products and test them on customers. There may be numerous reasons why a product is developed or modified to be sold in a particular market; new government legislation, changes in culture, the economy or even the climate may be responsible.

The creation of a marketing strategy for the development of a fashion product involves four stages. Each of the stages (discussed below) involves marketing research with the ultimate aim of testing a product for feasibility prior to its production, and to produce a plan for its production and marketing.

- 创意的产生；
- 评估和形成新产品理念；
- 评估和开发新产品；
- 新产品定价。

从20世纪70年代后期开始，大多数时装店开始开发自己的新产品系列，专家认为产品开发人员主要是创造产品并且针对消费者进行产品测试的。有很多原因可以说明开发或者修改一个产品并在某个市场出售的理由，如新的政府立法、文化、经济，甚至气候的变化，都有可能是其中的原因。

时装产品开发策略的产生有四个阶段，每一个过程都包括在生产之前根据市场目标对产品的可行性进行测试。

4.12.1 Creation of a customer profile／目标客户的描述

By identifying potential target markets for the proposed product, it is possible to prepare a customer profile for each one. Profiling characteristics such as age, gender, occupation and geographical location are considered, together with lifestyle characteristics as used in market segmentation.

Once these target markets have been identified, the attitudes and perceptions of potential consumers may be researched. Different groups of consumers have different needs, and by addressing the variables associated with buyer behaviour, it is possible to identify the product attributes that will appeal to each target group.

The information necessary to write a customer profile is available from several sources, both primary and secondary. For example, trade press, reports from fashion shows, sales staff, industry analysis and buyers can all be called upon to supply information.

The identification of specialized target markets is as important to the area of fashion retailing as it is to fashion design. Many fashion retailers (Next and GAP, for example) have deliberately targeted very specific niche markets, in an attempt to differentiate themselves from the competition. Emphasis has been placed

针对计划的产品对潜在的目标市场进行分析，就可以为每个目标市场确定明确的目标客户，描述消费者的特征，如年龄、性别、职业和地理位置，以及市场细分中用到的生活方式要素。

一旦确定了目标市场，就需要对潜在消费者的态度和认识进行调研。不同的消费群体有不同的需求，分析与购买行为相关的变量，就会清楚每个目标群体对产品的看法。

可以通过多种方式掌握描述消费者特征的必要信息，包括一手资料和二手资料。例如，可以通过贸易出版物、时装秀报导、销售人员、行业分析和采购商等获取信息。

特定目标市场的划分对时装零售领域和时装设计都是很重要的。许多时装零售商（例如奈克斯特和盖璞）就谨慎地把利基市场（译者注：利基市场是指向那些被市场中的统治者/有绝对优势

on the development and acquisition of appropriate merchandise to satisfy particular market segments.

的企业忽略的某些细分市场，指企业选定一个很小的产品或服务领域，集中力量进入并成为领先者，从当地市场到全国再到全球，同时建立各种壁垒，逐渐形成持久的竞争优势）作为目标，试图从竞争角度体现他们的差异化，重视恰当商品的开发和测试，从而有助于企业发现满意的细分市场。

4.12.2 Preparing a profile of the competitors ／确定竞争者的特征

Information about competitors' market size, market share, product range, consumers and marketing strategies comes under the scope of marketing research. With this information it is possible to analyse the relative strengths and weaknesses of the competition, and decide how much of a threat they pose.

Some of this information can be found from secondary data sources such as company reports, trade press, brochures and other promotional materials. Online sources also provide useful information for competitor research. It may also be possible for sales representatives to gather primary data from customers regarding competitors. Buyers, for example, will usually be contacted by a range of alternative suppliers and may be able to provide insight into competitors marketing intentions.

主要通过市场调研获得有关竞争者的市场规模、市场份额、产品系列、消费者和市场策略等方面的信息，有了这些信息就可以分析企业的相对竞争优势和劣势，以确定其面临的威胁。

其中有些信息可以通过二手资料获取，例如企业报告、商业杂志、宣传册和其他推销宣传材料等，网上资源也可以为竞争调研提供有用的信息。可以通过销售代表从消费者那里获取有关竞争者的一手资料，例如采购商通常会和很多备选供应商联系业务，他们可能会提供调查到的竞争者的营销意图。

4.12.3 Preparation of a marketing strategy report ／准备营销策略报告

Once the target market has been identified and a profile prepared for both the consumer and the competition, a marketing strategy must be prepared. The report will include general information about the market (size, structure, etc.) as well as particular information about the proposed target market. It will also contain information about the product, including the product's differential advantage and pricing policy. An evaluation of potential retail outlets will also be included, and an assessment of the resources will be needed to produce and market the new or modified product.

一旦明确了目标市场，明确了消费者和竞争者，就需要制定营销策略了。报告中包括一般的信息如有关市场的规模、结构等，同样也包括预期目标市场的特别信息，还包含产品信息、不同产品的优点及定价策略，潜在零售店铺的评估，以及对生产和销售新产品或者改良产品所需的评价资料都需要考虑进去。

4.12.4 The merchandise plan ／商品企划

This stage involves product testing, i.e. exposing prototypes of the product to fashion buyers. Any

这个阶段包括产品测试，如把产品样衣展示给时装采购商，应该考虑这些

further developments suggested by these 'experts' will be considered, and the prototypes modified, as is the usual practice with product testing.

专家提出的进一步的有关产品开发的建议和样品修改的建议，以及产品测试的情况。

These are the main steps in developing and evaluating a new fashion product. The steps are slightly different from those involved in the development of more conventional consumer products, but the information necessary for a successful launch (such as an evaluation of the concept, its acceptability, consumer attitudes and preferences, information on the market in general and testing the product) is very similar.

新的时装产品的开发和评估有几个主要的步骤，这些步骤与便利品的开发有少许的差别，但产品要成功上市所必需的信息（对产品理念的评价、产品的可接受度、消费者的看法及喜好、总体市场情况和产品测试）是非常相似的。

4.13 Forecasting fashion ／流行预测

Estimating future demand for goods or services is extremely difficult in any market, but particularly so in fashion. Anticipating what buyers are likely to do under a given set of conditions is made more difficult by the eclectic nature of fashions, so any predictions about the future should be flexible and open to modification as the seasons change.

估算产品或者服务未来的市场需求是很难的事情，尤其是时装行业。因为时装本身风格多样，所以要预测顾客在某种特定条件下会有什么样的行为比较困难，因此对将来的任何预测都应该灵活一些，并且随着季节变化对产品进行改良。

There is a problem with the use of formalized techniques for prediction in that many fashion professionals mistakenly believe that their creativity will be inhibited or that their fashion acumen and flair will be trivialized by this process. This is clearly not the case, and these methods should be used to assist the decision maker.

运用程式化的方法进行预测有一个问题，那就是多数时装专业人士都误认为他们的创意可能会被放弃，或者他们在时装方面的才智和鉴赏力在这个过程中会被忽视。很明显这不是事实，这些方法可以辅助决策者进行决策。

4.13.1 Uses of information ／信息的使用

The basis on which forecasts can be made is one of sound information. Past and present consumer purchases are analysed for trend data. The target market for your products must be clearly identified and described by using marketing research techniques. The use of geodemographic systems such as ACORN (A Classification Of Residential Neighbourhoods) can be used to identify and contact your target market, and collect information about attitudes, preferences and future buying intentions such as 'Are you likely to buy a new coat in the next three months?'

做出预测的基础是掌握完整的信息，过去的和现在的消费者购买情况分析可以作为预测的资料。企业必须采用市场调研方法明确地区分和描述自己产品针对的目标市场。地理人口细分系统如橡树果实体系（按居住人口进行分类的系统）的使用可以用来区分市场，并且保持与目标市场之间的联系，同时这种系统可以用来收集消费者的看法、喜好以及未来购买意图等信息，例如“你在未来的三个月里会购买新外套吗？”。

Millers and tanners who often work years ahead of the market can be contacted for primary data on future

可以联系市场上游的工厂业主和一线工人收集有关未来发展趋势的资

developments, as can fashion editors and buyers, who are in the forefront of current consumer behaviour. Secondary sources such as trade magazines and newspapers provide information which is readily accessible. Range plans covering such variables as material, product type, colour and price are also an important source of data.

料，也包括那些最先了解消费者消费行为的时尚编辑和采购人员，还可以通过商业杂志和报纸获取二手资料，长期计划中的材料、产品类型、色彩和价格等市场变量等也是重要的资料来源。

4.13.2 Further techniques / 信息的进一步处理

Information gained from the above sources will provide an analytical base for more specialized forecasting techniques. These include the use of ordinal scales to rank product alternatives as well as panels of up to eight people, who are asked to provide a consensus view of forecasts. A consensus is sought to avoid the bias introduced if the opinion of a single person regarding future sales potential was taken. Computer forecasting software has been specially developed for use in the fashion industry, which has facilitated the use of complex statistical techniques.

从以上渠道获取的信息是进行专业性市场预测的基础。顺序量表法的运用可以对产品替代性进行排序，也可以对8人小组进行提问以提供对预测的统一意见，达成一致观点可以避免因为采取一个人对未来市场预测的看法而导致预测失误。已经开发出的适合时装行业的计算机预测软件，可以辅助完成一些复杂的统计工作。

A form of product testing, called style testing, is used to involve the consumer in the forecasting process. A representative sample of target consumers is shown several provisional styles and ranges for future seasons. The consumers are then asked to state which they believe will be 'winners' and which are likely to be 'losers' in terms of customer appeal.

产品测试的一种形式称为款式测试，可以将消费者与流行预测过程联系起来，指的是给目标消费者中的代表提供下一季的几种暂定的时装款式及系列，然后对消费者提问，让他们根据个人的喜好确定哪些款式会成功以及哪些会失败。

Test marketing of new styles, colours or silhouettes often takes place using a 'sample, test, re-order' system. Small quantities of garments are made up and placed in selected retail outlets. Customer reactions may be monitored without incurring the costs of full production. Similarly marketing research is used to monitor sales performance at the start of each season to identify any variations away from the forecast that may occur.

新款式、新色彩或者新造型的产品的市场测试通常采用一种“样品、测试、重新整理”的方法，具体指的是制作少量的时装并且投放到选择的零售店，从而可以在没有产生任何生产成本的情况下监控消费者的反应。近似的市场调研也用来在每个季初监控产品的销售状况，从而可以识别出哪些变量对未来流行预测是没有任何意义的。

Fashion forecasting methods involve much organization and planning, and are not easy to establish in the first instance. All fashion businesses are involved in forecasting to some degree, and an increasing number of companies are being set up solely to provide specialist prediction services.

要在早期确立时装流行预测的方法是有难度的，因为方法的确定需要组织和计划。几乎所有的时装交易在某种程度上都涉及流行预测，新成立的很多公司就提供专业性的行业预测服务。

Fashion buying will always rely on a high degree of intuition and gut feeling about the market. When this is combined with a structured approach to planning and the use of research, more accurate forecasting is possible.

一般来说时装购买行为的产生很大程度上依赖于直觉，将这些与合理安排的方法相结合并且运用调研法就可以获得较为准确的预测。

这部分将重点分析市场调研方法中网

4.14 The Internet as a research tool ／调研工具：网络

Rather than go into specific details of web page design (on which there are numerous available sources), this section will concentrate on the usefulness of the Internet as part of research methodology. Rapid developments in technology and corresponding reductions in costs have meant that the use of the Internet for both business and social use has proliferated in the past few years. Businesses all over the world are considering whether e-commerce can improve profitability. Consumers are increasingly embracing online shopping, with the choice of goods available broadening all the time, particularly with regard to apparel. Designers and retailers alike have websites that can be found easily on the Internet (e.g. Next, Paul Smith, La Redoute).

The increased use of the Internet as part of the marketing process has similarly had a great impact on the marketing research industry. The number of marketing research companies that now provide specialist Internet research services ('e-research') has also grown considerably.

It is easy to be very enthusiastic about the use of the Internet for research, but as with all available research tools, care must be taken to ensure that it is appropriate to the particular study. As with the more traditional research methods, there are advantages and disadvantages. Conducting research via the Internet may increase the speed of research from design to results and reduce costs, as well as appearing to facilitate research on an international level. Problems related to research via the Internet include using samples that are not representative of the target population and rapid obsolescence of information, such as e-mail addresses. In spite of the problems, the Internet is increasingly being used in marketing research for both primary and secondary data collection, and is proving to be a very useful addition to the researcher's 'tool kit'.

络的使用方法，而不是讨论网页设计的细节（在网页上可以找到大量的信息）。信息技术的快速发展和成本的降低使得网络在商业和社会方面的应用在过去几年快速增长，遍布全球的业务都在考虑电子商务是不是真的能提高赢利。随着网络供应的产品日益丰富，消费者越来越喜欢在线购物，尤其是购买时装产品，因为在网络上很容易找到设计师和零售商的网站，例如奈克斯特，保罗史密斯，乐都特。

越来越多的企业使用网络来完成营销活动，这点对市场调研有着重要的影响，现在提供网络专业调查服务的公司数量也有了很大的增长。

消费者很容易对网络调研感兴趣，因此企业必须注意调研工具与调研项目的适合性。与其他传统调研工具一样，网络也有其优势和劣势。通过网络进行调研可以加快市场调研的速度并且可以降低成本，同样可以使调研在全球范围内展开。运用网络调研的缺点是选择的样本有可能不能代表目标市场，并且信息很快会过时，例如 E-mail 地址。不管其存在的缺点如何，网络在市场调研中的使用日益广泛，包括收集一手资料和二手资料，也给调研人员提供了更多的调研方法。

4.14.1 Online secondary data sources ／在线二手资料来源

Online commercial databases have been available to researchers for many years (e.g. www.FT.com – *The Financial Times'* website), providing access to news sources, trade publications and market reports. (It is useful to note that as with conventional sources, access to online

很长时间以来调研人员都可以获取网上的商业数据（例如 www.FT.com—金融时报的网址），可以获得最新的资料，商业出版物以及市场报告等（在这里需要指出，与传统

secondary data is not always free.) The Internet contains a wealth of information but it may be time consuming to find as there is no single index of information available, rather a range of search engines (e.g. AltaVista, Yahoo!, Google), and sources may not necessarily be logic-ally linked. Although online databases and search engines may be searched using keywords, the selection of appropriate keywords may be problematic. It is not always the most obvious keywords that will provide the best information. Searches using short phrases in quotation marks may provide more relevant results. The speed of searching and the breadth, if not always depth, of information available does make the Internet a useful tool for secondary data searches, however, particularly in exploratory research.

资料一样，要通过网络获取资料并不是免费的）。网络资源丰富，但会花费很多时间去寻找信息，因为可获取的信息并不是单一的，相反有很多搜索引擎（阿尔塔维斯塔、雅虎、谷歌），而且资料在逻辑上并不一定是相关联的。尽管在线数据和搜索引擎是运用关键词来搜索的，但选择恰当的关键词可能会是一个问题，并不是选择最明显的关键词就能够搜索到有用的信息，用引号标注的短语进行搜索可能会获得最紧密相关的结果。搜索的速度和获取信息的范围可以使网络成为很好的二手资料收集的工具，尤其是进行探索性研究的时候。

The Internet can be a particular useful resource for business-to-business research. It is possible to visit companies' websites which contain much useful information about products or services offered, financial information and an indication of the target market.

网络对企业间的研究是非常有用的，可以访问企业的网站，上面会有很多有关产品和服务的有用信息，财务信息，而且有的信息也会暗示企业的目标市场。

It is also possible to gain access to a whole range of market reports and articles online. Not all of these reports are free, which may limit access for some researchers. A useful source for market research information is www.marketresearch.com which offers more than 110 000 market research reports from over 550 publishers. Other online sources include:

通过网络同样也可以获取广泛的市场报告和在线文章等资料，这些报告并不都是免费的，会限制某些调研人员的进入。可以在网站 www.marketresearch.com 上获取有用的市场调研资料，网站上提供了 50 多家出版机构的超过 110000 份的市场研究报告。其他的在线资源还包括：

www.companieshouse.gov.uk
Provides free information on more than 2 million companies.

提供超过 200 万家企业的免费信息；

www.londonstockexchange.com
Provides a free annual reports service, giving information on the performance of over 1300 listed companies.

提供免费的年报，1300 家公司的市场业绩。

For the fashion industry, there are a number of websites providing access to a range of industry information. These include:

对时装业来说，也有很多提供行业信息的网站。它们是：

www.fashionweb.co.uk
A dedicated web portal for the fashion industry. Also offers a website design and hosting service.

时装业的门户网站，同样提供网站设计和托管服务；

www.fashion.net
Provides links for agencies, news, services and employment in the fashion industry.

可以链接到时装业的代理商、新闻机构、服务部门和人员招聘等；

www.fashioninformation.com

A mainly subscription-only service providing information on trend forecasting for fashion industry professionals.

www.wmd.com

Womens Wear Daily website – giving current information on all aspects of the fashion industry plus access to archived reports available by subscription.

主要提供订阅服务，专业提供流行趋势预测方面的信息；

《女装日报》的网站，提供最新的时装业各方面的信息，也可以订阅报告。

4.14.2 Primary data collection online ／在线一手资料的收集

The main methods of collecting primary data via the Internet are by e-mail or website-based surveys or by online discussion groups.

通过网络收集资料的主要方法是E–mail，或者基于网站的调查或者在线小组讨论。

With e-mail surveys, questionnaires are sent to respondents at their e-mail address. The questionnaires are then completed and returned online. The advantages of speed of both delivery and return are clear, as are cost savings over mail surveys. Disadvantages of this method are that e-mail is not completely confidential and that respondents selected as having e-mail addresses may not be representative of the research population. There may also be a time lag for replies as not everyone reads their e-mail regularly! It should also be noted that with the increase in use of the Internet, the amount of e-mail and therefore 'junk' e-mail has increased. The response rate to e-surveys, although often lower, can be compared to mail surveys as similar problems with unsolicited mail exist. Now most e-mail surveys are completed following an e-mail invitation to participate and is a useful means of conducting business-to-business research. The usual problems associated with questionnaire design are still relevant when designing e-mail surveys.

采用E–mail的方式，调查问卷通过E–mail邮寄给被调查者。优点是分发和回收速度快，也节约了成本。缺点是E–mail地址是属于私密的，而且选择的那些有E–mail的被调查者有可能代表不了调研总体样本的情况，同时因为每个人并不一定都习惯读邮件，所以答复时间可能会拖后。在此需要注意的是随着网络的广泛使用，邮件的数量和垃圾邮件的数量越来越多。E–mail邮件调查的回收率一般比较低，与邮寄问卷调研相比有同样的问题，那就是调研对象会收到未经请求的邮件。如今越来越多的E–mail调查都能通过邀请参与来完成，这也是企业之间研究的一种很有用的方法，调查问卷设计的一般问题对于E–mail调查也是一样存在的。

Web-based surveys consist of questionnaires posted on a particular website which are then completed by respondents who 'hit' that given site. Website surveys allow for more complex presentation, using both graphics and sound. This method relies on convenience sampling of users who access the website. These self-selected respondents may not be at all representative of the target population and as such this method should be used with care. It should also be noted that the costs of setting up a website of this complexity mean that it is more frequently employed by commercial research organizations.

基于网站的调查指的是把调查问卷粘贴在某个网站上，每个点击问卷网址的回答者就会完成调查。站点调查可以设计得比较复杂，可使用图表和声音，这种方法实现的基础是对访问网站的用户进行抽样。这些自主选择的回答者可能代表不了整体样本，因此应谨慎地采用这种方法。需要说明的是建立这样的复杂的一个网站需要一定的费用，但也暗示了企业网站可能会被商业调查组织频繁地利用。

Online discussion groups are frequently used for qualitative research in a similar way to focus groups, for new product development, product testing and evaluation. One key advantage of this method is the fact

定性研究中在线小组讨论方法使用频繁，它与焦点访谈法有些相似，适宜新产品开发、产品测试和评价方面的研究。这种方法的最大优点是可

that results are available immediately and a transcript of the discussion can be taken easily. Research costs are also reduced as travelling expenses, venue hire, etc. are not incurred. The fact that respondents are able to participate from their place of work, however geographically dispersed they may be, has meant that this method is increasingly being used in business-to-business research. An incentive may be paid to the respondents, however, as the costs of connection will be borne by them. Visuals and sound files may also be included within the discussion site, but as respondents cannot touch the items, this method may not be suitable for certain products, e.g. where softness of fabric is important.

以快速获得结果，分析讨论结果也很容易，因为不会产生差旅费、租用场地等费用，所以降低了调研成本。同时由于被调查者地理位置分散，各自在他们工作的地方参与调查，因此这种方法更适合企业之间的调研。调研组织者可以给回答者少许激励，但相关的费用需要他们自己承担。相关的视频文件也可以放在讨论的网站上，但是回答者不能直接回应这些视频，这种方法可能不适合某些产品，如为什么面料的柔软性很重要。

4.14.3 Using the Internet for research / 使用网络进行调研

The rapid developments in technology have meant that access to information via the Internet is becoming faster and easier for an increasing number of people. There is currently a great deal of enthusiasm about the Internet as a medium for both leisure and business activities, but this should be tempered with caution when considering the Internet as a means for conducting research. Problems associated with access, sampling response rate and quality of information, etc. all need to be considered against economies of time and cost. As with all tools available to the researcher, each must be considered for its appropriateness to the study and selected accordingly.

信息技术的快速发展使得大多数人通过网络获取信息变得又快又容易。网络作为休闲和商业活动的媒体受到越来越多人的欢迎，但是使用网络作为调研方式时需要谨慎些。除了考虑到时间和成本之外，还要考虑进入网站的风险问题，样本回收率和信息的质量等方面的影响。和其他调研工具一样，调研人员必须考虑调研方法与研究问题的适应性并且进行合理的选择。

4.15 International marketing research / 国际市场调研

International marketing research generally refers to marketing research undertaken in countries other than that in which the research was commissioned. The challenge for the researcher here is to provide information from a culturally diverse, rapidly changing world. Each country in which research is conducted will have its own unique characteristics and mores with which the researcher may not be familiar. At the outset certain factors need to be taken into account in the research design. These include:

Conceptual equivalence

Do concepts such as 'brand loyalty' have the same meaning and significance in each country selected?

Functional equivalence

Does a product have the same or similar function in the selected countries?

国际市场调研一般指的是市场调研在国家之间范围内展开，而不是指的那些委托调研。这里调研人员面临的挑战是从有文化差异的、快速变化的世界中获取信息。每一个进行调研的国家都有自己独有的特点，调研人员可能并不知道这些国家的风俗习惯。首先必须考虑调研设计的一些因素，具体包括以下内容：

概念一致性

如品牌忠诚度在选择的被调研国家里是否有着一样的意思和意义？

功能一致性

在选择的国家中某种产品是否有相同的或者相似的功能？

Scalar equivalence
Do scale measurements taken in selected countries produce the same or similar results?
Linguistic equivalence
Does language used when translated provide the same meaning for respondents, whether verbally or in written form?

标量一致性

在被选择的国家里标尺测量是否有相同或者相似的结果?

语言一致性

对回答者翻译的语言是否意思相同,是采用口语还是书面语?

4.15.1 Cultural influences / 文化影响

Researchers must also understand the culture in which the research will be conducted. Some subjects will be easier to study in some cultures but not in others, depending upon the research population selected. It should not be assumed that a 'one size fits all' approach will be successful. Research design may have to be modified between countries and cultures to ensure comparability of data. For example, in Arabic countries it is generally harder to obtain samples of women respondents. Issues regarding access and culture have to be carefully addressed. In many instances, international marketing research may be designed in one country but administered by local agencies because of their knowledge of local custom and practice.

调研人员必须了解进行调研地区的文化。不管选择的调查对象是谁,在某些文化领域有些问题是比较容易研究的,而在其他文化领域会有所不同,不要认为一刀切是可以成功的。不同国家和文化背景下调研设计应作调整,确保数据具有对比性。例如在阿拉伯国家,就很难选择女性调研对象。同时应该特别注意那些与宗教和文化有关的问题。在多数情况下,国际市场调研应该针对一个国家设计,而交由当地的代理商完成,因为他们更了解当地的习俗和惯例。

4.16 Summary / 小结

This chapter has covered the nature and scope of marketing research, starting with the survey research process:

- definition of the research required;
- decisions about the survey population;
- sampling methods;
- questionnaire design;
- data collection.

The chapter has also covered types of research design and approach, and the sources of data available to the fashion marketer. The application of marketing research to the development of new products and fashion prediction has been discussed, as well as a consideration of some of the issues around international marketing research design and the impact of the Internet on research methodology.

本章主要介绍了市场调研的特点和范围,从调研过程入手包括以下内容:

- 市场调研的定义;
- 调研总体样本的确定;
- 抽样方法;
- 调查问卷的设计;
- 资料收集。

本章同时也介绍了调研设计和调研方法的类型,以及时装营销者可以获取的资源,营销调研在新产品开发和时装流行预测方面的应用,以及国际市场调研设计应注意的问题和网络对调研方法的影响。

Further reading ／课后阅读材料

1.Collins, M. (1986), Sampling, in Worcester, R.M. and Downham, J. (eds), *Consumer Market Research Handbook*, 3rd Edition, Esomar, McGraw-Hill, Maidenhead.

柯林斯 · M.(1986)，抽样，伍斯特 · R.M.，唐纳姆 · J.，《消费者市场调研手册》第 3 版，欧洲民意与市场研究协会，麦格劳希尔集团出版，梅登黑德

2.Entwistle, J. and Rocamora, A. (2006), The field of fashion materi-alized: a study of London Fashion Week, *Sociology*, Vol. 40, No. 4, pp. 735–751, BSA Publications Ltd., London. DOI: 10.1177/ 0038038506065158.

斯特尔 · J.，罗卡摩拉 · A.(2006)，《时装物质化领域：伦敦时装周剖析》，人文社会版，40 卷第 4 期，735–751 页，BSA 出版有限公司，伦敦 . 索引号：10.1177/0038038506065158.

3.Hague, P. (2003), Marketing Research: *A Guide to Planning, Methodology and Evaluation*, 3rd Edition, Kogan-Page Limited, London.

海格，P.(2003)，《营销调研：规划，方法和评估》，第 3 版，Kogan–Page 有限公司，伦敦市场调查协会杂志，特刊：网络调研，41 卷第 4 期，1999，10.

4.Kent, R. (1999), *Marketing Research: Measurement, Method and Application*, International Thomson Business, London.

肯特，R.(1999)，《营销调研：评估，方法和应用》国际汤姆森商务出版，伦敦 .

5.Kotler, P. (2000), Marketing Management: *The Millennium Edition*, Prentice Hall, Englewood Cliffs, NJ.

科特勒，P.(2000)，《营销管理：千禧年纪念版》，普兰蒂斯出版社，恩格尔伍德克里夫斯，新泽西 .

6.Mouthino, L. and Evans, M. (1992), Applied Marketing Research, Addison-Wesley, Wokingham.

穆蒂尼奥，L.埃文斯，M.(1992)，《实用市场调研》，安德森 · 威斯利出版社，沃金厄姆 .

7.Proctor, T. (2000), *Essentials of Marketing Research*, Pearson Education Limited, Harlow.

普科特，T.(2000)，《营销调研的概要》，培生教育出版有限公司，哈洛 .

8.Richards, E. and Rachman, D. (eds) (1978), *Marketing Information and Research in Fashion Management*, American Marketing Association, Chicagos, IL.

理查兹，E. 拉赫曼，D.(eds)（1978），《营销信息和时装管理调研》，美国营销协会，芝加哥 .

9.Tull, D.S. and Hawkins, D.I. (1997), Marketing Research: *Measurement and Method*, Macmillan Publishing Company, New York.

塔尔，D.S. 霍金斯，D.I.(1997)，《营销调研：评估和方法》，麦克米伦出版公司，纽约 .

10.Webb, J.R. (ed.) (1999), *Understanding and Designing Marketing Research*, Academic Press, London.

韦勃，J.R.(ed.)（1999），《分析和设计营销调研》，美国学术出版社，伦敦 .

Part C
Target Marketing and Managing the Fashion Marketing Mix

第 3 部分　目标营销与营销组合管理

Chapter Five Segmentation and the Marketing Mix
第 5 章 市场细分与营销组合

5.1 Introduction and overview / 引言

This chapter will discuss the nature of market segmentation and the related strategies that are open to the fashion marketer. The preceding three chapters have concentrated on customers, in the context of the marketing environment in Chapter Two, as buyers with differing needs and social characteristics in Chapter Three and as a focus of research efforts in Chapter Four. This chapter attempts to draw together several themes to look at how to decide which market or markets to aim at, namely the target market(s).

Having determined the target market or markets, the next consideration is the positioning of the fashion marketing organization and its marketing efforts towards the target, and this will be covered later.

The chapter also forms an important link with the rest of the book by introducing the concept of the marketing mix. Having shown how an organization can position itself within a market, the next task is the planning and organization of controllable variables to meet the requirements of the market profitably. The particular combination of marketing variables offered to specific markets is known as the marketing mix, and this is described shortly.

本章主要讨论市场细分的特点以及与时装营销人员相关的市场策略。前 3 章的内容以顾客为中心，其中第 2 章主要内容是分析营销环境，第 3 章分析购买者不同的需求特点以及社会特性，第 4 章侧重于市场研究工作。本章主要讨论如何确定企业要针对的市场，即目标市场。

确定目标市场之后，下一步需要考虑的是时装企业的市场定位，以及针对目标市场的营销策划，这些内容将在后续章节讨论。

本章也引入了营销组合的概念，与这本书中的其他内容有着重要的关系。在了解了企业如何在一个市场中寻找自己的定位之后，然后对可控制的市场变量进行计划和组织，以满足预期市场的需求。针对特定市场的营销变量的组合就是通常所说的营销组合，稍后将会展开论述。

5.2 Mass marketing and market segmentation ／大众营销与市场细分

5.2.1 What is a market? ／什么是市场

To constitute a market a number of conditions have to be met. There should be a genuine need, the customer(s) should be willing and able to buy the product, and the aggregate demand should be sufficient to enable a supplier to operate profitably.

市场的形成需要考虑多方面的因素。前提是有真正的市场需求，消费者应该是有意愿并且有能力购买产品，同时总体的市场需求必须足够大，以便产品供应商能够盈利。

5.2.2 Mass marketing ／大众营销

Fashion marketers who assume that all customers in the market are the same are adopting a mass marketing or undifferentiated marketing approach. The assumption is based on the idea that customer needs do not vary and that the company can offer a standardized marketing mix that meets the needs of everyone. The standard marketing mix means the same product, method of distribution, prices and promotional effort aimed at everyone. The best example of this is China during the cultural revolution of the 1960s where the whole nation was offered the Mao outfit of dark blue jacket and trousers.

In Chapter Two, when considering the development of markets, it was noted that the aristocracy and wealthy classes were able to obtain products that met their precise needs. Most people in the pre-industrial revolution period dressed in a variety of styles which were greatly influenced by local skills and raw materials. Mass production methods, coupled with the experience of producing clothing for large armies, led to the possibility of mass markets for clothing. Indeed the practice of mass marketing linked to the military can be illustrated by the existence of the 'demob' suit issued to servicemen upon demobilization from national service.

Where a product can be standardized, perhaps because of the predominance of function over style, then it could be argued that a mass market exists. Also, when mass production methods enable considerable economies of scale, some items may be produced so efficiently that the product becomes a low-priced commodity. Certain items of underwear such as white Y-Fronts or one-size tights are certainly capable of consideration as products suitable for mass marketing. The reality, however, is that although the possibility of mass marketing of clothing remains, it has never been a major feature of fashion markets in any advanced economy.

那些认为“市场上消费者的需求是一样的”营销人员会采取大众营销或者无差异营销的方法，这种方法以消费者需求不发生变化为前提，企业只提供一种标准的营销组合满足市场上每个消费者的需求。标准的营销组合指的是企业向消费者提供同样的产品、采取同样的分销渠道、同样的定价和促销计划。

第 2 章在讨论市场发展时提到贵族以及富裕阶层有能力购买满足他们特定需求的产品。在工业革命前期，大多数人都穿着不同款式的时装，这主要是受到地方技术以及原材料等因素的影响。大批量生产的方式以及为庞大的军队生产时装的经验使时装业大众营销有了可能，其实质是因为将复员军人的套装分发给了社会服务人员，才使得大众营销与军队有了关联。

一件时装产品在哪才能标准化，又或者因为时装的功能性比款式更重要，所以才出现了大众市场。同样，当大批量生产方式形成相当大的经济规模时，企业就会过量地生产某些产品从而导致低价产品的产生。内衣产品中的某些品类如白色的男式短裤，或者单一尺寸的紧身衣，都是适合大众营销的时装产品。然而从实际情况看，市场上虽然有能够进行大众营销的时装产品，但是在任何先进经济体系中大众营销都不可能成为时装市场

Given choice and the diversity of suppliers, consumers have amply demonstrated the desire for individuality that clothing can give them and they have rendered elusive the idea of a mass market for clothing. This is not to argue that homogeneity is absent in the clothing market or that there is not just one mass market, but many different clothing markets. One of the big success stories of the last decade has been Zara who have targeted younger customers with fast fashion as competitive prices (Figure 5.1).

的主要特征。

消费者足以证明时装产品能够满足他们个性化需求，但前提条件是了解供应商的差异和不同。消费者给时装大众营销提出了难以捉摸的想法，这并不是说时装市场不存在同质性，也不是说只有一个大众市场，而是有许多不同的时装市场。过去十年最成功故事就是Zara，它主要以年轻的消费者为目标推出具有价格优势的流行时尚产品（图5–1）。

Figure 5.1 Zara, an example of successful market segmentation.

图 5–1 市场细分成功案例：Zara

Recognizing that the existence of many markets reflects the needs and purchasing capacity of clothing buyers leads to the idea of segmenting markets. Markets may be segmented or divided where, for instance, a group of consumers has a set of homogeneous needs that is different to other groups.

认识到众多市场的存在反映了时装购买者的需求和购买容量，就产生了细分市场的想法。举例来说，就是将有同质性需求的一群消费者与那些需求不同的消费群的市场进行细分或者区分开来。

5.2.3 Heterogeneous markets／异质市场

The extreme form of market segmentation is where everyone has different needs and purchasing capability, and this is described as market heterogeneity. An example of this would be if everyone had bespoke tailoring, which, given the economics of the prospect, is an unlikely scenario. The nearest example is the market for corporate clothing. Here large organizations may require custom-made uniforms or limited ranges of clothing for their staff to enable the achievement of corporate image and personnel goals. However, even within the corporate clothing market, there will be some homogeneity, with for example smaller regional and local non-competing organizations such as restaurants who are willing to accept similar garments for their staff. Security staff and cleaning personnel from many organizations may be provided with the same garments.

市场细分的极端形式就是每个人都有不同的需求和购买力，这称为市场异质性。举一个例子来说，就是假设每个人都预约定制时装，那就会有很好的经济前景。但这是不可能出现的情况，最相近的例子就是工作服市场。从这点来说，大型的企业需要给他们的员工定制制服或定制少量的服装，从而体现企业形象和员工目标的一致性。可是，即使在职业装市场也有同质化的特点，规模小的、区域性和地方性的非竞争组织如饭店就愿意给员工提供同样的时装，许多单位的保安人员和清洁工也有可能穿同样的服装。

5.2.4 Market segmentation／市场细分

Market segmentation is where the larger market is heterogeneous and can be broken down into smaller units that are similar in character. In practice there is always the problem of balancing the similarity of needs with the desire for substantial numbers of potential buyers.

Pressure to target more closely can lead to greater fragmentation of a market so that the overheads of promotional support and information overload for consumers can become associated with lower levels of market efficiency. An acceptable balance has been found by many firms in what is known as niche marketing, where a clearly defined segment is targeted with a narrow product range. Wolford, Tie Rack and Thomas Pink are examples of this approach. Niche marketing is just another form of market segmentation. The extreme form of meeting customers' needs along this continuum has already been described as market heterogeneity, where each customer is treated as being unique.

There are other pressures to aggregate consumers with needs that are 'similar enough', but this can lead to a situation where the resultant marketing mix is a compromise that satisfies no one. The desire for larger markets is understandable as large markets enable economies of scale in production and marketing, and can

市场细分指的是把较大的具有需求异质性的市场划分为需求相似的较小市场的过程，实际上如何确定潜在消费者的需求和欲望之间的共同特点一直是一个值得研究的问题。

营销目标所产生的压力会使得企业进行更为明确的市场细分，这样就会导致促销开支的增加以及促销信息超出消费者的承受范围，进而导致较低的市场运行效率。由此许多公司采用了一种可接受的平衡方式，那就是所说的利基市场，它指的是明确定义的以有限的产品类型为目标的细分市场，例如沃芙德、泰·瑞克和托马斯·品客。利基市场是细分市场的另一种形式，其满足的是消费需求的极端形式且很早就被定义为市场差异化，企业需要区别地对待这个市场上的每一位消费者。

还有其他方面的压力把具有足够“相似”需求的消费者凝聚到一起，但是这可能会导致陷入营销组合的境地，这种妥协，任何人都不会对它感到满意。较大规模市场的需求欲望可

command higher profits. The compromise solution of aggregating those who are 'similar enough' is vulnerable to competing businesses, who can demonstrate that they are better able to satisfy more closely targeted segments. These two pressures are shown in Figure 5.2.

以理解为跟大市场一样，这有利于形成生产和营销的规模效应，并且可以控制较高的收益。整合那些具有“足够相似”的需求市场的妥协处理方式对竞争激烈的行业是存在危险的，没有哪个企业能证明自己可以很好地满足目标市场的需求。这两种压力形式见图 5–2。

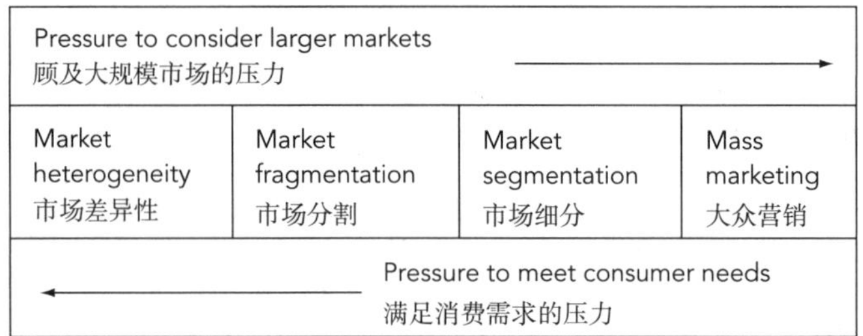

Figure 5.2 Factors influencing segmentation strategies.

图 5–2 影响市场细分策略的因素

5.3 Segmentation: rationale, bases and strategy / 市场细分：原理、基础和策略

5.3.1 The advantages of market segmentation / 市场细分的优点

By segmenting markets, fashion marketers gain several strategic advantages. Analysis of markets necessarily means consideration of competitors and their relative strengths and weaknesses in relation to customer needs. Such knowledge enables fashion marketers to decide whether to compete directly, if a strategic advantage is evident, or to position the company to exploit strengths and avoid retaliation from a stronger competitor.

The marketing research necessary to describe and segment a market usually leads to a deeper understanding of the customer that enables the most effective design of a marketing mix and the ability to respond to changes in the market.

Market segmentation enhances marketing planning in that it forces management to consider the relative costs, efficiency and effectiveness of the alternatives that segmentation reveals. Marketing planning is considered in detail in Chapter Ten.

通过市场细分，时装营销者可以获得战略上的优势。进行市场分析时要考虑与消费者相关联的竞争对手，以及他们的优势和劣势。如果战略优势明显，或者企业可以利用优势避免竞争者反击，这些优势和劣势将有助于时装营销者决定是否采取正面竞争。

营销调研过程中应该细分市场并且对其清晰地描述市场的特点，这样可以深入地了解消费者的需求，由此企业可以进行有效的营销组合设计，并且能够针对市场变化做出较快的反应。

市场细分强化了营销企划，因为企业在进行管理时需要考虑市场细分造成的成本、效率和效果等方面的问题。营销策划的内容在第 10 章阐述。

5.3.2 Segmentation bases ／市场细分的基础

Segments have been described above as groups of customers with similar characteristics. This section deals with ways of describing and analysing those characteristics. A larger market, say the womenswear market, may be divided or segmented into many different ways. There is no standard or preferred way to divide a market; however, it is important that the base(s) selected should relate to customers' needs.

Indeed it is not uncommon to find that fashion marketers use different methods for analysing the same market. What follows is an examination of some bases or dimensions that may be used to help categorize customers into meaningful and profitable segments.

市场细分就是分析消费需求相同的消费群体的特点，这部分主要讲的是描述和分析消费特点的方法。较大规模的市场如女装市场可能需要细分为多个不同的市场，并没有标准的或者最佳的方法来划分市场，可是最重要的前提是必须以消费者的需求为基础。

事实上，时装营销者都是用不同的细分方法来分析同样的市场，接下来的工作就是检验这些基础或者维度是否有助于把消费分为有意义并且具有盈利性的细分市场。

5.3.3 Segmentation based on descriptors ／基于描述的市场细分

One approach to segmenting markets is to describe the characteristics of potential customers. Such descriptions tend to look at demographic, geographical or personality characteristics of the buyer or a combination of the three measures. This approach is termed the descriptor perspective and has the merit that it is easily understandable and less costly owing to the availability of secondary data. An example would be to classify a market by age and income, thus for menswear we could show the market as shown in Table 5.1.

细分市场的一种方法就是描述潜在消费者的特点，这种描述主要考虑的是消费者的基本信息、地理位置以及个性，或者把三个要素综合起来衡量。这种方法称为愿景描述，与使用二手资料相比，这种方式较为容易理解并且成本较低。例如以年龄和收入为指标对男装市场进行细分，结果见表 5–1。

Table 5.1 Market segmentation in the menswear market: an example based on simple descriptors
表 5–1 男装市场细分：简单描述的例子

Income 收入 / Age 年龄	Low 低	Medium 中	High 高
16 ~ 25	A	B	C
26 ~ 35	D	E	F
36 ~ 55	G	H	I
56+	J	K	L

The next task using the table above is to quantify the various segments A to L and then analyse competitor activity within each segment. The fashion marketer can then make decisions about the positioning of the company within the market and in relation to

接下来的工作就是根据表中的信息衡量 A 到 L 这些细分市场，分析竞争对手在每个细分市场的市场策略。由此时装营销人员就可以确定自己在市场上

competitors. The concept of positioning is described later in this chapter.

The prime weakness of the descriptor approach is the assumption that the dimensions selected relate directly to clothing purchase behaviour. Clearly gender, age and income are significant variables in many clothing markets, but there is a danger in assuming that they are the only, or even the most important, variables in every market. Some of the main descriptors used in segmenting markets are shown in Table 5.2. Notice that some descriptors contain more than one variable. The family life cycle, for example, refers to age of head of household, marital status, and the age and number of children, if any.

的地位并且与竞争者展开竞争。市场定位的概念将在本章后面介绍。

描述方法最大的缺点就是假设所选定的指标直接与时装购买行为有关。很明显，在多数时装市场上性别、年龄和收入是重要的变量，但是把它们看作是每个市场上唯一的或者最重要的变量是有危险的。细分市场时的一些重要的描述方法如表 5–2 所示，可以看出一些描述方法包含多个变量。例如家庭生命周期指的是户主的年龄、婚姻状况以及孩子的数量。

Table 5.2 Market segmentation descriptor variables

表 5–2 市场细分的变量

Variable 变量	Potential categorization 分类
Gender 性别	Male/female 男性 / 女性
Age 年龄	<2, 2 ~ 5, 6 ~ 10, 11 ~ 15, 16 ~ 25, 26 ~ 35, 36 ~ 45, 46 ~ 64, 65+
Marital status 婚姻状况	Single, with partner, divorced, widowed 单身，已婚，离异，寡居
Occupation 职业	A,B,C1,C2,D,E Manual or non–manual 体力劳动或脑力劳动 Full– or part–time employment 全职或兼职
Income 收入	In decile bands, i.e. top 10%, next 10%, etc. 按不同的收入，如收入最高的前 10%、收入最低的后 10% 等
Net wealth 净收入	In decile bands or other bands, e.g. £0 – 4999, £5000 – 14999 按不同的收入，例如，0 ~ 4999 英镑，5000 ~ 14999 英镑
Education 受教育程度	Terminal age of education, e.g. <15, 16, 17, 18, 19, 20, 21 – 23, 24+ 接受教育的最大年龄，例如 <15,16,17,18,19,20,21 ~ 23,24+
Customer size 顾客体型	In height, weight, dress/suit sizes, e.g. petite, large 身高，体重，时装尺寸如：小号、大号
Religion 宗教信仰	Atheist, Christian, Muslim, Jewish, etc. 无神论者，基督教徒，穆斯林，犹太教徒等
Youth Subcultures 青年亚文化	Jazz, Goth, R&B, Rap, hip hop, punk, etc. 爵士乐，摇滚，节奏布鲁斯，说唱乐，嘻哈音乐，朋克音乐等
Family life cycle 家庭生命周期	Young single, young couple with no children, young couple with children, older couple with children, etc. 年轻的单身，没小孩的年轻夫妇，有小孩的夫妇，有小孩的年长夫妇等
Type of neighbourhood 居住环境	Urban/rural or, for example, ACORN 城市 / 农村，或者按居住人口进行分类的系统

续表

Variable 变量	Potential categorization 分类
Housing/area Region/country 地区 / 城市	e.g. North East, Coastal, Central, UK, Italy, 例如东北，沿海，中部地区，英国，意大利
Climate 气候	Hours of sunshine, rainfall, extremes of temperature 日照时长，降雨量，最高、最低温度
Lifestyle 生活方式	Groupings based on measurement of activities, interests and opinions 以活动、兴趣、观点为基础分组

5.3.4 Segmentation based on benefits and customer behaviour / 基于利益和消费行为的市场细分

Another approach considers the behaviour of, and benefits for, consumers of fashion products and services as the main dimensions in segmentation. Here the concern is with monitoring how the consumer behaves and the benefits she or he seeks from the product. Then and only then are descriptors considered. An obvious example may be the categorization of customers into those who are heavy spenders, moderate spenders or low spenders. For the fashion retailer operating a store card system the data should be readily available on a database along with other demographic information about customers, i.e. region, income, marital status, age, and so on (Table 5.3).

另一种细分方法是以时装产品或者享受服务的消费者的行为和利益为主要指标进行市场细分，这种方法的核心是了解消费者的消费行为以及他们想从产品中获得的利益。很明显的例子就是把消费者分为高档消费群、中档消费群和低档消费群。时装零售商要运行一个商店的卡片式记账系统，其数据库里就必须有顾客的居住地区、收入、婚姻状况和年龄等信息，见表 5-3。

Table 5.3 Market segmentation: behavioural and benefit variables

表 5-3 市场细分：行为和利益变量

Variable 变量	Potential categorization 潜在的分类
Purchase loyalty 购买忠诚度	Brand loyal to non-committed 品牌忠诚—非承诺的品牌忠诚
Purchasing mode 购买方式	From comparison shopping to convenient outlets only 购物中心—便利店
Usage rates 使用频率	Heavy users, medium users, light users, occasional users, non-users 经常使用者，一般使用者，很少使用者，偶尔使用者，不使用者
Expenditure 消费支出	High spenders to low spenders in deciles 高档消费层—低档消费层
Usage situation 着装环境	Working clothes, leisurewear, eveningwear, formal wear, e.g. weddings, and so on. 工作服、休闲服、晚装、正装，例如婚礼服等
Price sensitivity 价格敏感度	From very price aware and conscious to least price sensitive 对价格高度敏感—低度敏感
Benefits 利益	Easy-care garments, environmentally friendly fabrics and/or durability, etc. 易保养的时装、环保面料且 / 或耐穿性好等

An important consideration is the number of variables that may be interlaced to provide a basis for segmentation. It would be unusual to use only one variable to divide a market, but it is wrong to assume that using more variables (multi-variable segmentation) is without difficulties. The use of more variables provides greater precision for the analyst. The cost of more variables, however, is the danger of greater market fragmentation as described above. Benefit and behavioural bases for segmentation are rarely sufficient on their own and so they are usually combined with demographic data to display a fuller profile of the segments. Knowing that some customers want easy-care garments is one thing, knowing how many customers and how to reach them via distribution outlets and promotional efforts is another matter.

采用这种方法时，最关键的方面就是确定细分市场时变量的个数。一般很少选用一个变量来细分市场，但是选择多个变量（多变量细分）进行市场细分则难度会比较大。选择多变量进行市场细分可以使分析更为准确，可是多变量细分法的成本对上述的较大市场的细分有着一定的影响。以利益和行为为变量的市场细分显然是不全面的，因此通常也需要考虑人口方面的因素，从而形成比较完善的细分框架。了解到部分消费者需要易保养的时装是一回事，知道有多少消费者以及如何通过分销渠道和促销措施满足消费者这一需求又是另外一回事。

5.3.5 Criteria for selecting segments / 选择细分市场的标准

The bases for analysing market segments have just been described. Before developing a segmentation strategy one must select a segment or segments as a focus for marketing efforts. There are four main criteria that should be taken into account to achieve this.

前面已阐述了市场细分的基础，在制定细分市场策略之前，企业必须选择一个或者几个细分市场作为营销工作的重点，必须考虑到四个方面的因素。

◆ The segment should be measurable and easily identifiable. Before allocating marketing resources the target should be quantified. Producing garments to appeal to 'art lovers' may sound a good idea, but until it is known how to identify 'art lovers' and work out the market size little progress can be made.

◆ 细分市场必须具有可衡量性并且容易识别，在分配营销资源之前必须明确目标。生产迎合“艺术爱好者”的时装听起来是个好主意，但只有企业知道辨别谁是“艺术爱好者”，并且能够估算出市场容量时，这种策略才有可能取得成功。

◆ The chosen segment or segments should be relatively stable. Within the context of fashion this factor may seem ironic. However, fashion marketers invest considerable resources in building distribution networks and marketing information systems geared to particular groups or segments of customers and there must be the assurance that investment will yield long-term results. While styles may evolve over successive seasons, it is hoped that the core segment will remain loyal to the fashion marketer who leads and reflects their fashion tastes.

◆ 选择一个或多个细分市场应该相对稳定些。在时装行业，这个因素看起来有些讽刺意味。然而时装经营者为了满足特定消费群体或者细分市场顾客的需求，会将大量的资源投入渠道建设以及营销信息系统方面，但他们必须确保这项投入的长期收益。同样，尽管时装款式是按照季节特点设计的，但是经营者也希望核心市场的消费者具有较高的忠诚度。

◆ The segment or segments chosen should be accessible. Accessibility refers to both distribution and promotional efforts. The role of demographic data in simplifying decisions about reaching the chosen segments has been described in the previous section.

◆ 选择的一个或多个细分市场应该比较容易进入，这样也可以确保分销渠道和促销工作的开展。人口因素方面的资料有助于简化决策过程，从而满足细分市场的需求，这一内容在前面已有所介绍。

◆ The segment should be large enough to be profitable for the scale of operations of the fashion marketer. Opening a boutique for women aged 35 plus in a small country town may be a sensible move for a small entrepreneur, but not for a large multiple retailer. It cannot be stressed enough that the longterm goal should be profitability rather than sales or market share. It is far better to have 7% of a high margin market earning £500 000 profit per week than 15% of a low margin market earning £196 000 profit per week.

◆ 细分市场必须具有较大的容量以确保时装企业盈利。经营者在小城镇开一家规模小的，针对 35 岁以上女性的时装店是比较明智的决定，但对大规模经营者来说并不适合，不能只强调长期目标比促销和市场份额更有市场价值。每周在高利润市场中获 7% 即 500000 英镑的利润远比在低利润市场获得 15% 也就是 196000 英镑的利润要好得多。

Many companies describe their typical customers on websites, press releases or in advertisements, and this can give an indication of their target markets. However these statements can often be an aspiration rather than a reality as they are usually intended to flatter and attract consumers rather than defining the market segments in a way that informs marketing decision-makers. On their website, Warehouse describes their customers as 'Passionate about fashion, Knowledgeable about trends, Appreciates design and quality, Body confident, Independent and primarily 18–30, but Warehouse is about attitude not age!' This description is a nice complement to potential customers, but may not fully meet the criteria mentioned above for selecting a segment.

很多公司在网站、新闻公告或者广告活动中描述他们的典型顾客，这就暗示了公司的目标市场。然而这些描述通常只是一种希望而不是事实，因为这些公司一直都想满足或者吸引消费者而不是告知营销决策者来确定细分市场。在“WH”品牌的网站上，企业把他们的顾客描写为“热爱时尚，了解流行趋势，重视设计和质量，对自己身材自信，独立并且年龄在 18 ~ 30 岁的人，然而“WH”品牌强调的是一种观念而非年龄本身”。这种说法是对潜在消费者的补充描述，但是并不符合前文提到的选择细分市场的标准。

5.3.6 Segmentation strategies / 市场细分的策略

Segmentation strategies can range from the choice of one target market or segment within the market to the selection of several segments in the market, each with a different marketing mix. The selection of only one segment is known as concentration strategy and the selection of two or more segments is called a multi-segment strategy.

市场细分的策略包括目标市场的选择和一个或者几个细分市场的选择，每一个市场都有不同的营销组合策略。仅选择一个细分市场指的是密集营销策略，选择两个或多个市场称为多样化细分策略。

The determinants of a segmentation strategy are the company resources, the nature of the competition and the nature of demand in the particular fashion market, for instance, whether it is stable or volatile. A concentration strategy can enable the company to become expert in satisfying one segment of customers and so to acquire enough prestige and goodwill to foster loyalty among customers, Herbert Johnson (Hats), established in 1889, being one such example. The risk of a concentration strategy is that a downturn in one market can expose the company to considerable financial risk.

决定市场细分策略的因素是企业的资源情况、市场竞争状况以及特定市场的需求特点，而不考虑市场是否稳定。密集营销策略可以使企业成为满足某一细分市场消费者需求的专家，并且可以获得较好的声誉从而培养消费者对企业的忠诚度，成立于 1889 年只生产帽子的赫伯特·约翰逊就是一个例子。密集营销策略的风险是某个市场衰退就会使企业陷入相当大的财务风险。

A multi-segment strategy can provide a measure of stability in times of rapid market change by spreading risk across several segments. The same firm, while offering different marketing mixes, may find that the effort affords some economies of scale. For example, a company may target male and female segments via magazine advertising, and bulk purchasing of media space in magazines within the same publishing group may enable larger discounts to be earned.

多样化细分策略可以通过及时监控快速增长的市场变化将风险转移到各个细分市场，然而同一家公司采取不同的营销组合策略时会发现要实现风险转移的前提是企业必须拥有较大的市场规模。例如，一个企业可能通过杂志广告来瞄准男装或者女装市场，那么通过收购同一出版集团的各类杂志的广告版面可能获得较高的折扣，就能获利。

Many companies have changed from a concentration segmentation strategy to a multi-segment strategy in a desire to expand or maintain growth rates. Both Jockey and Sloggi now produce underwear for males and females, having expanded from single-sex segments of the market. Sometimes the expansion into new segments can have a number of teething troubles, as with Jigsaw's first attempts to move into menswear and Marks and Spencer's recurrent attempts to target younger women.

许多公司为了扩大或者保持市场增长率，会从集中营销策略转而采用多样化细分策略，乔基和斯洛琪两个品牌现在生产男女内衣，就是扩大了原有单一性别的细分市场。有时候进入新的细分市场会遇到很多暂时的问题，就像基戈索早期试图进入男装市场，以及玛莎百货反复尝试定位在年轻女性市场一样。

The size of the customers is changing. Few people have the figure of a catwalk model and retailers recognizing this are offering more ranges in a wider variety of sizes. Taller consumers can buy from Long Tall Sally, a retailer who offers longer-length clothing. Evans Collection specializes in clothes for women of size 14 and over. Petite ranges for shorter women are now being offered alongside the usual ranges in many stores; Principles Petite is one example.

消费者的时装尺码是一直变化的，很少有顾客的身材跟模特一样，零售商也认识到了这点，因而会提供更宽尺码、更多类别的时装。身材较为高大的顾客可以在高个子莎莉店那里买到衣服，它是一家提供加大码衣服的零售商，而埃文斯专门生产 14 号以及 14 号以下的女装产品。很多商店里针对身材较矮女性的尺码都沿用常规尺码，理论上的小号只是一个范例。

One leading clothing retailer, well known for floral designs, had tried to target a new market – that for boys between 8 and 11 – only to realize that particular age group often places great emphasis on distance from the feminine domain. Fortunately the lesson was learned after only a limited amount of experimentation with the new market segment and at small cost. Had the same retailer chosen a more masculine name and different outlets the outcome might have been very different.

以花卉设计而出名的一个知名零售商试图将 8 ~ 11 岁的男孩作为目标市场，但却发现这个特定的年龄群都不太喜欢女性化的设计元素，幸运的是他们花费很少的成本在新的细分市场进行有效的市场实验之后认识到了这个问题。同样的零售商选择比较阳刚的名字和不同的店铺，收入可能会大不相同。

5.3.7 Multi-segment strategies in practice / 实践中的多样化细分策略

The idea of segmentation has been taken on board by most of the high street retailers. Several large groups try to cover the whole market by having a variety of stores catering for different groups of customers. The Arcadia Group plc (formerly the Burton Group) was formed in 1998 at the same time

繁华商业街上的零售商已经接受了细分市场的这个观念，一些大集团试图通过不同的商店来满足不同消费群体的需求，从而覆盖整个市场。阿卡迪亚集团（以前的波顿集团）成立于 1998 年，那时刚好

as the demerger of Debenhams. Under the Arcadia Group are Burton, Dorothy Perkins, Evans, Outfit, Bhs, Tammy, Top Shop, Top Man, Wallis and Miss Selfridge. Dorothy Perkins and Burton offer affordable mainstream clothing for women and men, respectively, and Evans is the UK market leader for larger size womenswear. The group has a significant online presence with an e-commerce and Internet service provider called Zoom. In total the group has over 2500 outlets, is the second largest clothing retailer in the UK and has over 2.7 million active store card customers. In international markets the Arcadia Group has over 420 stores and operates in over 30 countries. Total sales for the group exceeded £1.85 billion in 2007.

Labels offered at Top Man are aimed at fashion orientated 15- to 25-year-old men looking for keen pricing. Burton aims at 25–40 year olds who are primarily socio-economic groups BC1C2; in 2007 they launched a premium Black Label featuring classic designs and higher grade fabrics for the less price conscious customer. Miss Selfridge offers clubwear, Wallis concentrates on stylish well-cut clothes. Thus within the Arcadia Group as a whole there will be some crossover of appeal for each brand, but the current emphasis of the group is on building distinctive labels.

与德本汉姆斯终止了合作关系。阿卡迪亚集团旗下有波顿、多萝西・珀金斯、埃文斯、奥菲、包豪斯、塔米、顶级店、极品男人、威尔斯和塞尔弗里奇小姐。多萝西・珀金斯和波顿主要提供价格实惠的时尚男女时装，埃文斯是英国市场上提供大号女装的领导者，公司有名为 Zoom 的电子商务系统和网络服务系统，总共有 2500 家专卖店，是英国第二大时装零售商，拥有 270 万个会员。阿卡迪亚集团在全球 30 多个城市拥有超过 420 家店铺，2007 年集团总销售额是 185 万英镑。

极品男人时装定位于渴望廉价产品的 15 到 25 岁的男性消费者，波顿主要针对 25 到 40 岁处于中等收入阶层的男性，2007 年发布了针对价格敏感度不高的消费群体，以经典设计和高档面料为主要特点的时装系列。塞尔弗里奇小姐主要供应俱乐部时装，威尔斯专注于裁剪精致的时装。在阿卡迪亚集团，每个品牌的消费群体可能会有所交叉，但集团目前的工作重心是建立有特色的商标。

5.4 Positioning and perceptual mapping ／定位和认知图

Positioning is to do with the perception of the firm and its marketing mix by the target market. Positioning is how customers see the market, although that perception may have been influenced by marketing action. The customers' perceptions include the role of the competition and may embrace some notion of an ideal offering.

The main method of determining a market position is the use of marketing research to construct a perceptual map of the market. A perceptual map is the consumers' view of the market, where consumers provide the main dimensions or criteria for making judgements. Ideally, these criteria will be the same ones identified when the firm considered behavioural and benefit bases for segmentation. Perceptual mapping involves complex statistical procedures, but is often shown as two- or three-dimensional diagrams. A hypothetical example of a perceptual map for positioning within the women's shoe market is shown in Figure 5.3.

定位指的是分析公司的发展规划，根据目标市场制定营销组合策略。定位就是明确消费者是如何看待市场的，尽管这点会受到企业营销活动的影响。顾客的感知包括竞争的作用，以及企业是否能够提供满足消费者需求的产品。

确定市场定位的主要方法是通过营销调研建立市场认知图，认知图是消费者对市场的看法，在这个图里消费者提出评价市场的主要尺度和标准。理论上来说，在企业考察细分市场时了解到的这些标准应该是一样的。认知图的建立包括复杂的数据统计过程，一般都以二维或三维坐标表示。图 5–3 是女鞋市场定位的认知图例子。

Figure 5.3 A market positioning example. 图 5–3 市场定位实例

An important point to be made about the perceptual map is that it is hypothetical and may have little to do with the realities of style and pricing. If typical consumers believe things about shoe stores that are reflected in Figure 5.3, then they will behave in such a way to affirm those beliefs, as described in Chapter Three. Thus some customers may never even enter a Ravel store as they think it may be too expensive for them, while others do not consider Marks and Spencer shoes as their perception is that they are poor on styling.

The essence of positioning is to get the product right in terms of customer needs and expectations and then to tailor the image of the firm's marketing offering to meet the aspirations of the chosen market segment. Thus in the example above, if Ravel was trying to position itself to meet aspirations then the perceptions on pricing need to be addressed. If prices are too high in reality then the purchasing policy should be reviewed. However, if the prices are in fact lower than shown by the perceptual map, then promotion efforts could emphasize, for example, the value for money aspect of Ravel shoes.

建立认知图的一个关键问题是认知图是假定的，可能与款式和价格的实际情况没有多大关系。假设图 5–3 给出的都是典型消费者信任的鞋店，那么他们即会采取适当的行为确认他们的信念，如第 3 章内容所述。可能有些消费者从来没有到过拉威尔的商店，因为他们认为那些产品他们消费不起；另外一些消费者则不会购买玛莎百货品牌的女鞋，因为他们认为这个品牌的鞋款式老旧。

市场定位的本质是提供能够满足消费者需求和期望的产品，然后就是建立企业形象以满足细分市场的强烈愿望。上述例子中，假设拉威尔品牌试图满足消费者的需求，那么它首先需要满足消费者对价格的期望。如果实际的价格过高，就必须重新审查一下企业的采购策略。可是，如果价格比认知图中的价格低的话，就必须加大促销力度，例如拉威尔物超所值的案例就说明这个道理。

5.5 The fashion marketing mix ／时装营销组合

The marketing mix is the range of variables that can be controlled by the fashion marketer to meet the needs of buyers profitably. Simply put, the marketing mix is getting the right product to the chosen market segment at the correct time, in the right place and for the right price.

营销组合指的是时装营销者控制一系列市场变量来满足购买者的需求。简而言之，营销组合就是在合适的时间、合适的地点，以合适的价格为选定的细分市场提供合适的产品。

Conventional descriptions of the marketing mix concentrate on what is known as the four Ps of marketing, namely Product, Price, Place and Promotion. This book does not deviate from that view but prefers the phrase Distribution decisions instead of Place decisions, as a synonym. Other approaches identify several other ways of dividing up the mix with between 2 and 12 components. The 4P approach is still the most popular among practitioners and academics, and has the merit of facilitating, the understanding about marketing activities.

一般的营销组合也就是通常所说的 4P，即产品、价格、渠道和促销，本书并没有脱离这个观点，只不过用分销替换了渠道的说法。其他方法是用 2 到 12 个要素来分析营销组合的。业内人士和学术界仍然采用 4P 理论，因为运用 4P 理论分析市场活动比较容易。

The last section ended with a discussion of positioning within a market and that should be the starting point for the development of a marketing mix. The positioning statement is a strategic decision taken by a company and the marketing mix is concerned with turning that decision into a reality via specific activities. To devise a combination of marketing elements, i.e. the mix, to meet customer aspirations while having a competitive advantage is the route to profitability.

最后一部分内容讨论某一个市场的定位方法，是营销组合策略的着眼点。定位描述就是公司的具体策略，营销组合是通过具体的营销活动来实现的。例如，设计营销组合要素时要满足顾客期望，同时企业必须具有竞争优势才能获利。

5.5.1 The planning and co-ordination of the marketing mix ／营销组合的计划和协调

All fashion firms have a marketing mix whether they consciously design one or not. The mix, as seen by the customer, works in varying degrees. Over-concentration on promotion to the neglect of adequate and timely distribution is a common feature of a flawed approach, as described in Chapter One. There is little point in advertising in magazines about the new range for a new autumn season in early September if retailers do not have the product in stock. Similarly, a public relations campaign to create an upmarket quality image can be easily undermined by a policy of almost continual discount sales.

任何企业不管是否有意识的设计，一般都有营销组合计划，从顾客的角度看营销组合可以在不同层面展开。就如第 1 章所讲的，过分地强调促销而忽视充分及时的分销计划是比较常见的问题。如果零售店里没有存货的话，企业 9 月初在杂志上宣传秋季的新品就没有任何的意义。同样，期望建立高端形象的公关活动很容易受到连续性的打折促销的影响。

All elements of the marketing mix should be co-ordinated towards the positioning objective. Thus a brand image may be reinforced by the pricing policy and the sales force should be sufficient to meet the needs of the distribution channels. Chapters Six to Ten deal in detail with the components of the marketing mix, and Chapter Ten will revisit planning and co-ordination, but the point should be noted now.

营销组合的所有要素之间必须相协调，如此一来，价格政策才会更加强化品牌形象，销售力量应满足分销渠道的需求。第 6 章到第 10 章将具体介绍营销组合的要素，第 10 章会再次提到营销组合的计划和协调，但在这里需要针对这点给出说明。

5.5.2 Alternative marketing mixes / 另一种营销组合

Firms may pursue a multi-segmentation strategy and offer different marketing mixes to different market segments. Therefore a designer dress offered at a higher price in department stores to an upmarket customer may be accompanied by a diffusion range with less design content and lower-quality fabrics at lower prices through chain stores to another segment by the same company. Different marketing mixes from the same company can coexist easily and are often unknown to consumers through the use of different company names and brands.

企业需要多元化的市场策略，并且针对不同市场制定了不同的营销组合策略。百货商店高价定位的设计师时装可能会由同样的公司在连锁店里同时推出，但是设计感较差，并且使用的面料档次较低。采用不同名称和不同品牌的同一家公司会制定不同的营销组合策略，但这些策略消费者是不知道的。

Table 5.4 Different marketing mixes aimed at similar menswear markets
表 5–4 同样的男装市场 不同的营销组合

Brand 品牌 / Strategy 策略	H&M 海恩斯·莫里斯	River Island 海岸
Segment 细分市场	20 ~ 35 岁 Male 男性 Mid–market 中端市场	15 ~ 35 岁 Male 男性 Mid–market 中端市场
Product 产品	Extensive range 品种类别丰富 Staples, Active lifestyle 主流的、积极的生活方式 L.O.G.G. Sports Casual/leisure L.O.G.G 系列运动便装 / 休闲装 Well–dressed formal wear 时尚正装	Casual/leisure 便装 / 休闲装 Broad range 产品类别多样 Different fibres and fabrics 不同质地和面料
Price 价格	Mid–range 中等定价 From tops at £4 to suits at £250+ 上装最低价 4 英镑，套装最低价 250 英镑	Slight premium over mid–range 比中等定价稍高 Tops from £25 to suits around £200 上装最低 25 英镑，套装大约 200 英镑
Distribution 分销渠道	Online shopping not available in UK in 2008 2008 年在英国没有网络购物 100+ high street stores 繁华商业街超过 100 家店铺	Online shopping available in UK 在英国有网络购物 200+ high street stores 繁华商业街超过 200 家店铺
Promotion 促销	Direct marketing, brochures, press advertising 直销、宣传册、报纸广告 Billboards 户外广告	Press advertisements 报纸广告 Strong visual merchandising 强大的视觉营销体系

An important principle to note in relation to the marketing mix is the principle of equi-finality. This means that there may be more than one way to reach a

与营销组合有关的，还需要提及的一点是等同效应，指的是有很多种方式可以达成目标，但达到营销目标的营销

goal, and that alternative routes or mixes may be equally effective in achieving marketing objectives. Table 5.4 gives a brief example of alternative marketing mixes to illustrate, in part, the principle of equi-finality.

组合策略必须有效。表 5–4 给出了另一种营销组合方式，在某种程度上说就是等同效应理论。

5.6 Summary / 小结

This chapter has introduced the concepts of segmentation and the marketing mix. Segmentation was discussed in terms of:

- ways of segmenting a market;
- criteria for selecting target markets;
- descriptor, behavioural and benefit dimension of segments;
- concentrated and multi-segment strategies, and their benefits and risks;
- examples from real fashion markets.

The chapter then went on to discuss market positioning and the relevance of the marketing mix to this, covering:

- building a strategy;
- co-ordinating the mix elements;
- alternative marketing mixes;
- customer perceptions of the marketing mix.

本章主要介绍了市场细分和营销组合的概念。市场细分从以下几个方面进行了阐述：

- 细分市场的方法；
- 选择目标市场的标准；
- 细分市场的描述、行为和利益；
- 集中营销和多元化营销策略以及它们的优势和风险；
- 实际的时装营销案例。

接着论述了市场定位以及与之相关的营销组合策略，包括：

- 制定营销组合策略；
- 协调营销组合要素；
- 另外的一种营销组合；
- 消费者对营销组合的理解。

Further reading / 课后阅读材料

1.Cahill, D.J. (2006), *Lifestyle Market Segmentation* (Haworth Series in Segmented, Targeted, and Customized Market), Haworth Press Inc., New York.

卡希尔 • D.J.(2006)，《生活方式的市场细分》(哈沃思系列丛书，市场细分，目标市场及定制市场)，哈沃思出版社，纽约 .

2.Cova, B. *et al*. (eds) (2007), *Consumer Tribes*, Butterworth-Heinemann, London.

科瓦 • B. 等 . (2007)，《消费群体》，巴特沃斯海尼曼出版社，伦敦 .

3.Dibb, S. and Simkin, L. (2007), *Market Segmentation Success: Making It Happen*, Haworth Press Inc., New York. International Thomson Business Press, London.

迪布 • S.，辛金 • L.(2007)，《市场细分的成功之路：让它出现》，哈沃思出版，纽约 . 汤姆森国际商务出版社，伦敦 .

4.Hooley, G. *et al*. (2008), *Marketing Strategy and Competitive Positioning*, 4th Edition, Financial Times/Prentice-Hall, Harlow.

胡利，G. 等 (2008)，《营销策略及竞争定位》，第 4 版，金融时报 / 普伦蒂斯—霍尔出版社，哈罗 .

5.McDonald, M. and Dunbar, I. (2004), *Market Segmentation: How to Do It, How to Profit from It*, Elsevier Butterworth-Heinemann, Oxford.

麦克唐纳 • M.，邓巴，I.(2004)，《市场细分：如何操作，如何赢利》，爱思威尔 • 巴特沃斯海尼曼出版社，牛津 .

6.Wedel, M. and Kamakura, W.A. (2000), *Market Segmentation: Conceptual and Methodological Foundations* (International Series in Quantitative Marketing), 2nd Revised Edition, Kluwer Academic Publishers, Boston.

威德尔·M.，镰仓·W.A.(2000)，《市场细分：概念和方法论基础（定量化营销中的国际系列）》，第 2 版，威科学术出版社，波士顿 .

Chapter Six　Designing and Marketing Fashion Products
第 6 章　时装产品设计与营销

6.1　Introduction ／引言

This chapter will examine the product element of the marketing mix and its pivotal role in the success or failure of businesses within the fashion industry. First it addresses the concept of fashion and its economic and social importance, followed by an analysis of the nature and attributes of fashion products. Then there is a description of how the industry is organized for the diffusion of new trends and an examination of the process of new fashion product development. Concepts are then applied by examining a retail buying sequence.

本章主要分析营销组合中的产品要素，以及其对时装产业发展成败的关键作用。首先论述时装的概念及其经济价值和社会价值，分析时装产品的特点和属性，接着描述流行趋势是如何传播的，举例说明时装新产品开发的过程，这些概念随后通过测试一个零售中的购物环节加以分析应用。

Later there is an assessment of the concept of fashion and other life cycles and the implications for marketing decision-makers. Finally the relevance and use of the concept when determining seasonal product mixes and planning and controlling the introduction of new ranges are examined.

稍后阐述时装的概念、产品生命周期以及对营销决策者的启示。最后论述时装的概念与企业在确定某一季产品组合以及对新产品系列进行计划和控制时的关联性。

In this chapter, the definition of fashion as a current mode of consumption behaviour has been applied specifically to clothing products. However, it is acknowledged that in its broadest sense the term can be used to describe any product or service consumed as part of a particular way of living. More specifically the contents of the chapter could equally apply to other clothing-related aspects of fashion, such as shoes, cosmetics, accessories or hairstyles, as outlined in Chapter One.

本章中把时装当前消费行为模式的解释仅仅用于对时装产品的分析，然而从广义上来讲，这个术语适用于生活消费中的任何产品和服务。更确切地说，本章的内容也适用于其他与时装相关的领域，包括鞋、化妆品、配饰或者发型等，就像第 1 章中所描述的一样。

6.2 The importance of fashion products／时装产品的重要性

6.2.1 The concept of fashion／时装的概念

The product element of the marketing mix is fundamental to the fashion design industry. The continual process of new product development and resulting change drives the whole industry and answers the demand from consumers for a constant stream of new ideas and offerings. Indeed it could be argued that without this constant generation and introduction of new ideas into the marketplace, the concept of 'fashion' would not exist.

营销组合中的产品要素是时装行业经营的根本。持续的新产品开发和市场变化驱动着整个产业的发展，同时企业通过不断产生的新创意和新产品来满足消费者的需求。可以说如果没有把这些新创意运用到市场中的话，时装的概念也无以存在。

Axiomatically, if consumers were not constantly engaged in the process of looking for new products or services to satisfy their emerging needs (and once having consumed them, allowing a set of new and different needs to emerge), the fashion process could not function.

很明显，如果不是消费者在尽力地去寻找满足他们需求的产品和服务的话（只要有人消费，就会产生一系列新的不同的市场需求），时装的设计、生产就没有任何意义了。

Thus the industry revolves around a time-based, i.e. seasonal, process in which new fashions are introduced into the marketplace and are adopted by enough consumers to warrant the description of 'fashion' in its proper context in the first place (as a current mode of consumption behaviour), only to wane eventually in terms of popularity, thus rendering them 'unfashionable'. While some product offerings will remain popular over several or even many seasons, others will fade very quickly; these differences are discussed further in the chapter. The important point to stress here, however, is that this regenerative process is intrinsic to the fashion industry and is very necessary for its continued survival.

因此时装业的循环发展，是基于一定时间段（例如季节性）的生产过程——在这一季新产品系列进入市场，并且被大多数消费者所接受，就见证了前文对时装概念的描述（即当下流行的消费行为的模式），然后需求逐渐减少，最后产品过时。一些供应商的产品可以在几个或者更多季节在市场上畅销，而其他的则很快退出市场，这些区别将在本章展开进一步阐述。这里需要强调的是，时装业的发展本身就有这样的循环过程，这也是产业获得长期发展的前提。

6.2.2 The economic importance of fashion／时装的经济价值

In 2006 the UK clothing market was valued at £13.9 billion at manufacturers selling prices and had been growing steadily for the previous few years. However, also in 2006, the number of UK clothing manufacturers reached an all-time low with large job losses to overseas suppliers of underwear and lower-priced garments. Many UK designers and fashion companies have been successfully exporting their ranges for many years; indeed the ratio of exports to imports has been rising steadily (in value terms) over the past few years. Nonetheless the UK remains a net importer of clothing.

按照时装生产商的销售价格来核算的话，2006 年英国时装市场总值为 1390 万英镑，并且在前几年一直保持稳定的增长。然而同样在 2006 年，英国时装制造商的数量达到最低，主要是因为大量的失业人员转移到了海外的内衣和低价时装供应商那里。多年来许多英国的时装设计师和时装公司都在出口他们的产品，并且取得了成功。事实上出口和进口之间的比率在过去几年是保持稳步增长的，尽管如此，英国一直都是时装产品的净进口方。

Although the percentage of household expenditure on clothing and footwear in the UK has slightly declined during the past decade, it still amounts to nearly 6% of the total of all consumer expenditure at current prices. Due to intense competition at the retail level and low-priced overseas sourcing and a strong pound, UK consumers have seen real reductions in clothing prices since 2000. While historically not as fashion conscious as their European counterparts, many UK consumers have become much more fashion aware and consequently much more discerning when it comes to appearance.

过去十几年，英国的家庭在时装和鞋类产品上的消费在逐渐减少，但按照现行物价计算，其消费额也达到了总体消费的 6%。自从 2000 年以来，由于零售市场以及海外低价产品的激烈竞争加之强势英镑的作用，英国时装消费价格有了很明显的降低。然而和欧洲市场上他们的对手不一样，许多英国消费者对时尚越来越关注，并且对流行时尚更为敏感。

To remain competitive many UK clothing manufacturers have chosen to follow an upmarket, high-cost route embracing high quality rather than competing with manufacturers elsewhere in the world who are able to maintain very low labour costs (and therefore offer volume-produced garments at very low prices). Others, however, have developed purchasing strategies that involve subcontracting work into low-cost countries while still maintaining a high design 'edge' over competitors.

为了保持竞争优势，英国时装制造商决定建立一个高端的，高成本并且提供高质量产品的市场而不是和那些生产低成本产品（提供大批量生产的低价时装产品）的制造商相竞争。然而其他制造商却采取了新的开发策略即将业务转移到劳动力成本低的国家，但同时在竞争者中还保持着较高的设计水平。

Clothing is now a global activity with China and the EU having 30.6% and 33.8% of world trade in clothing exports in 2006, respectively. Hong Kong with clothing exports of US$28.4 billion is much more active in this market than the USA with clothing exports of US$4.9 billion.

时装产业具有全球性的特点，2006 年中国和欧盟的出口分别占据全球市场的 30.6% 和 33.8%。中国香港在服装出口市场上表现更为活跃，远远超过了美国，其出口总值为 2840 万美元，而美国则为 490 万美元。

6.2.3 The social role of fashion ／时装的社会价值

It has often been suggested that fashion plays an important societal role in terms of individual wellbeing. This, it is maintained, comes through enhanced self-esteem and acceptance by peers and various other social groups through the 'correct' choice of clothing and use of other image-developing accessories. Therefore it could be argued that the primary objective in gaining greater understanding of the nature of fashion products and the process of new product development is to become more effective in targeting specific market segments and thereby satisfy some of the most basic needs within a society.

一般都认为时装在人们的生活中有着重要的社会价值。因为时装可以增强人们的自尊心，同龄人或者不同社会阶层的消费者通过选择合适的时装以及配饰从而认可时装的价值。使消费者了解时装产品的本质以及新产品开发的过程，其主要目的是能够有效地定位目标市场，从而满足社会个体的最基本需求。

Commercially this will lead to increased customer loyalty resulting in trust in what is being offered by the organization or the designer in question, resulting in improved sales performance and profitability. In the UK in particular, improved marketing capabilities have led to the maximization of design and manufacturing

从商业角度看，这样会增加消费者的忠诚度，从而使消费者信任企业或者设计师提供的时装产品，同时促进企业销售业绩的增长。尤其是在英国，市场容量的增长使设计和生产潜力都达到了

potential; British manufacturers cannot compete with low-cost producing countries on price and so have used their design and marketing talent as a basis to distinguish the UK in the marketplace.

最大化。英国制造商不能在价格上与那些生产低成本产品的国家的制造商相竞争，所以根据设计和营销水平才能区分哪些产品是来自英国的。

6.3 The nature of fashion products ／时装产品的本质

6.3.1 Product definition and classifications ／产品的定义和分类

Quite literally a product can be defined as anything that might satisfy a need that can be offered in the marketplace. Classifying products in terms of their characteristics and how consumers purchase them assists marketers in determining the appropriate blend of other marketing variables, i.e. promotion, pricing and distribution for the product in question.

Traditionally three categories have been used to define tangible product offerings, namely convenience, shopping and specialty, as shown in Figure 6.1.

产品指的是向市场提供的能满足人们需求的任何物品和劳务。根据产品的特点和消费者的购买方式对产品进行分类，有助于营销人员采取合适的营销策略，例如产品的促销、定价以及分销策略等。

传统上把有形产品分为三类，即便利品、选购品和特殊品，如图 6–1 所示。

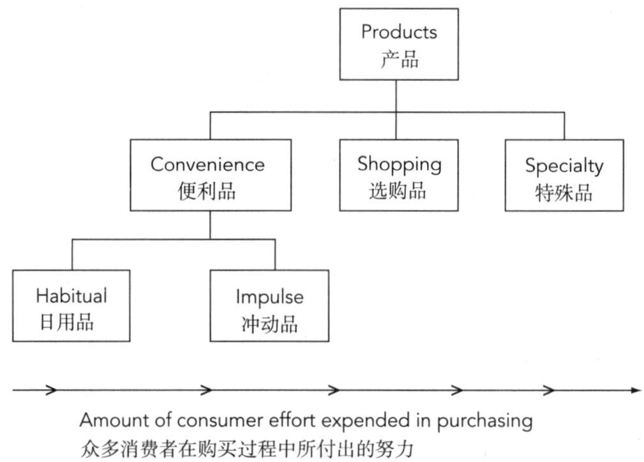

Figure 6.1 Classification of products. 图 6–1 产品的分类

Convenience goods ／便利品

Convenience goods are frequently purchased with little thought, effort or attempt to undertake comparisons with similar products. Convenience goods can be further subdivided into staple goods, purchased habitually and where brand loyalty is probably very strong, and impulse goods, purchased without any pre-planning or searching. It could be advocated that certain basic items of clothing

便利品是消费者经常购买的，购买时常不假思考，不做任何努力，也不会和其他类似的产品相比较。便利品可以进一步分为日用品和冲动品。日用品是经常购买的产品，消费者通常有着较高的品牌忠诚度。冲动品指

such as hosiery and underwear are often purchased as convenience goods, perhaps along with the family's regular one-stop shopping from the supermarket. Indeed many food retailers have capitalized on this approach by stocking such ranges alongside other non-food ranges.

消费者没有计划，不经过任何调研就购买的产品。比如袜子、内衣等都属于便利品，包括家庭在超市经常购买的产品。实际上食品零售商就是考虑到消费者对便利品的需求特点而采购食品以及其他非主食产品的。

Shopping goods ／选购品

Shopping goods are where consumers compare product attributes such as price, quality and design by shopping around. Products in this category will constitute high-volume markets similar to those of high street fashions. However, they will lack the seasonal variations intrinsic to the fashion industry and are likely to be purchased less frequently than most clothing items.

选购品指的是消费者购买时会检查并且比较价格、质量和设计水平的产品。这类产品与时装一样都有较大的市场容量，但是这类产品缺少季节性特点，与其他服饰品类相比，购买频率不高。

Specialty goods ／特殊品

Specialty goods are products with characteristics that differentiate them from the other two classifications, usually based on high-quality and higher-perceived value. Brand image is very important here; often customers will make the effort to seek out the exact product they require. It may be that they will also expect some degree of exclusivity in the product offering and will go out of their way to find it. More upmarket, branded fashion items obviously fall neatly into this category. However, over the past decade the demand for brand names in most garment categories and price ranges (triggered specifically by the mass market growth in sports and leisurewear) has dramatically risen. Therefore it could be argued that all except the most basic of clothing items could be described as specialty. As a result the high street has seen the development in recent years of what has come to be known as the 'capricious consumer'. By this we mean one who shops on a whim with little or no degree of store or brand loyalty but who has a keen eye for value for money with all the necessary design and brand name requisites. As a result, at the lower end of the market discount fashion chains such as Primark, H&M and Matalan find themselves the current 'value champions' on the high street through having low operating margins and still being able to offer viable customer propositions. At the premium end, brand-builders such as Gap and Next are still able to command premium prices despite having substantial operating costs, while companies such as Alexon with less brand strength found it difficult to sustain profitable operations.

特殊品具有不同的特点，一般指的是具有高品质和物超所值的产品。对这类产品来说品牌形象特别重要，因为消费者通常都会尽力寻找适合他们需求的产品。可能他们期望市场上能够提供独一无二的产品，并且他们会费尽心思去寻找这些产品。很显然，很多高端市场的品牌服饰产品都属于这一类别。然而过去十年里，消费者对大多数服饰品类的品牌性需求，以及物价水平（由大众市场运动服和休闲服快速增长引起的）都有了很明显的增长。因此可以这样说，除了最基本的服饰品类以外，其他产品都可以归为特殊品。近几年时装的快速发展促成了“多变消费者”的产生，这里我们所说的是那些因为一时冲动而消费，几乎没有品牌忠诚度的消费者，但是他们可以从设计和品牌名称方面发掘产品的价值。因此，市场销售终端的折扣店如普瑞玛克、海恩斯·莫里斯和玛塔兰发现他们在时装领域现有的“价值竞争”体系是通过获得较低营业利润才形成的，他们会继续实行这种策略。在高端市场的品牌创建者如盖璞和奈克斯特不顾运作成本的高低依然提倡高价，而品牌竞争优势较弱的艾莉森发现要维持赢利性的运营就比较困难。

6.3.2 Classifying products with a fashion element /按照时尚元素来划分产品

Although the categories above do apply to certain items of clothing in the fashion industry, they are slightly limited in use when one is trying to analyse buying motives and methods. It is probably more accurate therefore to classify tangible fashion products slightly differently, categorizing them as classics, fashions or fads.

尽管上述产品分类适用于时装产业的某些产品，但是当企业分析消费者的购买目的和购买方式时这种分类就有了局限性。因此较为准确的分类应该是把时装产品稍作区分，即分为经典产品、时尚品和潮流品。

Classics /经典产品

It is possible to use the term classic in several contexts. In terms of 'bundles of utilities', classics can usually be seen as the midpoint compromise of any style, i.e. total look or composite effect. Indeed, the term 'style' is often used to describe the classic in this context, complying with the basic laws of harmony in proportion, aesthetic sense and incorporation of balanced design features. Colour and pattern may vary but the classic customer does not seek the satisfaction of a new seasonal experience in the way that his or her fashion and fad counterparts do. However, it is likely that some satisfaction will be sought at the core of the product's tangible attributes, e.g. good quality, good fit and durability. Aquascutum is such an example as shown in Figure 6.2.

在很多章节中都提及"经典"这个词。在"综合效应"这一术语中，"经典"通常被看成是整体外观或综合效果较折衷稳妥的一些服装款式。事实上"款式"一词在本章通常是用来描述经典服装的品种，遵循时装设计中比例协调、美感和均衡的设计法则。时装的色彩和图案可能会有所不同，但经典产品的消费者不会购买仿冒的时尚品和潮流品来获得对新一季产品的满足感。有时消费者可能会比较满意产品的某些属性，如质量好、合体以及耐穿等。图 6–2 所示的雅格狮丹就是一个例子。

Figure 6.2 An example of a fashion classic. 图 6–2 经典时装的例子

In a product sense a classic is never out of style for its market segment and will rarely appeal to the majority. Design changes will be minimal; these changeless and always acceptable garments are found in all recognizable areas of fashion, e.g. the women's tailored suit with knee- or just above knee-length skirt or for men the City pinstripe, the double-breasted trench coat, the blazer; even denim jeans have their classic in the five-pocket Western style.

从产品感受方面看，经典产品在市场上是永远不会过时的，并且很少去迎合大众消费者的需求。产品设计很少改变，在时装领域这些不变的但一直被消费者接受的时装有很多，如裁剪精致的女式套装搭配长度在膝盖或者膝盖以上的裙子，或者男式的细条纹时装、双排扣大衣、轻便上装以及有五个口袋的西式牛仔服等。

Classic garments, sharing the quality of 'timelessness', will collectively make up the classic styles described above. At any given time, however, it will be possible to identify dominant and secondary styles. What should be added here is that although often described as timeless, classics also evolve gradually over many years according to the style of the age.

经典服饰承袭的是永恒不变的高品质，从而才成为了经典的款式，可是在某个特定时期需要区分哪些是主流款。在这里需要补充说明的是，通常所说的经典都是永恒的，但是多年以来经典逐渐地被认为是某个款式流行的年代。

Certain designers have also been described as classic, producing fashions that are seen by many as timeless and therefore can be worn despite the season and current high fashions. Barbour, Pringle and Nike provide good examples of brand names, while Paul Smith and Donna Karan are two examples of contemporary classic designers.

不管流行什么都可以穿着的时装，如巴伯尔、普林格和耐克主要供应品牌产品，而保罗・史密斯和唐娜・卡兰则只提供当季流行的产品。

Classic products may occasionally become fashionable, e.g. the ongoing revival of the Chanel suit, albeit with more up-to-date styling detail. However, it is more likely that the classic will form the basis for the annual slow, continuous change that forms fashion. There is a skill in combining the appropriate variations on the appropriate classics for any given moment in time to create an appropriate contemporary style.

经典产品也会流行起来，例如夏奈尔套装尽管没有太多的流行设计要素，但还是重新流行起来了。然而很有可能的是因为经典的不断变化才形成了时尚，有一种方法就是在特定时期将适当的变化融入经典设计之中，从而形成当季的流行款式。

Fashions and fads ／时尚品和潮流品

The distinction between a fashion and a fad is usually defined on the basis of their acceptance cycle. Fashions usually have a slower rise to popularity, reach a plateau with continuing popularity and then decline gradually; often this cycle relates to a season, whether autumn/winter or spring/summer. Mid-season modifications to the original fashions may be introduced with the specific intention of maintaining buying interest and encouraging further purchases from early as well as later adopters (see Chapter Three).

一般区分时尚品和潮流品主要考虑市场接受的周期。时尚品流行速度较慢，逐渐被大众接受，市场稳定后会慢慢下滑，往往这种情况跟季节有较大的关系。无论是秋冬季还是春夏季，季中的时候对原有的时装稍作修改后企业会有意地去进行宣传，从而保持消费者的购买热情并且鼓励后来者购买（见第3章）。

Fads, in contrast, will rise meteorically in popularity only to suffer an abrupt decline as they become adopted. As a fad becomes fashionable it also becomes unfashionable. Adoption of a fad is based solely on the

相对而言，潮流品被市场接受后总是昙花一现，之后市场需求就会急速下滑，潮流品既是流行时尚也是非流行时尚。接受潮流品的消费者只是想要一种

desire by the individual for a new experience that is not likely to become popular on a large scale. For this reason a fad tends to be viewed as non-viable in the commercial sense and usually eccentric in nature.

新的体验，因此潮流品不可能大规模地流行起来。正是因为这样，从商业角度看，潮流品是比较特殊的产品不可能长期存在。

Retailers like Zara, who operate a system of fast fashion where catwalk ideas can become translated into lower-priced fashionable items made available in stores within weeks, have contributed to the erosion between fashion and fad in some market segments.

类似 Zara 这种以快速时尚为主的零售商，将 T 台流行的服饰转化为低价的时尚产品，数周时间就可以到达店铺，这些产品不断地冲击着某些细分市场上的时尚品和潮流品。

6.3.3 Product attributes ／产品属性

In designing and developing new products, it is essential to understand what is being offered and therefore to appreciate the customer's perception of the product. As shown in Figure 6.3, there are four basics in terms of fashion design, namely silhouette or form, colour, texture or pattern and style or total look. However, the fashion consumer will tend to view the garment as a series of attributes. Some of these will relate more closely to the social or psychological needs of the consumer and therefore will not always be recognized by the individual. However, it is essential that the fashion marketer is aware of both the subconscious and the conscious aspects of the product to offer the best combination of need-satisfying benefits to the customer.

在设计和开发新产品时应该明确提供的是什么样的产品，从而满足消费者对产品的期望。如图 6–3 所示，时装设计有四个要素即廓型或样式、色彩、面料和图案以及款式或整体外观，但是消费者会把时装看作是一系列属性的组合，其中有些属性与消费者的社会和心理需求紧密相关，通常是很难被识别的。时装营销者必须认识到产品的潜意识和有意识两方面，从而为消费者提供满足其利益需求的产品。

Thus the product offering can be analysed at three levels. First, the *core* product that satisfies the most fundamental needs. Secondly, the product can be seen as the physical interpretation and presentation of the four design basics to create the most appropriate fashion for

因此企业提供的产品可以从三个层面进行分析：第一，产品的核心属是满足消费者最基本的需求；第二，产品的有形属性被看作是物品自身的描述，四个基础设计要素组合来

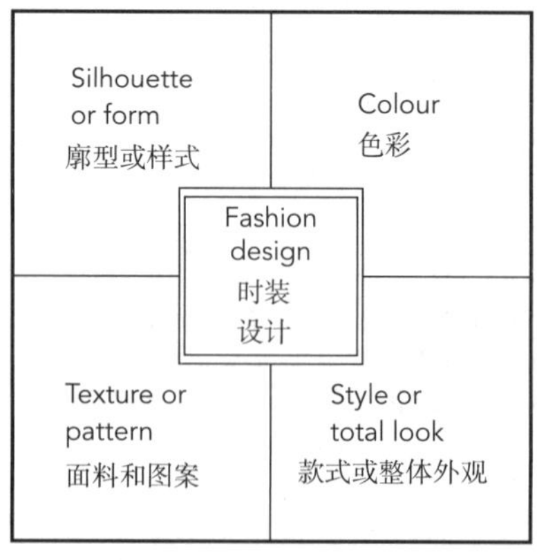

Figure 6.3 Four basics of fashion design.

图 6–3 时装设计的四要素

the market in question. Thirdly, there is the *intangible* product, i.e. the additional services and benefits that supplement the previous two levels and create the total product offering.

创造出满足市场需求的合适的产品；第三，产品的无形属性，指的是辅助以上两个层次的附加服务或者利益从而形成整体的产品概念。

Core attributes／产品的核心属性

The core of the product's attributes will revolve around the three basic tenets of clothing: protection, modesty and adornment. Since every garment will offer combinations of these functions to a greater or lesser degree, the consumer must decide how well the combination matches his or her basic criteria for purchase. Buyers will always look for those products that satisfy the maximum set of needs simultaneously. In practice, offerings will seldom satisfy all of them simultaneously and so each purchase decision will result in a compromise. The extent to which the customer has to make these compromises indicates the extent to which there are apparent gaps in the marketplace and therefore the need for more differentiation. This in turn helps to perpetuate fashion change.

产品的核心属性围绕着时装的三个学说，保护说、羞耻说和装饰说。任何一件衣服都是在不同程度上对这三种功能的组合，消费者必须确定这些组合是否符合他们购买的基本要求，购买者往往会选择那些能最大程度同时满足以上三个功能的时装产品。事实上，很少有产品能满足他们的这些需求，因此消费者也会折中考虑来决定是否购买。消费者做出多大的让步就说明企业的产品与市场需求有多大的差距，这点是需要认真分析的，如此一来有助于企业不断地进行产品的更新。

Tangible attributes／产品的有形属性

Tangible product attributes, or the interpretation and presentation of the four design basics to provide an overall style, will revolve around in the first place the set of design features which make up the actual product. For example, a basic ladies' blouse may offer variety in terms of shape (loose, fitted, etc.), sleeve type (set-in, raglan, dolman, etc.), type of collar and shape (one piece, two piece, pointed, round, etc.), any decoration or trimmings, etc. In addition, the designer must have regard to the appropriate use of fabric, texture, pattern and colour for any given season. These are set in the context of both overall style and, for instance, co-ordination with other garments and accessories to form a 'total look'.

产品的有形属性，或者说对以上四个要素进行解释和分析来形成整体设计，以设计要素中的第一位要素为主形成实际的产品。例如，基本款的女式衬衫在外形上可能有所变化（宽松、合体等）、袖型（装袖、插肩袖、蝙蝠袖等）、领型（一片领、两片领、尖领、圆领等）以及是否有装饰等。另外，设计师必须根据季节特点选择合适面料、图案和色彩，同时必须考虑时装的整体造型，例如与其他时装和配饰搭配来形成整体效果。

For example, it could be claimed that a hypothetical range of garments designed for the executive working woman offered high performance (durability, washability, etc.), an acceptable level of fashion for the given season, suitable styling for the executive role and versatility in wear. However, although the consumer may purchase specific items in the range at different times, it is highly likely that she would still expect co-ordination within the range to provide a suitable total look with whatever

举例来说，假设要给女性行政人员设计系列时装，那么这些时装就必须具有高性能（耐穿，耐洗等），符合季节特点，款式适合行政人员的职业特点并且容易搭配。尽管消费者会在不同的时间购买某类产品，但很有可能的是，她们依然会希望买到的时装能和系列中的其他产品搭配，从而

combination of garments she had purchased.

A designer and manufacturer should also strive to maintain standards of quality appropriate to the market which they have chosen to target. Quality control is becoming more and more important, although garment manufacturing does not have to comply with any British or European Standard in the way that product and engineering designs do. Therefore there is a variety of qualities of make and sizing specifications in clothing. Many consumers are quick to point out that a size 12 from one manufacturer or retailer may vary considerably from that of another. In 2006 the European Clothing Size Standard will aim to gradually replace national dress sizes and is based on body measurements. Metric sizing, anthropometric data, is derived from a major European study of sizing and benchmarking with similar international (ISO 3635) standards. If the European standard is widely accepted it will give the adopters of the standard a competitive advantage in world markets as both consumers and retail buyers will have greater confidence in the sizing information they use to make decisions. However, retail dominance since the 1980s has resulted in the introduction of more stringent quality control procedures. More discerning consumers now require quality of service and choice as well as product, and there are significant marketing implications in this.

Most retailers now employ teams of garment technologists whose remit is to work with in-house buyers and manufacturers to establish and maintain standards of make in line with given company policy. Quality manuals are used to provide guidelines on general standards such as fabric performance and size specification through to specifics such as the number of stitches per inch on seams which suppliers to use for component parts of the garment, such as trimmings.

The quality procedure in one large UK retail organization is as follows: retailers will require that buying samples (sample garments made to relevant quality standards) are approved before volume production. Once they have been checked by the technologist and buyer against established standards, two sample garments will be 'sealed', one to be kept by the manufacturer and one by the retailer. These samples will become the yardstick against which the quality of volume production will be measured. When volume garments begin to come off the production line a technologist will usually approve and seal a further three

形成完美的穿着效果。

设计师和制造商必须尽量保持目标市场上产品质量的一致性。虽然时装制造商没有按照英国或者欧洲的标准来进行产品设计和制造，但质量控制依然变得越来越重要。时装的生产和号码规格有很多不同的标准，因而大多数消费者会很快指出一个制造商或者零售商产品中的 12 码和其他制造商的产品的区别。2006 年，欧洲时装号型标准是以体型测量数据为基础的，其建立的目的就是逐渐地替代国内现有的时装号型体系。这个标准采用公制尺寸，其人体测量数据来源于欧洲人的尺寸和基准测量的研究成果，类似于国际标准（ISO 3635）进行的尺寸和基准测量研究成果。如果欧洲标准能被广泛接受的话，这将会使那些采用欧洲标准的企业在国际市场上更具竞争优势，同时消费者和零售采购商在购买时会更加信任这些尺码信息。然而自从 20 世纪 80 年代开始的零售限制导致产生了更为严格的质量控制程序，现在越来越精明的消费者对产品的选择和对服务质量的要求是一样的，其中蕴藏着重要的营销启示。

现今很多零售商雇用时装技术专家，这些专家与采购商和制造商一起合作来建立或者维持和企业政策一致的质量标准。质量手册只提供了一般的指导性标准，如面料性能和尺寸规格、缝制时每英寸的针数以及时装的其他组成部分如镶边等。

在英国大型的零售集团，质量控制程序如下：零售商要求批量生产前采购的样品时装（按照相关标准生产的样品时装）必须经过检验。技术人员和买方按照既定的标准检查完样品后，两件样品必须封样，一件由制造商保存，一件由零售商保存。这些样品将会成为批量生产的质量标准，当批量生产的产品下线时，技术专家一般会核查并且再选三件样品进行封样，确保产品达到质量标

samples, confirming that quality standards are being met and that the goods can be delivered into a central warehouse or direct to the store.

A further tangible attribute is seen in use of suitable packaging and branding. This is important in image creation, leading to differentiation in the marketplace which can be achieved very effectively through the use of labelling. Branding can be in the form of brand names, logos, trade marks, etc. Certain brand names have become so powerful that they are synonymous with the product. Consumers may talk of their Nike's instead of their training shoes, or of a Burberry instead of a raincoat. In the same way, suitable packaging is as import-ant in the fashion industry as any other.

Brand names are a very important vehicle for providing the customer with assurances regarding quality and consistency of standard, the brand name of Marks and Spencer is a case in point. They can also provide assurances as to the suitability of fashion content for the season in question. Strong brand names can be very advantageous when establishing overseas markets. Young Japanese consumers with very high levels of disposable income are dedicated followers of British fashion. Traditional labels such as Burberry have established strong links in Japan, as have designers such as Paul Smith, Mulberry and Vivienne Westwood.

As shown in Figure 6.4, companies can employ various strategies as regards the use of brand names, such as:

◆ A variety of names can be used with no obvious link, the caveat here being that substantial promotional budgets will be needed to establish each one in the mind of the consumer. The Arcadia group have Topshop, TopMan, Wallis, Miss Selfridge, Dorothy Perkins, Outfit, Evans and Burton as separate brands (Figure 6.4).

准，这样才可以将产品运到中心仓库/总库或者直接运送到店铺。

有形产品的另外一个属性是恰当的包装和品牌策略，这些对创建企业形象非常重要，可以通过使用商标来有效地实现市场差异化。品牌可以是品牌名称、标识、商标等。某些强势品牌名称代表的是企业的产品，消费者会谈论耐克而不是他们的运动鞋，同样会谈论巴宝莉而不是风雨衣。同样的道理，恰当的包装在时装业发展中也相当重要。

品牌名称是一种非常重要的媒介，它可以让消费者信任产品的质量是和行业标准一样的，玛莎百货就是这样的品牌，同时也可以使消费者确信其产品是符合季节流行趋势的。在拓展海外市场时强势品牌有很大的优势，有较高可支配收入的日本年轻消费者大多是英国时尚的追随者。传统的品牌如巴宝莉就和日本市场有着紧密的关系，拥有着保罗·史密斯，缪尔白瑞和薇薇安·韦斯特伍德等设计师。

如图 6-4 所示，就品牌而言企业可以采取不同的策略，例如：

◆ 使用不相关的多个品牌，这里需要指出的是企业可能需要大量的促销预算以建立每个品牌在消费者心目中的形象。阿卡迪亚集团就拥有顶级店、极品男人、威尔斯、塞尔弗里奇小姐、多萝西·珀金斯、奥菲、埃文斯和波顿等

Figure 6.4 Branding strategies: a continuum of approaches.

图 6–4 品牌策略：系列化措施

◆ Specific ranges may be given individual brand names; in this way some common link can be emphasized such as range co-ordination across several garment categories, or ranges that have been designed with a specific theme or purpose in mind. For example, Max Mara uses Max and Co as an affordable brand name for their younger market, Pianoforte for more expensive eveningwear and Marina Rinaldi for larger sizes.

◆ Use of only one brand name across the entire organization and its offerings can create a powerful image in the mind of the consumer. In time, use of well-established brand names can be stretched to introduce new products into different markets. This policy of brand stretching goes beyond brand extension, where new products are introduced into the same category. Use of this approach can increase the survival chances of new products and reduce launch costs. Indeed, brands that are too closely associated with particular types of products and do not use the power of relationship (in the consumer's mind) to extend and evolve into new formats and markets are likely to have very short lives. Towards the end of the 1990s the claim was that a new kind of brand was emerging – one capable of expressing a certain kind of attitude to life and somewhat reminiscent of the 'lifestyle' concept in the 1980s. Major brands are now becoming more 'elastic' in the sense that companies are increasingly defining them as a way of life and stretching them into new areas. Virgin now uses its name for airlines, music, broadcasting, broadband, trains, finance, soft drinks, mobile phones, health care, cosmetics, holidays, bridal wear and cinemas and an online car buying service. At a time where many companies are making similar types of products within similar price bands, functionality does not often succeed as a means of differentiation. Therefore it is essential that companies emphasize the emotional aspects of their brands in the hope that consumers will identify with sets of values that the brand is meant to represent. Even here, however, brands that stress highly intangible, emotional qualities must provide merchandise that is consistent with the brand promise.

The role that packaging plays within the tangible product offering will depend very much upon the nature of the product's image and the importance of branding and packaging within that. Although the main function of packaging is that of protection, it has often

多个品牌（图 6–4）。

◆ 给定每个品牌的品类范围，这种方法强调的是不同产品类别之间的关联性或者同属某一特定主题、特定目的而设计的产品系列。例如麦丝·玛拉集团的玛珂丝和蔻这两个品牌就是针对年轻消费市场的，而品牌皮安诺福特的主要产品是高档晚礼服，马瑞娜·芮娜迪则主要提供大码时装。

◆ 整个公司使用同一个品牌名称，可以在消费者心目中形成较强的品牌形象，最后还可以利用已建立好的品牌将新产品引入其他不同的市场。这种品牌扩张方式超出了品牌延伸的范畴，品牌延伸是把新产品引入到同一个品类的市场。采用这种方法增加了新产品成功的机会，降低了投入成本。事实上，品牌和特定类型的产品有着紧密的关系，如果不利用这种有利的关系进行品牌延伸并且进入新市场的话，企业就不会有长久的发展。20 世纪 90 年代末就出现了一种新的品牌，一种能表达 20 世纪 80 年代人们的生活态度，让人联想到当时生活方式的品牌。大多数品牌变得越来越具有弹性，由此企业就把品牌定义为一种生活方式，从而延伸到新的领域。品牌“维珍”如今在航空、音乐、广播节目、电台、列车、金融、软饮料、移动电话、卫生保健、化妆品、休闲度假、婚纱、影院和在线汽车购买服务等领域都在使用。同时许多公司也生产同一类型的具有相同价格区间和功能性的产品，作为差异化竞争的一种方式但并没有取得成功。因此企业需要强调他们品牌的感性特征，从而希望消费者能够识别品牌所体现的价值。即便这样，强调无形性和感性特征的品牌也必须提供与品牌承诺相一致的产品。

有形产品中包装的作用主要取决于产品形象、品牌的重要性和包装本身。尽管包装的主要作用是保护产品，但是它也是产品的本质特点，并且体现产品

become intrinsic to the overall offering and its status, as exemplified by labels such as Monsoon or Shanghai Tang, where the brand name and corporate colour scheme of fashion stores are reflected in the packaging design. The packaging may even have a functional use in its own right; continued use will help to reinforce brand and image with the customer.

的市场地位，就像曼休妮和上海滩两个商标一样，包装在其所授权范围内可能甚至有某种功能性作用，持续使用的话有助于强化品牌在消费者心目中的形象。

Intangible attributes ／延伸产品的属性

Intangible attributes, the additional services and benefits that supplement the core and tangible attributes, include services intrinsic to the purchase such as credit facilities, delivery arrangements, and after sales service such as alterations and money-back guarantees. Several UK fashion retailers such as, Selfridges and John Lewis, are beginning to follow the example of their American counterparts in providing customers with consultation as to personal image. This may include advice on the most appropriate garment styles for different body shapes and height, as well as colours most suited to the individual's complexion and hair colour.

Image and reputation of the seller, possibly because of an effective promotional campaign, constitute further intangible attributes. However, word-of-mouth recommendation, appealing shop interiors and exteriors and even satisfaction with previous purchases can all be contributory factors to the build up of longer-term loyalty. Lastly, there are consumers' quality and value perceptions, which are closely related to image and reputation but more often linked to customers' attitude towards price levels.

延伸产品，指的是用以补充核心产品和形式产品的附加服务和利益，包括提供贷款、免费送货以及退换货、退款保证等售后服务。一些英国的时装零售商像塞尔弗里奇小姐店和约翰·莱威斯商店就仿效美国的竞争对手提供给顾客个人形象咨询等服务，这种咨询包括为不同体型和身高的消费者推荐合适的时装款式，以及选择与消费者个人肤色和发色相搭配的时装色彩。

销售商的形象和声誉可能主要是因为其做了大量有效的推广活动，从而形成延伸产品。可是，每月推荐以及具有吸引力的店内图片和店外形象，和对前期购买的满意度等都有助于建立消费者对品牌的长期忠诚。还有一点就是消费者对产品质量和价值的认知，与企业的形象和声誉都有密切关系，但更多时候是和消费者对价格水平的看法有关的。

6.3.4 Licensing ／特许

The 1980s spending boom encouraged many big name fashion houses to expand their commercial activities through retailing and licensing. For many large investors, the appeal of high fashion lies not so much in their collections, but rather in the lucrative licences for perfumes and other products bearing the designer's name. Under a licensing agreement the designer will lend his or her name to products made by mainstream manufacturers. In spite of changing economic circumstances and problems associated with a strong pound and weak yen, the demand for British goods continues to grow in Japan. As a result, leading edge designers such as Paul Smith now have a high percentage of their business in Japan as licensing since

20 世纪 80 年代，消费高涨促使很多知名的时装店开始通过零售和特许扩大他们的销售活动。对于许多较大的投资者来说，高级时装的吸引力不只在于他们的时装发布会，更大程度是在于利润丰厚的香水以及标有设计师名称的其他产品。在许可协议条件下，设计师会把自己的名字借给主要的制造商使用。尽管受到经济环境变化、英镑强势和日元疲软等问题的影响，日本市场对英国产品的需求仍在不断地增长。由此带来的结果是，如保罗·史密斯等高端的设计师品牌自从 1986 年和 C.Itoh 签署许

the first licensing agreement was signed with C. Itoh in 1986; the company had sales of over £300 million in 2006. Burberry has signed a licensing agreement with Luxottica a world leader in premium eyewear developer and distributor to produce its first premium eyewear collection in 2007. Around £86 million, comprising 11% of Burberry's sales turnover, was derived from licensing in 2007.

可协议后至今在日本都有着较大的市场份额，2006 年销售额超过 3 亿英镑。巴宝莉就曾和与世界领先品牌“陆逊梯卡”签署过许可协议并在 2007 年举办了高档眼镜产品发布会，陆逊梯卡主要从事的是高档眼镜的开发和销售。仅 2007 年特许经营就给企业带来了大约 8600 万英镑的收入，这项收入占巴宝莉营业额的 11%。

In licensing, fashion houses such as Lauren and Dior must maintain a delicate balance between profiting from the prestige of their name and not simultaneously jeopardizing their exclusivity and high fashion image and reputation. Ralph Lauren concerns himself with every detail, from the quality of the product to how it is delivered and presented in the shops. Licensing royalties for Ralph Lauren were US$236 million in 2007.

特许模式中像劳伦、迪奥等品牌的时装店就必须保证在借助他们的品牌声誉赢利的同时，不损害品牌的高端时尚形象以及品牌声誉。拉尔夫·劳伦比较注重细节运作，从产品的质量到如何将产品运送到商店，以及产品如何在商店进行展示都非常关注，拉尔夫·劳伦 2007 年特许经营收益为 2.36 亿美元。

Cardin, in contrast, has more than 8400 licences for items ranging from scuba diving equipment to sunglasses and while it is now one of the highest turnover fashion companies with estimated sales of over US$1 billion in 2006, it has foregone its status as a high fashion house to become so.

相比较而言，卡丹大约有 8400 家特许店，其产品系列从水中呼吸器到太阳镜都有，据估算其 2006 年营业额为 10 亿美元，为目前营业收入最高的时装公司，并且一直处于高级时装公司的前列。

6.4 The fashion industry and new product development / 时装业和新产品开发

6.4.1 The role of the designer / 设计师的任务

The role of designer in the fashion industry is crucial to its success. The task is specifically one of interpreting society's current and anticipated mood into desirable, wearable, garments for every type and level of market. To do this effectively, designers must be in tune with the wider social, cultural, economic and political environment within which human beings conduct their daily lives; only then will their ideas truly reflect current prevailing conditions and the impact they are likely to have on future consumer needs. Thus the designer will draw on a wealth of ideas; the media and entertainment, other cultures, social attitudes and mores, historical and contemporary events all provide important sources of inspiration.

设计师对时装产业发展成败有着至关重要的作用。设计师的主要任务是分析社会环境、预测消费者的期望和穿着需求，以及每一类产品和不同消费水平的市场对时装的需求情况。要做到这些，设计师必须关注与人们日常活动有关的社会、文化、经济以及政治环境，只有这样他们的构想才会反映目前的流行信息，并且能够影响到未来消费者的需求。因此设计师需要丰富的想象力，媒体、娱乐业，其他的文化，社会观点以及风俗、历史和当今的社会事件等都给设计师提供了很好的构思源泉。

The skill in any good design really lies in maximizing the value that can be added to a set of basic raw materials. It is therefore dependent on the quality of the original design, its suitability for the market and the way it is made to meet customer requirements.

任何优秀设计作品的巧妙之处都在于将原材料的价值最大化，这主要取决于原创设计的水准，对市场的适合性以及满足消费者需求的方法。设计师必须擅长处理新产品开发与营销成本、产品生命周

Any designer should be skilled in striking the right balance between new product development and other marketing costs and the life expectancy and therefore anticipated sales and profit contribution of the product. However, serious concern is being expressed within the industry that the increased speed of the whole fashion cycle is beginning to stunt the growth of young designers and that the demand for new ideas and collections is so strong that the chance to develop ideas properly does not arise.

期、预期销售额以及产品利益之间的关系。可是值得关注的是时装业中整个时尚周期的快速交替性，这一点已经开始影响到年轻设计师的发展。同时，消费者对新创意和新产品的需求更为强烈，以至于并没有出现能够正确开发创意的时机。

6.4.2 The influence of haute couture ／高级定制时装的影响

In terms of influence the industry continues to operate in a hierarchical sense. The more renowned and internationally accepted designers (historically the haute couturiers, although this section of the industry is now in something of a downturn) continue to be a very significant source of new ideas regarding fashion direction. At the same time, however, influences from elsewhere will pervade. From the late in the 1980s the influence of 'street fashion' has been felt throughout the industry. The skill for many designers, and particularly those who are trying to appeal to the wider, mass market, will be to interpret the wealth of ideas and sources of inspiration into garments that are appropriate for high street consumption.

The point should be made here that haute couture and mass production are quite different. The former evolved from the desire for luxury and conspicuous consumption from the elite strata of society; the latter developed in response to the growing post-war affluence of the majority and the desire for an improvement in living standard and lifestyle. Thus it has historically been the function of mass production to select and adapt appropriate couture design to meet the needs of the public at large. While the recognized leading designers in Europe, America, Japan and elsewhere continue to act as sources of inspiration, their supremacy and unattainability for the masses is maintained by employing the best in fabric, make, embellishment, etc. and producing fashions that can only be afforded and worn by a select, fashion conscious and extravert few. However, even the leading designers are vulnerable; if their sense of direction and development is not consistently strong they will fail to develop a progressive adaptability. The stereotypical style that may result could leave the way open for new designers who have a better understanding of the way

从影响角度来看，时装业仍然是按照市场等级来运作的，具有较高声望以及被国际认可的设计师（习惯称为高级女装设计师，尽管这个领域产业的发展现在处于低迷时期）是时尚发展趋势中新创意的最主要资源。然而，其他方面的影响也开始蔓延，20 世纪 80 年代后期“街头时尚”影响着整个时装产业。对于大多数设计师尤其是那些想迎合大众市场需求的设计师来说，他们必须富有创意，并且能够把设计灵感融入那些适合街头时尚消费的时装产品。

这里需要提及的一点是，高级时装和大批量生产是完全不同的。前者主要源于消费者对奢侈品的欲望以及对社会名流奢侈消费的向往，后者是因为战后富裕人群的增加，以及人们期望提高生活水平和生活方式才发展起来的，因此长久以来大批量生产的作用就是选择和调整高级时装的设计，以此来满足大众的需求。然而欧洲、美国、日本和其他地方的一流时装设计师都被看作是设计灵感的源泉，他们在大众市场的霸权地位主要是依靠使用最好的面料、工艺和装饰来维持的，他们主要生产一些时尚选购者、时尚敏感者以及思想开放的少数消费者能够买得起并且穿得起的时装。可是即便是一流设计师也有弱项，如果他们的设计定位和产品开发理念跟消费需求不一致，他们就不会得到市场的认可。传统的经典款式为新设计师提

fashion develops.

供了拓展设计的基础，他们由此可以更准确地把握时尚流行的趋势。

6.4.3 Organization of the fashion industry ／时装业的组织

In recent years the haute couturiers have, along with established designers, tended to move towards greater brand differentiation to capitalize on their names and some have also decentralized their manufacturing operations to cut costs. Some manufacturers now produce and distribute designer collections, enabling haute couture or designer names to be made available to a larger market at more accessible prices through ready-to-wear ranges. The announcement by the French government in the early 1990s that it was planning to encourage new designers into haute couture indicated the fact that the couture market was in decline. Younger customers are being tempted away from the idea of luxury for its own sake and are now demanding clothes by the newer designers that are indisputably contemporary in their direction and approach.

Production capacity of the manufacturing sector in the industry will be split into different ways. Some will devote their entire production to retail own-label ranges, while others may run own-label (i.e. manufacturer) ranges alongside. The third possibility is to allocate certain capacity to manufacturing garments under licence (see earlier). Similarly, retail strategies may be based on 100% own-label ranges in store, or mixing retail label with manufacturer- and/or licensee-labelled merchandise.

Thus within the industry chain the process of converting basic raw materials into finished marketable goods will involve teams of people working together at each level. Yarn and textile producers will employ designers and technologists and may employ the services of colour consultants and fabric forecasters in their work. Teams comprising in-house designers, pattern cutters and sample machinists, production and sales personnel will work together in manufacturing organizations on the development of own label and licensed ranges.

At the same time their designers and production personnel will be working with buyers and merchandisers in retail organizations on the development of retail own-label merchandise; retail buyers and merchandisers will, in turn, be working with teams of their own in-house designers, quality controllers, garment technologists and possibly even store personnel during their planning

近年来，高级时装设计师和那些已成名的设计师都打算朝品牌差异化方向发展从而将他们的品牌名称资本化，有些则分散生产环节以节约成本。一些生产商现在也生产和分销设计师的设计作品，从而使得高级时装或者设计师品牌能以可接受的价格到达较大的市场。20 世纪 90 年代初期法国政府的一次公告就表示要鼓励新设计师进入高级时装设计领域，这点就说明了高级时装市场处于下滑趋势。年轻消费者已经不再有奢侈的想法，他们现在需要的是新设计师设计的时装，因为这些设计师跟他们属于一个年代。

时装业生产部门的生产能力可以按不同的方式进行划分。有些是将全部生产能力投入自有品牌的零售当中，有些则是同时还在运作自有品牌（如生产商）。第三种可能是分配一部分生产能力去做特许产品（如前所述）。同样地，采用零售策略的基础是拥有完全属于自己的品牌，或者与生产商联合的商标，或者是特许商标。

因此在时装产业链中，将原材料转换为可销售的成品时装的过程需要各个部门人员的共同努力。纱线和纺织品生产企业在运作时可以雇用设计师和技术人员以及色彩顾问和面料预测人员。在生产环节，包括经验丰富的设计师、样板裁剪师以及样衣师、生产及销售人员在内的团队会一起合作来促进自有品牌和特许品牌的发展。

与此同时，在零售环节，企业的设计师和生产人员也会和买方及采购人员一起合作来促进零售品牌的发展；在计划过程，零售采购商和业务员一般会和企业里有经验的设计师、质检人员、时装技术人员以及店铺人员一起合作。如

cycle. Retail dominance as described earlier has also led to retail buying and merchandising personnel working closely with yarn and textile producers in a bid to differentiate ranges at an even earlier stage in the chain. Fabric will be dyed or woven according to retail specification and subsequently ordered for the garment manufacturers.

前所述，零售控制同样会导致零售采购员和业务员与纱线和纺织品生产者紧密联系，以便在生产前期明确彼此的责任，有时企业采购的面料也会根据零售规格以及时装制造商的订单要求来染色和生产。

6.4.4 The sequence of events／流行大事件序列

There are four major stages of influence in the new product development and fashion diffusion and adoption process. These are, chronologically:

◆ 'The Colour Meeting' in Paris known as the *Concertation* where approximately 40 leading fashion industrialists representing major yarn, textile and garment manufacturers, top designers, stylists, colour consultants and fashion forecasters gather. Together they will establish the major colour trends (based on around 30 colours) that will dominate the fashion scene two years from the time of their meeting. The trends will usually be based on themes of darks, brights, pastels and neutrals. Work will then begin by various sections of the industry on interpreting and adapting the basic story to suit their own particular requirements. For example, the International Wool Secretariat and Cotton Institute will work on appropriate interpretations for their respective yarn and textile industries.

◆ The biannual yarn and fabric fairs where the new colours, textures and patterns will be presented as trends for 12 months ahead. These fairs are now held in most of the major cities of Europe.

◆ The biannual international fashion fairs in Paris, Milan, Tokyo, Shanghai, Moscow, New York and London where leading designers will present their latest collection ideas six months ahead of the season in question. Representation by the media is very strong at the international collections, showing the enormous influence the media now have on fashion awareness and acceptance.

◆ Reportage in the trade and commercial press of the designer collections is described above. The power and extent of modern-day mass communication systems are such that the media are instrumental in shaping and influencing the fashions that are ultimately accepted. This process is shown in Figure 6.5. Simultaneously, journalists now provide a two-way flow of information, reporting 'upwards' on street styles that have been a

有四个主要的阶段影响新产品开发、时尚的传播及接受。按年代顺序是:

◆ 巴黎“色彩大会”作为重要的发布活动，会吸引 40 多个知名时装企业家参加，他们代表了主要的纱线、纺织品生产商以及时装制造商、顶级设计师、造型师、色彩顾问以及流行趋势预测专家。他们一起创立色彩流行趋势（以 30 种色彩为基础），这一色彩趋势在会议之后两年的时间里都会主导时装界的发展。流行趋势一般是基于暗色、亮色、淡色和中性色等色彩而建立的，时装业不同部门接着就开始分析和调整流行趋势以适应他们自己特定市场的需求。例如，国际羊毛局和国际棉花协会一般选择适合纱线和纺织工业特点的色彩。

◆ 一年两次的纱线和面料博览会将提前一年发布色彩、材料结构以及图案方面的流行趋势，这类会议目前主要在一些欧洲城市举办。

◆ 一年两次在巴黎、米兰、东京、上海、莫斯科、纽约和伦敦举办的国际时装博览会上，顶尖设计师一般会提前半年举办他们最新的作品发布会。国际时装发布会中的媒体代表是非常有影响力的，也显示了现在媒体对时尚认知和接受的重大影响。

◆ 服装商贸部门的出版物中有关设计师发布会的报导在之前已有所描述。当前大量的信息系统所具有的影响力主要指的是媒体有助于形成时尚，并且影响最终被市场接受的时尚。这个过程在图 6-5 中有所表述。与此同时，新闻记者提供了两种信息传递的方式，即同时报导过

significant influence on top designers over the past few years (and often creating their own fashions and fads in the process), as well as 'downwards' on developments in the collections to the public.

去几年对知名设计师有重大影响的街头时尚的（通常在这个过程中也形成了自己的时尚品和潮流品）高端产品，以及设计作品面向大众发展的较低端产品。

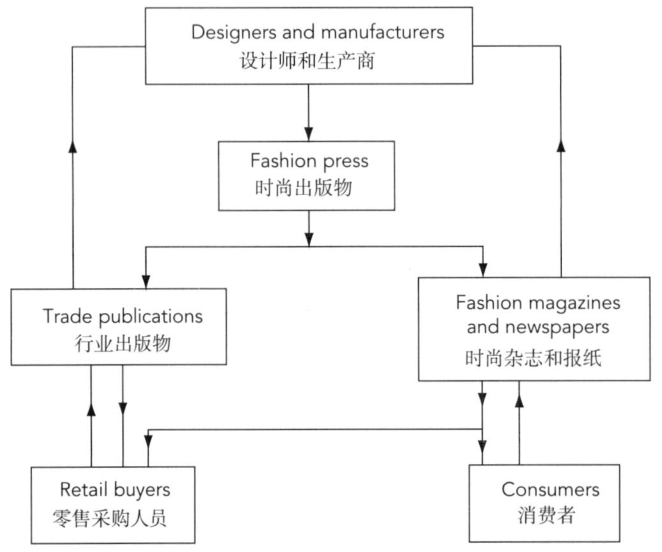

Figure 6.5 The two-way flow of fashion information. 图 6–5 时装信息传递的两种方式

6.4.5 The process for developing new products ／产品开发的过程

Change in the form of new product development is an intrinsic part of the culture of all organizations associated with the fashion industry whether directly in manufacturing or retailing or indirectly in the media or public relations. While product strategies will invariably be linked closely to corporate objectives, continual new product development will also enhance and strengthen image, brand name, etc.

Traditional models used to describe the new product development process will describe many stages from concept through to actual launch. However, the timescale to which the fashion industry works is such that several of these stages will function simultaneously. To demonstrate this, the example chosen to work through is that of a high street multiple retailer. Whether textile or garment manufacturer or retailer the principles and procedures described are very much the same since all are involved in the process of buying, sampling and selling. Obviously the timescales will vary according to how far back in the chain they go.

新产品开发方式的改变是所有与时装产业相关的组织中最本质的特点，不管他们是直接相关的生产商、零售商还是间接相关的媒体或公关组织。然而产品策略总是与企业发展目标有着紧密的关系，连续性的新产品开发同样也会增强企业影响力和品牌声誉。

新产品开发过程的传统模式涉及从理念定位到实际产品上市的多个环节，然而时装产业运作的整个周期有可能是多个环节发挥作用的。为了证明这一点，我们选择了商业街的零售商进行了阐述。无论是纺织品制造商还是时装生产商，或者时装零售商，产品开发的原则和过程几乎是一样的，因为他们的运作都涉及了采购、样品制作以及销售等环节，很明显根据企业发展远景的不同，整个周期的长短也会有所不同。

6.5 Retail buying sequence: autumn and winter season / 零售采购顺序：秋冬季

6.5.1 Early September / 9 月上旬

Analysis and development of new concepts take place, along with analysis of last year's range, to identify good and bad sellers based on performance and average weeks' cover. This is an indication of the rate at which a style is selling and the number of weeks it would take to sell out completely at the current rate. Lines which have averaged 10 weeks' cover, or less, will be seen as good sellers, anything above this will not have been such a success and is not likely to be repeated. If a line has averaged over 20 it will be deleted. The analysis will be by style, fabric, colour and price point and will form the basis for the range going forward. Supplier performance also will be examined, by line (rate of sale, prices and profitability) and by quality and reliability, for instance, in delivery.

At the same time an analysis of forward trends is conducted (working here with in-house design studio staff and colour and fashion forecasters if relevant). This is to gather new ideas, colours, fabrics, etc. that can be applied to the range.

The actual plan will be built up around improvements or revisions to existing products, additions to existing product lines and the incorporation of new products into the range.

分析和开发新的设计理念的同时，需要分析上一季的产品，根据市场表现和每周业绩确定畅销品和滞销品，这个分析说明了一款时装的销售率以及按照目前的销售情况需要几周才能把货品全部销售出去。销售周期为平均 10 周或者 10 周以内的可以被认为是畅销品，如果销售周期在 20 周以上的产品就会下柜。这一分析过程包括对产品的款式、面料、色彩及价格方面的分析，并为下一阶段产品开发提供了参考依据。供应商的表现同样也根据产品系列（销售额、价格和赢利性）以及产品质量和可靠性以及货物配送等方面进行衡量。

与此同时也会对发展趋势进行分析（和相关经验丰富的设计人员、色彩以及时尚趋势预测人员等一起工作），这样将新的创意、色彩和面料等信息集合起来，用于新产品的开发。

实际的过程是围绕着改进和修正现有的产品而进行的，加之对已有产品系列和新产品的改善和调整。

6.5.2 Late September / 9 月下旬

First stage screening, further development of concepts and initial product development are all now able to proceed. Initial presentations of range plan ideas for basic approval take place and the alteration cycle begins. Further research is now needed for concept development and is conducted by, among other ways, shopping trips to Europe and America. Initial buyer and supplier meetings take place to exchange ideas and give direction, while sampling and the alteration process also take place at this time.

第一阶段筛选，开始进一步对设计理念和新产品进行提炼，提出新产品系列的规划理念并且开始进行调整。此时设计理念的提炼需要进一步的调研，通过去欧洲或者美国等地购物来完成这项调研。初期的采购人员和供应商会议主要是为了交流想法以及设定产品开发的方向，样品生产也会同时进行。

6.5.3 Early to mid-October / 10 月中旬的早期

Second stage screening is conducted, while product development continues. Visits are made to the fabric

第二阶段筛选，继续进行产品开发，参加面料展销会，继续寻找供应商。如

fairs. Supplier development continues. Once the concepts and styles have been approved by the controller, a presentation is made at director level.

果总监认同了产品的设计理念和款式风格，主管就会公布新产品。

6.5.4 November to the end of January / 11 月到 1 月末

Product development is now finalized, and provision for test marketing within the proposed new ranges is planned. Sampling and negotiating with suppliers and agents is in full swing, culminating in agreement on prices. Range meetings take place with controller and directors at end of January for approval of final ranges. Sealed samples, as described, are taken and work now begins on accurate buying figures and phasing of deliveries.

Range plans at this stage will feature certain styles to be included as experiments or test lines at the beginning of the season. It may be that they have a higher element of fashion in them than the norm and are therefore seen as carrying more risk. However, flexibility will be built into the range to purchase more of the new ideas if they prove to be successful once launched.

产品开发到此结束，制定新产品系列的市场试销计划。全力进行样品制作，并和供应商及代理商协商，协商要点集中在价格方面。在 1 月末与总监和主管召开会议以最终确定产品系列。按照前面所讲的进行封样，并且按照实际购买者的体型和交货时间开始生产。

这一阶段的产品系列企划以某些款式为主，这些款式在季初会被作为实验品或者测试产品，这些产品本身更具有时尚元素，因此也更具有市场风险。然而一旦这些产品上市成功的话，就可以从新产品系列中获得更多新的设计灵感。

6.5.5 Mid-February / 2 月中旬

Marketers begin to develop the other mix variables, and prices are finalized. Other marketing tasks include liaison on contract preparation, and the development of in-store and other promotional ideas.

营销者开始研究其他组合变量，并且确定最终的价格。其他营销工作还有准备合同，发展店铺和策划促销方案。

6.5.6 April to May / 4 月到 5 月

Chasing production, quality checks and monitoring progress are the main pre-occupations now. Feedback from these is used in a continual review process.

追加生产，质量检测以及控制进度是这阶段最主要的工作，这些工作的反馈意见会被用到后续的审核程序中。

6.5.7 July to August / 7 月到 8 月

The first phase of the range is launched in stores. Phasing of deliveries according to pre-planning is set at approximately every six to eight weeks.

新产品系列进入店铺的第一阶段，根据先前计划大约间隔 6 到 8 周确定配货周期。

6.6 The product mix and range planning / 产品组合和产品系列企划

6.6.1 The nature of the product mix / 产品组合的本质

The product mix or product range is the assortment of goods a company offers for sale at any time. Before each season the organization must not only consider how it might alter or modify its classic (i.e. more basic)

产品组合和产品系列指的是一个公司在任何时候要销售的货品的分类。季前企业需要考虑如何调整和修改经典的（例如，基础系列）产品系列，这些经

lines, which are less liable to radical change, it also must undertake careful planning of its fashion ranges in terms of width, depth and fashion content (and simultaneously anticipate and plan for the risk involved). Decisions concerning the mix of products also will relate to changes in broader company objectives. These may range from sales and profit growth, via emphasis on increasing market share or targeting new markets to return on investment targets, etc.

典款不容易进行较大的改动，必须仔细地规划新产品系列的宽度、深度和产品内涵（同时预见可能的风险）。有关产品组合的决策往往与企业目标的变化有关联，这些包含销售额和利润增长率，通过强调市场份额的增长或者瞄准新的目标市场来获得投资回报。

6.6.2 The planning cycle / 企划周期

The frequency of the planning cycle is probably greater in the fashion industry than any other because of its seasonal nature. Changing customer preferences ensures a perpetual drive for change. Volatility in terms of the seasonal variety of products offered and the speeds of change in fashions require skill, creativity, a propensity for risk taking and in-depth knowledge of end-user requirements in order for companies to plan effectively, and implement and control what is being offered in any given season.

Traditionally companies have planned for two seasons, autumn/winter and spring/summer. However, many are now moving towards the incorporation of mid-season ranges. For some this will mean a totally new set of garments, accessories, etc. and for others it will merely involve adding top-up variety to the major lines that were introduced at the beginning of the season.

At every stage in the planning cycle the team, which may comprise any combination of textile and/or fashion designers, production managers, sales-people, buyers, merchandisers and store personnel, will focus on the permutation of fashions being offered. The following terms are used in the example below which highlights the two major stages.

因为时装业的季节性特点，其企划周期的频率可能会比其他行业高一些，不断变化的消费者的喜好是这种变化永久的动力。市场上供应的季节产品变化无常，时尚流行的不断变化要求企业有能力、创造力和承担风险的习惯，能深入了解终端消费者的需求从而使企业可以有效地制定计划，并且执行和控制某个季节市场上的货源。

按照惯例企业一般制定两个季节的计划，秋冬季、春夏季，然而现在有些企业增加了季中计划。这对于有些企业意味着要推出一系列全新的时装和配饰系列，而对于其他企业而言只是在季节开始的时候推出的主打系列里增加一些不同的产品。

在计划周期的每个阶段，以面料设计师、时装设计师、生产经理、销售人员、采购人员、业务员和店铺人员组成的团队的工作重点集中在上市产品的调整和安排方面。下面例子中所用到的术语就强调了这两个主要的阶段。

Garment category / 时装的分类

This refers to types of garments in a generic sense, i.e. as a whole class or group. This could be such terms as market being served, context of wear, fashion look or statement. For example, a manufacturer of men's and women's jackets may offer ranges that appeal to the same target market in terms of age, income, interest in fashion and other segment characteristics. Alternatively, the ranges may be functionally based on, for example, rugged outdoor use, and appeal to a wide age range.

这里指的是一般意义上对时装的分类，可以依照企业服务的市场、穿着环境及时装款式来分类。例如，男式或女式夹克的制造商会根据目标市场的年龄、收入、喜好以及其他的细分特征来向市场提供时装产品。有时也会按照功能特点对产品系列进行分类，比如适合户外使用的，年龄群较宽泛的时装系列。

As another possibility, the ranges may comprise a mixture of classic through to high fashion garments that have been manufactured using similar production methods and materials. However, owing to their fashion content their appeal lies at either end of the fashion spectrum. In such a situation it is highly likely that the manufacturer would differentiate the ranges by distinct promotional, distribution and pricing strategies.

还有另一种可能就是产品包含经典和高级时装系列，这两个系列产品都是使用相似的生产方法和原材料生产的。然而因为这些产品具有明显的时尚内涵，因此对终端消费者有着较强的吸引力，在这种情况下，制造商很有可能根据不同的促销、分销及价格策略来区分不同的产品系列。

Product line ／产品线

This is a breakdown of garment categories into fashions that are related in more specific, identifiable ways. Here an established variety of words or terms will probably be used to describe the breakdown into product types. Thus a casual jacket might be described as an anorak, a parka, blouson, yachting, donkey, etc.

产品线是以一种特殊的、可识别的方式与时装分类明细表联系起来的，有一些既定的不同词语和术语是可以用来描述产品分类的。休闲夹克可能会被表述为登山夹克、带帽厚夹克、夹克衫、帆船服、防雨工作服等。

Style ／风格

Each product line can be broken down into a variety of specific designs appropriate for the given season.

每一个产品线都可以细分为适合特定季节的不同设计风格的产品。

Width and depth ／产品线的宽度和深度

The dimensions in terms of number and variety in each stage of the planning process are shown in Figures 6.6 and 6.7.

Figure 6.6 shows how a hypothetical range of womenswear might be broken down into the following garment categories: tailored separates, blouses, casual tops and bottoms, and accessories. Casual tops have then been further broken down into specific product lines as follows: casual jackets, cardigans, sweaters and T-shirts. At the same time, the figure shows a possible percentage breakdown of total sales revenue and profits for the range by garment category. Table 6.1 and table 6.2——a further breakdown has been given within casual tops showing the percentage contributions of each to their own garment category and to the overall range.

Figure 6.7 demonstrates how stage 2 in the planning cycle could be applied to one specific style within the line of women's T-shirts. The figure also quantifies percentage sales revenue and profit of each style within the T-shirt range itself and as a contribution to the overall casual tops range.

产品企划过程中每个阶段以数量和种类两个维度进行划分，见图 6–6 和图 6–7。

图 6–6 给出了假设的女装系列是如何被分为以下时装类型的：定制的单件时装、女衬衫、休闲上装和休闲下装以及配饰。休闲上装又被进一步细分为专门的产品线：休闲夹克、开襟羊毛衫、针织衫以及 T 恤。同时，图中也给出了按时装类别预测的销售收入和利润的百分值列表。

表 6–1、表 6–2 进一步给出了休闲上装划分的设计企划以及每个产品对整个产品系列和所有产品线的贡献率。

图 6–7 给出了第二阶段的产品企划是如何应用在女装 T 恤产品线中的某个款式的。同样，图中也分析了每个号型在 T 恤系列产品中的数量占比、销售收入及销售利润百分比，以及 T 恤对整个休闲上装的贡献。

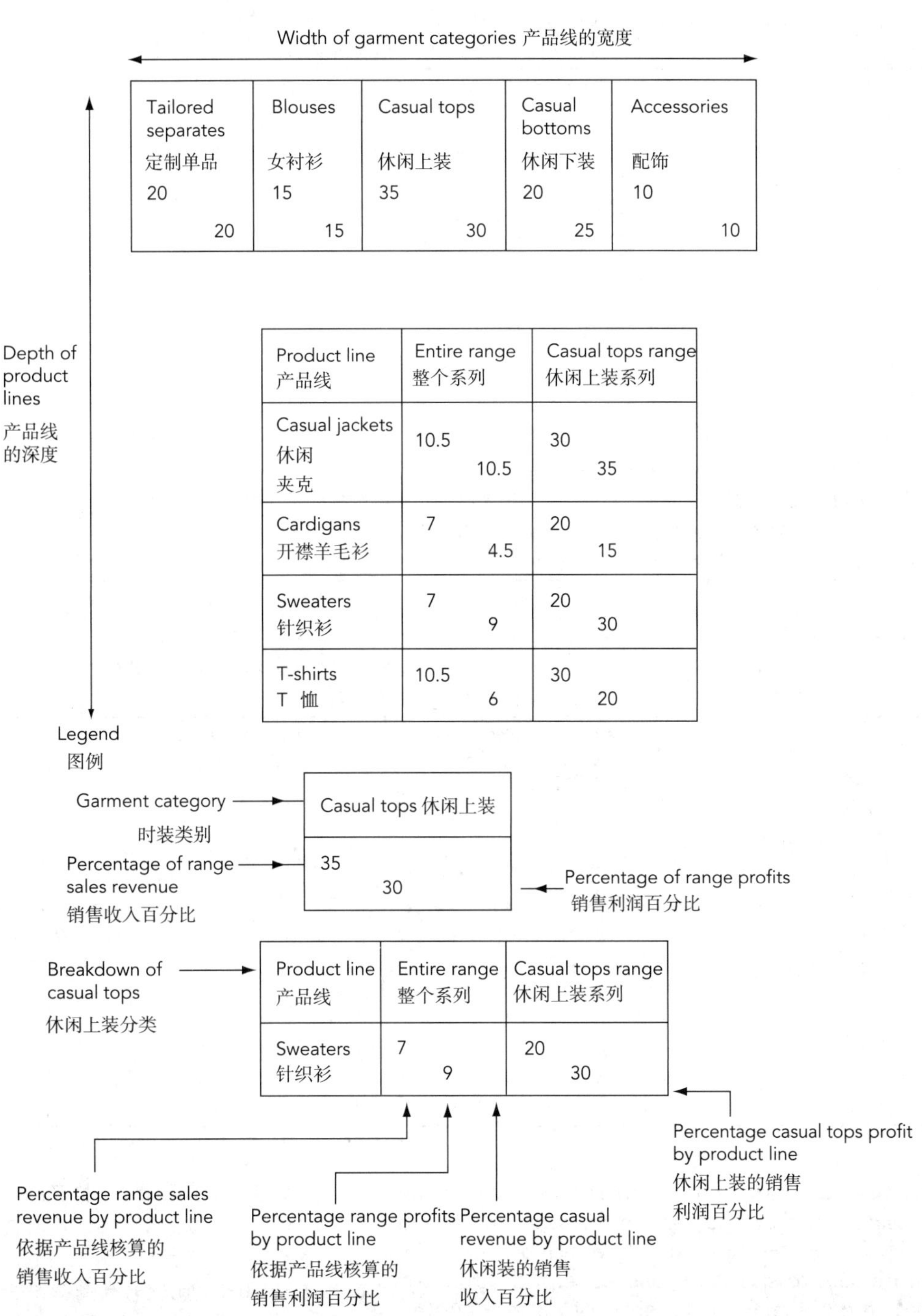

Figure 6.6 Stage 1 range planning: hypothetical womenswear range analysis.

图 6-6 产品企划的第一阶段：假设的女装系列分析

Table6.1 Range plan detail for style 1

表 6–1 款式 1 的产品系列企划细节

Design detail 设计细节	Round neck, long sleeve, single cotton jersey T-shirt. 圆领、长袖、纯棉针织 T 恤、明线装饰的罗纹领、直边袖口			
Pattern 图案	Single rib collar with top stitching, straight edge cuff. Printed triple stripe. 印花的三线条纹			
Colourways 色系	Navy with white stripe, ivory with navy stripe. 海军蓝搭配白色条纹、象牙色搭配海军蓝条纹			
Size range 号型系列	S	M	L	XL
Pack size 包装比例	2	4	4	2
Total quantity (units) 总数量	720			
Quantity per size (units) 每个号型的数量	120	240	240	120

Additional comments: 备注：

If manufacturer: Own label, to all UK licensees 制造商：自有品牌，英国范围内授权

If retailer: Basic, all-store line 零售商：基本款，全部店铺

Table6.2 Analysis of percentage sales revenue and profit contribution

表 6–2 销售收入占比和利润贡献分析

Style 款式	Percentage sales revenue 销售收入百分比	Percentage profit 销售利润百分比
Contribution to casual tops range: 休闲上装系列：		
Style 1 款式 1	12.25	9.0
Style 2 款式 2	12.25	9.0
Style 3 款式 3	7.00	7.5
Style 4 款式 4	3.50	4.5
Contribution to T-shirt range: T 恤系列：		
Style 1 款式 1	35	30
Style 2 款式 2	35	30
Style 3 款式 3	20	25
Style 4 款式 4	10	15

Thus in retail terms the T-shirt range would feature two basic styles that would go to all stores and amount to 70% of sales revenue. The more fashionable style 3 might be sent to specific branches, e.g. the top 50%. Style 4, the highest risk in terms of fashion content, might be featured in only 10% of stores and probably only at those stores most likely to sell high fashion garments. At the same time profit expectations would

从零售的角度看，T 恤产品系列有两个基本款，款式 1 和款式 2 这两个基本款在所有的店铺销售并且占到总销售收入的 70%。比较时尚的款式 3 则需要在特定的渠道销售，例如只在 50% 的店铺销售。款式 4 是最具风险性的产品，更为适合在其中 10% 的店铺销售，也有可能仅在销售高级时装的店铺销

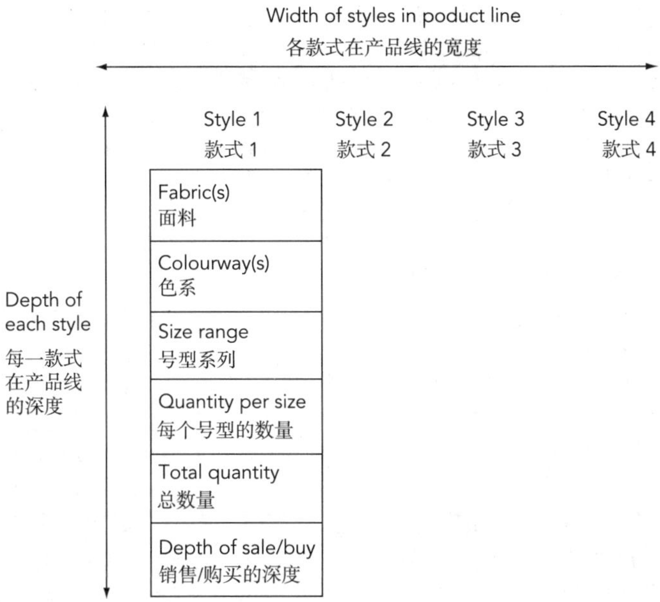

Width of styles in poduct line
各款式在产品线的宽度

Depth of each style
每一款式在产品线的深度

Style 1 款式 1	Style 2 款式 2	Style 3 款式 3	Style 4 款式 4
Fabric(s) 面料			
Colourway(s) 色系			
Size range 号型系列			
Quantity per size 每个号型的数量			
Total quantity 总数量			
Depth of sale/buy 销售/购买的深度			

Figure 6.7 Stage 2 range planning: women's T-shirts. Hypothetical breakdown of specific product line.

图 6–7 产品企划的第二阶段：女式 T 恤——假设的某个产品线的分类

vary: pro rata style 4 has the highest profit potential.

As the organization grows, it may be strategically sensible and profitable for it to diversify its ranges into non-garment categories such as accessories, luggage and home furnishings. However, these decisions will usually be taken at board level since they will relate fundamentally to the nature of the company's business.

The retail examples of Next plc, Ted Baker and Ralph Lauren demonstrate how it is possible over time to move into broader clothing and non-clothing areas from an established base. From its original target group of 25- to 40-year-old women, Next plc has established itself with appeal to a much wider age range. Success eventually led to the development of several differentiated womenswear ranges, menswear and childrenswear, footwear, jewellery, watches and giftware.

售。同时预期的利润也是不同的：款式 4 可能会具有最大的盈利潜力。

随着企业的发展，从战略和盈利角度来看，企业会将产品线延伸到非服饰领域如配饰、箱包和家居品。这一般是企业高层管理者做出这项决策，因为这些产品和企业的业务有着基本的关联。

零售商如英国潮品服饰连锁店奈克斯特连锁，泰德・贝克和拉尔夫・劳伦就说明了如何从基础领域进入更广泛的服饰领域或者非服饰领域。奈克斯特连锁从最早的 20 ~ 40 岁的目标群体扩充到了更广泛的年龄群体，最后获得了成功并且涉足女装、男装和童装，以及鞋袜、珠宝首饰、手表和礼品领域。

6.6.3 Range planning checklists / 产品系列企划检查项目

Improved technology means that planning teams are now better informed regarding sales histories for previous seasons. At any one time there are many dimensions of historical information available, e.g.

不断改进的技术使得企划团队能够较好地通报上一季产品的销售情况。在任何时候可以从很多的角度去评价分析过去的信息，例如每季中销售最好的和

seasonal best and worst selling styles, colours and sizes; customer sales patterns; geographical variations; specific rates of sale for garment styles; most popular price levels. The first essential stage in any planning cycle is to analyse what has happened in previous seasons to enable more informed decision-making so the firm can ultimately capitalize on previous success.

最差的款式、色彩和号型、顾客喜欢的图案、区域差异、特定款式的销售比、最受欢迎的价格水平等。任何产品企划周期中第一个必要的阶段就是分析上一季的市场情况，从而使决策信息更为充分，由此企业会在以后取得更大的成就。

Pre-planning checklists / 事前检查项目

The following pre-planning checklist indicates where the analysis should focus:

◆ Sales history: Good and bad sellers; most popular designs and why? Best/worst customers in relation to best/worst stores. Specific styles and why?

◆ Rates of sale of styles offered, reasons for variations. Although certain styles may appear to be faster sellers there may have been problems regarding others, e.g. availability.

◆ Colour/fabric/pattern trends. For example, were best sellers limited to only certain colours, fabrics, etc. and if so, which ones?

◆ Emerging trends: Are there any new trends emerging from sales of high fashion lines, e.g. colours, styles, fabrics? Which are applicable to the range in question, i.e. which will suit the intended target market? To what depth should risk be taken?

◆ Pricing: Were the price levels appropriate?

◆ Did the styles offered represent good value for money?

◆ Was the balance of price levels right?

◆ Was it similar to that of competitors?

◆ Were target profit margins achieved overall by various styles?

◆ If not, how can profit margins be improved?

◆ Competitors: How successful in the previous season in question? Regular analysis of competitors should have been carried out during the season via comparative shopping surveys, information from other manufacturers or retailers, trade press articles, publicly available financial information, etc. Have there been instances of successful practice that can be followed?

下面的事前检查表给出了市场分析的重点：

◆ 销售历史：畅销的和滞销的产品，最受欢迎的设计以及为什么受欢迎，最好的 / 最差的店铺中最好的 / 最差的顾客，独特的款式是哪些以及原因。

◆ 供货款式的销售比率变化的原因。虽然某种款式可能会销售得较快，但会对给其他工作带来影响，例如供货能力。

◆ 颜色 / 面料 / 图案的流行趋势。例如，是不是最好销售的产品局限在少数的几种颜色和面料？如果是这样，是哪些产品呢？

◆ 新的趋势：高级时装产品系列的销售是否有新的趋势？例如，颜色、款式和面料方面？哪些适合现在的产品系列？哪种产品更符合预期目标市场的需求？需要承担多大的风险？

◆ 定价：价格定位水平恰当吗？

◆ 供应的款式是否物有所值？

◆ 是否适合物价水平？

◆ 和竞争者有无相似之处？

◆ 是否能够通过销售不同的款式来实现预期的利润目标？

◆ 如果不能，如何提高销售利润率？

◆ 竞争者：上一季销售是如何取得成功的？在每个季节，通过店铺调查资料、其他制造商和零售商的信息、贸易期刊的文章、公开发布的财政信息等定期对竞争者进行分析，有没有可以借鉴的成功的实践经验？

Balance, cohesion and synchronization / 平衡、衔接力和同步化

Once ranges have been determined, the following will serve as a useful checklist to ensure balance, cohesion and synchronization:

◆ Garment categories: Is the percentage breakdown appropriate? Is the balance correct for customer requirements, and are there enough options to meet a variety of preferences and tastes?

◆ Product lines: Are the styles within each appropriate for the target market in terms of design content, style, fabric, colour, pattern and texture? The tension here will be between offering width or depth of range – where should the balance lie between offering safe lines and high fashions with more risk? Decisions regarding which new fashion directions should be incorporated are crucial; today's riskier lines could very easily become tomorrow's best sellers, as they become more widely accepted and therefore safer over time.

◆ Do the above two items fit the company image we are trying to portray? For example, the garment label or company name may be well established in a high fashion context.

◆ Is each range balanced? Is there cohesion in what is being offered or might there be too much emphasis on certain styles and not enough on others? If there seems to have been a tendency to favour one or two styles, might competitors be doing the same? If this is a possibility the market will be flooded when the ranges are launched. Are the proposed size ranges balanced?

◆ Is the range profile balanced over time? This is particularly important when styles are phased in over a season rather than launched simultaneously. Does the phasing ensure availability of interest in the range at all times?

◆ Are the design proportions synchronized? For example, when considering a range of men's outerwear, if jacket lapels are narrow, are shirt collar point lengths also small? Are ties slim enough to provide a small enough knot? Are widths of trouser bottoms and other design features in proportion to those of the jackets?

◆ Is there balance across the pricing structure? Are the price levels right? Is there a relative balance of prices across lines and garment categories?

一旦确定了产品系列，以下给出的检查项目对确保平衡、衔接力和同步化是有用的。

◆ 时装分类。百分比列表是否正确？消费者需求是否平衡？是否有足够的选择来满足不同的喜好和品味？

◆ 产品线。每个款式在设计风格、款式、面料、色彩、图案和材料、结构方面是否适合目标市场的需求？这里指的是产品线的宽度和深度，提供的保险的产品线与较高风险的高级时装之间的平衡点在哪？根据什么来确定新系列产品的方向是至关重要的，今天的具有市场风险的产品系列有可能成为明天的畅销品，因为这些产品随时间流逝慢慢被广为接受，反而更加安全。

◆ 上述的两个方面是否符合我们即将建立的企业形象？例如，在高级时装领域必须很好地建立时装的商标和企业名称。

◆ 每个产品系列是否平衡？供应的产品之间是否联系紧密，是不是过分地强调某些款式而忽略了其他款式？如果出现一个或两个款式热销的趋势，竞争对手就可能模仿么？如果这种模仿的范围扩大化，那么当产品系列上市的时候，市场就已经饱和了。既定系列的号型系列是否平衡？

◆ 产品系列是否一直保持平衡？这点尤其重要，特别是当按照季节特点而不是同时将产品面市时。按既定计划是否能确保任何时候每个产品系列都有收益？

◆ 设计比例是否一致？以男装外套系列为例，如果是窄的翻领，那么搭配的衬衫的领尖长度是否也要短一些？领带是否是细长的，以保证能形成小的打结？裤子的宽度和其他设计是否与夹克的宽度成比例？

◆ 价格体系是否平衡？定价水平合适吗？各产品线和每个产品项目间的价格是否相对平衡？

6.7 Fashion and related life cycles /时装与产品生命周期

6.7.1 The risks inherent in fashion /时装业本身的风险

The cycle of marketing activity begins and ends with consumer needs; as the most urgent set of needs is satisfied in the form of appropriate products, others emerge. In turn, these new needs become of prime importance and create the driving force leading to a desire for further new products. Nowhere is this process more apparent than in the fashion industry; the continual development and introduction of new products into the marketplace are axiomatic to its very existence.

Paradoxically, while an essential undertaking, no aspect of the marketing mix is as uncertain as the introduction and acceptance of new products, particularly when they have a fashion element in them. Implicit in the pluralist nature of today's fashions is the existence of several typical looks or styles in any given season, and the incorporation of many modifications and variations according to the market requirements. The result is that all levels of fashion conscious consumers are able to distinguish between styles that are currently popular and others that belong to previous seasons and are therefore deemed out-of-date. The ability of the individual to observe and react to these phenomena in a negative way ensures the perpetuation of the fashion cycle.

Implicit in the above is that at any moment in time a style considered unfashionable by some may yet be deemed fashionable by others. The net effect of this is that the product's profile will vary over time in terms of sales revenue, profits generated and the target market it appeals to as the fashion becomes more widely accepted and therefore less fashionable. To avoid or at least minimize the risk of failure of new fashions, a method of forecasting the onset of popularity with the rate and extent of possible adoption and diffusion patterns would be invaluable to marketers. Furthermore, the ability to recognize symptoms of decline or failure at an early stage or perceive changes in the nature of the target market during the season could lead to appropriate changes being made to promotion, pricing and distribution policies to maximize sales and profit potential.

营销活动的周期随着消费者的需求开始和结束，如果有合适的产品满足了消费者某次最急切的需求，其他需求就可能接踵而至。这些新的需求会刺激消费者追求新产品的欲望，并且给企业提供了新的动力。在服饰行业这点是最明显的，新产品的不断开发和上市就说明了有市场需求的存在。

不可思议的是，营销组合中没有哪个方面是像新产品的上市和为市场所接受这么具有不确定性的，尤其是产品设计中带有时尚元素的时候。如今时尚所具有的暗示性指的是任何季节都有几种经典的造型和款式，以及许多根据市场需求进行改动和变化的产品。结果是不同水平的、时尚意识较强的消费者会区分哪些款式是目前流行的，哪些是上一季的以及哪些是过时的款式。消费者个人会以消极的态度来观察这些现象并对这些现象做出反应，这样就确保了时装流行周期的长久不衰。

上面所讲的意思是某个时期一个被认为是不流行的款式可能会被其他人认为是流行的。实际的结果是产品介绍的信息会根据销售收入、利润及要满足的目标市场而有所不同，直到产品被广泛接受之后而过时。为了避免或者至少降低新产品系列的风险，对于营销人员说，根据市场接受度、接受范围以及传播方式预测流行是否开始的方法是非常重要的。此外，每个阶段对销售下滑或者销售失败的预见能力，以及整个季节过程中观察目标市场变化的能力会使企业对促销、价格和分销策略做出适当的调整，从而最大化销售额和销售利润的增长潜力。

6.7.2 Limitations of theoretical models / 理论模型的局限性

Although it has been argued that fashion is the synthetic creation of the seller, particularly with the growth of retail concentration in the last decade, the existence in terms of diversity of direction offered in the marketplace at any one time and the numbers of 'dictated' designs that fail every season are evidence enough that fashions are decided by the majority. Taken collectively the public is closer to the zeitgeist or 'spirit of the age' than any individual designer, manufacturer or retailer; it is the consumer who has the last word in what will or will not become fashionable. At the same time the majority of tastes do not swing from one extreme to another every season; in the main changes are gradual and incremental. The implication here is that historical data relating to sales patterns of previous seasonal successes and failures can, to a certain extent, be used as the basis for planning anticipated success rates for new styles (or at least estimating the degree of risk involved). However, the real skill lies in being able to identify the most appropriate seasonal fashion directions for the target market in question, while using historical data to plot the likely success rate of the new selections in an effective way.

While the concept of the product life cycle described below provides a useful framework for analysing sales revenue and profit patterns over time, such analysis will always be retrospective. Thus the model is not able to answer important questions relating to the why and how of product acceptance or failure, or why different rates of acceptance and success exist. However, if the seasonal performances of incremental product changes are analysed in the context of variations in the rest of the mix during the cycle, and their performance is compared over time, it is feasible that acceptance and diffusion trends can be identified on the basis of product attributes or bundles of utilities. The caveat here is that relying solely on this information and using it too literally can very quickly lead to boredom on part of the consumer, ultimately leading to purchase decisions being made elsewhere in the pursuit of fashion.

Therefore, the real value of the product life cycle concept lies in its use as a tool for planning and controlling anticipated as opposed to actual rates of sale, at the same time understanding how varying the

随着过去十年零售业的快速增长，可以说时尚产品是综合畅销品的卖点而创作的，任何时候市场上提供的产品都具有多样性，但每一季过后失败的产品都足以说明时尚的设计是否受欢迎是由大多数群体决定的。从总体上看，与任何一个设计师、制造商、零售商相比，公众都是与时代精神最接近的群体，消费者是最有权力确定哪些产品将会流行或者不会流行的。同时，每个季节大多数消费者的品味都不会从一个极端走向另一个极端，基本上品味都是慢慢地变化的。这里暗示的是：在某种程度上，上一季销售成功的或者失败的产品的销售数据可以作为预测新款式能否成功的参考（或者至少能够估算可能存在的风险）。然而真正的作用是能够确定最适合目标市场的产品走向，同时采取有效的方法，运用历史数据尽可能地增大新产品成功的概率。

下面所描述的产品生命周期概念为分析销售收入和销售利润结构提供了有用的模型。这些分析通常是回顾性的。因此这个模型不能回答为什么哪个产品被市场认可，哪个产品失败，或者为什么被市场认可和取得成功的概率不一样等问题。可是，如果在整个周期中对其余的营销组合变量分析时，也分析产品的季节变化特点，并且对比市场表现的话，就可以轻易地根据产品贡献或者组合效用来分析产品的市场认可度和流行趋势。这里需要提醒注意的是，单纯地依靠这些信息并且全部采用这些信息分析的话，可能会很快导致部分消费者的厌烦，最终导致消费者在追求时尚过程中做出另寻他处的购买决策。

因此，产品生命周期理念的真正价值在于它是被用作策划和控制的一种工具，与我们所预期的实际的销售率是有关的，同时考虑如何去改变其他营销组

emphasis of other mix variables can impact on product performance at different stages in the cycle. In the longer term, greater understanding of interrelationships will result in more effective planning for appropriate changes according to emerging sales and profit performance.

合变量来影响产品生命周期不同阶段中产品的市场表现。从长远来看，明确地认识这种关系有利于有效地根据销售额和盈利表现来调整计划。

6.7.3 The fashion product life cycle ／时装产品生命周期

The concept of the product life cycle is based on the proposal that all products have a finite 'life cycle' that can be plotted over a given period using the biological analogy of growth, development and decline. It proposes that all products will go through four major stages, namely introduction into the marketplace, growth, maturity and decline. However, it has already been pointed out that the nature of products in the fashion industry varies according to the rate, extent and timescale of acceptance of any new offering. Thus while fashion and fads do make up successful new product introductions, garments that are more classic in nature will never actually go 'out of fashion', nor will they rarely be 'in fashion', rather they will continue to meet established target market requirements. Thus the concept should be modified when analysing various fashion product classifications.

The life cycle of a fashion garment, extending over one or several seasons, probably comes nearest to the bell-shaped curve normally used to depict the product life cycle model (Figure 6.8).

产品生命周期理论的核心是建立在假设之上的，这个假设就是所有的产品都有有限的“生命周期”，并且可以采用生物类的成长、发展和衰退的原理在给定的时期对其进行分析。生命周期理论提出所有的产品都会经历四个主要的阶段，即市场进入期、成长期、成熟期和衰退期。然而，之前就指出了时装产品的本质是其会根据销售率、新产品被接受的范围和时间周期而改变。因此时尚品和潮流品会很快进入市场并取得成功，经典的时装从来也不会过时，同样也不会成为时尚的主流，但是经典的时装会不断地满足目标市场的需求。因此在分析不同的产品类别时应该改变这种认识。

时装产品的生命周期会长达至一个到几个季节，一般用近似钟形的曲线来表述产品生命周期（图 6–8）。

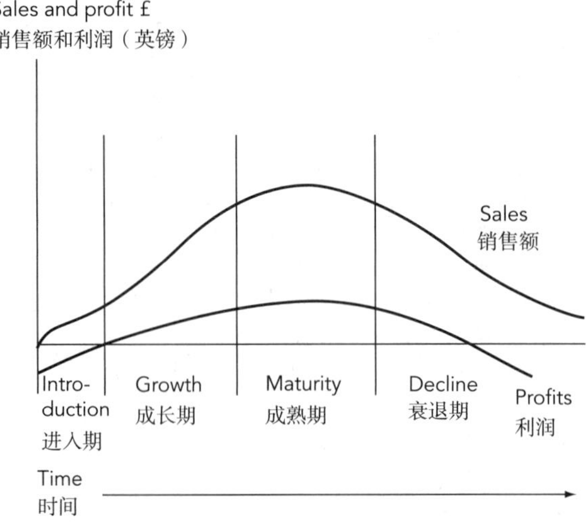

Figure 6.8 The fashion product life cycle. 图 6–8 时装产品生命周期曲线

The sales and profitability patterns and marketing implications of the model are described below.

以下描述的是这个模型的销售额、盈利模式以及营销含义曲线。

Introduction ／概述

New fashions take time to gain acceptance. Some consumers will be more innovative than the majority and, while they are willing to pay higher prices, unit costs could potentially still be high due to low sales. However, to counterbalance this, the high fashion element (and therefore exclusive nature) of the style at this stage may mean that customers are willing to pay very high prices, leading to generation of high profits. Selected promotion will emphasize image and high fashion nature; the main aim will be to educate and inform the customer as quickly as possible. The size of the market will, however, be limited. Distribution will tend to remain exclusive.

新的产品需要一段时间才能被市场接受。有些消费者会比大多数消费者具有创新性，他们愿意支付高价，单位成本高的原因主要是因为销售额较低。可是在这个阶段，为了保持平衡，时装款式中会有时尚性元素（以及独有的特色），也就暗示了消费者愿意支付高昂的价钱，从而就有了高利润。优秀的促销方案会增强企业形象并且强调高级时装的特色，最主要的目标是尽可能最快地培养和告知消费者。然而市场容量是有限的，企业必须拥有独立的分销渠道。

Growth ／成长期

Competition increases as the fashion gains exposure and begins to have wider appeal. Products will be modified to reduce costs and be offered at lower price levels. Sales will begin to rise sharply; new price bands will be established quite quickly. Distribution, still selective at this stage, will be wider as the fashion is diffused. Promotional emphasis will be on broadening exposure to gain acceptance of the fashion by the opinion forming element of the mass market.

当时装产品被大多数消费者接受时，市场竞争就会加剧，企业就会改良产品以降低成本并且以较低的价格供应市场。销售额会快速地增长，企业就会很快地形成新的价格带。当产品需求慢慢扩大时，分销渠道也会不断地扩张。这一阶段促销的重点是扩大产品的曝光程度，从而使得产品被大众市场的消费者接受。

Maturity ／成熟期

At this stage the fashion will have mass appeal; this period will be the longest in its life cycle. Competition will be intense, and prices will begin to fall to appeal to a very large market. Products will be further modified to achieve the ensuing lower price levels and profit potential will be falling. Distribution will be wide; promotional emphasis will be on reinforcement of what has by now become an established fashion.

在这个阶段，时装产品被广泛接受，这个时期是产品生命周期最长的一个阶段。竞争会变得更加激烈，产品价格开始降低以扩充更大的市场。企业会对产品进行改良以确保产品处于较低的价格水平，此时销售利润也会降低，企业应该继续扩大分销渠道，促销的重点是强化现有产品的特点。

Decline ／衰退期

The style is rapidly going out of fashion. Competitors are gradually eliminated as sales and profits are falling drastically and the prospect of being left with obsolete stock is near. Those left in the market may try

处于衰退期的时装款式慢慢地被市场淘汰。随着销售额和销售利润的快速下降，竞争者也会逐渐减少，结果就是过时产品的积压。市场上剩下的经营者

to extend the product's life by intensive advertising, extending distribution or searching for new segments. The alternative segments are likely to balance concerns about the likely success of the product against others such as price levels and the remaining life of the product.

会通过深入的广告策略、扩大销售渠道或者寻找新的细分市场等方式来延长产品的生命周期。选择新的细分市场与维持价格不变或延长产品剩余寿命的其他方法相比，更有可能确保产品的成功。

6.7.4 The fad life cycle ／潮流品的生命周期

The life cycle of the fad will tend to be very short, peaking quite sharply and declining almost as quickly as it rose in popularity (Figure 6.9).

The sales and profitability patterns and marketing implications of the cycle are described below.

潮流品的生命周期是非常短暂的，快速增长并且跟增长速度一样快速地下降（图 6-9）。

下面描述的是关于潮流品寿命周期中的销售额和盈利模式以及营销含义。

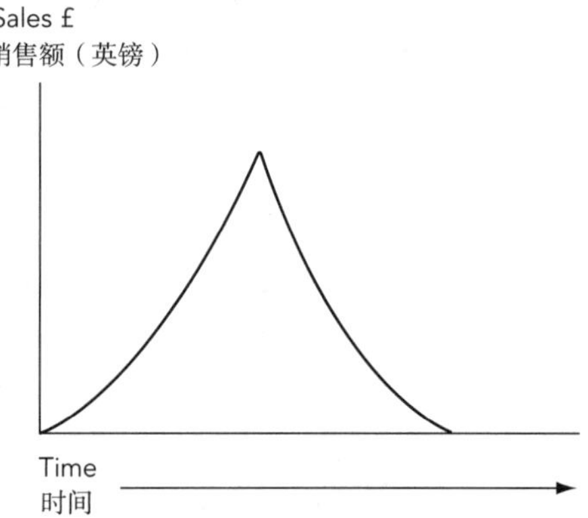

Figure 6.9 Sales of a fashion fad. 图 6-9 潮流品的销售额曲线

Introduction and growth ／投入期和成长期

In the case of a fad there is no introductory period coupled with rapid growth; the objective will be to capitalize on popularity as quickly as possible. However, the ability to do this will be restricted to a great extent by its 'fad-like' nature. Thus sales are pitched at a price the market will bear, probably higher than the fashion item it has been derived from, if this is applicable. Pricing strategy will aim to maximize profits even at launch stage, and the general emphasis will be on offering the new and different to a very specific type of consumer.

对于潮流品来说，并没有投入期和快速成长期，目标是尽可能地尽快扩大产品的普及率。然而因为其“潮流性”的特点，在很大程度上这点都是会受到限制的。因此，销售价格必须建立在市场可接受的水平上，如果对于企业有益的话，也可以将潮流品的定价高出时尚品的定价。即便是在产品进入市场的初期，价格策略的目标依然是提高利润，重点是要提供针对特定类型顾客的新产品和不同类型的产品。

Maturity and decline ／成熟期和衰退期

As maturity is reached, decline will begin very rapidly. Sales and profits will also decline; the emphasis here will be on getting rid of any remaining stocks as quickly as possible, either by reducing prices or by varying distribution channels. Promotional costs may be incurred in persuading new segments of the fad's dying appeal.

进入成熟期，销售量显著下降。销售额和利润同样也会下滑，此时的营销策略是通过降价或者通过不同的销售渠道尽快地将库存销售出去，同时为了给即将消失的潮流品寻找新的细分市场，可能会产生较大的促销成本。

6.7.5 The classic life cycle ／经典产品的生命周期

The style will have established itself over a time and, once established, will maintain its popularity with its target markets. Periodically the style will become fashionable; the shape of its curve, therefore, will tend to undulate gently (Figure 6.10).

一旦一个产品款式在一段时间内确定了自己的风格，就会在目标市场上流行起来。这个款式会周期性地流行，它的发展周期的曲线会呈缓慢波动状（图6–10）。

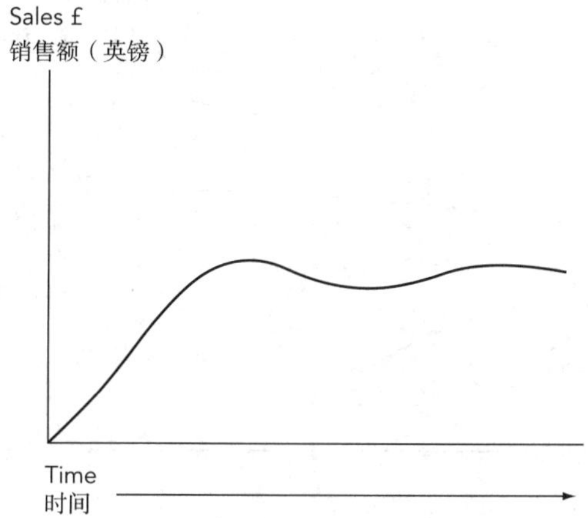

Figure 6.10 Sales of a fashion classic. 图 6–10 经典产品的销售额曲线

Sales and profitability patterns and marketing implications of the cycle ／经典产品寿命周期中的销售额、盈利模式和营销含义曲线

Classics will already be established in the mature stage of the cycle (although they will occasionally be revived as fashion). Distribution channels, price and profitability levels will rise relative to what the established market will bear. Promotional policies for classics will tend to be based on reinforcement of well-established, accepted styles. Over time the market for classics could increase as demographic shifts in the population lead

经典产品在产品成熟阶段就形成了（尽管有些时候会偶尔被认为是时尚品），分销渠道、价格以及盈利水平根据市场的承受能力而扩大和增长。经典产品的促销策略主要是通过口碑的影响力以及可接受的款式，经典产品的市场会随着人口转移所导致的大量人群进入

to larger numbers in mature age brackets (classics tend to be bought by older, more mature consumers). Earlier in this section the point was made that the life cycle concept would be most useful where analysis of decisions regarding product and other mix variables could be made regarding sales and profit patterns, and where analyses could then be compared over time.

A second dimension in terms of the concept's utility as a planning tool is where comparison can be made over time between the performance of specific styles of brands and broader market and sector trends. Analysis of life cycles here can be made at three related levels (as shown in Figure 6.11), from a general product classification or garment category through to specific product lines within each category and then to various garment styles or brand names (see Section 6.6).

成人年龄段而扩大（年长的、成熟的消费者喜欢购买经典产品）。在本章前面已经讲过，尤其是在根据产品和其他营销组合变量进行分析决策时，以及对整个过程进行对比分析的时候，产品生命周期概念是非常有用的，从概念作为一种策划工具的角度看，它的第二个特点是可以在整个过程中对时装品牌特定款式的市场表现，以及广阔的市场和行业趋势进行对比分析。产品生命周期可以从三个相关的方面进行分析（图6–11），即从常规的产品分类或者时装类别到每个类别中特殊的产品线，再到不同的时装款式和品牌（见6.6章节）。

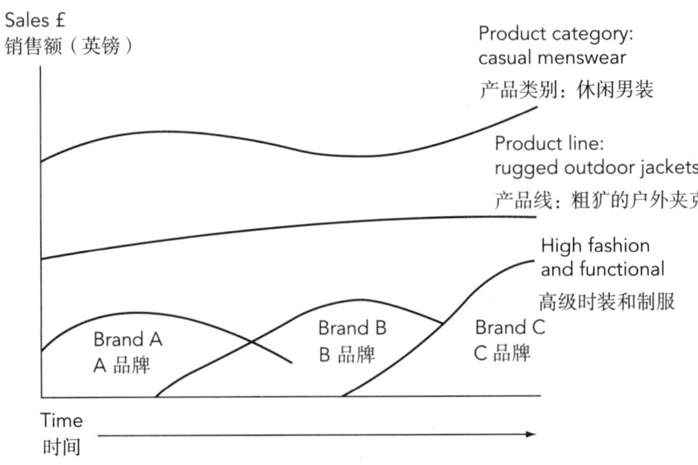

Figure 6.11 Hypothetical example of a three-level analysis within the general menswear sector.

图 6–11 对常规男装假设系列进行三个层面分析曲线

6.7.6 Fashion oscillations／时装市场的波动

Some empirical evidence exists to substantiate the proposition that fashions will oscillate over time from one extreme or opposite to the other. These extremes may be in the form of silhouette or shape, colour, fabric texture or pattern and overall style/total look; in other words the four basic design dimensions mentioned earlier.

时装会从一个极端波动到另外的一个极端，这可以通过一些经验性的证据得到证实，即这些极端可能是以廓型或者款式、色彩、面料、结构或者图案，以及整体造型和外观来表现的。换而言之，就是前面所说的时装设计的四个要素。

The driving force behind these oscillatory trends is the continual search by the individual to satisfy a variety of needs, ideally within one purchase decision, and the inherent inability of any one garment to satisfy all of them simultaneously. The net result is that a compromise has to be made between the ideal set of satisfactions sought and the reality of the product's potential set of satisfactions. This will ultimately open up possibilities for many different offerings, the spread of which will depend upon the extent to which compromise has had to be made.

这种波动趋势的驱动力是每个消费者都在不断地寻找能够满足他们不同需求的产品，比较理想的情况是消费者只有一种购买决定。任何一件产品都不可能同时满足所有消费者的需求，最终的结果是在消费者追求的满意度和产品潜在的满意度之间寻找一个平衡点，这也会给不同的产品提供发展机会，产品会有多大的市场主要取决于先前作了多大的让步。

However, every satisfactory purchase made will initiate new drives. These drives will be based on the perpetual need to search for different offerings to satisfy new needs. Paradoxically, therefore, as one design satisfies a combination of needs it extinguishes the very needs that produced it, simultaneously encouraging those needs least fulfilled by the design to come to the fore. The human drive for social approval results in the tendency for oscillations to reach extremes that are still universally adopted within market segments, e.g. miniskirts which are worn by a variety of body shapes and sizes within the youth market.

可是，一个满意的购买决定会产生新的购买动力，这些动力是建立在消费者期望寻找不同的产品来满足其新的需求的基础上的。因此矛盾的是，当一个设计满足一系列需求时，那么生产这类产品就是必要的，同时也会促使这些消费需求从设计层面转入到市场。人们希望得到社会认可的心理会导致市场波动到达极端，这种极端就是产品被细分市场完全接受，例如年轻市场中不同体型和身材的人都会穿超短裙。

Neglect of some essential design element or embellishment over a long period also can lead to a vigorous revival. The sudden upsurge of many fashions can be explained from such frustrations, the classic example being Dior's post-war 'New Look' or Alexander McQueen's famous 'Bumster' Trousers in the 1990s.

在一段时间内忽略一些必要的设计或者装饰要素，也可能使市场重新活跃起来，多数时装产品需求突然高涨可能就是因为这样的原因。典型的例子就是迪奥战前"新式样"或者 20 世纪 90 年代亚历山大·麦克奎恩著名的"低腰牛仔裤"。

Sophisticated mass communications have resulted in consumers becoming more fashion conscious and fashion aware. The trend now is towards the desire for considerably more diverse ranges of products in the marketplace and the need for more personalized, or customized, fashion. The general result of this is that fashion swings or oscillations are becoming shorter in a time-based sense, often leading to confusion in the marketplace. Here again, however, historical analysis of trends can help when trying to determine future developments.

多样化的大众传播工具使得消费者变得对时尚越来越敏感并且他们的时尚意识越来越强，现在的趋势是消费者期望能够在市场上得到更多的不同风格的产品，以及期望更多的个性化的或者定制的时装，通常的结果是时装波动周期会变短，从而使得市场比较混乱。然而这里还需要再次提及的是，对过去的流行趋势进行分析有助于确立未来产品的发展方向。

6.8 Summary / 小结

At the end of this chapter readers should be able to:

◆ understand the role and importance of the product element of the marketing mix in the fashion industry;

在本章的最后，读者可以：

◆ 理解时装业营销组合中产品要素的作用和重要性；

◆ analyse and describe the perceived attributes of fashion items by the intended target market;

◆ describe the fashion diffusion process within the industry and its bearing on the process of new product development;

◆ understand how product mixes and ranges are planned and controlled.

◆ 分析和发现既定目标市场所供应产品的感性特征;

◆ 说明时装产品的传播过程以及与新产品开发的关联性;

◆ 明白如何计划和控制产品组合及产品系列。

Further reading ／课后阅读材料

1.Baker, M.J. and Hart, S. (2007), *Product Strategy and Management*, 2nd Edition, FT Prentice Hall, London.
贝克·M.J.，哈特，S.(2007)，《产品策略和产品管理》，第 2 版，FT 出版社，伦敦 .

2.Barclay, I. *et al*. (2000), *New Product Development*, Butterworth-Heinemann, Oxford.
巴克莱·I. 等 .（2000），《新产品开发》，巴特沃斯海尼曼，牛津 .

3.Elliot, R. and Percy, L. (2006), *Strategic Brand Management*, Oxford University Press, Oxford.
埃利奥特·R.，珀西·L.(2006)，《战略品牌管理》，牛津大学出版社，牛津 .

4.Goworek, H. (2007), *Fashion Buying*, 2nd Edition, Blackwell Publishing, Oxford.
戈沃瑞克·H.(2007)，《时装采购》，第 2 版，布莱克威尔出版社，牛津 .

5.Jackson, T. and Shaw, D. (2000), *Mastering Fashion Buying and Merchandising Management*, Palgrave Macmillan, London.
杰克森·T. 肖恩·D.(2000)，《时装采购管理与商品管理》，帕尔格雷夫·麦克米伦出版社，伦敦 .

6.Pendergast, L. and Pendergast, T. (2003), *Fashion, Fad and Style*, UXL, MI.
德加斯特·L.，德加斯特·T.(2003)，《时尚，潮流和风格》，UXL，MI.

7.Trott, P. (2004), *Innovation Management and New Product Development*, 3rd Edition, FT/ Prentice Hall, Englewood Cliffs, NJ.
特罗特·P.（2004），《创新管理与新产品开发》，第 3 版，FT 出版社，恩格尔伍德克里夫斯，新泽西 .

Chapter Seven Pricing Garments and Fashion Services

第 7 章　时装定价与服务

7.1　Introduction／引言

This chapter begins by considering price first as a concept and then in relation to other elements of the fashion marketing mix. External and internal factors affecting price are examined. The principal methods of setting prices used in the fashion industry are outlined and an explanation of discounts and the concept of break-even are given. The chapter concludes with a discussion of pricing strategies and the administration and nature of price changes.

本章首先分析价格的概念，然后研究时装市场营销组合的其他内容，并且考察影响价格的内外部因素，阐述时装业采用的主要的定价方法以及折扣并给出盈亏平衡的概念，最后讨论定价策略、价格管理和价格变动的执行和本质。

7.2　Different views of price／关于价格的不同观点

According to economists, price is the point at which exchange between buyer and seller takes place, where supply and demand are equal. Anyone who has witnessed sales of out-of-season garments or clothing that have not enjoyed the popularity hoped for will notice that reductions occur to a point at which the stock is bought. However, price as an element of the marketing mix involves much more than the perspective of the economist.

按经济学家所说，价格是买方和卖方之间产生交换的一个点，在这个点上供需是平衡的。有人已亲眼见到过季的时装或不太受欢迎的衣服，价格就降到了库存货的进价。然而，价格作为营销组合的一个成分涉及的因素比经济学家的观点要多得多。

The accountant tends to concentrate on the relationship between costs of production and the need to provide a certain return on capital invested with the final price that is to be charged. Cash flow is a major concern of all accountants and as such,

会计往往倾向于关注生产成本和需求之间的关系，希望投入的资本能够在最终定价所产生的销售额之中获得收益。现金流是所有会计所关注的主要问题，定价同时也会影

price decisions can influence the volume of an item that is sold over time. For example, pricing bikinis at £8.99 each may mean that the entire stock is sold within four weeks of launch within a retail outlet. A higher price of £12.99 may mean that the same goal of selling all the stock takes eight weeks. Admittedly, in the latter case an extra £4.00 profit per pair has been earned, but at the cost of holding the stock for a longer period. An additional risk of charging £12.99 is having to reduce prices to shift stock that is particularly susceptible to changes in the climate.

响产品在一定时期内的销售量。例如，比基尼的定价是每件 8.99 英镑，就意味着一个零售点的所有库存要在 4 周内售完。以 12.99 英镑的较高价格出售，就意味着要用 8 周时间售完所有库存的商品。诚然，后一种情况每件可获得 4.00 英镑的利润，但是要以较长时间持有库存为代价。12.99 英镑的定价带来的额外风险是必须降低价格以消化库存，尤其是比基尼的销售很容易受到气候变化的影响。

Marketing personnel are interested in price decisions for many reasons. Prices that are set can determine the rate and extent to which marketing objectives are achieved. A company with a goal of achieving a 10% increase in market share will conclude that lower prices may give a competitive advantage that encourages purchases. Similarly, the goal of building a reputation for good quality may well lead to higher prices that follow from the higher costs of using better quality fabrics and imposing more quality checks in manufacture. Marketing managers are also interested in the price perceptions of buyers. As noted in Chapter Three, perception flows from an inner reality that may not be an accurate representation of true price levels. A company's products may be the cheapest on the market, but the advertising or the stores that sell the product may contribute towards an image that contradicts one of low prices. In such a case, opportunities may be missed as consumers do not even bother to check the accuracy of their perceptions. At the level of organizational buyers, from the manufacturer selecting fabric to the retailer acquiring stock, the awareness of price levels is usually a professional imperative. However, consumers vary considerably in their levels of awareness of prices. With branded products it is easier for consumers to make judgements, therefore comparison shopping is likely to be a common practice for many shoppers. Products from different manufacturers, even if within the same product category such as blue boot-cut denim jeans, present consumers with challenges to make direct comparisons due to differences in styling, quality of construction, quality of materials used and image.

营销人员对定价感兴趣的原因有很多，设定的价格能够决定营销目标实现的速度和程度。在市场份额中，具有 10% 增长目标的公司会得出一个结论，较低的价格可以产生竞争优势，鼓励顾客购买。同样，要建立良好的质量信誉就会产生较高的价格，因为使用高品质面料的成本较高，而且生产时需进行全面的质量检测。销售经理们也对买方的价格认知能力感兴趣，如第 3 章提到的，企业内部人员对价格的认知也不能用来确定产品的价格水平。一个公司的产品在市场上可能是最便宜的，但是广告和店铺所诠释的形象可能会与较低的定价产生矛盾。在这种情况下，企业可能会失去机会，因为消费者不会用心衡量认知的准确度。从组织采购者的角度看，从生产商选定面料到零售商获取库存，价格水平的认识通常具有专业性。然而，消费者对价格的认知会产生较大的变化，消费者更容易对品牌产品做出判断，因此比较购物就有可能成为许多购物者的习惯做法。来自不同生产商的产品，即使在相同的产品目录范围内，例如蓝色牛仔靴裤，也会从款式、生产质量、材料品质以及形象的不同上挑战消费者来做出直接的比较。

The above perspectives and salience of pricing decisions for companies mean that many people within a company may have direct and legitimate interests

上述定价策略的观点和特点，意味着公司内的许多人会从价格决策中获得直接的和合法的利益。影响和控制的核

in price decisions. The locus of influence and control will vary according to the organization of particular firms and to the relative importance given to financial and marketing matters. This is not an argument for the supremacy of marketing over other functional considerations, but a recognition that many disciplines should be involved in price decisions.

心会随着个别企业的组织以及对财务和市场问题的重视度而变化，这不是争论营销相对于其他功能因素的至高无上之处，而是要认识到价格决策涉及了许多的学科。

7.3 The role of price decisions within marketing strategy / 营销策略中价格决策的作用

The price levels for a product range selected by an organization can, along with other elements of the marketing mix, decide the success or otherwise in attracting certain target markets. Setting price levels too low may send confused messages and alienate some buyers who feel that the product may be poorly made. Excessive prices may inhibit other people who may feel other products, while not similar, offer better value for money. Others may feel that high prices are solely a premium for immediate ownership and that waiting for a short period may yield price reductions. Therefore price decisions help to determine who buys and how much they buy.

由一个组织机构选定系列产品的价格水平，连同其他营销组合要素一起决定销售成败或者吸引特定的目标市场。定价水平太低可能会传播混乱信息并且疏远一些购买者，使消费者感到产品做工太差。过高的价格可能会约束一些人，使他们觉得其他产品物有所值。尽管不是同类产品，有些人可能觉得较高的价格完全是直接所有权的溢价，并且期待着短期内可以降价。因此，价格决策有助于决定谁要买或者要买多少。

In relation to decisions about place matters, pricing decisions can secure access to certain outlets. To give retailers opportunities to achieve their profit margins, manufacturers must recognize the needs of the retailer's target market and the margins that are expected. If a retailer expects that an item will be a fast seller then a lower margin may be accepted. Similarly, higher margins are expected on slow moving items or risky new fashion products that may or may not be quickly accepted by the consumer.

在店铺选址的问题上，定价策略可以确保产品进入特定的销售渠道，给零售商提供机会获得利润。生产者必须认识到零售商目标市场的需求以及他们期望得到的利润，如果一个零售商期待一件商品较快地被卖掉，就必须接受较低的利润。同样，消费者可能会或者不会较快地接受那些流行较慢的或者时尚类的产品，此类产品通常可以获取较高的利润。

Product matters are related to price decisions in many ways. The nature and extent of the product line may limit the flexibility possible in setting prices. For example, a co-ordinated range of skirts, jackets, blouses and accessories may be so priced as to encourage the purchase of several items by the consumer. Rigidly sticking to a fixed profit margin on each product in the range could undermine a policy that would otherwise lead to higher sales and profits by varying margins of items within and between the co-ordinated product lines. If the prices of products were left as a sum of their costs of manufacture plus a fixed

产品决策与定价在许多方面有着联系，产品线的特点和宽度可能会约束设定价格的灵活性。例如，一件衬衣、夹克、短上衣以及其他物品进行定价时就会考虑，促使消费者的购买量增加。严格地规定系列中每件产品的边际利润，通过区分不同产品以及相关产品线的利润会带来较高的销售额和利润。如果以制造成本加上固定利润进行定价，那么就必须调整同一款不同型号时装的定价。一件 18 码外套的用料几乎是 8 码外套用料

markup, then variations in prices of different sizes of the same garment would be the obvious outcome. A size 18 overcoat may use nearly twice as much material as a size 8, yet few retailers would contemplate charging more for the larger one. In this sense, smaller customers subsidize larger customers, but in practice most manufacturers, retailers and consumers accept the notion of averaging costs and prices across different sizes.

的 2 倍，然而，零售商很少会考虑将大号外套的定价提高一些。从这个角度看，身材娇小的消费者所产生的销售额会补贴身材较大的消费者所耗费的超出材料的成本。但实际上，对于大多数生产商、零售商以及消费者而言，他们会接受不同尺码耗费同样的成本以及采取同样定价的观点。

Promotion and pricing decisions most closely relate with regard to the image that is being put forward to consumers. Most people perceive a relationship between price levels and quality, though not always a linear one. Usually, the expectation is that, high quality goes with high prices and low prices reflect low quality or possibly out-of-date or out-of-season clothing. The selection of a particular medium to reach a certain target market may mean that prices are not even mentioned in promotional messages. An accessory from Gucci, advertised in *The Times* with no mention of price, is such an example. At the other extreme a store selling garments aimed at low-income groups may make price a prominent feature of its window displays and advertising. Marks and Spencer originally began promoting itself as a store where everything was priced at one penny, but strategic repositioning and greater competition in the particular market segment have changed the company's practice since then.

促销和产品定价与企业传播给消费者的形象有紧密的关系，大多数消费者都意识到了价格水平和产品质量之间的关系，尽管这种关系不是线性的。通常人们的常识是高质量的产品价格较高，低价格反映的则是产品质量较低，或者可能是过时的或过季的时装。选择特定媒介针对目标市场进行推广的时候，价格信息通常不会出现在促销的内容中，在时代杂志上推广古琪品牌的配饰时就没有提及价格。而另一个情况是，一个针对低收入群体销售时装的商店可以在橱窗展示和广告上将价格作为最重要的卖点。玛莎百货早期进行产品推广时，每一个物品是按一个便士定价的。自此之后，企业在特定细分市场重新调整定位，加之较大的市场竞争力，使得公司的情况发生了转变。

The above discussion shows the interrelationship between price, target markets and other elements of the marketing mix. There is one particular area where pricing does differ from other elements of the marketing mix. All other elements of the marketing mix entail costs which it is hoped will lead to increased sales and profit. Pricing, while also affecting sales, will be a direct determinant of revenue out of which marketing and other costs are met.

上述讨论表明了价格、目标市场和营销组合要素间的相互关系。在某个特定的领域，定价和营销组合的其他要素是有区别的。营销组合的其他所有元素促使价格带动了销售量和利润的增加，定价同样也会影响销售量，它决定了营销等其他成本所对应的收入阶层。

7.4 External factors influencing price decisions /影响定价的外部因素

7.4.1 The nature of competition in the particular market /在特定市场中竞争的本质

At a broad level it should be noted that competition comes not just from other garment suppliers, but also from other products and services that compete for consumers' discretionary income. High prices for garments may encourage consumers to spend more money on other consumer durables such as high-

在宏观层面上，我们应注意到竞争不仅来自其他时装供应商，而且也来自那些竞相获得消费者可支配收入的其他产品和服务。时装的高定价会鼓励消费者把更多的钱花在其他耐用消费品上，例

definition televisions or on leisure activities such as holidays. The unattractiveness of the prices of garments in relation to other competing products and services should be kept in mind. The relative sales and trends of various sectors of industry, plus the inflation rates by sector, are indicators of how well or otherwise this inter-sector competition is being met.

如高清电视或者度假等娱乐活动。营销人员必须牢记，时装产品和其他竞争产品以及服务相比较，时装产品的价格是缺乏吸引力的。各种产业相关的销售收入和产业内各种机构的发展趋势，以及由各种机构拔高的通胀率，充分说明了产业内各部门间将面对的缓和或激烈的竞争。

The more homogeneous the product the greater the price competition. The fashion industry tries to encourage non-price competition by the branding and creation of unique designs and images for ranges. At the designer level of the market, such garments are in limited supply through exclusive outlets and, the creators hope, for limited periods. The ability of competitors to produce similar products is restricted by some legislative protection of the design. Consumer confidence in garment quality and the ability to purchase an up-to-date design immediately enable higher prices to be charged. For other products such as socks the latitude to command exclusivity or any special design point that can be reflected in a higher price is more restricted.

产品越单一，价格竞争越激烈。时装业试图通过创立自身品牌的独特设计或形象来鼓励非价格竞争。从市场的角度看，此类时装通过独家销售限制供应，而且品牌创立者还希望在限定的时间内销售。对产品设计的合法保护限制了竞争者生产类似产品的能力，因为消费者信任时装质量并且有能力及时购买到流行产品，所以时装的定价很高。对于袜子等其他产品而言，较高价格反映的排他性允许幅度或者某个特别的设计点都是更受限制的。

7.4.2 Joint or related demand for products ／产品的连带需求或相关需求

This may arise where the increase in demand for one product is accompanied by an increase in demand for another. Good weather may well spur demand for swimwear, sun hats and sunglasses, whilst poor weather may lead to an increase in demand for rainwear, hats and scarves. Retailers, well aware of these linkages, may design the layout of the store and adjust prices accordingly to make the most of complementary demand. Other examples include the purchase of a new tie that may stimulate the purchase of a new shirt. New colour themes for a season, if adopted, may stimulate a whole range of purchases. Thus a new evening dress may be accompanied by the purchase of new hosiery, underwear, coat, cosmetics, hairstyling, shoes and handbag. Such outcomes are the aspiration of many department stores. It is the relative pricing, besides the selection and co-ordination of appropriate items in the above list, that is crucial in deciding the successful sale. Manufacturers who produce such complementary items independently need to anticipate the needs of intermediaries and the ultimate customer when setting prices (Figure 7.1).

一种产品需求的增长可能会引起另一种产品需求的增长。好天气可以刺激泳装、太阳帽和太阳镜的需求，而坏天气可以引起雨衣、帽子和围巾需求的增长。零售商注意到这些联系，可以设计商店的布局并相应地调整价格，最大限度地利用互补性需求，其他例子还有新领带的购买可以刺激购买新衬衣。一个季节新的色彩主题被接受的话，可能会促使消费者购买整个系列的产品。因此购买一件新的晚礼服可以伴随着购买新的长统袜、内衣、外衣、化妆品、鞋子和手袋，这种结果是许多百货商店所渴望的。这正是“相对定价”的情况，还包括就下图所指各方面进行适当地选择和调整，这对成功销售而言是至关重要的。自行生产这种互补性商品的制造商，在定价时需要预测中间商以及终端顾客的需求（图 7–1）。

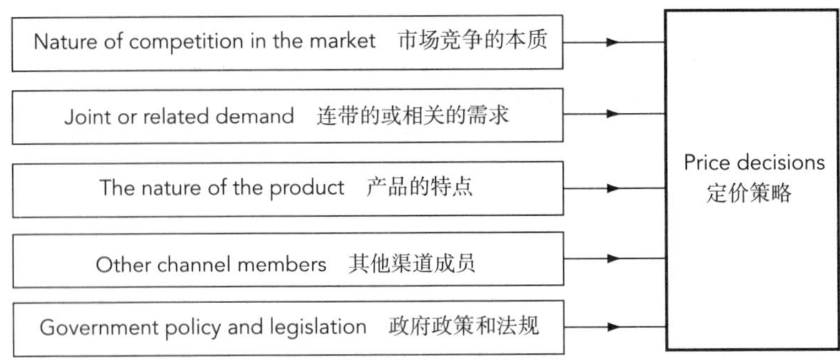

Figure 7.1 External factors influencing price decisions. 图 7–1 影响定价的外部因素

7.4.3 The nature of the product / 产品的特点

Whether the product is seen as an essential or not is a factor that influences the power of the seller in setting prices. Target markets differ considerably in what is seen as essential. A dinner jacket may be seen as a luxury by some, but as an essential item by a manager who has to attend many formal functions.

Some items of clothing and footwear are essential for protection and warmth. The rate of replacement of garments and the ability of consumers to defer purchase, obtain repairs, make clothes themselves or buy second-hand goods remain within the consumers' discretion. One related factor that influences the pricing of fashion products is the perceived life of the product. If a garment is seen as a 'classic' that will last for many seasons or years, such as a Barbour jacket or Burberry raincoat, then premium prices are more easily tolerated. In relation to other markets such as power supply, the fashion industry does not enjoy the privilege of producing items whose demand is insensitive to price changes. The nearest that the fashion industry comes to such demand is when there is only a limited supply of a unique design that is eagerly sought by buyers.

The speed with which some firms in the industry are able to produce garments that are similarly styled and made from comparable fabrics or fibres means such uniqueness does not go unchallenged for long. The issue here is not one of counterfeits, although that is a serious problem for some firms. The intrinsic difficulty of ensuring full protection for fashion designs is where the slightest difference in styling can be used as a basis for contesting a claim for breach of copyright.

不管某个产品是不是必需品，它都是影响卖方定价的一个因素。因为必需品不同所以目标市场也有差异，有些人会把晚宴夹克看作是奢侈品，然而对于经常出入正式场合的经理人而言，则会把它看作是必需品。

有些时装和鞋的核心功能是保护和保暖，时装的更换频率、消费者延期购买、获得维修、自做衣服或购买二手商品的能力由消费者自主决定。消费者对产品生命周期的感知也是影响定价的一个相关因素，如果一件衣服被看作一件“精品”，那么就会流行多个季节或很多年，消费者也很容易接受较高的定价，例如一件巴伯品牌的夹克或一件巴宝莉的风雨衣。时装业并不喜欢那些市场需求对价格变化不敏感的产品。当时装产品的需求对价格变化越不敏感的时候，采购商通常都急切地想采购到设计独特，供应量有限的商品。

行业中某些企业有能力生产款式近似、材料和纤维也很相近的时装，这意味着这种独特性会成为长期的一种挑战。这里说的并不是赝品的问题，对于某些企业来说这是一个严重的问题。确保时装设计得到全面保护的根本问题是款式上的微小差别，它能成为侵犯版权、争取索赔的一个基础。因此，无弹性需求

Inelasticity of demand is therefore limited in the fashion industry by the ease with which comparable alternatives can be quickly supplied.

在时装业很少见，因为很多其他的企业可以快速地生产替代品。

7.4.4 Other members of the distribution channel ／销售渠道的其他成员

If one member of the distribution channel is able to charge higher prices this may tempt those earlier in the chain of distribution to increase prices and share in the profit potential. The ability of manufacturers to change retail outlets and the willingness of other outlets to stock a profitable product range are key variables that influence the setting of prices at the retail level.

如果销售渠道的一个成员能够出较高的价格，这就可以吸引那些在渠道链前端的成员提高价格并且分享利润。制造商储存可赢利的系列产品的能力是影响定价的关键变量，最终可以改变零售终端和其他渠道的意愿。

Within certain sections of the retail clothing sector there are traditional margins that must be accounted for when setting prices. One large retail group, for instance, is known to have a company policy of multiplying supplier prices by 2.3 to arrive at a retail price. Such practices must be anticipated by manufacturers as, depending on the balance of power with the retailer, these traditional margins may be used as a mechanism to force down the manufacturer's selling price.

在某些时装零售部门，定价时必须考虑惯常的边际利润。例如，一个大型零售集团产品的售价会是供应商价格的2.3倍，这一点是众所周知的，这也是制造商所期望的。通过平衡零售商和制造商之间的权利，这些惯常的边际利润会被用作逼迫制造商降低价格的一种方式。

Changes in the costs of raw materials, labour or manufacturing at earlier stages in the distribution chain are factors that can influence the ultimate price to the consumer. With the growing internationalization of the clothing industry, the ability of retailers to procure stock from sources in different countries is greater than ever before. The power of suppliers to pass on price increases unchallenged is diminished except where the supply of a fabric or design is either unique or very well known, such as Gore-Tex or Lycra.

原料成本、劳动力成本或者在渠道链前端的制造成本都会影响最终消费者所面临的价格。随着时装业的日益国际化，零售商从不同的国家采购商品的能力比以前有了大幅度的提高，供应商毫不顾忌提价的权利也随之逐渐消失，除非他们的材料独特、设计知名度高，例如戈尔特斯防水面料或者莱卡面料。

7.4.5 Government policy and legislation ／政府政策或法规

As has been noted in an earlier chapter on the market environment, governments can influence the readiness of consumers to pay particular prices via policy related to inflation, investment and employment.

Government policy on taxation, in particular value added tax (VAT) and corporation tax, might be said to provide extra 'costs' that must be borne by the fashion consumer. The change of emphasis in taxation from earnings to expenditure in recent years has, at the macro-level, influenced demand for fashion products. The Office of Fair Trading, the UK Competition Commission and the European Commission are all

如在较前章节中提到的市场环境，借助膨胀、投资和就业等政策，政府能够影响消费者做好支付高价的准备。政府关于税收的政策特别是增值税和公司所得税，增加了消费者购物时的成本。从宏观上讲，近年来税收重点从盈利到支出的变化影响了时装产品的需求。商品交易处、英国竞争委员会以及欧洲委员会有责任保护公共和商业的利益，并且反对各种形式的价格垄断，这在本章后面会有所描述。

charged to defend the public and business against various price fixing methods, as described later in this chapter.

7.5 Internal factors influencing price decisions / 影响定价的内部因素

7.5.1 The ability to control costs / 控制成本的能力

The ability of the company to minimize costs is a major determinant on the price levels that can be set. As costs can be decreased so either profitability can be enhanced or the ability to compete at low prices can be strengthened.

公司缩减成本的能力是设定价格水平最主要的因素，因为可以降低成本，所以既能提高利润，又能增强低价竞争的能力。

7.5.2 Other elements of the marketing mix / 营销组合的其他要素

The relative importance of other elements of the marketing mix of the company is a factor influencing pricing decisions. The company competing directly on price to achieve high-volume distribution at low margins is in a very different position from the company setting out to create an image of high quality at premium prices.

公司营销组合中其他要素的相对重要性是影响定价的一个因素，公司在价格方面相竞争以获取高销量低利润，和那些设定高价并且创造高品质形象的公司是处于不同市场地位的。

7.5.3 The product range / 产品线

The breadth and depth of product lines and the price relationships between items in those lines are factors that must be considered when setting prices. A warm lining for a raincoat sold separately will need to be assessed not only in terms of individual cost, but also for the impact it has upon the total demand and profitability of the raincoat and lining together.

设定价格时，产品线的宽度和深度以及在产品线中不同产品之间的价格关系是必须考虑的因素。单独销售一件雨衣的保暖衬里时，不仅需要评定个别成本，而且需要评定衬里对此产品总需求和利润的影响。

7.6 Main methods of setting prices / 定价的主要方法

There are many ways of setting prices, but most are variants of the two principal methods, namely cost-plus pricing and market-based pricing. Cost-plus pricing is simply calculating the cost of raw materials, labour and overheads such as administration and adding an amount to cover profit to arrive at the selling price. Market-based pricing is founded on market research to find the optimum selling price which then acts as the main driving force on cost containment via design and quality control effort.

定价的方法有很多种，但大多数属于这两种主要方法的变体，即成本加成定价法和基于市场定价法。成本加成定价法是简单地计算原材料的成本、劳动力的成本以及管理方面的费用，再加上确定销售价过程中的附加利润，即构成了销售价格。基于市场定价法是以市场调研为基础寻找最恰当的销售价格，其通过设计和质量监控成为控制成本的主要驱动力。

7.6.1 Cost-plus pricing methods ／成本加成定价法

A cost-based method aims to ensure that no product is sold at a loss. The practice is common where the product is non-standard, such as designer wedding gowns, or where there are many small independent retailers supplying the market. Cost-plus pricing is also used with tender proposals, for instance, when a clothing manufacturer makes a proposal to supply uniforms to a large corporate client. A simple example is given below based upon a manufacturer supplying a retailer with zip-up tops made of cotton jersey.

The concept of the markup is explained in more detail below. In the example in Table 7.1, the profit margin per item is fairly low, but this may be deemed appropriate for an item that faces much competition and is expected to sell in very large quantities. The markups for the manufacturer and retailer have been set at 25% and 65%, respectively, as the minimum rates of return needed to service the capital required for each business, namely shareholder dividends or the cost of loans.

以成本为基础的定价方法旨在确保产品不会亏本销售，对于非标准化的产品，例如设计师品牌的婚礼服或者市场上有很多较小零售商供货的时候，其定价的操作方法是一样的。成本加成定价法也用于招标活动中，例如一个时装制造商计划给一个大公司的员工供应制服。下面给出了一个生产商供给零售商带拉链棉质紧身内衣的简单例子。

下面详述了涨价的理念。在表 7–1 的例子中，每件商品的利润都是相当低的，但有些人认为这种定价对那些面临大量竞争对手，而且希望获取巨额销售收入的商品而言是较为适合的。生产商和零售商的加价分别设定为 25% 和 65%，因为最小的收益必须足以支付开展每一笔业务的资金，即股东红利或贷款成本。

Table 7.1 An example of cost-plus pricing 表 7–1 成本加成定价法的例子

Item 商品	Details 描述	Quantity 数量	Unit cost 单位成本	Total cost 总成本（英镑）
Cotton 棉	Jersey 紧身内衣	1.5 m	£2.22/m 2.22 英镑 / 米	£3.33
Trim 辅料	Polyfil thread 涤纶线	1 1 卷	£0.09 0.09 英镑 / 卷	£0.09
	Metal zip 金属拉链	1 @ 20 cm 1 条 20 cm	£0.27 0.27 英镑 / 条	£0.27
	Knitted collar 针织领	1 1 个	£0.21 0.21 英镑 / 个	£0.21
Label 标签	With logo and care instructions 带有公司商标和使用说明	1 1 套	£0.06 0.06 英镑 / 套	£0.06
Labour to cut, make and trim @ 15 minutes 剪裁、制作和后整理的劳动力 15 分钟				£1.40
Cost of production 生产成本				£5.36
Manufacturer's markup @ 25% 生产商的加价 25%				£1.34
Manufacturer's selling price (excluding VAT) 生产商的售价（不包括增值税）				£6.70
Retailer's markup @ 65% 零售商的加价 65%				£4.36
Retail price excluding VAT 不含增值税的零售价格				£11.06
VAT @ 17.5% 增值税 17.5%				£1.94
Retail price including VAT 含增值税的零售价格				£13.00

The example assumes that all of the zip-up tops will be sold at the full price. If the retailer is determined to clear stock, but not to sell below the cost of any item, then the lowest 'sale' price will be £6.70 plus VAT. If the retailer sells at VAT exclusive prices of between £6.70 and below £11.06 then the technique of contribution analysis is being applied. Contribution analysis is a variant of cost-plus pricing and works on the idea that any excess of price over cost enables a contribution to be made to the cost of capital to run the business – simply put, some profit is better than no profit. Clearly the whole of a company's pricing cannot be based on covering costs alone, as fashion companies need to do more in order to survive and grow. More sophisticated variants of contribution analysis can be used to link price setting to several financial ratios.

这个案例中假设所有带拉链的棉质紧身内衣将以全价卖出，如果零售商决定清理库存，以不低于商品的成本价销售，那么最低的销售价将是 6.70 英镑加上增值税。如果零售商以 6.70 英镑到 11.06 英镑（不含增值税）的价格销售，那么就要应用毛利分析法。毛利分析是成本加成定价法的一个变量，任何超出成本的价格都会促使毛利的产生，以用于公司经营的成本，简单地说，有利润好于没有利润。显然整个公司的定价不能仅仅包括成本，因为时装公司为了生存和发展需要多加价，与毛利分析相关的更多复杂的变量能够把定价和财务比率联系起来（表 7–2）。

Table 7.2 Calculation of target buying prices **表 7–2 目标市场采购价格的计算**

Cotton jersey hooded top including 带帽棉质紧身内衣 VAT at 17.5% 含 17.5% 的增值税	£12.99
Less VAT at 17.5% 低于 17.5% 的增值税	£1.93
Retail price excluding VAT 不含增值税的零售价	£11.06
Less retailer's markup at 65% of buying price 低于零售商 65% 的加价的买价	£7.19
Retailer buying price or manufacturer selling price 零售商的进价或制造商的售价	£3.87

7.6.2 Market-based pricing methods ／基于市场定价法

These methods rely on a good knowledge of consumer price sensitivity and awareness levels. For example, market research may indicate that buyers in a certain target market may respond very favourably to a hooded top made of cotton jersey, if the item is priced at £12.99 (including VAT). If the retailer enjoys considerable purchasing power then the retail price of £12.99 can be used as a base to determine target buying prices for the retailer. The example in Table 7.2 shows how with a starting price of £12.99 the target retailer buying price or manufacturer selling price is determined.

Similarly, the manufacturer may then use the selling price of £3.87 as a target to challenge designers, pattern cutters and production staff achieve certain economies. In practice, many large UK retailers work very closely with manufacturers to decide prices that

这些方法依赖于对消费价格敏感度和认识水平的充分了解。例如市场研究表明，如果一件连帽棉质紧身内衣按 12.99 英镑定价（含增值税），那么某些目标市场上的购买者会作出积极的反应。如果零售商有较强的购买力，那么 12.99 英镑的零售价格就可以看作是确定目标市场中零售商采购价格的基础。表 7–2 中的例子说明的是以 12.99 英镑为基点，如何确定目标市场零售商的进价和制造商的售价。

同样，生产商可能使用 3.87 英镑的销售价作为目标挑战设计师、样品制作师和生产人员来实现经济效益。在实际操作中，英国许多大的零售商与制造商都有着紧密的联系，试图使定价与消费

attempt to match consumer expectations.

者的期望相符。

7.6.3 A comparison of markups and markdowns / 利润成本比率和利润售价比率的对照

A markup is where profit is expressed as a percentage of costs and it is shown by the following formula:

$$\frac{(\text{Price}-\text{Cost})}{\text{Cost}}\times 100$$

Thus a selling price of £30 with a cost of £20 gives a markup of 50%.

A markdown is where profit is expressed as a percentage of the sale price and it is shown by the following formula:

$$\frac{(\text{Price}-\text{Cost})}{\text{Price}}\times 100$$

Thus a selling price of £30 with a cost of £20 gives a markdown of 1/3.

Different firms use different approaches to calculate profit and selling price. However, all are variants of either a markup or a markdown. Indeed, knowing one it is easy to express profit in terms of the other. The formulae showing the interrelationship of the two main measures of profit margin are shown in Figure 7.2.

利润成本比率是利润占成本的百分比，用下列公式表示：

$$\frac{\text{利润}}{\text{成本}}\%=\frac{\text{售价}-\text{成本}}{\text{成本}}\times 100\%$$

因此，30 英镑的销售价格，20 英镑的成本，产生的利润占成本的 50%。

利润售价比率是利润占销售价格的百分比，用下列公式表示：

$$\frac{\text{利润}}{\text{售价}}\%=\frac{\text{售价}-\text{成本}}{\text{售价}}\times 100\%$$

因此，30 英镑的销售价格，20 英镑的成本，产生的利润占售价的 1/3。

这是企业使用两种不同的方法来计算利润。然而，所有方法都是衡量利润的变量。实际上，知道其中一个数据就能很容易地算出另一个数据。下面的公式表明了衡量利润的两个主要变量的关系，如图 7–2 所示。

$$\%\ \text{markdown on selling price}=\frac{\%\ \text{markup on cost}}{100\%+\text{markup on cost}}\times 100 \qquad \text{利润售价比率}=\frac{\text{利润成本比率}}{100\%+\text{利润成本比率}}\times 100\%$$

$$\%\ \text{markup on cost}=\frac{\%\ \text{markdown on selling price}}{100\%-\%\ \text{markdown on selling price}}\times 100 \qquad \text{利润成本比率}=\frac{\text{利润售价比率}}{100\%-\text{利润成本比率}}\times 100\%$$

Figure 7.2 Markup and markdown formulae. 图 7–2 利润成本比率和利润售价比率公式

Using the above formulae we can see that, for example, a markup on cost of 50% is the same as a markdown on selling price of 1/3.

Sometimes fashion retailers use a simple formula to calculate a retail selling price, including VAT, given a particular quotation from a manufacturer. The retailer wanting a markup of 120% and knowing that VAT is charged at 17.5% may simply multiply the quoted cost price, excluding VAT, by 1.375 to arrive at a tax inclusive retail selling price.

采用上述公式我们可以知道，分别按 50% 的成本利润率和 1/3 的销售利润率来计算利润得出的结果是相同的。

有时候当时装零售商从制造商那里获得一个详细的报价，他就会采用一个简单的公式来计算出包含增值税的零售价格。零售商希望 120% 的利润—成本比率并且知道需征收 17.5% 的增值税，那么就可以简单地用 1.375（120%+17.5%）乘以不含增值税的成本价格，得到的则会是一个含税的零售价格。

7.6.4 Discounts / 折扣

The issue of margins leads naturally into a discussion of the purpose and types of discounts that are offered. The principle of economies of scale applies by which both buyer and seller recognize that larger quantities enjoy larger discounts. For the manufacturer, selling large quantities to fewer buyers means lower delivery and other overhead costs. Retailers naturally appreciate such advantages for both manufacturers and wholesalers and will press within negotiations for the largest quantity discounts possible.

利润的问题很自然地引出了折扣用途和折扣种类的讨论，采购商和销售商同时认识到规模经济的原理并提出了大批购买产品可享有较大的折扣。对于制造商来说，向少数采购商出售大量的商品，运费和其他管理成本都会很低。零售商自然会认同低成本给制造商和批发商带来的优势，并且会在谈判时尽可能地要求最大的折扣。

Variations on the simple quantity discount are the cumulative and non-cumulative discounts available. Some negotiations may result in extra discounts becoming available should the buyer purchase certain minimum quantities over a fixed period, say one year. This extra discount may then become available as a rebate or credit against future purchases. The main aim of cumulative discounts is for the seller to encourage loyalty to the supplier and to induce small buyers to purchase more.

单一数量折扣的变量可用的有累积折扣数量和非累积数量折扣。如果采购商在固定的时期比如一年内会购买至少多少数量的产品时，在协商的时候就可以获得额外的折扣，这个额外的折扣是将来可享受购货折扣以及信用的保证。累计数量折扣的主要目的是销售商鼓励供应商的忠诚度并吸引较小的采购商购买更多的商品。

At the consumer level the retailer may encourage a customer to buy a jacket and a skirt, for example, by offering 10% off one item if both are purchased simultaneously. This type of discounting at the retail level operates erratically and is usually offered by the small outlets to tempt those potential consumers who are vacillating about a purchase.

从消费者角度看，零售商可以鼓励其购买一件夹克和一件衬衣，例如同时购买两件商品，每件商品提供 10% 的降价。这种非累计数量折扣形式在零售方面具有变动性，通常都是一些小型销售商用于吸引那些购买时犹豫不决的消费者时采用的。

Another common form of discount is the cash discount. Business to business discounts of this form usually take the form of a percentage reduction if payment is made within a fixed, usually short period. For example, 1.5% discount may be offered if payment is received within 30 days. Changes in legislation in the UK now allow retailers to charge different prices to consumers depending on the method of payment, be it cash or cheque versus a credit card payment. The obvious benefit for the retailer of a cash payment is improved cash flow and the avoidance of a payment of between 2% and 5% to the credit card company. The incidence of differential prices has yet to become widespread and, owing to the different charges levied by the credit card companies, is most likely only to be favoured by the small retailers.

另一种常见的折扣形式是现金折扣。如果在特定的期限，通常是短期内付款的话，商家对商家的折扣通常就会采用百分比降价的方法。例如：如果 30 天内收到货款，那么可提供 1.5% 的折扣。英国的立法调整之后，现在允许零售商根据付款方式的不同制定不同的价格，付款方式有现金支付、支票支付、信用卡支付，现金支付的好处是可以改善零售商的现金流并避免支付信用卡公司 2% ~ 5% 的手续费。很多销售商采用不同定价，由于信用卡公司会收取不同的费用，因此只有一些较小的零售商才会允许信用卡付款。

7.6.5 Break-even calculations / 盈亏平衡的计算

A central concern of marketing personnel in the fashion industry is balancing the relationship between price and volume. For example, a clothing manufacturer may manufacture 20 000 skirts and wish to know how many must be sold to cover costs. In other words, at what point will the manufacturer break even and begin to earn profits? The first example assumes the manufacturer is in a relationship where prices are fixed by fierce competitive pressures and tough negotiating from retail buyers.

时装行业中的营销人员最关注的是平衡价格和销量之间的关系。例如，时装生产商生产 20000 件衬衫并且希望知道卖出多少件可以赚回成本，也就是说，制造商在哪一点上可以达到盈亏平衡并开始盈利？这个例子是制造商在零售采购商激烈的竞争压力与艰苦的谈判中确定价格的基本前提。

Alternatively, a designer who owns a retail outlet may have considerable discretion over price levels, but wonder about the profitability of the different volumes that could be sold at different prices. Break-even analysis is a technique that can help decision-making needs in the two examples just given.

另外一个例子是，拥有一家零售店的设计师对定价有一定的判断力，但对以不同价格出售的不同销量的产品的获利情况有点疑惑。在前面刚给出的两个例子中，盈亏平衡分析法在决策时是非常有益的一种技巧。

Break-even analysis is an aid that can show the relationship between fixed costs, variable or marginal costs, total costs, sales revenue and output or volume. Fixed costs are those costs incurred by the fashion company that do not change as the volume of purchases or production changes. Some examples of fixed costs include business rates, purchase of a computer for wages and salaries for security staff. In practice, many fixed costs are variable in the long term, such as costs of plant for manufacturing. If these variations can be set aside, then a simple technique that can give a fairly sound guide to setting price level can be found in break-even analysis.

通过盈亏平衡分析可以体现固定成本、变量或边际成本、总成本、销售收入和产量或销量的关系。固定成本是时装公司产生的成本，不会因为采购量的多少或者生产的变化而变化。固定成本包括营业税、购买计算机的投入和保安人员的工资等。实际上固定成本在较长的一段时期内是变化的，例如工厂的制造成本。如果不考虑这些变量，那么在盈亏平衡分析中就会发现一种设定价格的简单方法。

Variable costs are those costs that are directly affected by the level of output; some examples are the amount of material used, the direct labour costs in pattern cutting, making up and tailoring, and packaging costs. Total costs are the sum of fixed costs plus variable cost per unit multiplied by the output or volume. Sales revenue is simply price multiplied by volume sold. In practice, the price taken for the calculations is one that is exclusive of VAT.

变动成本是那些直接受到产量水平影响的成本，例如材料用量，在裁剪和缝制时的直接劳动力成本以及包装成本。总成本是固定成本加上每单位变动成本乘以产量或销量，销售收入仅是价格乘以销量。在实际计算中采用的价格是不包括增值税的价格。

The formula that shows the relationship between the above variables is as follows:

$$\begin{aligned}\text{Revenue} &= \text{Price} \times \text{Volume} \\ &= \text{Total costs} + \text{Profit} \qquad (7.1)\end{aligned}$$

When revenue is less than total costs, a loss (or negative profit) will result.

如下公式表明了上述变量之间的关系：

$$\begin{aligned}\text{收入} &= \text{价格} \times \text{销量} \\ &= \text{总成本} + \text{利润} \qquad (7\text{–}1)\end{aligned}$$

当收入少于总成本时，就会亏本（或负盈利）。其中：

Where

Total costs = Fixed costs + (Variable cost per unit × Volume)

and

Profit = Profit per unit × Volume

At the break-even point, no profit is earned and all costs are covered by sales revenue. Hence

Revenue = Fixed costs + (Variable cost per unit × Volume)

or

Price × Volume = Fixed costs + (Variable cost per unit × Volume)

To determine the break-even point we can do some simple simultaneous equations where

FC = Fixed costs

VC = Variable cost per unit

V = Volume

P= Price

Thus we know that at the break-even point:

$$(P \times V) = FC + (VC \times V)$$

By taking (VC × V) from each side of the equation we get:

$$(P \times V) - (VC \times V) = FC$$

which, when simplified is:

$$V \times (P - VC) = FC$$

Next divide both sides of the equation by (P–VC):

$$V = \frac{FC}{(P-VC)} \qquad (7.2)$$

Of course (P–VC) is really the gross profit per unit.

To calculate the break-even volume, we divide the fixed costs by the difference between the price and the variable cost per unit.

If we wished to know the minimum price at which all the output was sold and covered all costs, i.e. the break-even price point, the formula is calculated as follows:

We know that at the break-even point:

$$(P \times V) = FC + (VC \times V)$$

If we divide each side by V we get:

$$P = \frac{FC}{V} + VC \qquad (7.3)$$

The value given here for price is the minimum that must be charged if the entire volume is sold and no profit is earned. In practice, a seller would wish to charge higher prices and earn some profit. The formula does at least help to establish a baseline for making pricing decisions.

总成本＝固定成本＋(单位变动成本×产量)

利润＝单位利润×销量

在盈亏平衡点上，没有赢得利润并且所有成本都包括在销售收入中，因此：

收入＝固定成本＋(单位变动成本×产量)

或

价格×销量＝固定成本＋(单位变动成本×产量)

为了确定盈亏平衡点，我们可以做一些简单的联立方程式，其中：

FC＝固定成本

VC＝单位变动成本

V＝数量（产量/销量）

P＝价格

因此，在盈亏平衡点上我们知道：

$$P \times V = FC + (VC \times V)$$

通过对方程的两边移动 $(VC \times V)$，我们得到：

$$P \times V - (VC \times V) = FC$$

可以简化为：

$$V \times (P - VC) = FC$$

方程的两边同时除以（$P-VC$）：

$$V = \frac{FC}{P-VC} \qquad (7\text{–}2)$$

当然，（$P-VC$）实际上是单位毛利润。

为了计算盈亏平衡值，我们通过固定成本除以价格和每单位变动成本之间的差来计算。

如果我们希望得到卖出了所有产品且包含了所有成本的最低价格，即盈亏平衡价格点，则按如下公式计算：

我们知道，在盈亏平衡点处：

$$P \times V = FC + (VC \times V)$$

如果两边同除以V，我们得到：

$$P = \frac{FC}{V} + VC \qquad (7\text{–}3)$$

如果卖掉所有产品且无利可得，这里给出的价格值就是定价的最小值。实际上，销售者都希望定高价并且获取利润。

以上公式至少有助于为定价设定一个底线。

7.6.6 Break-even analysis: an example / 一个盈亏平衡分析实例

A small retailer of knitwear in a franchise operation may have rental and other fixed costs amounting to £45 000 per annum. If 3000 items of stock for resale are purchased per year at say £16 each (excluding VAT), then the total variable cost is £48 000. Assume here that the sales assistants are paid a fixed wage of £45 000 that is included in the fixed costs. If sales assistants were paid a commission for each item of knitwear sold, then this would be a variable cost and would have to be added to the purchase cost per item. Thus the total costs for the knitwear retailer are £45 000 fixed costs plus £48 000 variable costs, giving £93 000 per annum.

一个拥有针织品特许经营权的小零售商在经营中每年会需要45000英镑的租金和其他固定成本，如果每年以每件16英镑（不含增值税）的价格购买3000件待售的商品，那么总的变动成本是48000英镑。假设支付售货员45000英镑的固定工资（包括在固定成本中），如果需要支付售货员卖掉针织商品的佣金，那么这将成为变动成本，而且需要算在每件商品的进货成本中。因此针织品零售商的总成本将是45000英镑的固定成本加上48000英镑的变动成本，即每年需93000英镑。

If the knitwear retailer wishes to calculate the minimum price that must be charged to cover costs and sell all the garments then formula (7.3) must be used:

如果针织品零售商希望计算最低的能够覆盖成本的价格，并且卖出所有的衣服，那么必须用到公式7-3：

$$P=\frac{FC}{V}+VC$$

Substituting we get:

代入数值后，得到：

$$P=\frac{45000}{3000}+16$$

Therefore, if a price of £31 (plus VAT) per unit was charged the business would break even.

因此，如果每件商品卖31英镑（加上增值税），那么就会达到盈亏平衡。

If the retailer, after undertaking market research into competitors' prices, wishes to charge £39.95 (including VAT) per item, the question is now to determine the minimum number that must be sold to break even. A price of £39.95, including VAT at 17.5%, gives a VAT exclusive price of £34.00.

如果零售商调查了竞争对手的价格之后，希望每件商品卖出39.95英镑（包括增值税），那么就可以确定达到盈亏平衡的最低卖价了，39.95英镑的价格包括17.5%的增值税，去除增值税后是34.00英镑。

Formula (7.2) is used to calculate the break-even volume, thus:

公式7-2用来计算盈亏平衡的数量，那么

$$V=\frac{FC}{P-VC}$$

Substituting values we get:

代入数值后，得到：

$$V=\frac{45000}{34-16}$$

which gives a volume of 2500 units to break even.

这里计算出的是2500件的销量就可以达到盈亏平衡。

If the retailer sells all 3000 garments then if the original formula (7.1) is used:

如果零售商全部卖掉3000件衣服，那么用最初的公式7-1：

$$\begin{aligned}\text{Revenue} &= \text{Price} \times \text{Volume} \\ &= \text{Total costs} + \text{Profit} \qquad (7.1) \\ 34 \times 3000 &= 45\,000 + (16 \times 3000) + \text{Profit} \\ 102\,000 &= 45\,000 + 48\,000 + \text{Profit}\end{aligned}$$

Thus the profit earned is £9000 or 8.82% of sales revenue.

$$\begin{aligned}\text{收入} &= \text{价格} \times \text{销售} \\ &= \text{总成本} + \text{利润} \\ 34 \times 3000 &= 45000 + (16 \times 3000) + \text{利润} \\ 102000 &= 45000 + 48000 + \text{利润}\end{aligned}$$

因此，赢得的利润是 9000 英镑或销售收入的 8.82%。

7.7 Pricing strategies in relation to new products ／新产品的定价策略

The pricing objectives derived from a marketing strategy in relation to new products are to achieve growth, maximize profitability or generate cash flow. The crucial decisions to be made prior to selecting a pricing strategy are the identification of the target market(s) and careful consideration of the other elements of the marketing mix.

营销策略中有关新产品定价的目标是实现销量增长，收益最大化或产生现金流。选择定价策略最关键的方面是了解目标市场并且仔细考虑营销组合的其他要素。

7.7.1 Market skimming ／撇脂定价法

This strategy is to charge high initial prices and then only reduce them gradually, if at all. A skimming price policy is a form of price discrimination over time and for it to be effective several conditions must be met.

First, the demand for the garments must be relatively inelastic. Inelastic demand only really exists for essential items that are in short supply or items that have a degree of exclusivity and a significant number of buyers who are relatively unconcerned about price. A limited edition luxury handbag by Furla would be an example of such an item. For the supplier the unit costs of producing a small volume must not be too high. Finally, the high-profit margins on each item in a skimming policy will attract competitors unless the seller can protect the garments from being copied. Such a situation usually applies to haute couture and to a lesser degree to designer ready-to-wear ranges.

这个策略是指产品上市初期先出高价，然后逐渐地降低价格。撇脂定价是一种随着时间调整的策略，要使其产生应有的效果必须满足以下几个条件。首先，市场对时装的需求必须相对稳定，无弹性需求仅存在于必需品中，这些商品供不应求或具有一定的独特性并有相当数量的买方且不在乎价格，芙拉限量版的休闲手袋就是这种商品的一个例子。对于供应商来说,生产少量产品的单位成本不能太高。最终，撇脂定价中每件商品的高额边际利润将会吸引竞争对手的加入，除非卖方有能力保护自己的产品不被仿制，这种情况通常会用到高级时装上，有时也会用于设计师系列产品的定价。

7.7.2 Market penetration ／渗透定价法

This strategy is the opposite of market skimming and aims to try to capture a large market share by charging low prices. The low prices charged stimulate purchases and can discourage competitors from entering the market as the profit margins per item are low. To be effective this policy relies upon considerable economies of scale in either manufacture or retailing or both. It also depends upon potential customers being

这是与撇脂定价相反的一种策略，旨在通过较低价格占领较大的市场份额。因为低定价时每件商品的利润都很低，因此能够刺激购买并且阻碍竞争对手进入市场。为了发挥这种方法的作用，生产商或零售商或两者都必须具有相当可观的规模经济，这同时也取决于那些对

price sensitive about the particular item and perhaps not perceiving much difference between brands. An example of this sort of policy may be seen in the plain 15 denier tights sold in supermarkets.

特殊商品的价格较为敏感且不在乎品牌差异的潜在客户，例如超级市场销售的15旦尼尔的平纹紧身衣裤。

7.8 Pricing strategies to match the competition ／参照竞争者定价的策略

Pricing objectives in relation to the competition include, as both active and reactive positions, an attempt to maintain price leadership, to stabilize prices or to discourage others from entering the particular market. Such strategies may also be linked to objectives concerned with building and maintaining the loyalty of other parts of the distribution chain. Aiming for stable prices while recognizing the traditional margins in the channels of distribution are the characteristics of the marketing activities of many fashion marketing companies.

与竞争相关联的定价目标包括主动地位和被动地位，试图将价格保持在领先者水平、稳定价格或阻碍其他价格者进入市场，这种策略和在其他销售渠道建立和维护消费者的忠诚度也有关系。需要时装公司在营销活动中了解分销渠道惯常的边际利润这一特征，进而同步设定稳定的价格。

7.8.1 Price leaders and followers ／价格领先者和价格追随者

In the case of the follower, the firm identifies a target market and sets prices in line with competitors who are serving the same market. A firm with limited marketing resources may simply shadow a competitor. Within fashion retailing it is quite common for sales assistants to visit other stores to monitor the price points for garments and accessories. Monitoring the competition is an essential part of any market research, but slavishly aping one's rivals' actions without a clear long-term goal is another matter. The leader in such a situation is usually the firm with the lowest costs and best profit margins. Followers hope to avoid a price war by stressing non-price aspects of competition such as a higher customer service level.

对于价格追随者，企业识别目标市场并按照服务于相同市场的竞争对手的价格确定价格，那些营销资源有限的企业可以简单地追踪竞争对手的定价。在时装零售领域，售货员通常会进入其他店铺了解时装和配饰品的价格，这是非常普遍的现象。在任何市场调研活动中，监视竞争对手情况都是非常重要的内容。但是也会出现一些企业原原本本地模仿竞争对手，没有一个清晰的长期目标，这会成为企业发展的一个瓶颈，这种情况下的领先者通常是拥有着最低成本和最高利润，追随者只能通过非价格方面的竞争避免价格战，例如较好的客户服务水平。

Market research may indicate, for example, that a certain income group targeted by the firm is willing to pay between £25 and £35 for a blouse. The same research also may find that the main competitor is pricing similar garments at £29.95. The conclusion may be to charge at the same price or marginally lower, say £29.50. Such a policy of price matching can avoid a price war while maintaining profit margins. The policy of matching the competition is particularly vulnerable to enterprising newcomers to the market who may

市场调研表明，例如收入确定的目标市场中的消费者希望花 25 英镑到 35 英镑买一件衬衣，同样的调研也可以发现，主要的竞争者通常会以 29.95 英镑给类似的时装定价，结果企业是按同样的价格卖出或者以 29.5 英镑的价格卖出而获得较低的利润。这样的价格策略可以避免一场价格战，而且确保了利润。

be able to upset the cosy reassurance that sometimes emerges in some sectors. An economic downturn with pressures on margins or the slow sales on some product lines can easily render this policy susceptible to change.

参照竞争对手定价容易使一些刚进入市场的新手利益受损，他们有时能够削弱某个行业发展的信心。在某些产品线中利润压缩或销售缓慢导致的经济低迷会轻易地影响这个策略而使其发生变化。

The large retail groups may incorporate an element of matching the competition within an overall pricing strategy, by allowing local managers some discretion in meeting local competition by adjusting prices where necessary.

大型零售集团可以在整个定价体系中引入一些方法来与竞争者相抗衡，例如允许当地经营者在需要的时候自行调整价格以应对同城竞争。

7.8.2 Price fixing / 限价

Overt or covert price fixing by sellers is illegal in the European Union (EU) and most western nations unless a defence can be made that such action is not against the public interest. Manufacturers are, in the main, prohibited from imposing retail prices upon retailers in the UK, and this is known as retail price maintenance. Manufacturers are sometimes able to use pressure relating to the supply or withholding of products or financial incentives to exert influence over retail prices and effectively inhibit competition. The EU has an aim of free movement of goods within and between the member states and the intense competition within the fashion market works strongly against price fixing tendencies. However, in 1993, the French perfume industry was able to claim a victory in the European Court by winning the right to exclusive distribution of perfumes, thereby protecting the margins of outlets against the so-called grey imports. In 2001, the battle over exclusivity and free competition in the setting of prices continued with a legal case between Tesco, the supermarket group, and Levi Strauss(Levi's) over the distribution and pricing of jeans in the UK with Levi Strauss winning the case for exclusive distribution. However, there are strong pressures with the EU to review legislation in line with WTO principles of free trade. The role of online purchasing in international trade is another factor that is undermining the ability of retailers to control prices via exclusive distribution.

在欧盟和大多数西方国家，公开或者隐性限价是违法的，除非制定一个保护措施使这种行为不危害公众利益。一般而言，英国禁止生产商对零售商限定零售价格，也就是众所周知的零售价格保护。制造商有时能够利用供给压力、扣留商品或财政刺激来给零售商施加影响，从而有效地抑制竞争。欧盟有一个目标就是希望商品可以在成员国内或在成员国之间自由流通，然而时装市场的激烈竞争却抑制了限价的势头。在 1993 年，法国香水业在欧洲法院以赢得了香水业独家销售的权利胜诉，以此保护了店铺的利润来打击所谓的水货。2001 年，专营权和自由竞争之战可以通过一个案例来说明。乐购是一家大型超市，其与李维斯之间因为牛仔裤的经销和定价而产生了争议，李维斯最终赢得了独家分销权。然而，根据世界贸易组织的自由贸易原则来审查立法的话，欧盟会面临很大的压力。在国际贸易中，网上购物成为削弱零售商通过独家分销权控制价格的又一个因素。

7.9 Price changes / 价格变动

Prices for clothing may need to change for a variety of reasons, but the administration and communication of those changes are important matters that can affect profits greatly. An overview of price changes is given

时装价格可能会因为各种原因而变动，但是那些变动的实施和沟通却会极大地影响利润。图 7–3 给出了价格变化

in Figure 7.3. Prices can increase because of higher costs, rising inflation, excess demand for the product or simply a misjudgement of prior price levels.

的情况，价格提升可能源于较高的成本、不断的通货膨胀、对产品的过量需求或先前设定价格水平时小小的失误。

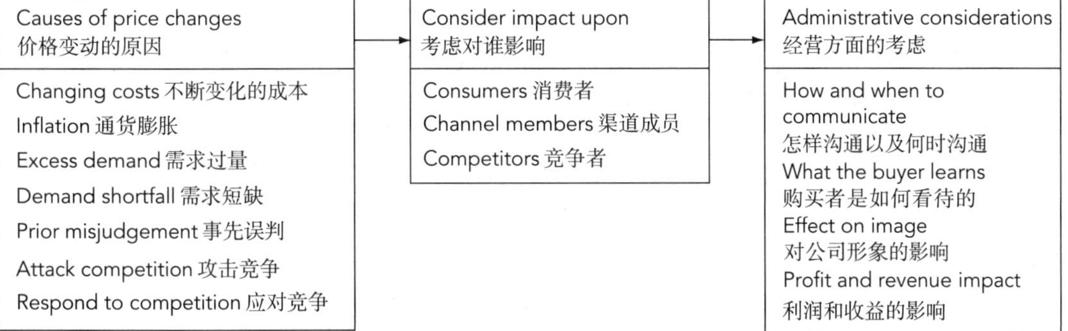

Figure 7.3 Price changes. 图 7–3 价格变动

Decreases in price can be attempts to drive out or meet competitors, to take advantage of lower costs or to generate more demand. As fashion is about change, garment prices usually fall over time. The only exceptions seem to be rare items previously owned by celebrities or clothing in short supply that is identified with a fast emerging cult.

Whatever the cause of the price change, it will affect customers, competitors and other members of the distribution channel. The uncertainty that accompanies the potential effect of any price change means that research and planning are essential. Buyer responses to price changes can be varied. For reductions, many may perceive the items to be end-of-season, unpopular, faulty or of lower quality. It also may be that buyers resist initial price reductions in anticipation of further falls. Price increases are only popular with those who bought at a lower price. Increases can signal that the product may soon be unavailable or that it represented good value for money with very low margins at the old price.

All price changes, when clearly marked, can attract attention and raise buyers' price awareness levels so that purchase values may then be reconsidered. As noted in Chapter Three, the concept of learning is important as price changes 'teach' consumers what to expect. Thus, if a store always marks items down by 20% after eight weeks, then a further 20% after another two weeks, some consumers will learn not

降价有可能将竞争对手驱逐或者与竞争者相抗衡，同时获得低成本的优势或者引发更多的需求。时尚通常是变化的，随着时间的变化时装价格也会降低。唯一的例外是社会名流最先拥有的稀有物品或者快速兴起的供应量少的时装。

无论价格变动的原因是什么，都会影响消费者、竞争对手和销售渠道的其他成员。伴随着价格变动潜在影响的不确定性，企业必须进行调研并且制定计划。买方对于价格变动的反应可能会多种多样，对于降价，许多人可能会理解为商品已过季、不受欢迎、有瑕疵或者质量差，买方也可能会预计到进一步降价而不接受早期的降价。那些低价购买商品的人们能够接受物价上涨，价格上涨体现的是产品很难买到或者物有所值，或按之前的价格销售的话只能获得很低的利润。

当清楚地标出价格变动时，就能吸引公众的注意力并且提高购买者的价格意识，购买者就会重新考虑购买价值。正如第 3 章所述，学习的理念很重要，因为价格变动教会了消费者期待什么。因此，如果一个商店总是在 8 周后标出商品降价 20%，再 2 周后又降价

to pay higher prices. The cycle of price reductions can therefore become reinforced as more people in the target market learn to avoid paying the premium prices.

The communication to consumers of price changes requires particular consideration. Changes promoted as 'massive reductions' can alienate those customers who paid higher initial prices, while simultaneously attracting the bargain hunters the supplier is seeking. How price changes are communicated depends upon the marketing objectives of the firm and the target markets being served. Indeed some target markets are defined by bargaining pricing as shown in Figure 7.4; the drawback of this for the fashion marketer is that loyalty is hard to engender with this type of customer. Announcing large clearance discounts in a sale in an outlet catering for higher income groups may be inconsistent with other aspects of the image. However, when the change is announced, it is imperative that the sales staff and customers are in no doubt what price is to be charged and when the change takes effect. Much damage to customer goodwill can be done by lack of care in announcing price changes. Given the practices of a minority of unscrupulous retailers, many consumers approach sales with a healthy degree of scepticism. Thus care is needed to avoid a small oversight being construed as a deliberate attempt to mislead.

20%，一些消费者就知道不需要高价购买商品了。当目标市场上的大多数人都学会了避免高价购买的时候，降价就会愈演愈烈。

企业需要特别重视向消费者传递价格变动的信息，“大幅度降价”的促销推广可能会疏远那些支付较高初始价格的消费者，同时会吸引供应商寻求的买便宜货的人。如何传递价格变动信息取决于企业的销售目标以及寻求的目标市场。的确，一些目标市场是根据交易价格来确定的，如图 7–4 所示。对时装经营者来说，这种方法的缺点是很难促使这些消费者产生忠诚度。在店铺进行的清仓折扣促销迎合了较低收入群体的需求，但反过来却会影响企业的形象。然而，在公布价格变动的时候，销售人员和消费者都不用考虑定价会是多少以及什么时候进行价格调整。在宣布价格变动时如果不顾及消费者的意愿，那么可能会给消费者带来负面影响。鉴于极少数肆无忌惮的零售商的实际行动，许多消费者会以一种理性的怀疑态度看待促销，因此，企业需要小心以避免小的疏忽被理解成为蓄意的误导。

Figure 7.4 Example of retail discounts. 图 7–4 零售折扣案例

7.10 Summary / 小结

This chapter has considered price, both as a concept and in the context of the marketplace in relation to the other elements of the fashion marketing mix.

本章从价格的概念以及内涵上阐述了市场价格与服装营销组合中其他要素间的关系。

Pricing decisions are:

◆ subject to a wide variety of influencing factors, internal and external;

◆ a strategic matter, and not to be approached in a short-term reactive way;

◆ to be made within the wider framework of a clear understanding of the target market, the firm's overall marketing strategy and the competition.

定价是:

◆ 受内部和外部种种因素影响的;

◆ 一个战略问题，难以按照短期的被动方式解决;

◆ 在清楚了解目标市场、企业整体营销策略和竞争情况的宽泛体系内进行。

Further reading / 课后阅读资料

1.Baker, R.J. (2006), *Pricing on Purpose: Creating and Capturing Value*, John Wiley and Sons, NJ.

贝克・R.J.(2006),《定价目标:创造与获取价值》，约翰威利父子出版社，新泽西.

2.Cram, T. (2006), *Smarter Pricing: How to Capture More Value in Your Market*, Pearson Education Ltd, Harlow.

克瑞姆・T. (2006),《精明的定价:如何在市场中夺得更高的价值》，培生教育出版集团，哈洛.

3.Cravens, D.W. and Piercy, N. (2005), *Strategic Marketing*, 9th Edition, McGraw-Hill, London.

克莱文斯・D.W.，皮尔斯・N. (2005),《策略营销》，第 9 版，麦克格劳希尔集团出版社，伦敦.

4.Nagle, T.T. and Hogan, J.E. (2007), *The Strategy and Tactics of Pricing: A Guide to Growing More Profitably*, 4th Edition, Pearson Education, London.

纳格・T.T.，霍根・J.E. (2007),《定价战略与战术:利润倍增指南》，第 4 版，培生教育出版集团，伦敦.

5.Ruskin-Brown, I. (2007), *Practical Pricing for Results*, Thorogood, London.

如斯肯－布朗・I.(2007),《实战定价成果》，萨尔古德出版社，伦敦.

Chapter Eight Fashion Distribution
第 8 章 时装分销

8.1 Introduction ／引言

This chapter examines the retail sector which for many people is the 'face of fashion', describing the structure of the industry and its constituent parts, and includes an outline of recent developments. It concludes with a brief examination of criteria against which retail marketing effectiveness can be judged. The large-scale retailers are all involved in marketing activities and most have specialist marketing departments.

本章探讨对许多人来说是“时尚的脸面”的零售界，描述行业结构及其组成部分，还包括规划近期的发展纲领。最后提出简单的可以判断零售营销效益的标准。大型的零售商都会参与营销活动，而且多数都有专门的营销部门。

8.2 The importance of fashion retailing ／时装零售的重要性

The retail industry is important to the marketing of fashion clothing in a number of ways. First, and most obviously, it is the mechanism through which the clothes reach the consumer.

Secondly, with the growth in applying information technology, it is also able to provide, within hours at most, detailed feedback of what the consumer is buying. This allows changes in the marketplace to be quickly assessed, thus helping range renewal, particularly in such areas as replacement sizes and colours. Benetton has the tills of all its shops linked directly to its marketing and design departments as well as to its dyeing facilities so that changes in demand can be quickly observed and production changed accordingly.

在很多方面，零售业对时装营销都是很重要的。

首先，也是最明显的是，它是通过一种方式将时装传递给消费者的。

其次，随着信息技术应用的普及，在短短的几小时内通过零售就可以得到消费者对于所购商品的反馈意见，这使得企业能够对市场变化快速地作出评估，从而有助于重新调整产品系列，尤其是尺寸和颜色的调整。贝纳通将所有的店铺和营销部门、设计部门以及染整机构相关联，从而快速地注意到需求的变化并且相应调整生产。

Thirdly, it facilitates the application of target marketing (see Chapter Five).

Fourthly, it has been active in the promotion of design awareness to the shopping public, two well-known examples being Habitat and Next, in terms of product design and store layout and equipment. Design also serves to promote market segmentation and to improve sales and productivity ratios in relation to increasingly expensive selling space.

Fifthly, manufacturers and designers can achieve stability by owning their own retail units. As Paul Smith has said of his retail side, 'it is a regular earner for us' (*Independent*, 9 August 1993, p. 19).

Finally, the retail outlet through its store image can create loyal customers who may provide a measure of stability in sales income and profits. A 1999 Verdict Clothing Report indicated that 86% of main users prefer their current main store, and that loyalty was highest in the south of England.

What goes into creating a store image? Various writers have offered suggestions, and Lindquist reviewed many studies and synthesized the following from them – merchandise, service, store atmosphere, promotion, clientèle, physical facilities, institutional factors and post-purchase satisfaction. Physical environment is an important influence on image, as Mary Jo Bitner (1992) outlines in a journal article. The main components of store image are shown in Figure 8.1.

Another factor in building store loyalty has been the introduction of store-based credit cards, which in addition to encouraging sales afford opportunities

第三，它可以帮助企业识别目标市场（详见第 5 章）。

第四，零售对公众购物的设计意识有提升作用，最著名的两个例子就是哈贝塔和奈克斯特的产品设计、店铺陈列和展示道具。设计也有助于市场细分，提高销售额和生产率，这些和逐步增长的高价品的销售空间有关。

第五，制造商和设计师因为拥有属于自己的零售部门，所以相对较为稳定。就像保罗·史密斯所形容的零售终端："这是我们固定收入的来源。"（独立杂志，1993 年 8 月 9 日，第 19 页）

最后，零售店可以通过店铺形象逐步积累忠诚的客户，零售店在销售收入和利润上具有稳定性。一份 1999 年的时装报告显示，86%的用户喜欢他们目前常去的店铺，而且英格兰南部消费者的忠诚度最高。

建立店铺形象考虑什么方面呢？各位作者提出了建议，林奎斯特审查了许多研究成果之后将其总结如下：商品、服务水平、店铺氛围、促销、客户、配套设施、制度因素以及购买后的满意度。如玛丽·乔·比特纳（1992 年）在期刊论文中所描述的，环境是影响店铺形象最主要的因素。店铺形象的主要组成要素见图 8–1。

另一个形成店铺忠诚度的因素是店铺推出的信用卡结算服务，除了鼓励销售

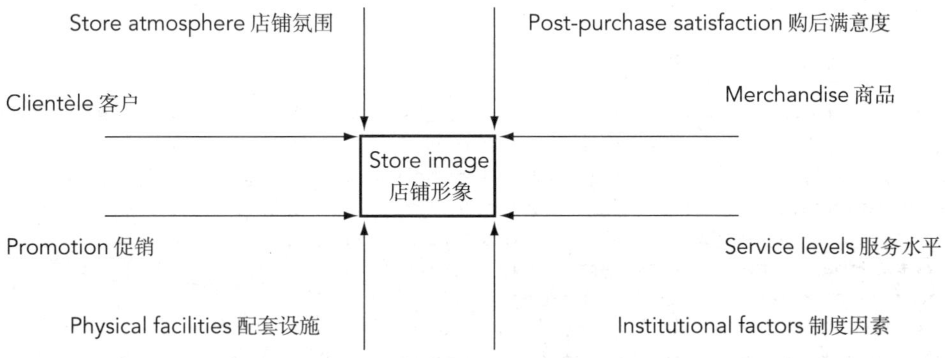

Figure 8.1 Components of store image. 图 8–1 店铺形象的组成要素

for database marketing. The Bhs Gold Card is one example and the Recognition FraserCard with more than 1 million cardholders is another.

以外还可以提供数据库营销的机会。Bhs 百货公司的金卡就是一个例子，另外一个例子是有 100 多万人持有佛雷泽卡。

Such is the importance of store image that some manufacturers and designers actively strive to be represented in certain stores. This, alongside other issues such as reliability, cost, stockholding capabilities and coverage of the market sought, is a major consideration in channel management.

这就是店铺形象的重要性，因此一些制造商和设计师都在积极努力以成为某类店铺的代表。在渠道管理中店铺形象和可靠性、成本、股权持有量和市场覆盖面等都是需要重点考虑的因素。

8.3 Structural issues ／结构问题

8.3.1 Basic structure ／基本结构

The industry has traditionally been divided into three distinct segments, which have over the years performed differently.

时装业历来都被划分为三种不同的部分，多年来都有着不同的市场表现。

Womenswear, the largest segment, has traditionally shown most growth, and was worth an estimated £31 billion in 2003.

女装是最大的细分市场，增长速度最快，2003 年的产值为 310 亿英镑。

Menswear has shown greater growth than womenswear in recent years as men become more fashion conscious. The men's outerwear market was worth an estimated £6.6 billion in 2004. However, just as it seems to do relatively better than womenswear when the economy is booming, so it seems to suffer greater decline in recessionary times.

近年来男装的增长高于女装，男性也体现出了较强的时尚意识。2004 年男性外套的市场价值大约是 66 亿英镑。然而，在经济蓬勃发展的时候，男装比女装发展相对较快，而在经济衰退期男装则会下滑很快。

Childrenswear is the smallest of the three retail markets, at an estimated £5.0 billion in 2004. In retail fashion terms it is a difficult market to cater for, but in recent years it has seen a growth in specialist retail chains such as Adams and the introduction of continental retail brands such as Chipie and Oilily. As children become more fashion conscious at a younger age, this affords new opportunities at all levels in the retail clothing industry.

童装是三个零售市场中份额最小的，2004 年估计达到了 5 亿英镑。从时装零售来看，童装是一个较难迎合的市场，但是最近几年专卖店连锁却发展很快，像亚当斯以及引入的零售品牌奇比和欧利莱。由于低龄儿童时尚意识的增强，给时装零售行业发展带来了新的机遇。

8.3.2 Concentration ／集中度

In common with other sectors of the retail trade, concentration in the fashion retail market has increased over the years. All three market segments described above are dominated by variety chains and multiples except at the designer level. Clothing retailing in the UK is perhaps most concentrated in the world. The top five companies in both womenswear and menswear account for over 40% of total sales. In the childrenswear market the top five retailers account for over 40% of sales. This has been achieved through

与其他行业的零售贸易相比较，时装零售市场的集中度近几年有了明显的增长。除了设计师主导的企业以外，上面所提及的三类细分市场都受到品种链和跨国公司的控制。英国时装零售业的集中度在全世界应该是最高的，位居前五位男装和女装公司占到总销售额的 40%，在童装市场中前五位零售商的销售额占了 40% 以上的份额，这主要是因

economies of scale, e.g. buying power, promotional spending and managerial expertise.

为规模经济效应产生的，如购买力、促销激励和管理经验。

It has been suggested that customers who want something other than the mass produced and marketed clothes provided by the major retailers will enable a considerable independent sector to thrive. Others point to entrepreneurial flair and ability to cater to local needs as reasons for their continued survival.

有人提议，有一些顾客想要一些不同于大批量生产以及区别于主要零售商销售的时装，这促使了个体店的发展。其他的观点则指出企业的资质和迎合当地需求的能力对其持续性的发展也是有影响的。

In this context those retailers who try to combine an element of exclusivity and the benefits of scale by trading from a limited number of outlets, such as Jigsaw, seem to have done relatively well in recent years.

在这种情况下，那些试图从少量零售终端获取独家经营权和规模效益的零售商近几年发展的相对较好，如拼图女鞋。

Multiple clothing retailers (with 10 or more branches) have over 25% of the market, variety chains slightly less and independents about 15%. Department stores, the last major grouping, have approximately a 7% market share.

拥有 10 余个或更多分公司的时装零售商已经占有了 25% 以上的市场份额，各种连锁店和独立店铺略有下降约占 15%。最后一个主要集团就是百货公司，大约占有 7% 的市场份额。

8.3.3 Numbers of outlets / “奥特莱斯”（品牌直销购物中心）的数量

The Department of Trade and Industry's (DTI) periodic retail enquiry shows a gradual decline in the number of outlets. Though most closures are small retailers, they nonetheless continue to make up the bulk of the specialist outlets. This to some extent is offset by an influx of European and American clothing companies setting up retail outlets in the UK, two examples of which would be Ouiset and The Gap.

贸易和工业部的定期调查显示，零售业“奥特莱斯”数量在逐渐地减少。虽然关闭的大部分是一些较小的零售商，但是它们依然是构成专业店铺不可缺少的部分，这在一定程度上是因为欧洲和美国的时装公司在英国设立了很多的零售“奥特莱斯”，其中的两个例子就是欧伊赛特和盖璞。

The 1996 retail enquiry figures put the number of outlets specializing in one or other of the three markets at 33000.

1996 年的零售调查数据显示，专营男装、女装或者童装的市场中就有 33000 个“奥特莱斯”。

The retail boom of the 1980s also resulted in a large increase in the amount of selling space, particularly in out-of-town locations. It also created greater demand for sites in town centres with Next, for example, taking over Combined English Stores so as to acquire additional prime selling space. There is now an argument for saying that the nation has too many shops, and some reduction in numbers is necessary. The development of non-shop outlets such as the Internet is likely to encourage this trend.

20 世纪 80 年代零售业的繁荣也导致了销售场所数量的快速增长，特别是城市的郊区。这也使得市中心区域产生了大量的需求，例如奈克斯特就接管“英国联合商店”从而获得额外的销售场所。如今有一个争论，那就是英国内的店铺数量太多，有必要减少数量，像非实体店的互联网的时装网店可能有助于店铺数量的减少。

8.3.4 Outlet size / “奥特莱斯”规模

To the extent that clothing retailers and particularly those who serve the upper market levels continue to

在某种程度上，时装零售商，特别是那些服务于高端市场的零售商会继续

trade from established city centre sites, there is limited scope for increasing the size of outlet, though Marks and Spencer did build a fifth floor onto its Marble Arch store.

在市中心设立店铺，但是此区域“奥特莱斯”面积扩大很有限，尽管如此，玛莎百货还是在伦敦的凯旋门建造了5层楼的购物中心。

Moving to out-of-town locations offers the potential for increasing store size but can affect the image of the store. Out-of-town supermarkets with their larger selling areas are offering an increasing range of clothing, much of it is fashion based. Marks and Spencer now has over 40 stores of over 100 000 ft^2 (10 000 m^2).

将店铺迁移到市郊，提供了扩大店铺经营规模的可能性，但会影响店家形象。拥有宽敞销售空间的城郊超大卖场提供了服装销售系列的增加，且增加的大部分都是时尚品，玛莎百货目前已拥有了40多家面积超过1万平方米的店铺。

8.3.5 Import and export ／进出口

In common with other UK industries there is a considerable amount of overseas trade and as in sectors of UK industry the degree of import penetration is high and rising. The value of exports is a small and decreasing fraction of UK imports of clothing.

The reasons for this state of affairs are many and complex and often apply equally to other sectors such as the exchange rate, comparative labour and other costs, together with tariffs and other barriers to trade such as subsidies and quotas. Free trade, that is countries being allowed to buy and sell goods and services worldwide without any restrictions, is theoretically desirable but the international textiles trade, like others, is regulated though less so with the ending of the Multi-Fibre Agreement in 2004, which resulted in a surge of imports from China. A subsequent attempt by the EU to reintroduce quotas in 2005 resulted in many millions of garments being temporarily stuck in European warehouses and many retailers fearing gaps in their product ranges.

与英国其他行业相比较，英国工业部门中海外贸易的进口渗透度较高而且还在增长，而英国的时装出口值很小，大概只有时装进口的一小部分。产生这种状况的原因是多方面的，也是很复杂的，往往体现在诸如汇率，相对劳动力和其他成本上，还有关税和包括补贴和配额的其他贸易壁垒。自由贸易，就是被国家允许的在全球范围内没有任何限制的购买和销售货物以及服务的贸易行为，在理论上这是可行的。不过国际纺织品贸易和其他的贸易一样，都受到一定的管制。在2004年多种纤维协定到期之后，极大地提升了各国从中国的进口量。随后欧盟试图在2005年重新引入配额，其结果是数百万时装被暂时扣留在欧洲的仓库，同时许多零售商也在担心他们产品线的缺口。

8.3.6 Exports ／出口

Exports are mainly restricted to high value and traditional sectors such as knitwear, where cost is less important as retail customers appreciate and are willing to pay for quality and style.

Much of the UK trade in textiles is with the other members of the EU, though the USA and the Far East are important markets. British retailers that expand overseas may provide useful export markets for the manufacturers who supply their UK stores.

出口主要限制了高价品和传统的业务如针织衫，消费者不关注此类产品的成本，愿意为质量和设计支付高价。英国纺织品贸易的大部分交易是与欧盟其他成员进行的，尽管美国和远东地区也是其主要市场，扩张海外市场的英国零售商给那些英国店铺供货的制造商创造了有利的出口市场。

8.3.7 The future for UK clothing firms ／英国时装企业的未来

Under increased pressure from low-cost producers, the British textile industry has steadily declined over the years as retailers have increasingly sought to import their merchandise from low-cost countries, originally in the Far East, particularly China.

多年来在低成本生产商的压力下，零售商越来越希望从低成本的国家进口商品，最早是远东地区，特别是中国，这导致了英国纺织业的发展持续下滑。

However, there is some hope: improvements in technology and manufacturing techniques hold out the possibility of UK manufacturers being able to meet the demands for small-scale production runs. Retailers' increasing reluctance to hold large stocks and consumer pressure towards more diversity and exclusivity encourage the need for small runs and put a premium on a fast flexible response that will tend to help UK-based manufacturers. Just-in-time (JIT) inventory control and a reluctance to commit budgets early in the season also offer the possibility of top-up orders even if the main order is initially placed overseas.

不过还是有一些希望：工艺和制造技术的进步使得英国制造商能够满足市场对少量产品的需求。零售商越来越不愿持有大量库存，在消费者多元化和注重个性的消费需求的压力下，极大地促进了小规模企业的发展，而且因为企业的应变能力更强，这将是有利于英国制造商的。即便主要的订单最初都集中在海外市场，然而即时库存控制以及不情愿在季初提交预算反而给企业提供了追加订单的机会。

Pressure from the dominant retailers has resulted in UK manufacturers increasingly making use of subcontractors, many of which are overseas. An increased emphasis on design is also being placed on the manufacturers, many of whom now have an in-house design capability, though in recessionary times these may be cut back.

来自主要零售商的压力导致了越来越多的英国制造商开始利用分包商，其中许多都是在海外。制造商对产品设计也越来越重视，许多制造商都拥有自己的设计团队，尽管这个团队可能会在经济萧条的时候被撤掉。

8.3.8 Relationships with manufacturers ／与制造商的关系

One option for clothing firms is to operate as both a retailer and a manufacturer, though this is becoming increasingly less attractive. The major disadvantage of this form of vertically structured form of organization is that considerable capital is tied up in manufacturing assets that, because of changing market conditions and increased overseas competition, provide progressively lower rates of return.

时装企业的一个选择就是经营中既可以是零售商，同时也是生产商，虽然这变得越来越缺乏吸引力。这种垂直结构的组织形式最大的缺点是大部分资金都用在了制造资本上，由于市场环境的变化和海外竞争的加剧，由此带来的回报率也在减少。

The major advantages for retailers with their own manufacturing concern were total control of the manufacturing process and security of supply, these advantages have been retained by the major retailers in their dealings with their suppliers because of their dominant role in the marketplace. Often suppliers are almost totally dependent on a particular retailer, who can in return for regular and substantial orders, demand total control over the manufacturing process and enforce narrow profit margins on the manufacturer.

零售商拥有自己的制造企业的最大优点是对制造过程和供应可靠性的完全掌控，在与供应商交易的时候，主要的零售商有着这样的优势，它在市场上是处于主导地位的。通常供应商几乎完全依赖于特定的零售商，零售商会以定期订单和大宗订单作为回报而要求自己完全控制产品的生产过程并且缩减制造商的边际利润。

Many retailers are cutting the number of suppliers they deal with. Bhs is reducing this figure from some 750 in the early 1990s to about half that number. Those that remain must meet strict terms on price, quality, delivery times, etc. Arcadia is another example of a retailer concentrating on a limited number of suppliers; over 40% of its products come from just 20 suppliers.

许多零售商正在削减供应商的数量，包豪斯将这一数量从 20 世纪 90 年代的 750 家缩减了一半，剩下的那些必须满足价格、质量、交货期等方面的严格要求。阿卡迪亚也是一个限制供应商数量的零售商例子，其超过 40% 的产品来自 20 家供应商。

At the same time, the reverse is occurring with some manufacturers who believe that the time taken to service small retailers would be better spent forging closer links with their major customers. An example of a supplier adopting this policy is Hardcore, the denim company.

同时，相反的情况是一些制造商认为花费时间向小零售商提供服务可以使其和核心顾客建立更为紧密的关系，硬核牛仔布公司就是一个例子，它就是采用这种方式的供应商。

8.3.9 Retail buying and selling / 零售采购与销售

In all large-scale fashion clothing retailers central buying is now the norm. Experienced buyers visit trade and fashion shows, overseas and UK suppliers, and use prediction services to make decisions on what to buy for the coming seasons. Often the initial order will be for only part of the expected sales, the rest being confirmed later in the season as actual sales figures allow management to estimate likely demand more accurately.

所有大型的时装零售商目前采取的都是集中采购的方式，经验丰富的采购商会参加贸易展和时装秀，拜访海外以及英国的供应商，并且借助预测服务确定下一季采购什么产品。通常最早的订单只会占到期望销售额的一部分，剩下的将会在当季后期确定，因为根据实际的销售数据表可以较为准确地估算将来的需求。

Specification buying is becoming increasingly prevalent, whereby buyers place orders against rigorous predetermined standards of fabric quality, trim, etc. Many leading high street fashion retailers have extensive laboratory facilities to monitor the quality of the clothes they sell. Some retailers also employ staff to allocate stock to their various outlets to maximize likely sales – these staff apportion new stock to the outlets by using past sales figures to estimate potential demand for new lines. Getting the allocations right maximizes sales and minimizes the likelihood of having excess stock in some branches which might, without a system of branch transfers to reduce it, result in this stock having to be cleared at a cost of heavy reductions. The biggest cost for all retailers is stock, so intelligent buying, good stock control and effective merchandising (see Chapter Six) are of paramount importance.

规范化的采购越来越普遍，即采购商会根据预先确定的面料质量和辅料标准下订单。很多领先的繁华商业街时尚零售商都有大量的实验设施以控制他们所销售的时装的品质。一些零售商为了扩大销售额，会雇用人员将库存商品分配给零售店，这些人员根据以往的销售数据表估测新产品的潜在需求，进而向各店铺发货。分配合理的话可以使销售额最大化，从而降低分店存货过量的可能性，如果店铺之间不能调货以降低库存的话，那么就必须大减价来清理库存。所有零售商最大的成本就是库存，因此理智的采购、良好的库存控制和有效的销售（详见第 6 章）都是极为重要的。

In this context several fashion retailers have adopted a concept known as 'edited retailing', whereby the customer is offered a limited though changing choice of merchandise that is highly co-ordinated, offering

关于这一点，有些时装零售商采用了称为“编辑零售”的概念，据此会给消费者供应有限的但有着多样选择的产品，以及提供相配套的产品线。编辑零

a high degree of product range compatibility. The concept of edited retailing is shown in Figure 8.2.

售的概念如图 8–2 所示。

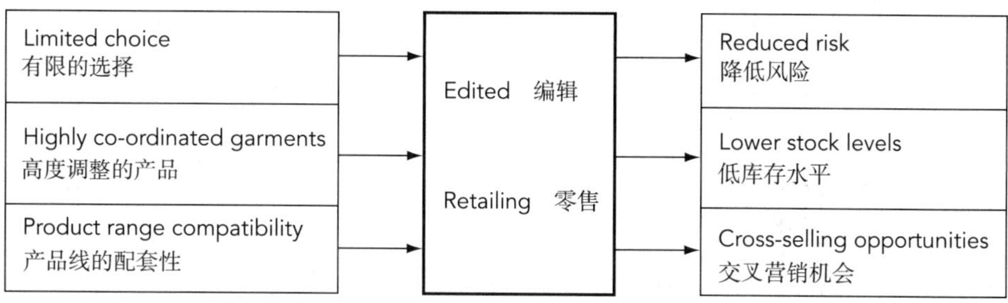

Figure 8.2 The edited retailing concept. 图 8–2 编辑零售的概念

Next is a good example of this approach. As well as reducing risk, stock holding, etc., it offers great scope for cross-selling, in effect buying the whole 'look'. As George Davies states in his book, *What Next*?, 'The exercise taught me one of the keys to success in retailing ... the trick is to give the illusion of choice.'

零售品牌奈克斯特是一个采取这种方法的很好的例子，这种方法可以降低风险和库存等，而且给交叉销售创造了空间，实际上也就是购买全系列的产品。就像乔治·戴维斯在他的书中写到的，奈克斯特是什么？这一实例告诉我们取得零售成功的一个关键因素……诀窍就是给消费者提供选择的幻想。

8.4 The industry's components ／产业构成

The retail fashion industry consists of many parts, the most important of which are outlined in this section.

时装业的零售包括很多方面，本节主要讲述最重要的几点。

8.4.1 Wholesalers ／批发商

Market trends ／市场的发展趋势

The wholesale sector is in serious decline; the reasons for this are increased retail concentration and a more volatile fashion driven clothing market. Jaeger, perhaps anticipating these trends, withdrew in 1987, as did Jacques Vert in 1998.

The large multiples and department store groups deal directly with their suppliers, often overseas companies, through central buying departments. They are therefore able to avoid using wholesalers and the associated costs. Indeed Marks and Spencer, the market leader in many areas of the retail market, was one of the first, if not the first, to deal directly with a manufacturer (Corah) and so break the grip of the wholesalers. Besides financial savings and

批发业严重下降的原因是零售业集中度的增加，以及时尚变化对市场的驱动，积家或许预测到了这种趋势，在 1987 年退出市场，同样地，雅克·沃特在 1998 年也退出市场。大型的跨国公司和百货店通过中心采购部门直接和海外的供应商交易，因此可以避免批发这一环节以及与此相关的费用。事实上，在多个领域的零售市场中处于领导地位的玛莎百货，如果不是第一个，也是最早一批的其中之一，直接与制造商科拉交易，并没有让批发商参与到交易中。除了节省开支和更好地控制产品质量以

better control over product quality, dealing directly with suppliers allows retailers to satisfy their, or more correctly, customers' needs. A measure of exclusivity in terms of fabric, design content, etc., enables them to differentiate themselves from their competitors.

The extent to which customers see the retailer's own label as better value than other brands improves sales, especially in recessionary times when customers are even more value conscious.

Although they carry fewer overheads and staff than manufacturers or retailers, the number of wholesalers and their market share will continue to decline. No longer needed by the large retailers they find themselves catering to a diminishing number of small firms, many of whom find their services of little or no use.

外，直接与供应商交易可以使零售商更好地满足顾客的需求，在面料、设计内容等方面的独家经营权使得零售商和其他竞争对手形成了一定的差异。

在很大程度上，顾客看待零售商自有品牌比其他品牌更有价值，其销售额有所提升，尤其是在经济衰退期，顾客的这种价值意识更强。尽管相比于制造商或零售商而言，批发商承担的管理费用和雇用的人员较少，但是批发商的数量和他们的市场份额依旧还会持续下降。大型的零售商不再需要批发商，但是批发商却发现他们可以为数量逐渐减少的小型公司服务，然而小公司当中有很多认为批发商所提供的服务用处不大或者根本没用。

Functions ／职能

The traditional functions of wholesalers are to:

- provide finance;
- break bulk;
- transport goods to the retailer;
- provide information or advice.

These may be attractive to small-scale retailers but are irrelevant to major retailers or small chains. Within the ranks of small retailers, those serving upper market levels will tend not to use them either.

Why is this the case? Each function will be examined in turn.

◆ ***Provision of finance***: Financing stock is attractive, but even if this is less costly than other forms of finance it could be counterbalanced by possibly paying higher prices and being restricted in one's choice of stock.

◆ ***Break bulk***: This is an attractive proposition if applied to large volume, homogeneous goods in constant demand. This to some extent applies to 'basics' such as T-shirts but for short-life fashionable clothing it is not appropriate.

◆ ***Distribution of goods***: Numerous distribution companies exist that offer a high-quality, reliable and comparatively inexpensive service to suppliers and

批发商的传统职能是：

- 融资；
- 分装；
- 货物配送；
- 提供信息和建议。

这可能对小规模的零售商有着一定的吸引力，但与主要零售商和小型连锁店却没有关联。在小型零售商的排行中，那些服务于高端市场的零售商同样也不会选择批发商。为什么会这样呢？下面将依次对每个职能进行分析。

◆ **融资**：投资是具有吸引力的，尽管这可能比其他形式的资金筹集成本要低，但是有可能需要支付的高价会抵消低成本这一优势，同时也会限制股票的选择。

◆ **分装**：对于有恒定需求的大批量、同质产品的时候，这种提议是很有吸引力的。这在一定程度上也适用于“基本款”的时装，如T恤衫，但对于短期流行时装而言是不适合的。

◆ **货物配送**：许多配送公司都会给供应商和零售商提供高品质的、可靠的以及相对廉价的配货服务。

retailers alike.

◆ ***Provision of information or advice***: A knowledgeable wholesaler may be able to offer this, but other arguably more relevant sources exist, e.g. trade shows, the trade press, prediction services and agents.

◆ **提供信息和建议**：懂行的批发商能够提供这些，但是也有更多其他资源存在，例如贸易展、行业出版物、预测服务公司以及代理商。

8.4.2 Mail order ／邮购

Since the 1970s the mainstream mail order sector, providing large catalogues running to over 1000 pages, has declined in importance. Its two main advantages, easily available credit and a generous returns policy, are now offered by the high street stores. In addition, the agents who operated the catalogue were servicing on average fewer customers each year, and many catalogues are now promoted on the basis that no agency is necessary. The sector still tends to suffer from a residual downmarket image, though its image is improving. Another drawback is goods returned which can average 30%.

In recent years the more successful mail order operations have tended to be the smaller specialist newcomers catering to a specific target market, often with a higher socio-economic profile than the mainstream catalogues. These offer the convenience that is attractive to many with limited time to shop as well as an element of exclusivity and a more positive image. These specialist catalogues offer the opportunity to service niche markets profitably, sometimes where a store-based retail system would be much less successful. They are now facing increased competition from mainstream catalogues, which are featuring more designer merchandise, and of course the Internet.

从20世纪70年代开始，主流的邮购业就提供了超过1000页的目录，现在已经没有那么重要了。它有两个主要优点，即容易得到信任而且有较好的退换政策，现在高级品牌店也开始提供这种服务。此外，管理目录的代理人每年只服务少许的客户，因为现在很多目录都在进行推广，所以没有代理商是必然趋势。邮购业在受众的眼里仍然被看作是剩余的面向大众市场的形象，尽管他们在改善自身的形象，另一个缺点是邮购的退货率平均是30%。

近几年较为成功的邮购业务往往是那些迎合特殊目标市场的新加入者，往往比主流目录具有更高的社会经济属性。邮购提供的便利性、专业性以及更为正面的形象吸引了很多购物时间有限的消费者。这些专业的目录提供了服务于小众市场的机会，有的时候那些以店铺为基础的零售体系更加难以取得成功。邮购业务现在面临着来自主流目录的竞争，这些目录的特点是包含更多的设计师产品以及提供网络服务。

8.4.3 Discount clothing retailers ／时装折扣店

As with other sectors of retailing, there exists a significant discount presence that caters almost exclusively for the lower end of the market. Sited in low-cost premises and offering keen prices on clothing of a lower quality than that available in many major multiples, they operate on very high levels of stock turnover. A second variety of discount store is the outlets run by the major retailers to dispose of excess stock from their normal branches.

如同其他行业的零售一样，时装行业也会为迎合低端市场的需求而采取折扣销售。折扣店选址位于租赁成本低的地段，提供的是一些比大多数跨国公司售价低的低品质时装，所以他们的库存周转率很高。

折扣店的第二种形式是由主要零售商监管的名品折扣店，主要处理正常销售渠道中的库存产品。

Thirdly, the introduction of factory outlet centres such as the one in the Hornsea Freeport shopping village may affect sales in full-price outlets. However, it could be argued that they benefit both retailers and manufacturers since they provide outlets for out-of-date and substandard products that, if sold through normal retailers, could damage the brand's image. They also allow the retailers to dispose of surplus stock, so helping them to offer new lines to their customers.

第三种方式是工厂店，如在霍恩锡自由港购物村的一个工厂店，这种渠道可能会影响全价销售商品的店铺的销售额。然而，因为折扣店销售的是过时的产品或者疵品，这会给零售商和制造商带来好处，这一点目前还是有争议的，如果通常正常渠道销售的话，可能会损害时装品牌的形象。折扣店也允许零售商处理剩余的库存产品，以帮助他们为顾客提供新的产品线。

8.4.4 Multiples and variety chain stores ／跨国公司和各种连锁店

The former are businesses with at least 10 outlets selling predominantly one merchandise group such as clothing or shoes. The latter, as the name suggests, sell a variety of merchandise, the three major variety chain stores with a significant clothing turnover being Bhs (part of Arcadia), Marks and Spencer, and to a lesser extent Woolworths.

Having a place in most of the nation's high streets and out of town developments, these shops represent the success story of British clothing retailing. Their sales and market share have increased year after year at the expense of other retailers. For many years the fashion element in their ranges was minimal, as mass market tastes were only gradually influenced by fashion and good profits could be earned by large volume orders placed with suppliers. Adopting a more fashion orientated range increased the degree of risk through entering a more volatile market that was difficult to monitor.

With a growing fashion awareness among their customers and increased competition from smaller, more fashion orientated retailers, they have moved to provide more fashionable ranges, often using established designers. In this they have been helped by advances in information technology such as Electronic Point of Sale (EPoS), and manufacturing techniques that make the supply and retailing of smaller quantities profitable. The adoption of segmentation policies, most notably by the Arcadia Group (see Chapter Five), has also allowed them to provide a more fashion-focused offering to their customers. Overemphasis on segmentation, though, has caused at least one failure, La Mama, where there were insufficient pregnant career women of means to justify its existence. One prerequisite of

跨国公司至少拥有10家“奥特莱斯”销售同一类商品如时装或者鞋子的商业集团，连锁店顾名思义销售的是多样化的产品，三个主要的占有较大营业额的连锁店分别是包豪斯（属于阿卡迪亚集团）、玛莎百货和沃尔沃斯。

这些连锁店在英国主要的街道和市郊都有店铺，他们代表的是英国时装零售业的成就，与其他零售商相比较，他们的市场份额在逐年增长。多年以来，连锁店产品系列中的时尚元素较少。因为大众市场的品位逐渐受到时尚的影响，所以供应商下单量大的话会赚较高的利润。当消费者接受一个以时尚为主导的产品系列后，企业就进入了一个不稳定的难以控制的市场，这自然会增加企业的风险。

由于顾客时尚意识的增强以及来自一些较小的、以时尚为主导的零售商的竞争压力，连锁店开始向市场提供更为时尚的产品系列，通常也会采纳设计师的作品。在这一点上，先进的信息技术如电子销售网点，以及制造技术的进步使得少量的时尚产品的供应和销售也可以产生利润，这给连锁店提供了很大的帮助。采用市场细分策略最典型的就是阿卡迪亚集团（见第5章），这使得企业能够向顾客提供更为时尚的产品。然而过度地强调市场细分可能会导致失败，例如拉·玛玛，因为怀孕的职业女性很少，所以很难确保品牌的存在，市场细分的一个先决条件就是市场必须足够大而且易于评估。

segmentation is that the market should be sufficiently large to justify catering to it.

These shops tend to have prime sites which guarantee high levels of customer exposure to their merchandise. Location is of prime importance to retailers, perhaps best summed up in the universal saying, 'There are three things of importance in retailing – location, location and location.' The enabling of consumer choice within a select shopping area is a key to success as shown in Figure 8.3. One charge levelled at these chains is that they have succeeded in creating a dreary uniformity in the high street, each one having its Bhs, Next, Miss Selfridge, etc., with the same corporate fascias and colour schemes and, more importantly, the same merchandise catering to the same middle market needs. This is a view the retailers naturally take issue with, though they are nonetheless trying to offer a more individualistic service, in which they are aided by systems such as ACORN, MOSAIC and Townprint (operated by Arcadia), which allows them to build up a picture of the market in their immediate catchment area.

这些店铺往往位于黄金地段，从而可以确保大多数消费者能够接触企业的产品。选址对于零售商而言是重要的，这也是国际上公认的一种说法："零售中有三个至关重要的因素，那就是选址、选址和选址。"如图 8–3 所示，让消费者能够在一个选定的购物区域选择购物是成功的关键所在。这些连锁店的定价取决于他们在繁华商业街区所营造的令人乏味的统一性，每一条街上都会有包豪斯、奈克斯特、塞尔弗里奇小姐等店铺，这些店铺有着相同的企业招牌和配色，而且最为重要的是提供的都是面向中端市场需求的产品。这是零售商自然会关注的方面，尽管如此，他们从来不会试着提供个性化的服务，这些服务可以借助橡树果实、马赛克和城印（由阿卡迪亚集团运作）系统来实现，同时也可以让零售商绘制一张现有市场分布的图片。

Figure 8.3 Example of the importance of location. 图 8–3 选址重要性的例子

8.4.5 Department stores /百货店

Though only small in number, only a few hundred, with some 7% of the overall retail clothing market, department stores have an important role to play in retailing fashion clothing. While catering to a wide market they are particularly attractive in terms of their strong AB customer profile and appeal to older customers. For mid- to upper-market labels they often provide the only suitable outlet, other than the designer opening his or her own store. This would not only demand a considerable capital investment, but also entail obtaining a suitable location for which, because of their relative scarcity, there is often great competition.

尽管百货店的数量较少，只有几百家左右，占有时装零售市场总额的7%，但是在零售领域其依然发挥着重要的作用。为了迎合较大市场的需求，它们主要吸引的是A类和B类顾客，并且满足年长顾客的需求。百货店也会为中高端市场的品牌提供一些适合的销售场地，而不是像设计师一样开设自己独立的商店。这不仅需要较大资金的投入，而且需要选择一个合适的位置，因为场所相对有限，所以往往会造成激烈的竞争。

As those involved in purchasing fashion clothing are involved in an exercise in comparative shopping, department stores have the advantage that they have under one roof a wide variety of clothing from expensive designer labels to comparatively inexpensive basics. In addition, department stores have a growing range of own label merchandise, such as the Linea range in House of Fraser.

时装购买活动中，消费者习惯于比较购物。百货店就有这样的优势，因为其提供的是多样化的产品，从昂贵的设计师品牌到相对廉价的基本款都有。另外，百货店也会开发自有品牌，如佛雷泽的房子，百货店的林雅系列。

Having a variety of concessions enables them to offer a range of other labels in addition to own label and bought-in manufacturers' brands.

因为在谈判的时候可以给予不同程度的优惠，所以百货店除了自有品牌以及购买制造商品牌以外，还会提供一些其他品牌的产品。

Many department stores have reduced the number of their departmental product groups but remain strongly committed to clothing. John Coleman the boss of House of Fraser thinks its upmarket, designer fashion-led offer successfully differentiates it from Debenhams.

许多百货店减少了产品部门的数量，但时装部门依旧还存在。佛雷泽的房子百货的老板约翰·科尔曼认为其店内提供的高端、设计师品牌系列使其和德本汉姆斯百货相比具有差异性，因此获得了较大的成功。

Department stores often attract high concentrations of overseas visitors, many of whom spend considerable sums of money.

百货店通常也会吸引海外游客，这些游客的消费也是相当可观的。

8.4.6 The independent sector /个体零售商

Independents have over a number of years been losing out to the multiples and variety chains, who have economies of scale. In addition many have succumbed to large increases in rents as leases came up for renewal, which has less of an effect on those others who often own the freehold of the site from which they trade. The introduction of a uniform business rate has also proved disadvantageous to many, resulting in

个体零售商多年来一直都是输给跨国公司和连锁店的，因为后两者能够实现规模效益。此外，因为续租之后租赁成本的大幅上涨，很多经营者都放弃了，而对于那些对场地拥有永久产权的经营者而言，这一点对他们并没有太大的影响。商业税率的产生给许多的经营者带

massive increases in rates in areas until now favoured as low-rate areas. Some of these pressures are shown in Figure 8.4.

来了麻烦，这直接导致税率的大幅增长，直至现在税率才有所降低。小型时装零售商的压力如图 8–4 所示。

Figure 8.4 Pressures on the small fashion retailer. 图 8–4 小型时装零售商的压力

At the upper market levels independents are still strong and are positively encouraged in some locations such as Covent Garden. However, owners and developers tend to favour large retailers as they are better able to afford high rents and are more reliable in terms of meeting long lease commitments. Nonetheless in the late 1980s and early 1990s, when most major chains were registering declines in sales and or profits, as a category independents fared relatively better.

A measure of exclusivity has provided some relief from these pressures through exclusivity of supply being granted to favoured independents. However, this may be subsequently lost to larger retailers.

在高端市场中，个体店仍然有着较强的竞争力，而且某些区域也在鼓励这种店铺的发展，如伦敦的考文特花园。然而，业主和开发商还是比较欢迎大型零售商，因为他们能够承受高额的租金而且在达成长期租赁协议方面更加有保证。尽管如此，在 20 世纪 80 年代后期和 90 年代初期，当大多数连锁店销售额和利润都出现下滑的时候，个体零售店却有着较好的发展。独家经营的产品供货也更加青睐个体零售商，这种专营权也使得个体零售商面临的压力有所减少，这可能会使业主失去一些较大的零售商。

8.4.7 Supermarket involvement ／超市的介入

Historically the supermarket groups have not seen the fashion clothing market as particularly attractive, preferring to concentrate their own expertise and other resources on food, though competitive pressures are changing this.

Sainsburys became involved through the Savacentre operation which was originally a joint venture with Bhs. ASDA has the highest profile involvement through George, its in-store clothing operation set up by George Davies, the ex-Next chief executive. Tesco is developing an extensive and more fashionable clothing offering under its own label. Supermarkets are particularly strong in children's clothing having a 16% share in 2004.

有史以来超级市场都不认为时装市场是具有吸引力的，他们关注的是自己的专长以及其他的如食物等商品，尽管来自竞争的压力改变了这种观念。萨瓦中心是和包豪斯组建的合资企业，经过萨瓦中心的运作，塞恩思伯里超市也成为了其中的一员。借助乔治・戴维斯，也就是奈克斯特的前任首席执行官的帮助，阿斯达（Asda）超市也涉足了时装销售，乐购超市则在自己的商标之下经营着很多种时尚类的产品。超市中童装的销售增长较快，2004 年其销售额占据了总销售额的 16%。

8.5 Trends in retailing ／零售的趋势

The retail fashion market has seen considerable changes in recent years, as have other sectors of the retail trade. Some of the more important are outlined below.

近年来时装零售市场以及零售贸易的其他行业都发生了很大的变化，下面对一些主要的方面进行阐述。

8.5.1 Franchising ／特许经营

Franchising is defined by the International Franchise Association as a contractual relationship between franchiser and franchisee in which the franchiser offers or is obliged to maintain a continuing interest in the business of the franchisee in such areas as knowledge and training; wherein the franchisee operates under a common trade name, format or procedure owned by or controlled by the franchiser, and in which the franchisee has made or will make a considerable capital investment in his business from his own resources. The reasons for its success as a retail format are the advantages offered to both franchiser and franchisee as outlined below.

根据国际特许经营协会的定义，特许经营指的是特许人和受让人之间的一种契约关系，根据契约，特许人要在技能传授、人员培训等方面为受让人提供持续性的帮助；受让人按照合同约定在统一经营体系下从事经营活动，受让人在特许人的监督下使用特许人拥有的商标、商业模式及经营管理经验等资源，受让人也可以投入一定量的资金或者个人的资源。特许经营作为一种零售形态能够取得成功的原因是其对经销商和加盟者的发展有着以下优势：

Advantages to franchisee ／特许经营的优势

◆ Obtains the benefits of the name, reputation, brand image, etc. already established with the public.

◆ Less need for own capital as the franchiser helps to obtain capital; banks tend to be more sympathetic to requests for loans to the more established franchises than to those without the backing of a franchiser.

◆ Help in a number of areas, e.g. staff training, site selection and purchase of equipment and stock.

◆ Benefits of any national advertising, e.g. Benetton spends a multi-million pound budget to run the Benetton racing team.

◆ Exclusive sales territory granted for the duration of the franchise agreement.

◆ Less risk of business failure. A survey in 1986 undertaken for the *Financial Times* showed that after five years 80% of small businesses had ceased trading, while less than 20% of franchised businesses had failed – an example of the Pareto (80/20) rule.

◆ 能够从已在公众当中建立的名称、声誉和品牌形象中获取利益；

◆ 个人资金的投入减少，因为特许人能够协助获取资金。比起那些没有特许人支持的经营者而言，银行更愿意给这些已经发展成熟的经营者提供贷款；

◆ 协助受让人进行员工培训、选址以及设备采购和股票交易；

◆ 从全国性的广告中获益，例如贝纳通花费数百万英镑的预算来支持贝纳通赛车队；

◆ 特许协议期限内在某个销售区域独家销售产品；

◆ 经营失败的风险较低。1986 年由金融时报开展的一项调查表明，5 年之后 80% 的小型企业将会停业，不到 20% 的特许经营会失败，这也是帕累托（80/20）原理的一个例证。

Advantages to franchiser ／对特许人的优势

◆ Rapid expansion is possible without causing cash-flow problems.

◆ 'Tied' outlets for products/service.

◆ Initial fee plus regular royalty payments.

◆ Less risk. The franchisee puts up the capital and as his or her own boss has a direct incentive to make a success of the venture.

Many niche retailers, so popular in the 1980s, were franchises. One of the earliest and most successful for many years was Tie Rack.

According to the British Franchise Association, any company offering a franchise to set ethical standards must have run its own outlets successfully for a minimum of one year.

◆ 不会造成现金流的问题且有可能进行快速扩张；

◆ 捆绑在一起的奥特莱斯的产品和服务；

◆ 加盟费加上特许经营费；

◆ 风险较小，加盟商提供资金自己成为老板，直接控制经营的成败。

许多特色店都是特许经营的，在20世纪80年代的时候非常普遍，这么多年来最早建立、也是最成功的案例就是泰・瑞克。

根据英国特许经营协会的规定，任何想进行特许经营的公司需要建立一套道德标准，自己开设的奥特莱斯至少要成功经营一年。

8.5.2 Concessions ／特许授权

Also known as shops within shops, they can be defined as space leased by the host retailer to another retailer, wholesaler or manufacturer from which to sell its merchandise.

One of the earliest examples was Jaeger as concessionaire and Selfridges on Oxford Street as the host retailer. This concept expanded greatly in the 1970s and 1980s. Debenhams, before its takeover by Burton in 1985, had over one-third of its selling space and income from concessions. Since then Debenhams and many other retailers have reduced their dependency on this type of operation.

Examples of concessions are Moss Bros, which is both a host retailer and a concessionaire, CC formerly Country Casuals, Liz Claiborne and Jacques Vert. Many fashion clothing concessions operate in department stores, sometimes trading from a very small sales area.

Possible advantages to the host retailer provided by concessions include:

◆ flexibility through short-term contracts;

◆ benefit of specialist expertise in buying and merchandising;

特许授权也称为店中店，可以被定义为主店将店面租给其他零售商、批发商或制造商，他们可以在店内销售自己的产品。

最早的一个例子就是积家和牛津街上塞尔弗里奇百货的合作，前者是受让人，而后者是主店。这一概念在20世纪70年代和80年代有所扩充，1985年在波顿接受德本汉姆斯百货之前，其有超过1/3的销售场地和收入都是来自授权。自那时起德本汉姆斯百货和多个其他零售商开始减少了对授权这种形式的依赖性。

特许授权的例子还有就是莫斯・布鲁斯，它既是主店又是受许人，受让人还有CC也就是之前的乡村休闲、丽资・克莱本、和雅克・沃特。百货店里有很多种特许授权店，有的时候是一个很小面积的专柜。

授权带给主店铺的好处包括：

◆ 短期合同具有灵活性；

◆ 可以从采购和销售的专业性中获益；

◆ additional interest to customers;

◆ reduction of certain costs, such as fixtures and fittings, training and wages;

◆ reduced stockholding costs and risk;

◆ guaranteed income for the store.

Possible advantages to the concessionaire include:

◆ no high start-up costs for their own retail outlet;

◆ good exposure to host shop's high volume of customers;

◆ concessionaires can test market at a relatively low-cost new ideas that, if successful, could result in expansion and ultimately opening their own stores and, if not, still enable them to relinquish the concession.

◆ 为顾客带来额外利益；

◆ 降低某些固定成本如设备、装潢、培训和工资等；

◆ 降低库存成本和风险；

◆ 店铺的收入有保证。

授权带给受让人的好处包括：

◆ 比自己开店的启动费用低；

◆ 使产品可以接触主店铺大量的客流量；

◆ 受让人可以相对较小的成本进行市场测试，如果成功的话，就可以扩张并且开设自己的专柜，如果不成功就可以放弃授权合作。

There are of course disadvantages. In respect of the host retailer these revolve around the possibly adverse effect that poor concessions have on the store's image and the competitive threat to its own sales by the concession. One quoted acceptable industry figure is 8:2, eight sales to be generated from people to the store by the concessions for every two lost by the store to their concessions. The major disadvantage to the concessionaire is the high cost of the space leased, whether charged as rent per square foot or as a percentage of sales, which can be well over 25% of turnover.

当然也有一些缺点。就主店铺而言，有一些负面的影响，那就是较差的授权会损害店铺的形象并且对自己的销售产生竞争性威胁。引用行业的数据 8 比 2，即 20% 的顾客会被店铺所忽视，80% 的销售额来自授权店铺带来的客流量。对受让人而言，最大的缺点是高额的租赁成本，无论是按照每平方英尺收取租金还是按照销售额百分比收取租金，租金都会占到营业额的 25% 以上。

8.5.3 Physical distribution／**物流**

There are several transport companies who specialize in the clothing sector. This involves considerable investment in warehousing and equipment. In addition to moving and storing clothing, many customers are demanding additional services such as pressing garments.

有很多物流公司专门从事时装运输，这需要大量的资金投入修建仓库以及购买设备。除了运输和存储时装以外，许多客户还需要额外的服务如时装整烫。

Like others involved in the fashion industry the specialist carriers are having to change to meet new demands. Increasingly, their clients are looking for a complete supply chain with JIT supply at the end of it to allow better stock management. This situation is well developed in other parts of the retail industry, notably in the food sector. Deliveries of new seasonal lines are also taking place later and later, so allowing less response time. Some fashion retailers have already contracted out the distribution side of the business.

与时装行业其他的参与者一样，专业的运输公司需要调整以满足行业新的需求。他们的客户希望拥有完整的供应链从而可以及时供货，并且可以很好地管理库存，这种情况在其他的零售领域发展较快，如食品行业。新季产品的交货也越来越晚，从而可以缩减相应时间，因此一些时装零售商将分销业务外包给了其他公司。

The physical delivery of goods is also important to the mail order sector. Next employed as one of its selling points a better system of getting clothing to its

对邮购订单而言，按时交货同样很重要，奈克斯特雇用了一些人派送货品给邮购客户，这也是该品牌的一个卖点，

mail order customers, and Empire Stores now promises a 24-hour delivery service.

帝国的店铺承诺 24 小时之内交货。

8.5.4 Supply chain management ／供应链管理

Managing the whole supply chain is becoming increasingly important to industry in general but more so in the retail sector and especially fashion retailing where customers, demand is always changing and has given rise to the term 'fast fashion'. One example of this in practice is Next doubling the frequency of injections into its ranges to every six weeks rather than twelve, this requires enhanced supply chain management skills. Retailers are therefore encouraged to contract out most or all of this process to specialists such as TNT Fashion Group or Kewell.

Its importance in a fashion retailing context can perhaps be best summed up as follows:

'The whole industry will continue to move further towards having faster and more flexible supply chains, not just in order to get the latest looks onto the shelves quicker, but also because it de-risks your business'.

Source: M.D. Supermarket clothing retailer quoted in Mintel Womenswear retailing, April 2004.

在整个行业中，供应链管理变得越来越重要，尤其是零售行业，他们的顾客需求经常变化，所以也就产生了“快时尚”的概念。其中的一个例子就是奈克斯特，以间隔 6 周而不是 12 周的时间就会增加新品系列，这就需要加强供应链的管理，因此一些零售商都把供应链管理外包给了专业公司，如梯恩梯时尚集团和科威尔。

供应链在时装零售领域的重要性可以归结如下：

“整合行业将会继续朝着拥有快速且灵活的供应链系统而努力，这不仅是为了是最新品以最快的速度展示在货架上，而是因为这样可以降低经营的风险。”（出处：M.D 超市的时装零售，引自敏特女装零售，2004 年 4 月）

8.5.5 Service provision ／提供的服务

Many retailers in a variety of sectors now see the provision of a high level of service as a way of establishing a competitive advantage.

In the retail fashion sector high levels of personal service together with good product knowledge and knowing customers' likes and dislikes have traditionally been seen as a strength of the independent sector. Provision of a high level of service is likely to be seen as increasingly important in the more mature age market, which demographically and economically will become more important in the future. The growing tendency to promote shopping, and particularly clothes shopping, as a leisure activity is another reason for offering high levels of customer service.

Common areas of service include late night shopping, free parking (for out-of-town sites only), a liberal returns policy, pleasant decor, helpful staff and a variety of payment methods. For clothing retailers another important area is that of changing facilities, which in some stores are non-existent and in others

不同行业的多个零售商现在都意识到了提供高水平服务是一种建立竞争优势的方式。

在零售行业，高水平的个性化服务，加上专业的产品知识，以及对顾客偏好的了解等都被认为是个体店的优势。在面向成人市场的时候，高水平的服务变得更加重要，因为从人口统计和经济学的角度看，成人市场会成为未来重要的市场组成部分。刺激购物作为一种休闲活动，尤其是在时装购买方面有着较大的增长趋势，这也成为了商家提供高水平顾客服务的另一个原因。

一般的服务范围包括：深夜购物、免费停车（仅指市郊区）、自由的退换政策、舒适的店面装修、热情的员工以及多样化的支付方式。对于时装零售商而言，还有一个重要的区域就是试衣设

range from poor to luxurious.

施，在某些店里没有试衣间，而其他店里的试衣间则是从最差到最豪华的多个级别的都有。

However, such provision is expensive and refurbishment costs are high, particularly so at higher market levels. The provision of high levels of personal service can conflict with a need to reduce operating costs in the form of staff levels, with many larger retailers moving towards employing part-time rather than full-time staff.

然而，提供较好的试衣间花费很大，装修成本也很高，尤其是定位高端市场的店铺。提供高水准个性化服务与降低运营成本之间是相矛盾的，由此很多大型零售商开始雇用一些兼职人员而不是全职人员。

8.5.6 Internationalization／国际化

UK fashion retailers have been slow to expand overseas. Early examples such as M & S venturing into Canada and later Europe met with only limited success. Other UK fashion retailers with an overseas presence include Arcadia, Jigsaw and Paul Smith.

英国时装零售商开始逐渐向海外市场扩张，最早的例子就是玛莎百货冒险进入加拿大和欧洲地区，只取得了很小的成功，英国的其他零售商也进军海外，包括阿卡迪亚、积家和保罗·史密斯。

The successful retailers in this context tend to be those who establish their operation with a local partner, at least in the initial stages. Examples of such ventures are Arcadia entering the Spanish market through concessions in department stores, as has Laura Ashley in Japan. Marks and Spencer has an international franchise operation that enables it to recruit suitable local partners in markets where it feels the need to have one. The perceived high risk in relation to relatively low rates of return has in the past tended to discourage such expansion.

在扩张的时候，取得成功的零售商在最初阶段都是和当地的合作伙伴共同来经营的，如阿卡迪亚进入西班牙市场的时候就是通过授权进入百货店的，就像罗兰·爱思进入日本市场一样。玛莎百货拥有一个国际特许经营部，如果需要的话，他们会通过招募的方式选择当地的合作伙伴而扩张市场的。因为相对较低的收益率带来的是较高的风险，因此在过去这种扩张并不被看好。

The retailers' overseas competitors have in the past few years been attracted to the UK in increasing numbers, particularly from continental Europe, with some building up a considerable branch network, such as the Spanish retailer Zara. Two of the major British mail order concerns, Grattan and Empire, are owned by Otto Verace, the German mail order house, and the French company La Redoute, respectively, and Renown (Japan) bought Aquascutum.

在过去的几年里，英国零售商的海外竞争者也被吸引进入了英国市场，而且数量增长较快，其中一部分来自欧洲大陆，他们建立了庞大的分销网络，例如西班牙零售品牌Zara。英国两大邮购销售商格拉坦和帝国，分别隶属于德国邮购集团奥图·范思哲和法国的乐都特，日本的邮购销售商丽娜则收购了雅格狮丹。

8.5.7 Teleshopping／电话购物

Electronic ordering through the medium of a domestic television set and telephone can take place via a computer terminal. In America, the department store group Saks became the first upmarket retailer to enter the market in 1993. Its first one-hour show brought sales of $575 000 of its

使用家用电话或者手机借助电脑终端就可以完成电子订单。在美国，萨克斯百货店在 1993 年以高端零售商的身份进入市场，旗下自有品牌的休闲装在发布 1 小时之后就带来了 575000 美元的销售额。

own label casualwear range.

Teleshopping has the potential to effect major changes in shopping patterns. Its impact on the retail fashion market in the UK, in such areas as mail order, will develop over the coming years, influenced by consumer acceptance and its own cost effectiveness. Digital television will offer increased possibilities in this area, particularly in respect of those who lack the time or enthusiasm for more conventional shopping, though developments in this area are likely to be heavily influenced by the growth of internet shopping.

电视购物对人们的购物方式产生了很大的影响，对英国时装零售尤其是邮购销售业务也产生了影响，电视购物具有成本优势，而且人们开始接受这种方式，所以在未来几年会得到进一步的发展。数字电视为这种销售方式提供了更好的发展机会，尽管网络购物对这种销售方式也会产生较大的影响，但是电视购物仍然受到那些时间紧迫，追求便利购物的消费者的欢迎。

8.5.8 Retail branding ／零售品牌

Branding as in other areas of retailing now plays a crucial role. It helps to differentiate one retailer from another and is both a consequence of retail concentration and a factor in its continued growth.

The attractiveness of brands or labels in terms of product has encourage some manufacturers to diversify into the clothing market and *vice versa*, often through the licensing of the brand name (see Chapter Six). Its importance to consumers is greater in the north than the south. Younger consumers also attach more importance to branding than do older age groups, as peer pressure to be seen with the 'right' label is not an issue with the latter.

Advertising (see Chapter Nine) plays an important part in building brand awareness and loyalty, and many major retailers spend heavily in this area.

品牌在其他零售行业同样发挥着重要的作用，它有助于消费者区分不同的零售商，也是零售集中所产生的结果，同时也是企业发展过程中重要的因素。

从产品角度看，品牌或者商标的吸引力在于能够鼓励一些制造商增加产品种类以进入时装市场，或者通过许可授权品牌名称给其他经销商（见第 6 章）。品牌对北方消费者要比南方消费者有着更大的影响，同样相比于老年消费群体而言，年轻消费者更加关注品牌，因为拥有品牌产品的话在同伴当中就不会成为落伍者。

广告（见第 9 章）对建立品牌知名度和品牌忠诚度有着重要的作用，所以很多零售商在广告方面的花费都很大。

8.6 The Internet ／互联网

8.6.1 Growing importance ／重要程度增加

As a distribution channel the Internet is becoming ever more important as the factors that previously limited its development, as detailed below, have declined.

◆ Limited access – now widespread, available in most homes, also thorough laptops or mobile phones, it can even be accessed from the local library.

◆ Security of payment – advances in encryption have allayed fears in this area, even though such fears appear as somewhat irrational given many people's willingness to give credit card details over the phone,

作为一个分销渠道，互联网变得更为重要，之前提到过的限制其发展的因素逐渐减少了，如下所述：

◆ 访问受限。现在网络已经很普遍了，在大多数家里都可以通过笔记本、手机上网，甚至当地有些图书馆也可以上网。

◆ 支付的安全性。加密技术的进步减轻了人们对支付安全的担忧，尽管如此，这些担忧依旧还存在，因为人们都不太情愿通

which is arguably a less secure medium.

◆ Cost of access – now largely limited to a small separate monthly fee though increasingly included in a bundle of other computer/communications services.

◆ Need physically to examine the merchandise – as customers come increasingly to trust retail and other labels this, coupled with a liberal returns policy, is less of a deterrent.

Various predictions exist for Internet usage with virtually all suggesting very strong growth in general and as a retail channel. Those who have adopted a so-called 'clicks and bricks' approach, i.e. having both an actual shop presence and Internet site, have tended to be more successful; the classic site's only failure being Bo.Com, which launched amid much hype in 1999 only to crash the following year.

过电话来告知信用卡的详细信息，而这种方式被认为是缺少安全保证的。

◆ 上网费用。尽管很多公司都会将上网费和电脑以及通信服务捆绑销售，但是采用较多的还是包月付费。

◆ 需要亲自验货。消费者越来越信任零售商和一些品牌，有了货品自由退换政策，自然就减少了消费者的顾虑。

各种各样的预言指出互联网的应用将会整体上促进销售的增长，而且会成为重要的零售渠道。那些接受点击购买，即拥有实体店铺和线上店铺的企业将会获得较大的成功，唯一一个失败的案例就是 Bo.Com，1999 年上线，第二年就倒闭了。

8.6.2 Limits on growth ／发展的限制

In general, the Internet as a medium of distribution shares many of the problems of mail order and teleshopping, namely returned goods, delivery costs and other logistical problems.

Clothes shopping is often seen, particularly by the young, as a 'social experience' and as such will continue to take place in a physical environment, be it high street, shopping mall or other venue.

Another issue is that of cannabalization, which also applies to other forms of home-based shopping: Internet sales may take place at the expense of other company outlets.

一般而言，互联网作为一个分销渠道，也有着和邮购销售和电话购物一样的问题，如退换货，运输成本以及物流方面的其他问题。

对于年轻人来说购买时装是一种社会体验，这种体验在实体店更为明显，如高街品牌、购物中心或者其他渠道。

另一个问题是互联网的销售额可能会威胁公司其他店铺的销售。

8.6.3 Retailers' use of the Internet ／零售商使用网络

This revolves around the following potential advantages:

◆ Cost savings – a physical presence on the high street or other location can involve considerable costs which can be avoided or reduced.

◆ Greater opportunities to segment the market more effectively and cheaply.

◆ The possibility of creating a truly global market.

◆ To complement and support the physical retail network where present.

这有着以下几种潜在的优势：

◆ 节省开支——在繁华商业街或其他区域开设实体店成本很高，而使用网络可以避免或者降低成本；

◆ 给有效地且廉价地进行市场细分提供了更多的机会；

◆ 开创一个真正的全球市场；

◆ 补充和支持实体的零售网络。

8.6.4 Internet marketing strategies /互联网营销策略

The following options, derived in part from the work of Dholakia and Rego (1998), can be adopted:

◆ Ignore it.

◆ Develop a basic site.

◆ Use the site to direct customers to high street or other locations.

◆ Link the site with a more traditional mail order operation, i.e. as an ordering mechanism.

◆ Use it to support dialogue with customers, i.e. in the area of customer complaints.

◆ Use it as a sales tool in its own right.

◆ Offer an individual service, thus making the individual the basis of segmentation and relationship marketing more of a reality.

In broad terms the strategic option(s) taken will be determined by the level of retailer commitment in terms of cost, linkages to existing retail formats and involvement with customers. This indicates perhaps that the greatest number of strategic options is available to well-established and well-funded clothing retailers. To obtain a current overview of strategies, positioning and segmentation issues the reader is recommended to visit a range of the growing number of websites.

In spite of its undoubted growth in recent years, there is still in, the industry, a degree of scepticism over its long-term impact; perhaps best summed up by one Chief Executive of an upmarket classic menswear retailer quote in the October 2005 Mintel report on Menswear Retailing.

'In reality the Internet is just a more efficient way of catalogue shopping which never got over 9–10% of clothing spending'.

以下内容来自德霍拉吉亚和力高（1998）的部分著作，可供选择：

◆ 忽视它；

◆ 建立一个基本网站；

◆ 用网站引导顾客去繁华商业街区或其他地方；

◆ 借助传统的邮购订单链接到网站，例如订购的商品；

◆ 通过网络和顾客交谈，例如顾客投诉的处理；

◆ 把网络当做一种销售工具；

◆ 提供个性化服务，使个体成为市场细分的基础，并且将关系营销转变为现实。

从广义上来说，选择什么样的策略取决于零售商在成本、与其他零售渠道的链接以及顾客参与等方面的承诺，这就说明了同时采取多种策略只适用于那些已建立的、资金充裕的零售商。为了对策略、定位和市场细分有一个基本的认识，建议读者访问一些相关的网站。

毫无疑问，网络近几年获得了快速的发展，但行业内对其长远的影响程度还存在着一些质疑，或许高档男装市场的首席执行官 2005 年 10 月在敏特零售周刊上有关男装零售的报告是对此最好的总结。

“事实上互联网比目录销售更为有效，因为目录销售在消费者时装消费中所占的比重从未超过 9% ~ 10%”。

8.7 The 'grey market' /灰色市场

Previously a number of clothing retailers, including some major supermarket groups, had obtained high-profile, high-margin fashion brands from a variety of sources other than the brand owner, the so-called grey or parallel market. The retailers benefited in terms of increased footfall and extra sales, often at better margins

以前，一些时装零售商包括一些主要的超市都会从各种各样的渠道中获取知名度高、利润高的时尚品牌，而不是从品牌所有者那里采购，这就是所说的灰色或平行市场。零售商从增长的客流量和超出的销售额中获利，通常都会有

together with increased publicity. Their customers had the opportunity to purchase expensive brands at a considerable discount. However, the brand owners or rather their usual stockists lost sales at the normal margin price, but perhaps more importantly the brand may risked losing credibility. This potential devaluation of the brand equity, the brand owners argued, represented a considerable loss on their investment in research and development and marketing support in creating and maintaining the brand, and can act as a disincentive to developing new brands or products.

The victory of Levi Strauss over Tesco in the European Court and China joining the World Trade Organization has virtually eliminated this problem. However the selling of fake merchandise remains a problem particularly for upmarket fashion brands.

较高的边际利润而且会扩大宣传，顾客则有机会在打折的时候购买到昂贵的品牌商品。然而，按照正常价格计算的话，品牌所有者或者他们的供货商的销售额就会下降，而最为重要的是品牌面临着信用缺失的危机。品牌所有者认为，这种潜在的品牌价值贬值将会使他们在创建和维持品牌发展过程中的研发、市场维护投入落空，这都可以看作是开放新品牌或者新产品的不利因素。

在欧洲法庭上李维斯胜诉乐购和中国加入世贸组织事实上已经消除了这个问题，然而对于高端时尚品牌而言，销售假冒伪劣商品依旧是一个很大的问题。

8.8 Retail marketing effectiveness ／零售营销的效益

Obviously the overall measure of success is long-term profitability. A subgoal of this is usually to increase sales in relative terms on an annual or a seasonal basis. Other indicators are sales per square foot and sales per employee. Selling a lower proportion of merchandise at reduced margins is also an indication of effective marketing as well as astute buying.

Another indicator is the conversion rate, or the number of customers who buy as a proportion of the total number who enter the store. The conversion varies by consumer segment, as shown in the example of a menswear retailer (Table 8.1).

A low conversion rate may be due to a variety of factors such as inappropriate price points, unattractive merchandise, or staff lacking product knowledge and

很显然，长期收益是衡量成功的总体评价标准，其子目标通常是年度销售额或者季度销售额的增长，其他因素包括每平方英尺的销售额以及每一个员工的销售额，降低边际利润来销售较少量的商品体现的同样是有效营销。

另一个指标是转换率，或者是进入店铺的所有顾客中有多少购买了商品。消费者细分的标准不同，转换率不同，如表 8–1 所示的男装零售商的例子。

较低的转换率可能是由若干原因造成的，例如定价不准确、商品缺少吸引力，或者员工缺乏专业知识以及销售技能。

Table 8.1 Entrant to buyer conversion 表 8–1 进店消费者到购买者的转换率

Segment 细分市场	Entrants (%) 进店的消费者	Buyers (%) 购买者	Conversion from entrant to buyer (%) 从进店消费者变成购买者的比率（%）
Fashion 时尚	7	4	16
Fashion-aware 时尚关注者	23	18	21
Classic 经典型消费者	9	14	42
Mainstream 主流人群	42	51	37
Downstream 追随者	19	13	28

Source: Drapers Record 18–7–87. 来源：德雷珀斯杂志记载 18–7–87

selling skills.

As much of the marketing effort in the industry comes from the retail sector, the large retailers invest considerable money and effort in market research (see Chapter Four) to measure its effectiveness.

时装行业中的很多营销措施都来自零售部门，大型零售商在市场调研方面会投入大量的资金和精力以衡量市场的有效性（见第 4 章）。

8.9 Summary ／小结

At the conclusion of this chapter the reader should be able to:

- ◆ understand the importance of the UK fashion retailing business;
- ◆ describe the retailer's relationship with the manufacturing sector;
- ◆ explain the importance of imports and exports to the UK fashion retail industry;
- ◆ outline the structure of the industry;
- ◆ indicate how retail marketing effectiveness can be assessed.

作为本章的结论，读者应该具备的能力：

- ◆ 了解英国时装零售的重要性；
- ◆ 描述零售商和制造商的关系；
- ◆ 了解进出口贸易对英国零售行业的重要性；
- ◆ 概述时装行业的结构；
- ◆ 指出如何实现零售商的营销效益。

Further reading ／课后阅读材料

1.Bitner, M.J. (1992), Servicescapes: the impact of physical surroundings on customers and employers, *Journal of Marketing*, Vol. 56, pp. 57–71.

比特纳·M.J.（1992 年），《服务场景：真实环境对顾客和员工的影响》，营销学报，Vol.56, pp.57–71.

2.Cox, R. and Brittain, P. (2004), *Retailing: An Introduction*, 5th Edition, FT Prentice Hall, London.

考克斯·R.，布瑞坦·P.（2004），《零售：概述》，第 5 版，普伦蒂斯·霍尔出版社，伦敦.

3.Davies, G. (1991), *What Next?* Arrow Books, London.

戴维斯·G.（1991），《奈克斯特是什么？》，阿罗书籍出版社，伦敦.

4.Dholakia, U.M. and Rego, L.L. (1998), An empirical investigation of web page effectiveness, *European Journal of Marketing*, Vol. 32, No. 7/8, pp. 724–736.

霍拉基尔·U.M.，雷戈·L.L.（1998），《一份网页效果的实证调查》，欧洲营销学报，Vol.32, No.7/8, pp.724–736.

5.Fashion Multiples (2008), Verdict Research, London.

《服装连锁店》（2008），裁定研究（译者注：英国零售咨询公司）出版社，伦敦.

6.Fernie, J. *et al.* (2004), *Principles of Retailing*, Butterworth-Heinemann, London.

弗尼·J. 等（2004 年），《零售法则》，巴特沃思·海纳曼出版社，伦敦.

7.Harris, D. and Walters, D. (1992), *Retail Operations Management*, Prentice Hall, London.

哈里斯·D.，沃尔特斯·D.（1992），《零售业务管理》，普伦蒂斯·霍尔出版社，伦敦.

8.Marciniak, R. and Willans, J.R. (2008), Fashion Retailing, Blackwell, London.

马尔辛尼克·R.，威兰斯·J.R.（2008），《服装零售》，布莱克威尔出版社，伦敦.

9.Retailing (1999), Verdict Research, London.

《零售》（1999），裁定研究出版社，伦敦.

Chapter Nine Fashion Marketing Communications
第 9 章　时装营销传播

9.1 Introduction ／引言

Promotion, widely regarded as the fourth P of marketing, is now being renamed marketing communications to which perhaps reflect its growing importance and increased profile within the marketing mix.

In this chapter the role and scope of marketing communications will be explained, with an emphasis on fashion marketing communications. Fashion is different!

促销被公认为营销过程中的第四个 P，现在被冠名为营销传播，这体现了它在营销组合中日益增长的重要作用和不断提升的地位。

本章主要围绕时装营销传播，探讨营销传播的作用和范围。时装是与众不同的！

9.1.1 Defining marketing communications ／营销传播的定义

The definition of marketing developed by the Chartered Institute of Marketing is widely regarded as a useful one:

Marketing is the management process responsible for identifying, anticipating and satisfying consumer requirements profitably.

Communication, from the Latin communis (a oneness of thought), is defined as 'imparting or – an exchange of information' (*Oxford Dictionary*).

If we combine the definitions of marketing and communication we might define marketing communications as:

A management process responsible for communicating with customers in order to inform and satisfy their needs and wants.

Therefore the focus of marketing communications

在市场营销定义中，英国特许营销协会所给出的定义应用更为广泛：

市场营销是为了追求利益而识别、预测和满足消费者需求的管理过程。

“传播”一词来自拉丁语“communis”（思想的统一），被定义为“信息的传递或交流”（牛津词典）。

如果我们把市场营销和传播的定义结合起来，那么就可以定义营销传播：

营销传播是负责与消费者沟通，由此来了解和满足消费者需要的管理过程。

因此营销传播的焦点仍然在消费者身

is still on the consumer, but with the additional dimension of statisfying the consumer's need for information. It may perhaps be useful to reiterate that consumers cannot be 'persuaded' to buy something they do not want or need. The skill in marketing communications, just as in marketing, lies in understanding the consumer and informing them about the benefits of your product above any other competing offers. The starting point of this mutually bene-ficial exchange must be informing them of your fashion offer.

上，只是增加了满足消费者对信息的需求这一点，或许有必要重申一遍：消费者是不会被"游说"去买一些他们不想要或不需要的东西的。营销传播与市场营销一样，关键在于理解消费者并且让他们产生这样一个观念：你们的产品比任何一家的同类产品都要好，这种互益性的交流必须以告知消费者提供的是时尚产品为出发点。

9.1.2 The historical background ／历史背景

Marketing communications goes back a long way. The earliest example of a promotional tool may well have been the town crier who would literally call out in the streets the availability of goods or services of a seller. This would presumably have been an effective method of promotion as the general populace had low literacy levels, and the media (newspapers, for example) were therefore non-existent.

营销传播可以追溯到很早以前，最早被人们认识的促销方式可以说是在大街上叫卖的小贩，他们大声吆喝，宣传自己的产品和服务。这种方法在当时来讲可能是一种有效的促销方式，因为当时公众普遍文化水平不高，媒体（例如报纸等）根本不存在。

Visual symbols, for example, an image of a needle and thread for a tailor, might have been painted above the shop premises. The traditional sign for a barber's shop, a red- and- white-striped pole symbolizing blood and bandages, still remains today as a legacy of the time when barbers also doubled as dentists and surgeons.

一些视觉符号，如一根针和一卷线的图片就代表裁缝，而这一图片可能被印在商店的招牌上。传统的理发店的标志是镶着红白相间条纹的，象征着血和绷带的柱子，这一传统在当时是纪念理发师作为牙医和外科医生的双重身份，一直沿用至今。

Today we find that visual symbols are an integral part of modern marketing communications, perhaps reflecting the old saying: 'a picture is worth a thousand words'. This is reinforced by the commonly held belief that we retain 70% of what we see, compared with 30% of what we hear.

如今，视觉符号是现代营销传播中不可或缺的一部分，这也印证了那句古话："一图抵千言。"而这种理念又被我们传统的观念所加强，我们能够记住 70% 的视觉信息，但只能记住 30% 的听觉信息。

Another good example of the usage of visual imagery as a communication tool is the advertisements by Benetton, which relied on controverside images as a tool of brand recollection, separate perhaps from the Benefton product itself.

另一个充分利用视觉形象作为传播手段的例子是贝纳通的广告，它们把具有争议性的图片作为品牌传播的工具，这些图片应该是从贝纳通的产品中分离出来的。

9.2 The marketing communications environment ／营销传播环境

Trevor Beattie (1999), one of the gurus of advertising who was responsible for memorable and successful campaigns, including Levi's 501s, said: 'If we whisper, we can't be heard.'

特雷弗·贝蒂（1999 年），这位主要负责大型广告宣传活动的大师，作品包括李维斯的 501 系列产品，他曾经说过："如果我们轻声细语，我们的声音就无法被听到。"

Today's consumer is constantly bombarded by visual stimuli in the form of advertising, logos, junk mail, celebrity gossip magazines, Internet pop ups and so on. It is therefore not surprising that marketing communications have to strive hard to stand out from the crowd. The modern consumer is subjected to a much more complex array of messages and media in an increasingly competitive retail environment when compared to the consumer of the past. Furthermore, modern marketing communications must take into account the fact that today's consumer is more sophisticated and discerning than the consumer of the past. It is no longer sufficient to say that your product is the best. In today's competitive retail environment where competing products are quite similar, the consumer wants to be entertained as well as informed – this is sometimes called infotainment. Marketing communications must give the consumer a reason to purchase your product over other similar products, and creating a strong brand with an equally strong brand identity may be a way of succeeding in the competitive retail marketing environment. Nowhere is this more important than in the highly competitive and saturated fashion market, where very similar products vie for the consumer's attention.

如今的消费者正在不断地被各种各样的视觉刺激物所围绕，包括广告、商标、垃圾邮件、名人八卦杂志、网络弹出窗口等，营销传播必须努力在此基础上脱颖而出。现代的消费者处在一个日趋激烈的零售环境中，因此与过去的消费者相比，他们面对的是一系列更加复杂的信息和媒体。同时现代营销传播必须考虑到这样一个事实，那就是今天的消费者比以往的消费者更加复杂、更具有识别力，如今说你自己的产品是最好的已经不再奏效了。在今天异常激烈的零售市场环境下，相互竞争的产品非常相似，而消费者既想从中得到乐趣，同时又想了解相关信息，这有时会被称为娱乐信息。营销传播必须给消费者一个“选购了你们的产品而没有买其他同类产品”的理由，由此在同类品牌中创建一个强势品牌形象，这可能就是在竞争激烈的零售环境中获胜的方式，在企业不断提供同质化商品来抢夺消费者的激烈竞争环境下和高度饱和的市场中，没有什么比这个更重要了。

9.3 The traditional approach to promotion / 传统的促销方式

9.3.1 Communication theory / 传播理论

Communication theory suggests the following fairly straightforward model of communication:

Sender → Message → Receiver

The sender is the producer or seller of the goods; the message is what the sender wishes to say, which may be encoded in symbols (visuals/music); and the receiver is the consumer or the target market. However, it is not always this simple, as the receiver may not receive the intended message or interpret (decode) it in the way the sender intended. When the message is obscured or misunderstood it is called noise; this is some sort of interference. Marketing communications is not an exact science; measuring and evaluating the effectiveness of a message in terms of feedback is not always a simple process.

Another model that marketers use to describe the process of communication is AIDA:

A Awareness

传播理论揭示出以下直线型传播方式。

发送者→信息→接收者

信息的发出者是产品的生产者或销售者；信息就是发出者要说的话，它们被编码成符号形式（图像 / 声音）；而信息的接收者是消费者或者目标市场。然而传播的过程并非如此简单，因为信息的接收者可能没有按发出者所预想的那样接收和解读信息。当信息模糊或者被曲解的时候，就成了噪声，这对人们来说就是一种干扰了。营销传播并非严谨的科学，从消费者的反应来估计和判断信息的有效性，不是一个简单的过程。

另一个市场营销人员用来描述传播过程的模型是 AIDA：

A 意识

I Interest
D Desire
A Action

I 兴趣
D 欲望
A 行动

This model suggests a linear process whereby the consumer moves from unawareness of the product to awareness, then takes an interest in the product, which in turn leads to desire for the product, which results in an action – a purchase.

这一模型揭示出直线型的心理过程，消费者对产品从不认识到认识，再到对产品产生兴趣，继而产生购买欲望，最终导致行动——购买产品。

In many texts on marketing communications the promotional mix is traditionally listed as:

- advertising;
- sales promotion;
- public relations;
- personal selling.

在许多关于营销传播的书籍中，促销组合一般包括以下几种：

- 广告；
- 营业推广；
- 公共关系；
- 人员促销。

Furthermore, each of these tends to be explained with examples from a diverse range of industries. It is the aim of this chapter to explore each aspect of the promotional mix in relation to fashion.

而且，对每项的解释都附有来自各行各业的实例，这一章节的目的就是解读促销组合中有关时装的部分。

9.3.2 An integrated approach to marketing communications ／营销传播的整合措施

According to McGoldrick (2002), the marketing communications objectives should be clearly defined at the outset. They may be some or all of the following:

- develop new customers;
- increase expenditure by existing customers;
- increase store traffic;
- increase product sales;
- develop the store image.

根据麦戈德里克（2002）的观点，企业最初就应该清晰地定义营销传播的目标，这些目标可能是以下列出的部分或全部：

- 开发新客户；
- 增加现有顾客的消费；
- 增大店内客流量；
- 提高产品销售额；
- 提升店铺形象。

Therefore, the overall strategy of the organization should be the starting point of all marketing communications. This should in turn follow what is known as an integrated approach, where each and every communication from the organization has the same 'handwriting'. A more comprehensive definition of integrated marketing communications (IMC) is:

因此组织的整体的策略应该是营销传播的出发点，继而需要遵循整合的原则，公司的每一个传播活动都要有相同的标识。更为全面的整合营销传播定义是：

> IMC is a concept of marketing communications planning that recognizes the added value of a comprehensive plan that evaluates the strategic roles of a variety of communications disciplines (e.g. general advertising, direct response, sales promotion and public relations)... and combines these disciplines to provide clarity, consistency and maximum communications impact.

> 整合营销传播是一个营销传播规划的概念，即意识到整体规划的附加值，这一规划对不同的传播形式，如一般性广告、直接反应性广告、促销、公关等的战略作用进行评估，并将这些形式结合起来，从而达到明确的、持续的和最大的沟通效果。

Therefore at the outset organizations should ask themselves:

- What do we want to achieve?

因此在最初阶段，组织应该自问：

- 我们想要实现什么？

◆ How should we achieve this? (perhaps most importantly)

◆ How can we measure success?

The organization may well use its internal capabilities to initiate a campaign; however, it is becoming more recognized that the services of an agency are required to develop a creative campaign and buy media space.

◆ 我们如何才能实现？（这也许是最重要的）

◆ 怎样衡量成功？

组织可能会好好地利用它们内在的能力去着手商业活动，但是，人们越来越认识到有必要通过代理机构的服务来策划富有创意的广告，抢占媒体空间。

9.3.3 Developing and communicating a brief ／策划和传播概要

A brief is an outline of the objectives that the company wants to achieve with its marketing communications. The fashion company may well have established, usually by some research, that a campaign is needed to do one or a combination of the following:

◆ Confirm with present consumers that theirs is a credible brand and therefore prevent the customers from straying into the outlets of a competitor who may have a high-profile campaign. This might be the 'follow-my-leader' campaign prompted by the competition.

◆ Introduce a new product range/brand. This might be when a retailer launches an accessory collection, or a childrenswear offer, or opens a new outlet in a new city.

◆ To inform potential consumers that the brand has changed in some way. This might be a repositioning campaign.

The company will communicate 'the brief' to a number of agencies and they will then 'pitch' for the account, normally by making a presentation to the company outlining their marketing communications plan in terms of:

◆ creative treatment (the encoding of the message in symbols, e.g. visuals/music);

◆ media strategy (which channels of communication would be appropriate, bearing in mind the target market, e.g. MTV, *Vogue*);

◆ evaluation (feedback mechanisms to measure the success of the campaign).

This means that the agency should have the capability to deliver all these aspects of a campaign and have personnel involved in

◆ creativity (graphics, copywriting, etc.);

◆ media planning (access to space);

◆ research (before, during and after the

概要是公司要通过营销传播想要实现的目标的提纲。时装公司或许已经通过一些调研，使人们知道商业活动需要做到以下的一方面或几方面：

◆ 使现有顾客坚信你们的品牌是可信的，以防顾客流失到更受瞩目的竞争者的商业活动中，这可能就是竞争所促成的“跟着我的样子学”的商业活动。

◆ 引入新的产品系列或品牌。指的是零售商可能会发布饰品系列、童装系列，或者在一座新城市开设新店。

◆ 让潜在顾客知道，你们的品牌已经发生了某种改变，这就是重新定位的广告。

公司应将“概要”传播到众多经销商中，接着经销商就会瞄准这些目标。通常的方式是向公司展示他们的营销传播计划纲要，主要包括以下几方面：

◆ 创新型的处理方式（将信息编码成符号，如图像／声音）；

◆ 媒体策略（哪种传播方式更适合，牢记目标市场，如：MTV 或《时尚》杂志）；

◆ 评估（建立反馈机制来估测商业活动的效果）。

这意味着经销商要有足够的能力来完成活动的各个方面，并且要有人员参与：

◆ 创意（图表、广告撰写等）；

◆ 媒体策划（进入媒体的途径）；

◆ 研发（活动前、活动中、活动后）。

campaign).

There has been a great deal of consolidation in the advertising agency sector in the recent past, including mergers and acquisitions within both the domestic and overseas sectors. This strengthens the capabilities of the agency to provide a complete package to the client and can facilitate integration of the various elements of the campaign. One recent developments is advertising agencies launching fashion only subdivisions, e.g. J. Walter Thompson (JWT) has created LABEL@JWT dedicated to the fashion sector. This implies advertising agencies have recognized that fashion requires a different approach and treatment in comparison with everyday commodities.

近来在广告领域已经出现了许多整合现象，包括国内和国外一些公司的合并和收购，这大大增强了公司为客户服务的能力，并且更易于整合商业活动的不同方面。广告公司启动的分类广告是这方面最新的进展，例如：智威汤姆逊广告公司创立的LABEL@JWT就为时装领域做出了贡献。这表明广告公司已经认识到，与日用品比较，时装需要不同的处理方式。

9.3.4 An integrated approach /整合措施

Fashion brand retailers are increasingly looking towards an integrated approach to their marketing communications strategies which can give some synergy and also cost economies.

If every aspect of the promotional mix is integrated then the effect is likely to be stronger and long lasting as the imagery and treatment, i.e. the handwriting, is consistent every time it is used – be it in an advertisement, on the web, in a store, or on the letter head. It becomes distinctive and is:

- Recognizable
- Repeated
- Reinforced
- Reiterated
- Recalled.

时装品牌零售商日益希望采取一种针对他们的营销传播策略的整合措施，这些策略可以发挥协同作用，同时能减少成本投入。

如果促销组合的每个方面都融为一体，那么其效果可能会更显著并且持久，因为传播中的文字每次使用的都是一样的，无论出现在广告中、网络上、商店里，或是印刷在信头。它与众不同，并具有以下特点：

- 易于辨认；
- 反复出现；
- 巩固形象；
- 重复使用；
- 便于记忆。

9.3.5 Case study example /案例分析

A middle market retailer of women's, men's and children's clothing launched a marketing communications campaign which comprised of a series of television, magazine, and cinema advertisements. The garments featured in the advertisements were made available to the press via the retailer's public relations department. The public relations department also informed the store personnel, via briefing sheets, of the exact details of the garments (by code number, colour and size availability) which were to be featured in magazines and in the intermissions of specific popular television programmes and cinema films.

一个经营女装、男装和童装的中等市场零售商举办了一次营销传播活动，该活动包括电视、杂志和电影广告。零售商的公关部门负责将广告展示的时装提供给媒体，公关部门也以简报的形式将时装准确的细节信息告知店铺的人事部，这些信息包括代码、颜色以及现有的尺寸，并且会在杂志、热播电视节目空档和电影里对时装的细节进行特写。

These were further detailed by region in relation to stores within each region. The programmes and films were itemized, as were the approximate timings of the advertisements.

The briefing notes also alerted staff to the in-store layouts and visual merchandising treatments that were to support the external communications. As one member of staff commented: 'We knew what was being advertised and when, and could direct customers to it on the shop floor.' According to senior management, areas which had underperforming stores now found new customers.

每一地区不同的店铺会进一步地细化这些信息，并且会列出节目、电影以及广告的时间段。

简介资料也可使全体员工更关注店内陈列和视觉展示，从而可以支持外部的传播活动。正如一名员工所说："我们知道什么时间什么商品正在做广告，可以在现场引导消费者感受这一产品。" 据高级管理人员所说，原本商店业绩不佳的地区现在也已寻求到了新顾客。

9.4 Fashion advertising ／时装广告

Above the line (paid-for) advertising in fashion is relatively low in comparison with other goods e.g. FMCGs – fast moving consumer goods, which probably reflects the fact that less money is spent by consumers on fashion than on food, transport, leisure, fuel, housing, etc.

Fashion companies in the middle market, where the majority of fashion is purchased, have traditionally relied on their stores, i.e. their physical presence in the market place, being a showcase for their products. However, as competition has increased, this marketing tool (the store itself) has not had as much impact. If the consumer does not see or visit your store because they think it is not the store for them, then their physical presence alone is not enough. Fashion stores therefore advertise in order to stand out from very similar stores carrying similar merchandise.

International upper market fashion brands like Chanel, Louis Vuitton, Versace etc., are heavily reliant on advertising to maintain brand awareness. We will now consider the communication channels which are available to fashion companies.

相比其他商品如快速消费品而言，线上时装广告（付费的）较少。这或许反映出这样一个事实，与食品、交通、休闲、燃料、住房等相比较，消费者在时装上的花费较少。

定位有着大量需求的中端市场的时装公司习惯于依赖他们的店铺，例如在陈列柜里展出他们的商品以证实他们在市场中是真实存在的。但是随着竞争日益激烈，这个营销工具（即店铺本身）并没有那么大的影响。如果消费者认为你的商店不适合他们而不来光顾，那么仅仅是商品的实际存在是不够的。因此，时装店开始登广告以使得自己能够从众多的出售相似商品的同类商店中脱颖而出。

国际高档市场的一些时装品牌，如夏奈尔、路易威登、范思哲等，很大程度上都依赖于广告以保持消费者的品牌意识。下面我们将谈及一些适合时装公司的传播渠道。

9.4.1 Television advertising ／电视广告

This is the most expensive method of advertising because it reaches the maximum number of people. However, for fashion retailers it is not always cost-effective as the fashion consumer or the target market may not see the advertisement. Also, it may be lost among other non-fashion advertisements, and a short three-minute commercial cannot always show the

电视广告是一种最昂贵的广告方式，因为它触及的人数最多。但是，对于时装零售商而言，这并不总是划算的，因为时装消费者或目标市场可能并没有看到广告，而且时装广告可能会被其他广告所掩盖。再说，短短三分钟的商业广告并不可能介绍企业的全

full range of items available. Television advertising is, however, a useful medium for brand image creation. For many fashion companies, targeting specific programmes which are likely to be watched by the target market may give some precision and an opportunity for the promotion of international brands such as Levi's and Nike.

部商品。然而电视广告是创建品牌形象的一种有效的方法，许多时装公司把目标锁定在一些特定的节目，因为目标市场有可能观看这些节目，从而有机会推广国际品牌，如李维斯和耐克。

9.4.2 Outdoor advertising ／户外广告

Ambient media denotes advertising on billboards, the Underground, street furniture, taxis, etc. It is relatively inexpensive, and its main advantage is that it can be highly targeted to transport users within the area of the fashion stores. A disadvantage is that it cannot give a lot of information as people will only have a moment to glance at it, and it must not be too distracting in content as it could cause people to lose concentration.

环境媒体是指出现在广告牌、地铁、街道设施、出租车上的广告，这一广告形式费用低，最主要的优势在于它可以集中针对时装店附近的乘坐公共交通工具的乘客。缺点则在于它无法提供很多的信息，因为人们总是匆匆扫视而过，而且它的内容不能过于分散，否则会使人难以集中注意力。

9.4.3 Magazine advertising ／杂志广告

Advertising in magazines is by far the most effective method of above the line advertising, as it can be fine-tuned to the target market of the magazine. Magazines provide media packs, which outline their target market and pricing strategy. For example, Vogue is renowned as a style bible all over the world and has a very clearly defined target market: 'To be in Vogue is to be in fashion.'

The media pack gives demographic details on the age profile, social classification, income level and education of its core readership, and a lifestyle profile is provided for their potential advertisers. The Vogue reader 'is style conscious ... enjoys an affluent, active lifestyle', dining out, pursuing cultural activities, taking frequent holidays and, of course, shopping at upmarket stores, and spending on clothes.

In addition, there are very specific comparisons with other magazines and instructions and costs associated with advertising in the publication. There is also an offer to bring advertisers together with complementary products to share the costs of a Vogue promotion; this is co-operative advertising and can be useful for advertisers who cannot afford the full cost (sourced from the Vogue Media Pack).

A fashion brand/retailer can be fairly confident when advertising in specific magazines that they can

杂志广告是目前最有效的广告形式，因为它可以准确定位于杂志的目标市场。杂志会提供媒体包，说明的是杂志的目标市场和定价策略。例如，《时尚》杂志闻名世界，被认为是一本介绍时尚的权威杂志，《时尚》杂志对于目标市场有非常明确的限定，即“看《时尚》，就时尚。”

媒体包同时也提供了一些人口方面的信息，如年龄概况、社会等级、收入水平以及核心读者群的受教育程度。另外，媒体包还为潜在的广告商提供了一份读者生活方式的基本信息。《时尚》杂志的读者“讲究品位……过着富足、活跃的生活”，他们是酒店常客、追求文化熏陶、经常度假，当然也会出入高档店铺选购时装。

此外，还与其他杂志进行专门比较，并给出了在出版物上做广告的须知和费用，《时尚》杂志还允许广告商连同他们的互补产品一起均分《时尚》杂志上的促销费用。对于无法承担全额费用的广告商而言，这种联合广告是非常有利的。（资料来源于《时尚》杂志媒体包）

在特定杂志上登广告，时装品牌或零售商可以相当有信心，他们的目标市场与这些

match their target market with the magazine target market and therefore not waste the advertising budget.

杂志的目标市场相匹配，他们的广告预算就不会白白的浪费。

Launched in the UK in 2004, Grazia is a weekly glossy which features the very latest in not only fashion, but also celebrity lifestyle. This magazine and other celebrity-focused publications have had a major impact on the fashion marketing communications mix, which will be discussed later in this chapter.

《红秀》于 2004 年在英国开办，这是一本时装周刊，其主要内容不仅包括最新时装消息，还包括名人生活方式方面的最新信息，该杂志与其他以名人为焦点的出版物对于时装营销传播组合有着重要影响。稍后我们将在本章中讨论。

9.4.4 Radio advertising ／广播广告

Radio advertising is not used very much by the fashion industry, since it is difficult to communicate the brand image by sound. The exception to this might be to alert listeners to a sale event – department stores that have a one-off extended trading period or 12-hour event happening that very same day use the radio to stimulate drivers to go into town.

时装界并没有广泛使用广播广告，因为很难用声音来传播品牌形象，但却可以通过广播广告提醒听众注意打折销售活动。例如，某百货公司一次性地延长营业时间，或者是在同一天里的 12 小时活动，都可以用广播刺激消费者到此购物。

9.5 Sales promotion ／营业推广

This method of promotion revolves around offering a discount on merchandise on production of a coupon often given away in a magazine. The cost of this obviously requires budgeting into the original promotional strategy, but provides a method of immediate feedback on the success of the promotion and would perhaps turn new or occasional shoppers into regular purchasers.

这种促销方法以商品打折为主，会在杂志中提供商品优惠券。这种方法的成本显然要计算到促销策略当中，这是一种能立刻反馈促销效果的方法，也许还能将新顾客或流动顾客变成老主顾。

Owing to the seasonal nature of fashion, mid-season and end-of-season sales are the most frequent methods of sales promotion and an effective way of reducing the stockholding in order to make space for new merchandise; however due to the rise of the 'fast fashion' phenomenon, which is the consumers' constant demand for newness, stores are often in continual markdown.

由于时装的季节性，季中和季末甩卖是促销中最经常使用的方法。这种方法能有效地减少存货堆积，从而为新产品腾出空间。但是由于“快时尚现象”的出现，即消费者对新事物的持续需求，商店经常连续减价。

9.6 Public relations ／公共关系

In fashion marketing, public relations (PR) is a very effective method of promotion; however, this method of communicating the fashion brand or a particular item is not always obvious to the untrained eye.

时装营销中，公共关系是一种非常有效的促销方法，但是对于那些缺少经验的人而言，则很难发现传播信息当中的时装品牌或者特色商品。

According to Harrison (1995), there is no universally accepted definition of PR, and perhaps this reflects its relatively new and still developing role within marketing. We might use the Institute of Public Relations (IPR) definition as a useful description of the role and responsibility of PR: 'Public Relations is about reputation – the result of what you do, what you say and what others say about you'.

In essence PR can be seen as managing the corporate identity. This can simply be getting goods into the public arena at one end of the spectrum, or at the other extreme, refuting any adverse publicity that the company may face. Therefore, it is important for an organization to have a PR department in place in order to be prepared for adverse reactions from the press or public. PR, if used effectively, can be seen as the guardian of the corporate reputation.

In fashion marketing, PR may be done by an in-house department, or by an external agency. It might be suggested therefore that PR should aim to:

- raise or confirm the profile of the brand/retailer;
- place products in the public arena;
- enhance other parts of the promotional mix;
- communicate with influential media.

In fashion marketing, PR is responsible for ensuring that magazines have merchandise to feature in fashion shoots, comparative offers and editorial features. This is a role 'behind the scenes' that is not always immediately apparent. Editorials are usually taken from press releases and may be very credible to the reader as an editorial is not an advertisement on behalf of the company, but an endorsement by an influential style leader. The success of PR can be measured using the value of how much the amount of space generated would have cost if it had been a traditional advertisement. The space is calculated using advertising rates and is known as 'rate-card value'. PR com-panies can demonstrate to their clients how much 'free' publicity has been generated using this method.

Of course, the brand has little control over how the product may be used in an editorial piece – it may be criticized as having the worst value for money in a comparison with other competitive products.

据哈里森于1995年所说，对于“公共关系”这个词，并没有公认的定义，也许这刚好说明了公共关系是相对较新的方式，而且在营销中的作用在逐渐显现。或许我们可以采用公共关系协会针对公共关系的作用及义务给出的定义：“公共关系关乎名声，是由你所做的、你所说的以及别人的评论所构成的结果。”

本质上来说，公共关系可反映企业形象的整体特征。一方面，它可以仅仅只是将商品展示在公众面前；另一方面，它也可以驳斥公司可能面对的负面宣传。因此对于一家公司而言，拥有一个恰当的公关部以应对媒体或公众的异议，是非常重要的，因为有效的公关活动可以维护公司声誉。

时装营销中，公共关系可由公司内部的部门或公司外部代理商负责。因此，公共关系必须实现以下目标：

- 提高或巩固品牌或零售商的形象；
- 将商品展示给公众；
- 强化促销组合的其他方面；
- 与有影响的媒体打交道。

时装营销中，公关部门负责确保杂志突出商品的特点、相对优势以及编辑特点，这是一个“幕后”的角色，所做出的贡献并不都是显而易见的。评论通常来源于新闻稿，在读者眼中有一定的可靠性，因为评论不是为了维护公司利益的广告，而是得到了权威时尚人士的认可。公共关系的成败可以用相较于使用传统广告而产生的空间量的增加值来衡量，而空间量则使用广告费来计算，即众所周知的“广告收费的价值”，公关公司向顾客展示用此方法可以产生“免费”宣传的效果。

当然，品牌企业是无法控制发布评论的消费者是如何使用商品的。例如，某一品牌的商品可能会被批评为同类商品中最没有价值的。但这必须冒险。处理好公共关系与杂

However, this is a risk that has to be taken, and close relationships between PR and magazine companies exist to limit damage to brands' reputations.

志公司的关系，就是为了将对品牌名声的伤害降到最低。

Other responsibilities of PR are also in event management, which could include arranging fashion shows, gala events, exhibitions and sponsorship deals. This makes it sound like a very glamorous career, but of course there is crisis management to consider, especially when the brand (or a celebrity by association) gets bad publicity. Contrary to the popular saying not all publicity is good publicity, as the bad tends to get repeated before any good news. For example, despite increased sales and a high-profile advertising campaign the previous fortunes of the company are often reported in the press:

'... once ailing, M&S stages a come back ...'

公共关系的其他职责还包括大型事务管理，例如安排时装秀、庆典活动、时装展以及赞助的协商等，这使得公共关系听起来好像是一份迷人的工作，然而其职责当然还包括危机的处理，尤其是当品牌（或与其合作的名人）的宣传效果不好的时候。事实上有时是与传言相反的，并非所有的宣传都是有利的宣传，因为好消息出现之前，坏消息总是屡次出现。例如尽管销售增长、广告宣传引人注目，可是该公司先前的负面信息还总是在新闻报道中被提及：

"……一度境况不佳，玛莎百货筹划东山再起。"

9.7 Celebrity endorsement and sponsorship ／名人代言和赞助

PR also has an important role to play in the use of celebrities by brands. Celebrity endorsement is a particularly powerful form of promotion and is increasingly being used by companies. Linking a well-known personality with the brand can give many benefits. If a well-known personality endorses a product or wears a brand through a sponsorship deal, we may well understand that they are being paid to promote the product. However, the effect is one of credibility, particularly if the personality is admired, in which case they imbue the product with their attributes of good taste, attractiveness, etc. Endorsement can give credibility to a brand that advertising alone cannot give. If a brand is linked with a personality who is outstanding or popular in their chosen field of endeavour, then the brand and the personality will begin to share similar characteristics, and the identity of the brand and the person become linked and begin to share similar characteristics. Sportswear brands have used celebrity endorsements to great effect in matching the brand with the personality.

公关还在选用名人代言品牌中起着重要的作用，名人代言是特别有力的促销形式，越来越广泛地被公司所采用。将名人与品牌结合在一起，会使公司获益匪浅。如果某位名人为某商品代言，或在赞助活动中穿戴某品牌商品，我们可以清楚地知道他们是在接受代言费用后在为这一产品宣传的。但是其效果是具有可信度的，尤其是当这一名人备受崇拜时，他们会使产品的品位和吸引力大大提升，代言可以给一个品牌带来广告无法带来的可信度。如果一个品牌和一位在某一特定领域卓有成就或者备受喜爱的名人联系起来，那么这一品牌就和这一名人开始分享相似的特点。运动品牌使用名人代言，使品牌和名人联系在一起，就产生了良好的效果。

The major disadvantage of this is if the endorser 'falls from grace', by being accused of some scandal or wrong doing, then the product with which they

名人代言的最大弊端就是假如代言人"失宠"了，或由于丑闻或错误行为而被指控，那和他们紧密联系在一起的商品也注定在劫

are linked will inevitably suffer a similar fate, and can become tainted with the same public disapproval. One of the worst things a celebrity endorser can do is publicly announce they don't wear or use the product with which they are linked. Overexposure is also a problem when the celebrity has too many products to endorse. It then seems as if they cannot possibly be in this for anything than the money, and this loses credibility for the brands involved. Sometimes the celebrity is bigger than the brand and viewers remember the celebrity but not the product with which they were connected. Contracts may overcome some of the disadvantages and problems for brands when linking up with people who are, only human after all. Levi's overcame this by using Flat Eric, a puppet!

难逃，也将一同受到公众的谴责，最糟糕的就是代言的名人不得不当众宣布他们不再穿用那些和他们有联系的商品了。代言过多是另一问题，即同一名人为多个商品代言。这无疑会使人们想到是利益驱使，从而失去对该品牌的信任。有时名人比品牌更有影响力，观看者只记住了名人，而忘记了与其关联的商品。明星毕竟也是凡人，因此当将品牌和名人联系起来时，合约可以帮助品牌克服一些不利的因素和问题，李维斯使用玩偶弗莱特·埃里克来代言就避免了这方面的问题。

Case studies – choosing the right celebrity / 案例分析——选择合适的名人

An own label retailer with a strong brand and market share was considering using celebrity endorsement for an advertising campaign. In order to establish which celebrities out of a large number would be suitable, they undertook some market research. The faces of the celebrities were shown to customers within the store environment and customers were asked to match the store personality to the celebrity personality. From this research there were five clear winners among the celebrities, and these five were subsequently used in an advertising campaign.

一个拥有自主品牌、驰名商标、可观市场份额的零售商，计划通过名人代言进行广告宣传。为了在众多名人中选择最合适的代言人，他们进行了市场调查。在商店里，他们向顾客展示每个名人的照片，询问他们哪一位明星的气质和商店的特色相匹配。通过调查，有五位名人脱颖而出并最终确定为广告模特。

Kate Moss has become one of the most famous models in the world since she shot to fame for Calvin Klein, shortly after being discovered in an airline check-in queue. However, as has been widely documented – whether accurate or not – an alleged revelation of substance abuse led to a number of her high-profile brand contracts being terminated. For example, H&M as a brand aimed at impressionable youth rapidly withdrew their support for her, but many including Rimmel which is positioned as an edgy London brand were to continue their affiliation. Indeed it would now appear that Kate Moss has more contracts than she had before. At the time of writing she is the face of Dior, Louis Vuitton, Belstaff and Burberry among others. It will be interesting to observe how this continues. Indeed, in Autumn 2006,

凯特·摩斯在机场登记处被星探挖掘，随后为凯文·克莱恩代言，并成为世界上最著名的模特之一。然而，因为不知虚实的大量报道爆出其吸毒丑闻后，各大品牌纷纷与她解约。比如海恩斯·莫里斯，目标群体是易受影响的年轻人，他们就不再支持凯特了。但是许多品牌包括芮谜，一个被定位为不安分（自由尝试、无拘无束）的伦敦品牌，选择与凯特续约。实际上，相比之前，凯特合约不减反增，写此书时，凯特正代言迪奥、路易威登、贝达弗和巴宝莉等品牌，继续关注此事的发展态势颇有意思。实际上，在2006年的秋天，凯特就与顶级店合作发布了个人时装系列。

she teamed up with TopShop to launch her own fashion range.

Sienna Miller is widely attributed with popularizing the 'boho' look in summer 2005. Many retailers had failed to spot the trend and were left to play a very swift game of catch up, which gave them the expert-ise to use fast fashion techniques. This demonstrates the power that a celebrity being photographed by paparazzi and appearing in weekly gossip columns can have on the fashion supply chain.

西耶娜·米勒在2005年夏天推广波西米亚潮流时得到广泛认可，许多零售商没能捕捉到该流行潮流，只能流于跟风的俗套。这样的案例给零售商们提供了一些快时尚反应的经验，这也体现了名人被狗仔队偷拍等一类的信息对时装供应链的影响。

It is often prohibitively expensive for companies on a limited budget to use a top model or celebrity so they may look for one who is tipped to become a star in the future, this is known as 'seeding', and worked well for Eva Herzegovina and Wonderbra. However, if the 'star' does not materialize, the brand will not get the coverage either.

对于预算有限的公司而言，聘请顶级模特和明星的费用令人望而生畏。因此他们会寻找刚出道的新人，这种方式被称为“播种”，品牌伊娃·何塞格维娜和魔术胸罩就是通过这种方法获得收益的。然而如果该明星不被受众认可，品牌自然也就不能得以推广。

The casual clothing brand Criminal used Steven Marks a self-confessed drug smuggler as an ironic figurehead for its publicity.

休闲时装品牌“罪犯”在品牌推广时，使用的是一个自首的毒品走私犯斯蒂文·马科斯的头像，极具讽刺意味。

David Beckham is an example of a celebrity who has become a brand in his own right.

作为名人中的范例，大卫·贝克汉姆凭借自身头衔已然成为了最上位的品牌代言人。

When selecting a suitable celebrity, fashion marketers try to achieve a match between the characteristics of the brand image they wish to project and the perceived qualities of the celebrity. In practice this is often accomplished by the use of focus groups who discuss their impressions of both celebrities and brands.

在挑选合适的名人时，时装市场营销人员试图找到个性气质与品牌形象特点相匹配的名人，在实际操作中，只有通过销售团队针对名人和商品的印象展开讨论来实现。

9.8 Personal selling ／人员促销

In fashion marketing the role of the sales assistant generally varies according to the type of outlet.

在时装营销中，售货员所起的作用因店铺类型不同而有差异。

Fashion outlets for the youth market tend to be self-service as the 'fashion enthusiasts' are quite happy to select, try on and purchase garments without much help or interference. However, the older consumer may require a personal service in terms of advice and alterations. Therefore, the type of sales assistant recruited by a fashion company tends to attract and reflect the target market in terms of age, size, demographics and lifestyle; although legislation against age discrimination may counterbalance this exact reflection of the brand by employees.

年轻群体的时装卖场更为自由，因为这些时尚爱好者很喜欢随性挑选、试穿、购买个性时装，不希望别人给予太多的建议，上了年纪的消费者则希望售货员可以提供建议和选择。因此，尽管反对歧视老年人的立法规定可能会与企业意图通过员工准确展示品牌的理念相矛盾，可是时装公司在招聘时，还是要寻找那些在年龄、体型、人口特征和生活品位上能够吸引和反映目标市场的销售人员。

9.8.1 Personal shoppers become personal stylists ／购物顾问成为个人造型师

This type of service is offered by upmarket retailers and is now increasingly a feature of the mass market. A selection of merchandise is provided from which the customer can make a selection in some privacy and comfort. It is also popular for the busy, time constrained, working executive or for a special-occasion purchaser. As in the cult of celebrity, everyone wants their own personal stylist and stores are catering to this demand by providing a stylist service. TopShop was the first fashion chain to pick up on the trend.

此类服务最初由高级零售商提供，时至今日已日趋成为大众市场的特色。商品的最终选择基于顾客的个人喜好和舒适感，这在日理万机的高层工作人员和为特殊场合而购买时装的消费者当中也很流行。追求名人时尚的同时，每个人都想拥有个人造型师，商家正是适应这种需求推出了形象设计服务，顶级店是第一个捕捉到此时尚风潮的商家。

9.8.2 Direct marketing ／直接营销

Direct marketing can be the purest form of one-to-one personal communication if it is used correctly, but all too often it tends towards the unimaginative mass mail out and misses golden opportunities. How many times have you received a mail shot which seems to take no account of your previous purchase history (you've never bought childrenswear from them, which might suggest you don't have children), and furthermore, they have spelt your name incorrectly? This does not engender confidence that it is the personalized invitation it purports to be.

如果使用恰当的话，直接营销是一对一人员传播最直接最有效的方式，但是在大多数情况下，发出的大量邮件都石沉大海并错失了许多好机会。有多少次你收到的邮寄广告是根本没有考虑你的购买记录的（你从未向他们买过儿童时装，可能意味着你没有小孩），此外商家是否写错了你的名字。这样的话，企业就很难赢得客户的信任，也感受不到为自己量身定做的初衷。

One shining example of how to use direct marketing effectively is that of the retailer Boden, which by being a predominantly mail order business, has enabled them to hone their skills in this area.

如何有效地开展直销，有一个鲜明的例子就是零售商波登，这是一家领先的邮购订单公司，在长期的磨练中直邮业务的技术越来越熟练。

Credit card and loyalty schemes allow brands/retailers to create databases which can provide direct marketing opportunities. Stores use the store card details of their customers to invite shoppers to launch events. Mobile phone and e-mail alerts direct to customers can be a strong reminder of the brand.

品牌经营者和零售商们通过信用卡和会员优惠制度建立了顾客数据库，为直销提供了更多的机会。商家可以通过赊购卡邀请顾客购买商品，而手机和电子邮件的提示也有助于加强消费者对品牌的印象。

9.9 Visual merchandising to visual marketing ／从视觉推销到视觉营销

In fashion marketing communications, one of the most important tools is the retail environment itself and deserves to have its own separate place in the promotional mix.

在时装营销传播中，最主要的手段之一就是卖场环境设置，在促销组合中应该单独考虑这一要素。

There is no single definition of what visual merchandising is, combining as it does for different commentators, different parts of the total retail environment experience. However, this one can be utilized as a broad approach to a definition:

Visual merchandising is the physical representation and communication cue of the brand or retailer, through creative grouping and presentation of merchandise in windows and in the store.

Visual merchandising is seldom just window display, as the store design and layout also plays a role in the creative treatment of the retail experience. The window, however, is a stage on which the retailer 'struts its stuff' as it is normally the first thing that the customer comes into contact with and this attracts the audience.

Visual merchandising, and store design and layout are now becoming widely regarded as important promotional tools to differentiate fashion store images in a crowded environment. Store designers often incorporate elements of the design process into promotional tools such as in-store graphics, but more are now visible in wrapping materials, carrier bags, T-shirts (which are then carried and worn), and become a powerful and free promotional tool out on the streets.

However, visual merchandising cannot be separated from the rest of the marketing mix. No amount of creativity and promotion can sell merchandise that customers do not want. But assuming that the product, price and place elements of the mix are correctly assembled to match the target market, visual merchandising as a part of the promotional mix is an attractive component of store presentation.

Since it is said that we retain 70% of what we see, compared with only 30% of what we hear or read, then it would be fair to assume that the visual representation of the brand must be an important tool in fashion marketing communications.

Store windows attract customers at a distance and they carry a number of subtle messages which customers use in order to decide whether to enter or not. New and on trend merchandise, the style of the mannequins, the styling of the garments all indicate to potential customers whether this is their type of store. Once inside the store, displays can be used effectively as signage so as to avoid too many

视觉推销没有单一的定义，要结合不同时装评论家和总体零售环境的不同方面来确定，因此也有了更为广泛的定义。

视觉推销是品牌或零售商的实物的展示和交流，主要是店内有创意的分类陈列及橱窗商品的展示。

视觉推销不只是橱窗展示，店面设计和内部装潢以及商品陈列在体现零售创意服务方面的作用不可小觑。橱窗是零售商“大显身手”展现精品服饰的平台，因为通常顾客最先接触并且被吸引的是橱窗中的商品。

视觉推销、店面装潢和商品陈列成为重要的宣传手段，有利于店铺形象在参差不齐的市场中脱颖而出。一些设计师将设计元素融入宣传手段中，比如室内装潢，以及现在更具视觉化的包装材料、手提袋、T恤衫（可以携带或穿着），这些已成为街头免费的宣传手段。

然而，视觉推销却不能独立于其他的营销组合要素。没有什么创意或促销能够让顾客买不想要的东西，但是假如能够恰当地组合产品、价格和地点因素并且符合目标市场的话，视觉推销就会成为促销组合的一个组成部分，也会成为店铺陈列当中极具吸引力的要素。

据说人们的记忆中70%来自视觉，30%来自听觉，因此可以很准确地假设，品牌的视觉陈列展示是时装营销传播中的重要手段。

商店橱窗可以远远地吸引消费者并潜藏着微妙的信息，让消费者决定是否进入。新颖时尚的商品，模特的风格，衣服的款式都给消费者暗示该店是否符合他们的品味。一旦进入店内，陈列的商品就成了标识，从而可以避免过多的书面信息。然而，有一种叫做“快时尚”的货架，现已成为店铺的特色，

written messages. However there is one fixture in stores that has recently become a feature and that is the 'fast fashion' fixture, often labelled with a sense of urgency:

通常贴着具有紧迫感的标签:

- Get it before it goes!
- Buy it now or regret it later!

- 走过路过，不要错过!
- 机不可失，时不再来!

The fixture and the signage provide the busy but 'fashion enthusiast' consumer with a short cut communication to the latest deliveries. A small number of garments are on this fixture which signals exclusivity and rarity, although thousands may exist in the apparel pipeline, this encourages an impulse purchase based on the premise that the opportunity may not arise again.

此类货架和标识让繁忙但热爱时尚的消费者最便捷地了解到了新品，少量时装被摆在此货架上，以显示其具有个性且很稀有，虽然在流水线中还有成千上万的时装，但这却极大促进了消费者的购买欲望，毕竟机会只有一次。

9.9.1 Store design and layout / 店面设计和布局

There exists a whole industry based on store design and layout. However the psychology of attracting customers, via design and visual merchandising, is by no means an exact science.

整个行业是以店面设计和布局为基础的，然而通过设计和视觉推销来吸引消费者的心理学理论绝不是一门精密的科学。

Zara, in particular, presents a designer type environment which suggests exclusivity by using a lot of space in between merchandise, yet has affordable middle market pricing.

Zara 就通过商品间较大的空隙，创造了一个设计师风格的环境，彰显了品牌的特色，并且价格大致在平民消费得起的中档市场定价范围之内。

Even money retailers are recognizing the value of presenting an aesthetically pleasing environment, which in turn encourages customers to stay longer and inevitably spend more than they intend. But they also attract the bargain hunter with a pile it high, sell it cheap offer, which is consequentially an untidy image by the close of business, but it would appear that customers are prepared to forgo a cleanly merchandised environment for a keen price.

即使一些时装零售商意识到了提供美感愉悦的环境能够带来一些价值，如可以延长消费者在店铺内的逗留时间，而且还可能比预期花费更多。但是他们有时也以囤货多、价格低来吸引四处寻购便宜货的消费者，打烊的时候卖场就会一片凌乱。然而有些消费者为了找到更廉价的商品，他们通常不会选择那些一干二净的购物环境。

Visual merchandising can of course be used to discourage the 'wrong' target market; stores who do not put the prices of garments in the window suggest high prices. Closed, heavy doors, buzzer entry systems, small windows (like Tiffany jewellers) and uniformed 'greeters' are all visual cues to some people to stay away. In general, the bigger the price signs the cheaper the stock, and vice versa.

视觉推销当然也可能防止选择错误的目标市场。没有把衣服的价格挂在橱窗的商店意味着价格偏高，密闭厚实的门，带蜂鸣器的入口，小窗户（比如蒂凡尼珠宝商）以及身着制服的迎宾员都是显性的暗示，令某些消费者望而却步。总的来说，标价越高，商品存货成本越低，反之亦然。

Layouts in fashion are different in different types of stores. A department store will use a hard surface 'race track' around the perimeter with carpeted areas at each brand concession to slow the footfall and encourage browsing. A 'boutique' layout may look haphazard, but is meant to stop and delight

店铺类型不同，时装陈列方式不同。百货店会用硬质的材料把每个品牌销售区所在的红地毯围绕起来，有利于消费者慢下脚步浏览。精品店的内部陈列看起来随意，但目的是在每个转角都能让顾客停下来愉悦地欣

the customer at every turn. A 'supermarket' type of layout is suitable for large value, discount, out of town (i.e. premium priced floor space) stores where trolleys are used.

赏商品。超级市场类型的陈列适合批量大、折扣低的城郊店（高价卖场），在那里手推车是常用的工具。

Colour, music and fragrance are all used to attract and to some extent control the customer's response and experience by activating their full range of senses. Colours can be either exciting or restful – busy environments use dramatic colours like red to signal sales, vibrancy, etc., whereas more leisured shopping environments with more expensive prices promote calm by using restful colours. It all depends how long you want customers to stay. Music with a fast-tempo has the same effect, it promotes a fast shop; whereas classical music promotes a leisurely stroll. Fragrances developed by brands and retailers are sold alongside the clothes. If a customer identifies with the brand and its values it is likely they will buy into the fragrance by association.

颜色、音乐和气味不仅影响顾客对商品的形象感知，而且在某种程度上也会调整人们的购物情绪和行为。颜色可动可静，比较热闹的环境使用夸张的颜色，如红色，以引导销售，活跃气氛。而休闲的购物环境，商品价格比较昂贵的店铺会选择柔和的色彩，使人能够心情平静，当然这还取决于你想要顾客逗留的时间长短。快节奏的音乐有着同样的效果，就是促使快速选购，但是经典音乐却提供的是一个闲逛的环境。品牌香水通常会和衣服一起搭售，如果消费者认可该品牌及其价值，那么他们就会掏腰包顺带购买香水。

9.9.2 Visual marketing / 视觉营销

Visual merchandising is much more than just 'dressing dummies'. It presents customers with a vision of what garments might look like on them before they have tried them on, and is therefore a stepping stone to a purchase. It offers ideas of how to achieve the desired look, and encourages extra sales of items especially accessories.

视觉推销不仅仅展示"衣着光鲜的人体模特"，一方面是在顾客试穿之前，向顾客展现时装穿在身上的效果，是消费者购买的重要前提；另一方面，体现了如何实现理想的穿衣效果，同时促进了配饰品的销售。

Visual merchandising could therefore be renamed Visual Marketing, reflecting that it combines with the product, price, place and promotion and further underlines its importance in the fashion business.

因此，视觉推销可以重命名为视觉营销，它集产品、价格、地点、宣传于一体，这种描述进一步突出了其在时装销售中的重要性。

9.10 International marketing communications / 国际营销传播

Increasingly, as fashion brands/retailers expand beyond their domestic boundaries, their marketing communications have to translate visually and literally into international markets.

随着时装品牌或零售商的业务超越国界，他们的营销传播无论在视觉还是在文字方面都将不得不打进国际市场。

Marketing communications strategies must therefore be capable of international standardization or adaptation in order to benefit from economies of scale, e.g. one advertisement that can be used globally rather than the expensive multiple generations of advertisement for different markets.

为了从规模经济中获益，营销传播策略一定要有国际水准或适应性，例如：广告要能够在全球范围内使用，而不是那种为不同市场服务的调整多次的昂贵广告。

This puts considerable strain on the creative

这就对国际化促销信息的创意性处理提

treatment of international promotional material, and has led to criticism over a lack of innovation. The future internationalization plans of a company may need consideration when generating ideas for brand names and strap lines. An example of this is the brand name Next, which is difficult to pronounce in some languages, and their advertising strap line, which was innovative and imaginative in the English language: 'Bringing fabric to life', but translated badly into most foreign languages as a rather confusing combination of 'resuscitating dead material': not exactly the image with which the company wished to be associated!

出了更高的要求，也导致因为缺乏创新性而受到批评。当思考品牌名称和广告标语时，一定要考虑到公司未来的国际化战略规划。以奈克斯特品牌名为例，在一些语言中很难发音，他们的广告标语，在英语中很有创意、想象丰富，“赋予纺织品以生命”，但当翻译成其他语言时，却很糟糕，成了“死亡的材料复活”，并没有达到公司希望消费者所能联想到的形象。

Since so many companies are operating globally now, it is not surprising that their logos (visual communication cues) are popular, rather than relying on heavy text which may need translation. The Burberry plaid speaks for itself, as does the interlinked Cs of Chanel and the Nike swoosh. And rather than, including a text that signals a company's presence,

London Paris New York

in a discreet place on an advertisements, a website address is now the norm, which obviously gives far more detail and lists all their locations in whatever language is required.

现如今，既然这么多公司都在全球化运营，他们的图标（视觉传播符号）很流行也就不足为奇了，而不需要依靠那些复杂的且需要翻译的文本材料。巴宝莉的彩格图案本身就是它的代言，还有香奈尔的连环 C，耐克的对勾。在不显眼的地方，用文本的形式表示出公司的地点，

伦敦巴黎纽约

一般会有网址，这样有利于以不同语言提供更详细的信息，并且根据语言需求列出公司的地址。

Observers of Vogue in a variety of markets and languages will see that their advertisements are the same the world over, relying on strong imagery and brand handwriting rather than text.

《时尚》杂志的观察家发现，即使市场不同、语言各异，他们的广告却能在全球通用，依靠的是强大的形象和品牌标识而非文本材料。

9.11 Ethics in marketing communications／营销传播中的道德标准

Legal constraints in terms of advertising have been introduced by most governments on the grounds of deception and false representation; however, the extent to which advertising is controlled varies between countries. Advertising to children is completely banned in Sweden.

由于广告中有欺骗和虚假陈述现象的出现，广告方面的法律约束已经被多数政府采纳。然而国家之间广告控制程度却有很大差异，例如针对儿童的广告在瑞典是完全禁止的。

In the UK, the advertising industry is self-regulatory, which in essence means that the industry controls itself and there should therefore be no offensive advertising or false claims made. However, this is not always the case, and there are instances when perhaps for shock tactics a company will flout the rules. The self-regulatory system means that it is the responsibility of the consumer to complain

在英国，广告业具有自律性，实质上指的是广告业的自我监控，因此没有侵犯性的广告或虚假的广告。然而并非总是如此，有时为了实现震撼的效果，公司可能会忽视法规。这一自律体系也意味着消费者有责任对广告提出投诉（在英国），每一个举报都会认真受理，如果专家组认为举报属实，广告

about an advertisement (in the UK). Even one single complaint will be investigated and if the panel agrees then the advertisement must be modified or withdrawn.

一定要修改或撤销。

If advertising agencies suspect that their creative treatment may cause some offence or is controversial in the UK they can approach the regulatory bodies and gain some advice. Some companies may just go ahead with the campaign and hope for the best.

同样，在英国如果广告公司怀疑他们的创意有可能会引起冒犯或者争议，那么他们可以咨询监察机构以获取建议，然而一些公司有可能坚持使用这些广告，并且希望会有好的结果。

The Advertising Standards Authority (ASA) has some case studies on fashion brands (www.asa.org.uk) which demonstrate the process from complaint to compliance. The brands range from Opium, Harvey Nichols to Diesel, Gucci and of course the ubiquitous French Connection (fcuk).

广告标准局（ASA）有一些关于时装品牌的案例研究（www.asa.org.uk），包括从被投诉到符合要求的过程，这些品牌包括鸦片香水、哈维·尼克斯到迪赛尔、古琦，当然还有无处不在的法式连接。

9.12 Evaluating the effectiveness of marketing communications / 营销传播的有效性评估

The issue of evaluating the effectiveness of any promotional effort is an area that generates a great deal of debate among academics and practitioners alike.

任何一次有关促销活动有效性的评估往往都会引起学术界和从业者的激烈争论。

Some campaigns are reasonably easy to evaluate in terms of increased sales. However, the problem lies in measuring success over a longer period and the effectiveness of different elements of marketing communications. Was it the advertisements on television or the money-off vouchers in magazines that was responsible for increased sales? Research is the key tool to use to establish answers to these types of question.

一些活动由于销售量增加而很容易评估，但难题是对较长时期进行的有效性评估和对营销传播中不同要素的有效性评估。到底是电视上的广告还是杂志上的代金券导致了销售的增加？调研才是解答这类问题的关键工具。

In the UK there are a number of agencies involved in the collection and analysis of data on consumers' viewing and recall habits in the case of advertising. More difficult and expensive to calculate are the changes in attitude towards a brand over time. This requires research before, during and after promotional effort. Some methods of measuring brand awareness can be carried out before, during and after a campaign, this type of research tends to be qualitative and can be done by the company itself, an independent market research company, or a media agency.

在英国，有许多机构从事收集和分析消费者对于广告的看法和回忆行为的数据。难度系数高、费用昂贵的是计算出在一定时间段内顾客对一个品牌的态度上的变化，这需要在促销活动之前、之中和之后进行调研。一些品牌意识测试的方法可以在活动前、中、后使用，这属于定性研究，公司自身、独立市场调研公司或者广告公司都可以完成。

Recall tests question whether the brand is salient (uppermost) in the consumer's mind, the recall can

回忆测试的问题是这一品牌在消费者心里是否是最在意的，回忆可以涉及现在的或

be related to present/previous advertising or can just be a question of when did you last shop in 'XXXX'?

The brand personality of a store can be ascertained by a number of variables as a means of comparison with the competition, in advertising evaluations these might include:

◆ Exciting advertisements , versus , boring advertisements

◆ Different from the rest , versus , the same as the rest

◆ Strong image/handwriting , versus , weak image/handwriting.

Just showing advertisements to respondents without the brand name visible and assessing their recognition will answer some of these questions.

Respondents can be asked 'If this brand was a person what sort of personality would it have?' This can give interesting insights into the perception of the brand.

Like most research into consumer behaviour this area is fraught with complications, conflicting opinions and evidence. It can however yield some useful results if undertaken and applied to a marketing problem correctly.

者过去的广告，也可以设计为一个问题，如：你最后一次光顾 ×× 店是什么时候?

与竞争对手相比较，一家店铺的品牌特色会由许多变量来确定。在广告评估中包括：

◆ 令人兴奋的广告还是无聊的广告；

◆ 与众不同还是大同小异；

◆ 视觉冲击力强的形象 / 字体还是视觉冲击力弱的形象 / 字体。

只需将广告展示给被调查对象，不要告知他们品牌的名称，他们的评价将为这些问题找到答案。

可以向被调查对象提问："如果该品牌是一个人，那么这个人有什么样的个性?"这有助于对这一品牌进行更深入的分析。

和大多数消费者行为研究一样，这一领域的情况也很复杂，有时观点和证据上会存在分歧，然而如果能够针对问题选对方法的话，那么就会得到有价值的结论。

9.13 New directions in fashion marketing communications / 时装营销传播的新动向

Whilst the demise of traditional communication channels has been widely reported, it is highly unlikely that they will disappear. Rather, they will change, develop and integrate with other tools as part of the route to the customer. It will be a test of the skills and a recognition of opportunities for marketing communicators to monitor and adapt to opportunities and changes in the fashion environment.

虽然有很多的报道指出传统的传播渠道已失去了一席之地，但其不可能完全消失，它们将跟随其他传播方式而变化、发展，并且和其他方式相整合，对于营销传播者而言，这将会是他们监控并且作出调整以适应营销环境中的机会和变化的一项能力测试和新的机会。

Media proliferation and direct marketing opportunities / 媒体推广和直接营销机会

The Internet has allowed fashion brands/retailers to establish a presence, communication channel and transactional websites. The Internet allows companies to be international, even global, without the costs normally associated with this strategy, i.e. setting up stores overseas.

网络可以告知时装品牌或者零售商的存在、建立沟通渠道和交易的网址。网络可以使公司全球化，无需像在海外开店那样付出高额成本。

Vogue, *Marie Clare*, *Elle* and *Cosmopolitan*, and the celebrity inspired titles of Hello, OK and Grazia, along with satellite and cable television channels, have crossed international boundaries and therefore provide opportunities for international marketing communications for global fashion brands.

《时尚》、《玛丽·克莱尔》、《世界时装之苑》、《白领时尚》，以及名人带动的《你好》、《OK》、《格拉西亚/红秀》，连同卫星和有线电视等都已经打破了国与国的界限，为全球时装品牌提供了国际化营销传播的机会。

Mobile telephones (GSM) and e-mail have facilitated text message (SMS) alerts to those who sign up for it. Digital technology, whilst in its infancy, is widely regarded as the next most important method for reaching target markets.

移动电话、电子邮件可以帮助注册客户传递文本信息。数字技术虽然还处在初级阶段，却被认为是下一个直抵目标市场的最重要的方式。

As Seen on Screen, www.asos.com, gives the fashion consumer a direct opportunity to buy what the celebrities have been spotted wearing.

通过 www.asos.com，时装消费者可以直接买到他们发现的名人穿的时装。

Viral marketing is beginning to take off as it is such an easy medium to employ. Simply send your favourite advertisement to your friends, and in no time the advertisement has travelled the world at a little or no expense. Tracking these advertisements give companies an opportunity to test consumer reaction before launching an orchestrated campaign – it is said that the Levi's 'Flat Eric' campaign was born this way.

病毒营销现在也在开始流行，其简单易于操作。只需把你最喜欢的广告发送给朋友们，无需花很多钱，该广告就会迅速漫游到世界各地。追踪这些广告，使公司有机会在开始精心安排活动之前测试一下消费者的反应，据说李维斯的“弗莱特·埃里克”活动就是这样诞生的。

Product placement is a subtle form of promotion where brands are featured in films or television programmes. Although it is shortly to be deregulated in Europe, it is not yet clear how important this will become, but having established that the consumer finds PR and celebrity endorsement more credible than traditional advertising channels, it is likely to be a strong tool.

隐性广告是一种微妙的促销形式，主要指的是在电影或者电视节目中体现品牌特点。虽然欧洲对其管制已经取消，但其重要性还并不明朗。然而我们已经发现消费者认为名人代言要比传统的广告更可信，看来隐性广告将会是一种有效的方式。

There is some evidence that user generated word of mouth, usually associated with Internet chat rooms or blogs, is becoming an increasingly popular medium similar to viral marketing, but the content is customer centric. Although companies could, in theory, join in the debate, the unregulated nature of this medium could be a problem in terms of corporate image.

有证据表明在聊天室或博客上发表言论的用户，与病毒营销有着相似之处，其内容主要是以顾客为中心的。虽然理论上来说，公司可以加入其中的讨论，但这种媒体的无序性有可能产生一些影响企业形象的问题。

9.14 Summary / 小结

This chapter has aimed to establish that fashion is different when considered in the context of the promotional mix. Fashion has caught up with the pack by moving away from an over-reliance simply on store presence. In an increasingly competitive

本章旨在强调促销组合背景下时装的独特性，时装已不再单纯地、过度地依赖商店的展示。在竞争日益激烈的营销环境中，寻求营销传播的整合方法，我们称之为“沐浴

marketing environment and looking towards an integrated approach to marketing communications, we might call this 'bathing in the brand', where every aspect has a unique handwriting or signature which cannot be mistaken for another store. This is where the store environment, graphics, display and advertising are in the same style and send a cohesive message regarding image and the product on offer. As fashion becomes increasingly global, the marketing communications may need to reflect or overcome cultural, language and geographical differences.

在品牌之中"，处处体现独特的有别于其他商店的印记。店铺环境、平面形象、陈列、广告都要具有统一的风格，共同表现公司的形象和产品信息。由于时装业变得更加国际化，因此营销传播中就需要体现并且克服文化、语言和地理方面的差异。

Useful websites ／参考网址

www.asa.org.uk
www.asos.com
www.brandrepublic.com
www.brandchannel.com

Further reading ／课后阅读材料

1. Harrison, S. (1995), *Public Relations: An Introduction*, Routledge, London.
   哈里森・S. (1995)，《公共关系导论》，劳特利奇出版社，伦敦 .
2. McGoldrick, P.J. (2002), *Retail Marketing*, McGraw-Hill, Maidenhead.
   麦戈德里克・P. J. (2002)，《零售营销》，麦格罗希尔国际出版公司，梅登黑德 .
3. Milligan, A. (2004), *Brand It Like Beckham*, Cyan, London.
   米利根・A.(2004)，《贝克汉姆的品牌效应》，塞恩，伦敦 .
4. Pringle, H. (2004), *Celebrity Sells*, John Wiley and Sons, Chichester.
   普林格尔・H.(2004)，《明星叫卖》，约翰・威利父子公司，奇切斯特 .
5. Shimp, T.A. (1999), *Advertising, Promotion and Supplemental Aspects of Integrated Marketing Communications*, Dryden Press, London.
   森普・T.A.(1999)，《整合营销传播的广告、促销及其他》，德里登出版社，伦敦 .
6. Tungate, M. (2005), *Fashion Brands: Branding Style from Armani to Zara*, Kogan Page, London.
   唐盖特・M.（2005），《服装品牌：从阿玛尼到 Zara 的品牌风格》，科乾图书出版有限公司，伦敦 .
7. Yadin, D. (2000), *Creative Marketing Communications*, Kogan Page, London.
   亚丁・D.(2000)，《创意营销传播》，科乾图书出版有限公司，伦敦 .
8. Yeshin, T. (2001), *Integrated Marketing Communications (CIM 2001)*, Butterworth-Heinemann, Oxford.
   叶士恩・T.(2001)，《整合营销传播（CIM 2001）》，巴特沃斯海尼曼，牛津 .

Chapter Ten Fashion Marketing Planning

第 10 章 时装营销规划

10.1 Introduction ／引言

Putting all aspects of a marketing mix together to achieve the goals of the organization is the most important fashion marketing task. Activities must be planned, co-ordinated and effectively implemented, and the results monitored. This chapter deals with the fashion marketing planning process, beginning with a broad overview of the process of planning fashion marketing, and continuing with the central role of the mission statement and marketing objectives.

The analysis of marketing activities and the marketing environment by a marketing audit are described. A synopsis is given of SWOT (strengths, weaknesses, opportunities and threats) analysis, a crucial underpinning to the development of a fashion marketing strategy. Consideration of strategic alternatives follows with reference to earl-ier material on segmentation and competitor analysis.

The chapter concludes by presenting a framework for producing a fashion marketing plan and examines some important issues concerned with the implementation of plans.

时装营销最主要的任务是将营销组合的各方面内容集合在一起，以期达到团队目标。营销活动一定要经过规划、协调，才能有效进行，其结果要加以监控。本章主要涉及时装营销规划程序。首先全面概述规划时装营销的过程，继而阐述经营宗旨及营销目标的主导地位。

本章还阐述营销审计对营销活动和营销环境的分析，并对时装营销发展策略起决定性基础作用的 SWOT（优势、劣势、机会、威胁）分析进行概述。战略备选方案的思考引用前面关于市场细分和竞争者的分析资料。

本章最后提出制定时装营销规划的基本框架，并且研究计划实施所涉及的重要问题。

10.2 The planning process and objectives ／规划过程和目标

10.2.1 The planning process ／规划过程

A marketing strategy is a specification of those markets the firm wishes to target with marketing activities and

营销策略是对公司致力于定位的市场的营销活动和如何创造和实现自己的

how competitive advantages are to be created and achieved. A marketing strategy is developed within the broader framework of corporate strategy and goals. The focus of this chapter will naturally be upon fashion marketing plans, but the whole context of the fashion marketing planning process should be kept in mind. Figure 10.1 shows the broader view of the process.

竞争优势的详细说明。营销策略是在更广泛的公司策略和目标的框架内制定的。这一章节的重点很自然落在时装营销规划上，而且要牢记整个时装营销规划程序。图 10–1 显示了规划过程全貌。

Figure 10.1 The fashion marketing planning process. 图 10–1 时装营销规划过程

Fashion marketing planning has been described as a process. It is a continuous activity and if undertaken correctly should be self-improving. The process requires the setting and communication of standards, effective implementation or corrective action and timely feedback on performance. The starting point in the process is taken from the marketing objectives, although, as noted above, these are subject to wider corporate decisions.

时装营销规划被描述为一个过程。它是一项持续性活动，如果合理实施，能够达到自我完善。整个过程需要标准的设定和沟通、有效执行或纠正行动的偏差、决策执行中的适时反馈。这一过程的起点是营销目标。尽管上文提到这些都从属于更广意义的公司决策。

10.2.2 The mission statement ／经营宗旨

The mission statement should begin by asking what business is the firm in and what kind of business would it like to be in? Normally this should be defined sufficiently broadly to allow flexibility but still be specific, for example, providing fashionable eveningwear and accessories rather than selling dresses. It also should be defined in terms of customer need, bearing in mind the firm's strengths in relation to the competition. Mission statements should be short and inspiring for company employees; they provide reasons for the firm's survival and growth and

公司的经营宗旨首先应从提出这样的问题开始：公司经营何种业务？公司想要致力于经营何种业务？一般说来，应充分定义经营宗旨，允许一定的灵活性，但是仍要明确。比方说，提供时尚晚礼服和配饰而不是销售普通女装。也应该从顾客的需求方面定义，同时牢记公司的竞争优势。经营宗旨应该简短，对公司职员有鼓舞作用；它能为公司的生存与发展提供依据，并且是判断企业

are a touchstone for judging corporate behaviour and development. Mission statement should be communicated to all interested stakeholders in the firm, employees, suppliers, customers and shareholders. They are in effect an enduring sense of purpose for the organization.

行为及发展的试金石。经营宗旨应该传达给公司里每一位利益相关者，职员、供应商、顾客和股东。实际上他们凝聚公司的持久的方向感。

For example River Island has the aim of providing 'design choice and value' as part of the mission statement. The company also has a full range of operating principles that derive from the broad mission statement and these are communicated in the annual report and are used in advertising copy and personnel communication initiatives. As its mission statement Levis Strauss has 'People love our clothes and trust our company. We will make the most appealing and widely worn casual clothing in the world. We will cloth the world.' Part of the Mango mission is 'Dressing the urban and modern woman, meeting her daily needs, is the formula which we have analysed, adapted and applied to each country we operate in.'

例如，“河岛”品牌的部分经营宗旨定位是提供“设计选择与价值”。公司还从总体的经营宗旨中导出一系列经营原则。这些都会在年报上进行交流，并且应用于广告宣传材料和人才交流上。再如“李维斯”的经营宗旨是“人们喜爱我们的时装，信任我们的公司，我们要生产出全球最具吸引力、最受欢迎的休闲装。我们要扮美世界”。“芒果”品牌的部分经营宗旨是“装扮都市摩登女郎，满足她的日常需求，是我们分析研究、适应和运用于每一个我们所经营地区的准则”。

10.2.3 Marketing objectives /营销目标

These will be more specific than the broad mission statement and will include quantified data such as profit levels, number of new business customers and market share. As shown in Figure 10.1, marketing objectives derive from corporate objectives. The latter are broader and include all aspects of the company's operations such as production, personnel and safety, as well as marketing objectives.

营销目标比内容宽泛的经营宗旨更为具体，并且包括量化数据，例如利润水平、新增客户业务数额及市场份额。如图 10–1 所示，营销目标来自企业目标。后者范围更广，除了营销目标外，还包括公司运营的各个方面，如生产、员工及安全。

Marketing objectives should be clear, written, measurable and attainable, but still challenging. They also should be specific and stated in relation to time constraints. Two examples of marketing objectives are: 'Our aim is to increase sales turnover from £31.3 million to £35.7 million in the next financial year, and to increase the gross profit margin by 5.2%' and 'to increase the share of sales via our corporate website from 4.3% of sales turnover to 8.5% within the next six months.'

营销目标应该清晰、书面化、可衡量并且可以达到，但还应具挑战性，也应具体，有时间限制。以两个营销目标为例:“我们的目标是在下一财政年度，把营业额从 3130 万英镑提高到 3570 万英镑，使毛利增长 5.2%”和“在接下来的 6 个月，通过我们企业网站，把销售份额从 4.3% 增加到 8.5%”。

10.3 Marketing audits and SWOT analysis /营销审计和 SWOT 分析

10.3.1 A marketing audit /营销审计

To achieve marketing objectives the current situation must be analysed. Periodic reviews of the marketing goals, operations and performance

要达成营销目标，应该分析当前形势。对营销目标、运营及时装公司业绩的定期审查被称为营销审计。这一概念和财务审计很

of fashion companies are known as marketing audits. The concept is very similar to financial audit, but unfortunately the former are carried out less frequently than the latter. The marketing audit involves a set of detailed questions that are asked to determine the status of the firm in relation to its objectives, customers, competition and marketing environment. One of the main reasons for a marketing audit is to identify areas where corrective action may be needed. The marketing audit is usually organized into two main categories covering the firm's internal and external environment.

相似，但遗憾的是，和财务审计相比，营销审计较少进行。营销审计涉及一系列具体问题。这些问题决定公司在企业目标、顾客、竞争和营销环境中的地位。进行营销审计的主要原因之一是为了确认哪个区域需要进行调整。营销审计通常分成两类，涉及公司的内部与外部的状况。

The audit of the external marketing environment covers the items identified in Chapter Two. Common frameworks adopted for the external marketing audit include LEPEST or STEPLE analyses, both of which cover Legal, Environmental, Political, Economic, Social and Technological aspects of the environment. The framework in Chapter Two elaborates on the above factors and distinguishes between controllable and partially controllable variables that require monitoring and analysis. The external audit should examine current activity and projected trends in both macro- and micro-marketing environments. It is imperative that all assumptions are made explicit in the audit, so that later modifications can be made to facts about developing events. For example, an assumption about forecast inflation rates for the next 12 months will have an impact upon the company's pricing policy. Thus data from the Retail Price Indices can be used later, if necessary, to revise plans. Likewise, anticipated changes in the bank rate will impact upon consumer purchasing power and thereby impact upon sales of garments.

外部营销环境审计包括在第 2 章所涉及的内容。一般用于外部营销审计的框架包括 LEPEST 分析或 STEPLE 分析。[译者注：LEPEST 分析或 STEPLE 分析是指是利用环境扫描分析总体环境中的政治 (Political)、经济 (Economic)、社会文化 (Socio–cultural)、科技 (Technological)、法律 (Legal)、环境 (Environmental) 等 6 种因素的模型。最近扩展又增加了教育 (Education) 与人口统计 (Demographics)。这也是在做市场研究时外部分析的一部分，能给予公司一个针对总体环境中不同因素的概述。这个策略工具也能有效地了解市场的成长或衰退、企业所处的情况、潜力与营运方向。] 两者都涉及法律、环境、政治、经济、社会和科技方面的因素。在第 2 章的框架中详细叙述了以上因素，并且区分了可控制的变量以及需要监测和分析的部分可控制变量。外部审计应该检查当前的活动和在宏观和微观的营销环境中的可预测的发展动态。在审计中，所有的推测都必须清晰明朗，这样可以修正新产生的结果。例如，对于下一年通货膨胀率的预测，会对公司的定价策略产生影响。因而，如果需要，零售价格指数的资料就会被用来修改计划。同样，银行利率变动的预测将影响消费者的购买力，从而影响衣服的销售。

The scope of an internal marketing audit would cover detailed analysis of sales, profits and market share data by product life and product range. As with the external audit a series of questions are asked about objectives, activities and achievement. For example, the adequacy of the size of the sales force may be

内部营销审计通过产品寿命周期及产品范围对销售额、利润和市场份额数据进行详细分析。对于外部审计，要提出一系列关于目标、活动和成就方面的问题。例如，评估销售规模是否足够与分布趋向的改变有关，生产线下线频率也要进行审查。营销审计可能还会质疑价格是如何确定的，竞争对手的价格资料的完整

assessed in relation to changing distribution trends or the frequency of product line deletions may be examined. The audit also may question how prices are set, the sufficiency of data about competitors' prices or the effectiveness of dealing with customer complaints. The whole range of marketing activities are subject to audit and are judged against customers' perceptions and marketing objectives.

性和解决消费者投诉的有效性。整个营销活动都需要经过审计，并且评估要以消费者的感受和营销目标为准则。

10.3.2 SWOT or situational analysis / SWOT 或形势分析

The outcome of a marketing audit is usually a detailed document specifying achievements and suggesting, where necessary, corrective action. Another use of the audit is the construction of a SWOT analysis, which is also known as a situational assessment of the firm. The SWOT, in essence, is the key issue emerging from the audit.

营销审计的结果通常是一个详细的书面文件形式，详述业绩和建议，如有必要，会提出调整措施。审计的另一用途是进行 SWOT 分析，即对公司进行环境的评估。从本质上来讲，SWOT 分析是审计的关键。

SWOT analysis considers both internal and external factors about either the whole company or a particular fashion product line or range in relation to customers, competitors and trends in the marketing environment. Strengths and weaknesses concern internal factors and opportunities and threats concern external factors. Figure 10.2 shows some components of a SWOT analysis.

SWOT 分析要考虑到与营销环境中的顾客、竞争对手和趋势相关的整个公司或一个特殊的时装产品生产线或者类别的内部和外部因素。优势和劣势涉及内部因素，而机会和威胁涉及外部因素。图 10–2 展示 SWOT 分析的一些构成要素。

Figure 10.2 Strengths, weaknesses, opportunities and threats. 图 10–2 优势、劣势、机会和威胁

Obviously the marketing audit is a good starting point to prepare a SWOT analysis; however, not all companies undertake regular marketing audits. The first marketing audit is invariably the most difficult for most companies as benchmarks or experience may be unavailable. Subsequent audits can begin with the preceding audit and marketing plan.

显然，营销审计是准备 SWOT 分析的一个良好开端。但是，并不是所有的公司都定期进行审计。对于大多数的公司来说，初次营销审计是最困难的，因为他们没有任何标准或者经验。后续的审计可以从前期的审计和营销计划开始。

A few guidelines are given below to enable the preparation of a simple SWOT analysis. The SWOT should be concise and specific, and communicate the key issues facing the firm. The items identified should be related to each other and not simply an *ad hoc* collection that does not point to future action. A clearly written analysis is helpful when it points to solutions or direct consequences. For example, 'A new outlet of a large competitor threatens our childrenswear department. Allow for a potential slowdown in sales turnover of 8–10% in next 12 months.' The alternative for the above childrenswear department may be to change the marketing mix to meet the threat more directly.

An important dimension of the SWOT analysis is the need for objectivity. This argument equally applies to the marketing audit. Fashion marketers charged with producing a marketing plan can sometimes be too close to the firm to be objective, as identifying certain weaknesses can be construed as admitting past failures. Outsiders, such as marketing consultants, can bring a broader and more objective perspective, but they are expensive and they take time to get to know the operations and procedures of the particular firm. At times, it can be most useful to employ a manager from another department or branch of the same company or a retired senior executive to bring objectivity coupled with company knowledge to help with the SWOT analysis.

以下阐述几个简单的 SWOT 分析准备的指导方针。SWOT 分析应该简明具体，并且要传达公司面临的关键问题。提出的项目应该彼此相关，不只是专门汇总那些将来不一定致力于开发的方面。如果直指解决方案或直接结果，清晰的书面分析会很有助益。例如，“大竞争对手采取的新一轮批发销售会对我们的童装部产生威胁。估计会使未来 12 个月的营业额减少 8% ~ 10%”。上述童装部门的备选方案可能会是改变营销组合以直面这个威胁。

SWOT 分析的一个重要方面是要求客观性。这一点同样适用于营销审计。负责制定营销计划的时装营销人员有时和公司走得太近，难以做到客观，因为指出某些劣势，就意味着承认过去的失误。而一些局外人，例如营销顾问，他们就会从更宽广、更客观的角度来看待。但是请他们费用昂贵，而且他们需要花时间去了解这个公司的业务和程序。有时，最有效的方法是雇用同一公司另一部门的经理，或者退休的高级主管，他们的企业知识和客观能够帮助公司进行 SWOT 分析。

10.4 Marketing strategy ／营销策略

10.4.1 Strategic choice and marketing tactics ／战略选择与营销战术

If the marketing objective describes 'What' has to be achieved, then the marketing strategy details 'How' the objectives are to be achieved.

Marketing strategy consists of important long-term decisions to which the competition cannot react quickly. It is the relationship of the firm with its environment. As marketing is an activity that is closely concerned with that environment, there is often considerable similarity between the corporate and marketing strategies within a firm.

The terms strategy and tactics need to be distinguished. Strategy is doing the right thing and is ultimately the search for effectiveness. Tactics are doing things right; they lead to efficiency. Unfortunately, some firms who apparently do not believe in planning

如果把市场目标形容为要取得“什么”，那么营销战略就是详述“如何”取得这一目标。

营销战略是由竞争中不能快速反应的至关重要的长期决策组成，涉及公司与其所处环境之间的关系。由于营销与环境息息相关，公司与公司内部营销策略之间有很大的相似处。

“战略”与“战术”这两个术语要区分开来。战略是指做正确的事，并且最终寻求效果。战术则是正确做事，战术追求效率。遗憾的是，正如第 7 章关于促销价格的讨论中所讲的，一些很显

have allowed short-term tactics to override strategy, as shown in the discussion of promotional pricing in Chapter Seven. Therefore, deciding upon the correct strategy and moving in the right direction are important for firms and require considerable effort.

然不信任规划的公司已经允许短期战术来代替战略了。因此，制定正确的战略，向正确的发展方向前进对公司来说是很重要的，而且需要艰苦的努力。

The SWOT analysis shows how the fashion firm will fare in the future and this should be compared with the marketing objectives that were established earlier. Often there will be a gap between objectives and the current situation and the larger the gap the more risky or adventurous the marketing plan must be.

SWOT 分析显示时装公司将来如何发展，这应与早期设立的营销目标相比较。通常目标与现状之间都有一定的差异。这个差异越大，这项营销计划风险越大。

From the SWOT analysis the firm should be able to make detailed assessment of the competition, its own distinctive strengths and which market segments to aim for.

利用 SWOT 分析公司能做出竞争的详细评估，了解自己与众不同的优势以及明确定位于哪一个细分市场。

10.4.2 Assessment of the competition / 竞争评估

A framework for assessing the competition is the same as the one used for the SWOT analysis, and some sample items are shown below:

- employment statistics and levels of expertise;
- organizational structure;
- number and location of distribution outlets;
- manufacturing capacity and flexibility;
- links with intermediaries;
- market share statistics;
- key products and services offered;
- promotional expenditure and impact;
- customer service levels;
- market segments targeted and trends;
- price levels;
- growth status – whether contracting, stable or growing;
- particular challenges to the firm;
- areas of vulnerability from the firm;
- environmental policies.

评估竞争的框架与 SWOT 分析所运用的相同。主要项目如下所示：

- 就业率统计与专业技术水平；
- 组织结构；
- 分销店的地点和数量；
- 生产能力和灵活性；
- 与中介机构的联系；
- 市场份额统计；
- 关键产品与提供的服务；
- 促销开支与影响；
- 客户服务水平；
- 细分市场定位与潮流趋势；
- 价格水平；
- 发展状态——是缩减、稳定还是增长；
- 公司面临的特殊挑战；
- 公司的弱势领域；
- 环境政策。

10.4.3 Selecting marketing segments / 选择细分市场

Market segmentation involves identifying separate market entities, with different needs and characteristics, so that the firm may specialize the product offering or marketing programme by segment or target.

市场细分需要以不同的需求和特征来识别各自独立的市场实体，这样公司能够根据细分或定位来提供专门产品或营销计划。

Market segmentation was discussed in detail in Chapter Five along with consideration of a positioning

市场细分已在第 5 章中与公司市场定位一起详尽阐述。细分策略，例如密集性

statement for the firm. Segmentation strategies, such as concentration and multi-segment strategies, were also described. Examination of the company's resources and the assessment of the competition, as determined in the sections above, should help to decide the precise strategy. Segment size, identification, profitability, access and stability also should be considered at this stage.

营销策略和差异性策略也已阐述过。如上述章节所指，公司资源考察和竞争评估有助于选定周密的策略。在这个阶段还要考虑细分市场的规模、可识别性、获利能力、可进入性和稳定性。

10.4.4 Determining a marketing strategy / 确定营销策略

The Ansoff matrix can be a useful tool to aid in the development of marketing strategy. A version of the matrix applied to fashion marketing is shown in Figure 10.3.

安索夫矩阵可以成为有助于营销策略开发的有用工具。用于时装营销的矩阵形式如图 10–3 所示。

Fashion markets 时装市场	Fashion product or service 时装产品或服务: Existing 现有的	Fashion product or service 时装产品或服务: New 新的
Existing 现有的	1 Consolidation or market penetration 合并或市场渗透	2 Fashion product or service development 时装产品或服务开发
New 新的	3 Fashion market development 时装市场开发	4 Dive rsification 多样化

Figure 10.3 The Ansoff matrix applied to fashion. 图 10–3 用于时装的安索夫矩阵

In the main, strategies are considered that offer new products or services to existing customers as in quadrant 2 or the same products or services to new market segments as in quadrant 3. High-risk options should only be considered if the planning gap, identified above, is achievable given company resources. The higher the quadrant number in the figure, the riskier the option.

就一般而论，营销策略被认为是向象限 2 中现有的消费者提供新的产品或服务，或者被认为是向象限 3 中新的细分市场提供原有的产品或服务。如果上述被认可的规划缺口是可实现的已知的公司资源，高风险的选项应当给予考虑。表格中象限的序数越大的选项，风险则越大。

Consolidation can be seen as a risk-aversive strategy; however, under certain circumstances it can be a shrewd move. When the market is in recession or the company is facing restructuring, for example, a consolidation strategy may be the best option. Market penetration is simply achieving a greater share of existing markets and may be gained by offering comparative advantages in pricing or services or by more effective advertising.

合并可以被看作是一种规避风险的策略，另一方面，在处于某种不好的境遇中时，它能成为解决问题的一个高招。当市场不景气或者公司正面临重组时，合并策略可能是最好的选择。市场渗透可能就单单是获得现有市场的较大份额，也可能通过市场上所出售商品在价格或服务上的相对优势获得，或者通过更加有效的广告宣传获得。

Market development concerns the marketing of existing products in new markets. Thus a small fashion retailer may open another store in a new city or a clothing manufacturer may start exporting to Japan. Donna Karan offered online shopping for DKNY products in 2005. Sometimes market development may be evident when a new use for an existing product is found. For example, Harris Tweed has been used in a range of trainers produced by Nike as well as being used for trim in braces and belts.

市场开发关系到现有产品在新市场的营销。因此，一家小规模的时装零售商或许会在一个新的城市里开另一家店面，或许某个成衣生产商开始向日本出口。唐娜·卡兰于2005开始提供DKNY品牌商品的网上购物。有时候，当一种现有产品的新用途被发掘出来，则其市场开发策略可能是清晰的。例如，耐克公司生产的海丽丝粗花呢被用于教练服系列，同时还被用于吊带和腰带的饰物。

Fashion product or service development is the mainstay of most fashion marketing firms, although the rate of introduction of new market offerings varies considerably. This strategic option has been extensively discussed in Chapters Five and Six.

虽然新市场上供应的琳琅满目的商品传入的速度相当快，但是时装产品或服务的开发仍然是大多数时装公司的支柱。这项战略选择已经在第5章和第6章详细地讨论过了。

Diversification is where new products are developed for new markets. The degree of difference from existing markets and products can range from marginal to massive, and the greater the difference the larger the risk. A minor form of diversification for fashion firms is vertical integration where, for instance, a manufacturer sets up or buys some retail outlets or vice versa. A company manufacturing men's suits which enters the formal womenswear market would be making a relatively small change in direction and some expertise in design, manufacture and marketing may be transferable.

多样化经营即为新的市场而开发新产品的战略。现有市场与现有产品的差异等级从小到大排列，差异越大风险就越高。时装公司多样经营的次级模式是纵向一体化的，比方说，生产商开设或买下几家零售商店，反之亦然。一家生产男士套装的公司进入女装礼服市场应该在经营范围和一些设计的专业技能以及成衣上要作出一个相对小的变化，并且其商品销售业务也可能发生转变。

The most common move for fashion companies is into fragrance markets, Ted Baker and Guess? being two such examples. Where there are totally unrelated products and markets in a diversification move, the organization is called a conglomerate. The licensing arrangements of some larger French fashion houses make them appear like conglomerates with home furnishing, sunglasses, cutlery, shampoo, cigarette lighters and dozens of other non-clothing items all sold under the same brand name. The main benefit of diversification is to spread the risk of trading across more than one market.

时装公司最常见的转型做法就是进军芳香类产品市场，“泰德·贝克”和“盖斯”这两个品牌就是实例。一个在多样化的进展中靠完全不相关的产品及市场运行的公司可谓集团公司。一些大的法国时装店的特许协定使它们看起来像是集团公司，集团公司的家纺、太阳镜、刀具、洗发剂、打火机和各种非时装产品皆冠以统一品牌出售。多样化经营的主要益处是分散单一市场中较大的贸易风险。

Having selected the correct marketing strategy to pursue attention must be paid to more detailed planning. A marketing plan must be devised with specific marketing mix(es) for the selected target market(s).

选取正确的营销战略后，为获得顾客的关注，还需要制定更加详细的计划。营销计划必须要为已选定的目标市场以特定的营销组合方案来进行设计。

10.5 The fashion marketing plan／时装营销规划

The fashion marketing plan is a document that details marketing action for a specified period. It states what has to be done when, how and with what effect. The plan gives details of the marketing strategy and how the firm will achieve its marketing objectives. The plan also allocates responsibilities and resources, schedules major activities and enables senior management to monitor the implementation of the fashion marketing strategy.

There are variations in how a plan should be structured. These variations are minor and usually just reflect the house style of the fashion firm. The following sections cover the main components of a marketing plan.

时装营销计划是一份特定阶段营销活动的详述文件。该计划说明何时以何种方式采取什么措施，将取得何种效果。计划中将给出营销战略和公司该如何达到其销售目标的细节。该计划还分配好责任范围、可用资源，安排主要活动，并使高层管理人员能监督时装营销战略的落实。

一份计划无论怎样被构造总会有变更，但这些变更较小，并且通常只反映时装公司的独特风格。营销计划的主要部分如下。

10.5.1 Summary for senior management／针对高层管理人员的摘要

This is self-evident and usually concentrates on profits, sales and resources. Many companies suggest that the summary should produced on a single side of a paper.

不言而喻，这部分通常关注利润、销售额和资源。许多公司建议将摘要单独成页。

10.5.2 Marketing objectives／营销目标

These should be stated concisely and be related to the mission statement. A number of related marketing objectives may be grouped such as promotional objectives.

这部分应该简明扼要，并要涉及任务说明。许多营销目标可以被分成组，例如促销目标。

10.5.3 Situational analysis or SWOT／环境分析或 SWOT 分析

As noted above, the SWOT should be related to the competition and produce a coherent and related set of recommendations.

正如上文提到的，SWOT 分析应当针对竞争而提出一系列合理相关的建议。

10.5.4 Marketing analysis／营销分析

This is an assessment of market segment options, the competition, the marketing environment and major trends.

这是一个对细分市场、竞争者、营销环境和主流趋势的综合评估。

10.5.5 Marketing strategy／营销战略

This is a statement of how objectives will be met by reference to segmentation and positioning of the product.

这是一份涉及市场细分和产品定位如何达成目标的报告书。

10.5.6 Marketing mix programmes / 营销组合计划

This section should detail product, price, distribution and promotional activities. This is probably the most detailed part of the plan as it states what is to happen along with the scheduling and co-ordination of activities. The plan should also show the allocation of tasks, accountability for implementation and costs of the activities.

这部分应当细化产品、价格、分销和促销活动。这一部分可能是整个计划中最详细的。因为它阐明了在整个计划安排和相应的活动进行中将要发生的事情。计划中还要表明任务的分配、实施过程中的责任义务以及活动的开销。

10.5.7 Forecast results and budgeting / 预测结果和预算

The forecast sales and profits from the plan should be given along with market share data and other relevant quantifiable criteria. Some firms place the expected results in Section 10.5.2. To facilitate calculations and comparisons, it is helpful to place revenue and profit data with information on costs and budgets. Some approaches to budget setting were described in Chapter Nine. The total budget is derived from the marketing mix programme costs mentioned above.

计划中的预计销售额和预计利润应与市场份额数据及其他相关的量化标准一同给出。一些公司将预期结果放在了10.5.2 部分。把收入和利润的数据与开销和预算的信息放在一起有助于估算和比较。在第 9 章中已经介绍过几种预算设定的方法了，而总预算是根据以上提到的销售组合计划的花销得出的。

10.5.8 Resourcing and implementation issues / 资源和实施问题

This item is to outline any staffing or physical resources that may be needed to enable the plan to be effected. For example, the introduction of a marketing database, for direct mail activities aimed at regular customers, may have major implications for staff training in information technology and the purchase and maintenance of computer equipment. Possible resistance from staff or fashion intermediaries to certain strategic changes should also be identified, along with recommended action to overcome or minimize negative effects. For example, the importation of garments made in a country that generates polarized political opinion may meet opposition from sections of the workforce or certain active consumer groups.

这部分就是要列出能够使这项计划生效的必要的人力和物力资源。例如，销售数据库的引进和针对老主顾的直邮方案，都将对信息技术方面的人员培训及购置和维护电脑设备产生较大的影响。应该指出从人员或时装中介机构到某些战略改变可能出现的阻力，同时应提出建议措施以克服或将消极影响降到最小。例如，进口持不同政见的国家所生产的服饰，很可能面临着劳动力部门或某些消费群体的反对。

10.5.9 Marketing control and evaluation / 销售控制和评估

Measurement of the plan is essential so that corrective action can be taken if necessary. Given the objectives and expected results specified above, this section of the plan details the frequency and nature of measurements to be taken. Mechanisms for comparing actual with planned results and the reporting procedures must be

对计划的衡量是必不可少的，这样可以适时采取矫正措施。前面已经明确了目标和预期结果，这节则是要细化测定的频率和性质。现实与计划的结果比较机制和报告程序要体现在这部分计划

shown. Some plans incorporate contingency corrective action in the event of deviations from the plan.

中，有些计划包含了应对偏离计划的意外事故的纠偏措施。

10.6 Implementation and organizational issues ／实施与组织问题

10.6.1 Planning horizons ／规划周期

The time scales for fashion marketing plans vary considerably. All plans are related to the fashion calender, usually two seasons, as noted in Chapter Six. They are also linked to the target market and the nature of the product life cycle. Chapter Six also describes product life cycles from the high-fashion fad to the fashion classic and these are major factors in the time scales adopted in the fashion marketing plan. All planning may be carried out for a variety of purposes, but one should strive never to forget its most basic function which is demonstrated in Figure 10.4.

时装营销规划的时间范围千差万别。所有规划都和时装销售进程有关，一般分为两季，正如第 6 章指出的。它们同样与目标市场和产品生命周期的所处阶段相关。第 6 章也描述了从前沿时尚到经典时尚的产品生命周期。这些是时装营销规划中特定时间段内最需要考虑的要素。实施规划的目的有千万种，但最基本的职能切不可忘记。这一职能如图 10–4 所示。

Planning helps in anticipating and avoiding proble 规划有助于预测及规避问题

Figure 10.4 The value of planning – an irony. 图 10–4 规划的价值——出其不意

Most fashion firms will have long-range plans lasting from three to five years or longer, medium-term plans for one to three years and short-term plans that may over one season or up to a year.

All three types of plan need to be co-ordinated, therefore short-term plans become part of medium-term plans, and so on. The more complex and changeable the marketing environment that the firm faces, the greater the tendency to need long-range plans and to review fully and update those plans regularly. Except for a very small minority of firms supplying stable items of clothing, possibly functional classic items such as uniforms, most fashion firms are confronted by a volatile and competitive marketing environment.

大多数时装公司会制定长期规划（3 ~ 5 年或更久）、中期规划(1 ~ 3 年)、短期规划（1 季或 1 年）。

三种规划必须相互协调，短期规划应为中期规划的一部分，依此类推。企业所处的营销环境越是复杂多变，企业越需要长期规划统揽全局，并进行周期性调整。除了少数公司专门生产固定类别的时装，比如说制服之类的传统功能性服饰，多数时装公司都处在多变及充满竞争的营销环境之中。

10.6.2 Organizational culture ／组织文化

Another factor influencing marketing planning is the organizational culture of the firm. As noted in Chapter One, fashion is about change and many managers, in coping with the demands of immediacy, adopt a short-term perspective. Large parts of the fashion industry do appear to lurch from one deadline to another, with

企业的组织文化也影响营销规划。正如第 1 章提到的，时装业应对的是变化。许多管理者为了及时性的需要，采取短线操作。大多数时装公司其实忙于应对一个又一个的“最后期限”，结果管理者只顾日常事务和短期业务。鉴于时装

the consequence that many managers concentrate on dealing with daily matters and short-term issues. Given the high failure rate of fashion firms and the constant uncertainty in the market, many managers feel that long-term planning is of limited value compared with concentrating on doing immediate tasks well. Another factor inhibiting long-range planning is the mobility of staff within the fashion sector. High labour turnover and headhunting (staff poaching) activities can mean that staffing changes can jeopardize the planning process and the security of marketing plans from the competition.

公司的高失败率和市场持续不稳定，许多管理者认为长期规划还不如集中精力做好眼前事情有价值。另一个约束长期规划的因素是时装产业从业人员的流动性。员工流动率高和"猎头"行为意味着人员变动会危及规划过程以及竞争中营销规划的安全保障。

The establishment of a marketing plan, particularly in a rapidly changing environment, can mean a substantial change of resources within the marketing department of a fashion firm. For example, the decision to place more emphasis on support for retailers via in-store promotion and merchandising may mean a reduction in the advertising and publicity budgets. These changes also may mean staff redeployment or redundancies that can demoralize staff and lead to reduced enthusiasm for implementation of the plan. The lesson to be learned is that encouraging participation in the marketing planning process and concern for, and communication with, those involved in implementation is crucial for success.

特别是在变幻莫测的环境中，营销规划的制定往往需要时装公司营销部门内部大规模资源变动。举个例子，如果企业决定采取店内促销和商品促销的方式支持零售商，那就有可能削减广告和宣传上的预算。这些变化也许将导致人员的重新调配甚至是裁员，不仅会打压员工士气，还会挫败实施计划的积极性。从中吸取的教训是：企业想要成功，鼓励员工参与整个营销计划，鼓励员工关心和融入实施的各个环节。

10.6.3 Internal marketing／内部营销

Internal marketing is the process of encouraging employees in all functional areas to have a customer focus and do their best to help deliver a good customer experience. A number of writers, e.g. Hulbert *et al*. (2005) and Dunmore (2002), argue that this aspect of a marketing plan is vital if objectives are to be achieved. Much marketing activity depends on the co-operation of other functional areas within the firm and without their support many projects may not be either completed or auctioned on time. Different departments have their own plans and a prime task of senior management to co-ordinate the various plans. However, fashion marketers do have a clear interest in making sure colleagues in other functional areas understand the rationale for the marketing plan and their supporting role within it. Thus the marketing plan needs to be 'sold' within the firm before it can be fully realized.

内部营销是指鼓励各职能部门员工尊承"以客为本"的信念，竭诚为客户提供优质客户体验的过程。赫尔伯特（2005 年）和邓莫尔（2002 年）等一些作家认为：要想实现目标，这些方面是至关重要的。许多销售活动需要公司内部相关职能部门通力合作完成，没有他们的支持，很多项目将无法按时完成或竞卖。不同部门有不同的规划，管理高层的首要任务就是协调好这些规划。不过，时装营销人员应清楚地认识到，必须确保相关职能部门人员理解营销计划原理以及他们在其中所起的支撑性作用。营销计划必须首先在公司内部推广，才能全面实现。

10.6.4 Management styles／管理模式

The previous sections argue that planning for the long term, within the fashion sector, is difficult. It is important

前几节我们已经讨论了在时装界制定长期规划并非易事。我们必须充

to note that long-term plans are essential for survival and growth, and that means commitment from senior management to long-term planning. The approaches adopted by some fashion executives can be summarized by the management styles shown below:

◆ *Management by conjecture*: i.e. Why worry about the future?

◆ *Management by crisis*: i.e. Let's deal with problems when they arise.

◆ *Management by subordinates*: i.e. Each fashion marketer does their own thing.

◆ *Management by prayer*: i.e. Things will get better, we hope!

The flaws in each style above are easily spotted. The approach advocated in this text is management by objectives, as described in an earlier section.

All fashion firms should plan for the long term. The resources and energy they allocate to that process are a function of the target market, organizational culture, product life cycles, the particular marketing environment and the commitment from senior management. A prudent approach for many fashion firms seems to be to plan on a rolling principle so that short-term plans always exist and they are reviewed and modified appropriately to meet new circumstances and challenges.

分意识到长期规划对企业存活并进一步扩大至关重要，这需要上至管理高层下至具体执行人员的一致付出。一些时装公司高管采用的管理办法大致可归为以下几类：

◆ 推测管理：即“为什么担心未来？”

◆ 危机管理：即“问题出现时让我们一起解决。”

◆ 隶属管理：即“每个时装营销者做好自己的事。”

◆ 祈祷管理：即“我们祈祷境况愈来愈佳。”

以上几种管理办法的不足之处显而易见。本文所倡导的管理办法是目标管理法，这在前面章节已阐述。

每个时装企业都应该为自己的发展作长远规划。投入其中的资源和精力是由目标市场、组织文化、产品生命周期、特定营销环境和高层管理的投入所组成的函数。大多数时装公司采用谨慎的做法，即利用循环原理制定计划，这样做可以保证短期计划长期存在，使企业能在自我反省与修正的过程中不断迎合新的环境与挑战。

10.7 Summary／小结

This chapter has dealt with further marketing planning, covering:

◆ the organizational mission;

◆ marketing objectives;

◆ marketing strategy.

Strategic alternatives were further examined in relation to:

◆ marketing audits;

◆ SWOT analysis.

Strategic marketing plans can be constructed more easily in the light of the information thus obtained. The chapter concluded by emphasizing the importance of adequate long-range planning in the context of organizational culture, internal marketing and management styles.

本章着重讨论深层营销规划，包括：

◆ 组织使命；

◆ 营销目标；

◆ 营销策略。

进一步的策略选择涉及：

◆ 营销审计；

◆ SWOT 分析。

基于已获得的信息，构建策略性营销规划并非难事。本章最后强调在组织文化、内部营销和管理模式的背景下，适宜的长期规划的重要作用。

Further reading ／课后阅读材料

1.Baker, M.J. (2007), *Marketing Strategy and Management*, 4th Edition, Palgrave Macmillan, Basingstoke.

贝克・M.J. (2007),《营销策略与管理》，第 4 版，帕尔格雷夫・麦克米伦出版社，贝辛斯托克 .

2.Dibb, S. and Simkin, L. (2008), *Marketing Planning: A Workbook for Managers*, Thomson Learning, London.

迪博・S.，西姆金・L. (2008)，《营销规划——管理者手册》，汤姆森学习出版集团，伦敦 .

3.Dunmore, M. (2002), *Inside Out Marketing: How to Create an Internal Marketing Strategy*, Kogan Page, London.

邓莫尔・M.(2002)，《营销内外——如何创建内部营销策略》，柯刚佩奇出版社，伦敦 .

4.Gilligan, C. and Wilson, R.M.S. (2003), *Strategic Marketing Planning*, Butterworth-Heinemann, Oxford.

卡罗尔・吉利根，威尔森・R.M.S. (2003)，《战略性营销规划》，巴特沃斯・海内曼，牛津 .

5.Hulbert, J.M. *et al.* (2005), *Total Integrated Marketing: Breaking the Bounds of the Function*, Kogan Page, London.

赫尔伯特，J.M. 等 . (2005)，《整合营销：打破职能界限》，柯刚佩奇出版社，伦敦 .

6.Kotler, P. and Armstrong, G. (2008), *Principles of Marketing*, 12th Edition, Pearson/Prentice Hall, Harlow.

科特勒・P.，阿姆斯特朗・G.(2008)，《营销原理》，第 12 版，培生教育出版社，哈洛 .

7.McDonald, M. (2007), *Malcolm McDonald on Marketing Plans: Understanding Marketing Plans and Strategy*, Kogan Page, London.

麦克唐纳德・M.(2007)，《麦当劳营销规划：通晓营销计划和策略》，柯刚佩奇出版社，伦敦 .

8.Westwood, J. (2005), *The Marketing Plan Workbook*, Kogan Page, London.

维斯特伍德・J.(2005)，《营销规划手册》，柯刚佩奇出版社，伦敦 .

9.Wood, M.B. (2007), *The Essential Guide to Marketing Planning*, Financial Times/Prentice Hall, Harlow.

伍德・M.B. (2007)，《营销规划基础指南》，金融时报 / 培生教育出版公司，哈洛 .

Glossary of Fashion Marketing Terms
时装营销专业术语

Advertising is persuasive and/or informative non-personal communications paid for by a clearly identifiable sponsor.

广告：是指由明确特定的出资人付费而进行的劝说性或告知性的非人员介绍。

Break-even analysis shows the relationship between fixed costs, variable or marginal costs, total costs, sales revenue and output or volume.

盈亏平衡分析：显示出固定成本、可变成本或边际成本、总成本、销售收入以及产量或规模之间的关系。

Causal research is used to determine the relationship between variables, e.g. the relationship between advertising and repeat purchases.

因果分析：用于测定变量之间的关系。例如：广告宣传与重复购买行为之间的关系。

Concessions also known as shops-within-shops, can be defined as space leased by the host retailer to another retailer, wholesaler or manufacturer from which to sell its merchandise.

特许商店：也称店中店，是指由主零售商租赁给其他零售商、批发商或制造商用以经营的区域。

Consumer behaviour provides a framework for identifying consumer needs and target markets, and enables the anticipation of consumer responses to marketing action.

消费行为：为界定消费者需求和目标市场提供框架，同时帮助准确预测消费者对于营销行为的反应。

Cost-plus pricing is simply calculating the cost of raw materials, labour and overheads, and adding an amount to cover profit in order to arrive at the selling price.

成本加成定价法：一种简单核算原材料、劳动力以及其他成本开销，再加上一定数量计算出利润，得出销售价格的计算方式。

Demographics is the study of changes in the size and make-up of the population.

人口特征：是关于人口规模和人口结构变化的研究。

Descriptive research provides an accurate description of the variables uncovered by the exploratory research.

描述性调研：对探索性调查所发现的变量予以精准地描述。

Exploratory research is an attempt to uncover any variables that may be relevant to the research project as well as an investigation of the environment in which the research will take place.

探索性调研：尝试找出任何可能与所研究项目有关的变量，同时也对研究环境进行探查。

Family life cycle is an attempt to classify people

家庭模式的生命周期：试图以户主年

according to the age of head of household, marital status, and the age and number of children.

Fashion is about continuous change, clothing and related products and services, and the exercise of creative design skills. Fashion is a current mode of consumption behaviour applied specifically to clothing products and related services.

Fashion classics can usually be seen as the midpoint compromise of any style, i.e. total look or composite effect. Colour and pattern may vary, but the classic customer does not seek the satisfaction of a new seasonal experience in the way that the fashion and fad counterparts do.

Fashion fads will meteorically rise in popularity only to suffer an abrupt decline as they become adopted. As a fad becomes fashionable it also becomes unfashionable.

Fashion marketing is the application of a range of techniques and a business philosophy that centres upon the customer and potential customer of clothing and related products and services in order to meet the long-term goals of the organization.

Fashion marketing concept attempts to embrace the positive aspects of high concern for design, customers and profit by recognizing the interdependence of marketing and fashion design personnel.

Fashion marketing plan is a document that details marketing action for a specified period. The plan gives implementation details of the marketing strategy and states how the firm will achieve its marketing objectives.

Fashions usually have a slower rise to popularity, plateau with continuing popularity and then decline gradually; often this cycle relates to a season, whether autumn/winter or spring/summer.

Franchising is a contractual relationship between franchiser and franchisee in which the franchiser offers, or is obliged to maintain, a continuing interest in the business of the franchisee in such areas as knowledge and training; wherein the franchisee operates under a common trade name, format or procedure owned by or controlled by the franchiser, and in which the franchisee has made or will make a considerable capital investment in his business from his own resources.

Geodemographics are systems derived from statistical analysis of census variables to discover

龄、婚姻状况、家中孩子的年龄及数量为依据划分人群。

时尚：是关于连续的变化、时装和相关产品及服务以及创造性设计技巧锻炼的话题。时尚特指应用在服饰产品及其相关服务的消费行为的一种现行模式。

经典：通常可被看作某些风格 / 款式（如整体形象或混搭效果）的折中点，色彩和款式虽有异，但经典款式的追捧者不会像其他追求时尚者那样在每一季新的流行款式中寻求满足。

风尚：是指能以最快的速度在大众中普及，正“如日中天”却又急转直下。当“一时流行”的变成“普遍流行”的，就意味着它已不再流行。

时装营销：是指一系列技术和某种经营理念的运用，而这一经营理念是把时装和相关产品和服务的顾客和潜在顾客作为中心以求实现公司长远目标。

时装营销观念：是指通过认识营销和设计人员的相互依存关系，接受的对设计、消费者和利润三方面高关注度的积极营销观念。

时装营销规划：是指对特定时间段内采取的营销手段进行详述的文件。它详细描述营销策略的执行情况，并指出企业应怎样达成营销目标。

流行：通常会经历从缓慢上升到流行、持续流行的高峰和逐步下降三个时期，这个循环通常与季节相关，春夏季、秋冬季都如此。

特许经营：是指一种特许人与加盟商之间的契约关系。根据契约，特许人要在技能传授、人员培训等方面为加盟商提供（或者说按照契约规定必须保证）持续性的帮助；加盟商按照合同约定在统一经营体系下从事经营活动，特许人授予其共用商标、经营模式等经营资源，同时也可投入一定量私人资金到此业务中去。

地理人口统计：是指对居住地，通常是人口普查区域所进行的与购买行为和媒

residential areas, usually census enumeration districts, that are linked to purchasing behaviour and media usage.

Innovation is anything the consumer perceives to be new, and could include an 'old' product introduced into a new market.

Intergated Marketing Communications is a concept of marketing communications planning that recognizes the added value of a comprehensive plan that evaluates the strategic roles of a variety of communications disciplines (e.g., general advertising, direct response, sales promotion and public relations) ... and combines these disciplines to provide clarit, consistency and maximum communications impact.

Lifestyle or **psychographics** is a classification of consumers based on activities, interests and opinions (AIOs).

Markdown is where profit is expressed as a percentage of the sale price.

Market-based pricing is founded on market research to find the optimum selling price which then acts as the main driving force upon cost containment via design and quality control effort.

Market penetration pricing tries to capture a large market share by charging low prices. The low prices charged stimulate purchases and can discourage competitors from entering the market as the profit margins per item are low.

Market research is used to refer to research into a specific market, investigating such aspects as market size, market trends, competitor analysis, and so on.

Market segmentation is where the larger market is heterogeneous and can be broken down into smaller units that are similar in character.

Market skimming pricing charges high initial prices and then only reduces prices gradually, if at all. A skimming price policy is a form of price discrimination over time.

Marketing is both a way of thinking about the firm from the perspective of the customer or potential customer, and a management process concerned with anticipating, identifying and satisfying customer needs to meet the long-term goals of the organization.

Marketing analysis is an assessment of market

体用法相关的人口普查变量的统计分析的系统。

创新：是指从消费者的眼光被认为是新鲜的事物，也包括进入新市场的老式产品。

整合营销传播：是指充分意识到综合规划所带来的附加值的营销传播规划概念。这种综合规划能够评定出不同传播准则（如：一般广告、直接反应广告、促销和公关）的战略地位，并把这些准则结合起来创造出明晰、一致和最佳的传播效果。

生活方式/消费心理学：是指一种基于消费者活动、兴趣和看法的对消费者进行分类的方法，简称 AIOs。

利润售价比率：以利润占售价百分比的形式表示。

基于市场的定价：是指通过市场调研得到最适宜的销售价格，并将其作为最主要的推动力在设计和质量控制方面努力控制成本。

市场渗透定价：是指以低价进入市场以赢得高的市场占有率。低价进入市场能刺激购买，同时由于单位利润率低，能阻止竞争者进入市场。

市场调研：是指对特定市场的规模、走向、竞争者分析等诸方面的调查研究。

市场细分：是指市场具有异质性，并且能被分解为具有相同或相似特征的较小单元。

市场撇脂定价：是指最初以高价进入市场，然后再逐步降低价格，直到最后。撇脂定价策略是一种随时间的变化而价格有所区别的形式。

营销：不仅是一种从顾客或潜在顾客的角度对公司的思维方式，而且也是预测、识别和满足消费者需要，来实现组织团体长期目标的管理过程。

营销分析：是指对市场细分可选的、

segment options, the competition, the marketing environment and major trends.

竞争、营销环境和主要趋势的评估。

Marketing audit involves sets of detailed questions that are asked to determine the status of a firm in relation to its objectives, customers, competition and marketing environment.

营销审计：包括一系列被询的详细问题，以确定公司经营目标、顾客、竞争和营销环境的状况。

Marketing environment is all the influences beyond the control of fashion companies that affect marketing action. It includes consideration of the social, cultural, technological, economic and political contexts within which fashion marketing occurs.

营销环境：是指超出时装公司控制范围的对营销活动有影响的所有因素。包括对时装营销发生时所处的社会、文化、科技、经济和政治背景的考虑。

Marketing intermediaries are the main channels that help to get fashion products and services from the manufacturer to the consumer.

营销中介：是指帮助时装产品及其服务从生产商送达顾客的主要渠道。

Marketing mix describes the specific combination of marketing variables used by a fashion marketer to meet the needs of specific groups of customers known as target markets. It comprises decisions made about products, prices, promotion, services and distribution that are assembled in a coherent and profitable way to represent what the firm is offering to the consumer.

营销组合：是指为了满足特定的消费群体即目标市场的需要，时装经销商将营销变量以合理、有利的方式进行组合，包括对产品、价格、促销、服务和分销的决策，展示公司对顾客提供的全部货品。

Marketing research covers investigation into all aspects of the marketing of goods or services, such as product research and development, pricing research, advertising research and distribution research, as well as all the aspects of market analysis covered by market research.

营销调研：是指对所营销的产品或服务各方面的调查研究。如：产品调研和开发、价格调研、广告调研、分销调研，还有市场调研所涉及的市场分析的各个方面。

Marketing strategy is a specification of those markets the firm wishes to target with marketing activities and how competitive advantages are to be created and achieved.

营销策略：是指公司针对目标市场，为了创造和获得竞争优势所采取的营销活动的细则。

Markets are places for buying and selling, for exchanging goods and services, usually for money. To constitute a market there should be a genuine need, the customer(s) should be willing and able to buy the fashion product, and the aggregate demand should be sufficient to enable a supplier to operate profitably.

市场：是指通常以货币形式，买卖、交换商品和服务的地方。构建市场一定要有真正的需求，顾客愿意且有能力购买时装产品，并且该需求聚集到足够的程度，使得供应商能够有利可图。

Markup is where profit is expressed as a percentage of costs.

利润成本比率：以利润占成本的百分比表示。

Mass marketing assumes that all customers in a market are the same. It is based on the idea that customer needs do not vary and that the company can offer a standardized marketing mix that meets the needs of everyone.

大众营销：假定同一市场中所有顾客需求都是相同的。这基于顾客的需求不用分成不同类别的看法，并且公司可提供标准化营销组合方式来满足每位顾客的需求。

Multi-Fibre Agreement (MFA) came into existence

多种纤维协定：1974 年作为临时性

in 1974 as a temporary expedient and is basically a framework for regulating trade in fibres, fabrics and clothing between developing low-cost countries and the industrialized countries.

Multiples are businesses with at least ten outlets selling predominantly one merchandise group, e.g. clothing or shoes.

Niche marketing is where a clearly defined segment is targeted with a narrow product range.

Opinion leadership refers to the degree of influence exerted in a given choice situation.

Perception is the process whereby buyers select, organize and interpret simple stimuli into a meaningful and coherent picture of the world.

Personal selling is interpersonal promotion carried out by the sales staff of a retailer, wholesaler or manufacturer.

Positioning is to do with the perception by the target market of the firm and its marketing mix. Positioning is how customers see the market, although that perception may have been influenced by marketing action.

Price is the point at which exchange between buyer and seller takes place, where supply and demand are equal. Price is the amount of money that is exchanged for fashion products and/or services.

Product can be defined as anything that can be offered in the marketplace that might satisfy a need. Products may be classified as convenience, shopping or specialty goods.

Product life cycle is based on the proposal that all products have a finite 'life cycle' that can be plotted over a given period using the biological analogy of growth, development and decline.

Product mix or **product range** is the assortment of fashion products that a company offers for sale at any point in time.

Promotional mix is the particular combination of promotional methods and media used by an organization to achieve its marketing communication goals. It includes advertising, sales promotions, public relations and selling.

Publicity is media coverage that is not paid for and has a mass audience and a high level of credibility.

Public relations aims to establish and maintain a favourable image through a pre-planned, long-

权宜之计出台，是调节发展中低成本国家和工业化国家之间在纤维、纺织、时装贸易方面的基本框架。

连锁店：是指至少有 10 家大卖场销售绝大多数是同一经营团体的产品，如时装或鞋。

利基营销 / 针对性营销：是指以一个窄的产品系列来定位一个清晰、确定的子市场。

意见领袖：指的是施加在一个给定的选择情境下的影响力。

感知：是指购买者选择、组织和将简单的刺激物阐释为世界上有意义、合理的图片的过程。

人员促销：是指由零售商、批发商或生产商的人员完成的人与人之间的促销活动。

定位：是指以公司的目标市场和营销组合的感知来进行的活动，定位是顾客对市场的看法，这种感知也会受到营销活动的影响。

价格：是指买方和卖方进行交易的基点，供需双方都认同。是时装产品或者服务交换时的货币量。

产品：可以被定义为市场上提供的满足需求的物品。产品分为便利品、选购品或特殊品。

产品寿命周期：是基于所有产品都有有限的“寿命周期”说法，这个寿命周期可以用类似于生物的成长期、发展期和衰败期的一定时期变化绘出寿命曲线。

产品组合或产品系列：是指公司在某一特定时期所提供待售的时装产品的搭配。

促销组合：是指为了实现营销沟通目标，公司所运用的促销方法和广告媒介的特别组合。它包括广告、促销、公共关系和销售。

公众的关注：也是一种媒体形式，不需付费，有大众参与和较高的可信度。

公共关系：通过精心筹划的长期计划，致力于在公众中建立和保持良好的形象，

range programme by communicating with its publics, including consumers, suppliers, shareholders, trade customers, employees, unions, government, pressure groups and the local community.

不断与包括消费者、供应商、股东、贸易客户、雇员、工会、政府、压力集团和当地社区在内的公众进行沟通的活动。

Sales promotion involves promotional activities that add value to fashion products or induce consumers or intermediaries to buy or provide an incentive for channel effectiveness.

促销：是指增加时装产品价值的促销活动，吸引消费者或中间商购买，或为销售渠道的有效性提供刺激。

Sampling involves selecting a small number of people from the larger survey population whose characteristics, attitudes and behaviour are representative of the larger group.

抽样：是指从大量的被调查人群中抽取少量在性格、态度和行为方式上具有代表性的代表。

Social class refers to divisions of people according to their economic position in society, whether they are aware of that position or not.

社会阶层：是指不考虑人们是否意识到，但根据人们的经济情况而对人群进行的细分。

SWOT (strengths, weaknesses, opportunities and threats) analysis considers both internal and external factors about either the whole company or a particular fashion product line or range in relation to customers, competitors and trends in the marketing environment.

SWOT（优势、劣势、机会、威胁）分析：是指整个公司或某一特定的时装产品生产线或系列在营销环境中涉及顾客、竞争者和趋势的内在和外在因素。

Variety chain stores sell a variety of merchandise. In the UK, the four major variety chain stores with a significant clothing turnover are Bhs, Marks and Spencer, Little-woods and, to a lesser extent, Woolworths.

百货连锁店：销售各种各样的商品。在英国，最主要的四大营业额可观的百货连锁店是：包豪斯、马克斯与思班赛公司、利特伍兹，还有稍小的伍尔沃斯。

Acknowledgements
致 谢

Fashion is a fascinating subject which stimulates a great many questions, an essential requirement for any academic endeavour. As mainstream marketing educators, the authors of this book brought a range of different expectations and experiences to the area of fashion. All of us have working, teaching, training or consultancy experience in the field of fashion marketing and wanted to write a book that would address real issues and would contribute, in a small way, to make the fashion industry and fashion students more aware of how marketing can enable them to be more effective in their work.

For several years the University of Northumbria has run an undergraduate course in fashion marketing. Our experiences of teaching on this course coupled with the paucity of UK texts on the subject convinced us of the need to write the book. Our research and experiences have led us to challenge the way we think about marketing and recognize the special role of design in the process. In many sectors with creative output, it has long been noted that designers need to know about marketing and marketers need to know about design. It is hoped that this book meets the needs of both groups, though in truth designers may learn more about marketing than vice versa.

Many people have helped me with the second edition of this book via comments on the first and second editions and stimulating conversations and inspirations.

The following people are sincerely thanked for their knowledge, help and friendship: Sheila Atkinson, Christine Sorensen, Patricia Gray, John Willans and Gaynor Lea-Greenwood. My co-authors have been very supportive over the years and have been good

时装是一个激发许多疑问、满足学术努力的基本要求、令人着迷的学科。作为时装营销教育工作者，本书作者带来一系列关于时装领域的不同的期望和体验。我们都拥有时装营销领域的工作、教学、培训和咨询经历，并且想要撰写一本阐述实际问题并且有助于时装业和学时装的学生们更多了解营销，如何能使他们在其工作中更加有效的书。

多年来，诺桑比亚大学一直开设大学本科时装营销课程，我们拥有这门课程的教学经验，再加上目前英国这一学科教材的匮乏，使我们认识到写这本书的必要性。这些研究和经验是对营销传统看法的挑战，并意识到设计在整个过程中的特殊作用。在产生创新性成果的许多方面，长久的一个共识是设计师要懂得营销，营销商要了解设计。希望本书能够满足这两者的需求，不过事实上设计师更应该了解营销。

许多人在本书的第 3 版写作中给予我帮助，他们对第 1 版和第 2 版提出建议，具有启发性的谈话和灵感令我受益匪浅。

首先感谢希莉亚·阿特金森、克莉斯汀·索伦森、帕特丽夏·格雷、约翰·威兰斯和盖纳·里－格林伍德，感谢他们给予我的帮助和友谊。我的合著者几年来一直支持着我，他们是我要好的同事、

colleagues, critics and sources of ideas. Richard Jones, Prof. Christopher Moore, Dr. Sandra Connor, Ruth Marciniak, Prof. Neville Harris, Alan Fyall, Fiona Raeside, Helen Carter and Julie O'Sullivan have all contributed their ideas and friendship over the years. Madeleine Metcalfe at Wiley-Blackwell is due special thanks for her encouragement, patience and tenacity in helping me finish this third edition. Special thanks are also due to my wife Janice for great support.

评论家和思想的源泉。理查德·琼斯、克里斯多夫·莫尔教授、桑德拉·康纳、露丝·马西尼克、奈维尔·哈里斯教授、艾伦·法伊奥、菲奥娜·瑞森德、海伦·卡特、茱莉亚·欧苏利文几年来不断给予我建议和帮助。特别感谢威利—布莱克威尔出版社的玛德琳·梅特卡夫，第3版的完成离不开她的鼓励、耐心和锲而不舍。还要特别感谢我的妻子詹妮丝的大力支持。

As usual there is a disclaimer: many people have helped me, but I accept total responsibility for all errors in the book.

免责声明：本书的写作，得助于多人，书中疏漏，责任在我。

Mike Easey
March 2008

迈克·伊西
2008年3月

List of Contributors
参编者简介

Sheila Atkinson, *MSc, MBA, PGCEd, AMCIM*. Her working experience includes buying and merchandising for the Burton Group plc and management of design education in further education. Sheila has extensive teaching experience in UK and Chinese Universities and has training and consultancy experience in fashion marketing. Sheila Atkinson produced Chapter Six with Mike Easey, on the design and marketing of fashion products.

Mike Easey, *BA (Hons), DipM, MCIM, CertEd*, is Director of Collaborative Ventures in Newcastle Business School at the University of Northumbria. He has worked for three multinationals in marketing research, promotion and marketing planning positions. He is an experienced Marketing Consultant and has undertaken an extensive range of consultancy work including marketing for fashion manufacturers and fashion retailers. He is also a university external examiner in fashion marketing, a QAA Specialist Subject Reviewer in Marketing and a member of the editorial board of the *Journal of Fashion Marketing and Management*. Mike Easey produced Chapters One, Three, Seven and Ten and co-wrote Chapter Five with Christine Sorensen and Chapter Six with Sheila Atkinson.

Patricia Gray, *MSc, Dip MRS, PGCEd*, previously a Lecturer in Marketing Research in Newcastle Business School, is currently working as a Researcher with Newcastle University. Her experience includes numerous

希莉亚·阿特金森

工学硕士，工商管理硕士，持有教育学研究生证书，英国特许市务学会会员。她的工作经历包括负责伯顿股票上市公司商品购买和推销以及为进修者讲授设计教育管理。希莉亚在英国和中国的大学有众多的教学经历，并且在时装营销培训和咨询方面拥有丰富的经验。希莉亚·阿特金森和迈克·伊西合写了本书第 6 章时装产品的设计与营销。

迈克·伊西

荣誉文学学士，市场营销文凭，英国特许市务学会会员，持有教育证书。任职诺森比亚大学的纽卡斯尔商学院合作风险系主任。他曾为三家跨国公司工作，其领域涉及营销调研、商品促销和定位营销，是一位经验丰富的营销顾问，担任大规模系列化产品的顾问，包括为时装生产者和时装零售商做顾问。他同时兼任大学时装营销方向的对外主考者、英国高等教育质量保障局营销方向评论专家和《时装营销与管理》期刊的编委会成员。迈克·伊西编写了本书第 1 章、第 3 章、第 7 章和第 10 章，和克莉斯汀·索伦森合写了第 5 章，和希莉亚·阿特金森合写了第 6 章。

帕特丽夏·格雷

工学硕士，市场调研文凭，持有教育学研究生证书，曾任纽卡斯尔商学院营销调研课讲师，现任纽卡斯尔大学研究员。其工作经历包括在许

consultancy tasks and she has worked in publicity for the arts and for Millward Brown Market and Social Research. Patricia Gray produced Chapter Four on fashion marketing research.

多公司任顾问，她目前从事艺术品宣传以及在米渥布朗集团（全球十大市场研究机构之一）市场和社会调研部工作。帕特丽夏·格雷编写了本书第 4 章时装市场营销调研。

Gaynor Lea-Greenwood, *MA, BA*, is a Senior Lecturer in Fashion Marketing at Manchester Metropolitan University. She has worked at a senior level in the fashion industry including a major role with Miss Selfridge. Along with consultancy experience for fashion retailers, she has extensive knowledge of international sourcing and promotion. She is an active researcher, external examiner for UK Universities and Acting Editor of the editorial board of the *Journal of Fashion Marketing and Management*. Gaynor is currently working on a new textbook on *Fashion Marketing Communications* for Wiley-Blackwell. Gaynor Lea-Greenwood produced Chapter Nine on fashion marketing communications.

盖纳·里–格林伍德

艺术学硕士，文学学士，曼彻斯特城市大学时装营销高级讲师。她是时装业界的佼佼者，同塞尔弗里奇小姐（英国名牌百货公司）一样拥有举足轻重的地位。除了拥有时装零售商顾问的经验之外，她在国际资源和促销领域还拥有渊博的知识。她是一位活跃的研究员，英国国立大学对外考官，《时装营销与管理》期刊的编委会执行编辑。盖纳目前在为威利—布莱克威尔出版社编写“时装营销交流”的新教科书。盖纳·里–格林伍德编写了本书第 9 章时装营销沟通。

Christine Sorensen, *MA, PGDip, BA (Hons) PGCEd, DipM*, is a Senior Lecturer in Marketing in Newcastle Business School. She has worked for three companies in marketing positions including the print industry and franchising. Christine has considerable experience of marketing training for small business and has appeared on radio to discuss developments in promotion. Christine Sorensen produced Chapter Two on the fashion marketing environment and co-wrote Chapter Five with Mike Easey.

克莉斯汀·索伦森

艺术学硕士，研究生文凭，持有文学教育学荣誉研究生证书，纽卡斯尔商学院市场营销课高级讲师。她为三家公司做营销定位方面工作，包括出版业和特许经营。她在为小企业营销培训以及出席广播电台讨论促销开发方面拥有相当丰富的经验。克莉斯汀·索伦森编写了本书第 2 章时装市场和营销环境，和迈克·伊西共同编写了第 5 章市场细分与营销组合。

John Willans, *MSc, DipM, CertEd*, until his recent retirement, was a Senior Lecturer in Fashion Marketing and Retail Distribution in Newcastle Business School. His background includes work with the retail sector and with textile marketing in Huddersfield. John Willans wrote Chapter Eight on fashion distribution. John is currently working on a new textbook, with Ruth Marciniak, on Fashion Retailing for Wiley-Blackwell.

约翰·威兰斯

工学硕士，硕士文凭，持有教育证书，直到最近退休，他一直是纽卡斯尔商学院市场营销和零售分销课高级讲师，他的背景包括在零售部门以及哈德斯菲尔德大学讲授“纺织品营销”工作。约翰·威兰斯编写了本书第 8 章时装分销。约翰目前正和鲁斯·马西尼克为威利—布莱克威尔出版社编写一本关于时装零售的新教材。